GLOBAL INTERNATIONAL
ECONOMIC MODELS

CONTRIBUTIONS
TO
ECONOMIC ANALYSIS

147

Honorary Editor

J. TINBERGEN

Editors:

D. W. JORGENSON

J. WAELBROECK

NORTH-HOLLAND
AMSTERDAM · NEW YORK · OXFORD

GLOBAL
INTERNATIONAL
ECONOMIC MODELS

Selected Papers from an IIASA Conference

Edited by

BERT G. HICKMAN *1924 -*

Department of Economics
Stanford University
Stanford, California
U.S.A.

1983

NORTH-HOLLAND
AMSTERDAM · NEW YORK · OXFORD

© ELSEVIER SCIENCE PUBLISHERS B.V., 1983

ISBN 0 444 86718 x

Publishers:

ELSEVIER SCIENCE PUBLISHERS B.V.
P.O. BOX 1991
1000 BZ AMSTERDAM
THE NETHERLANDS

Sole distributors for the U.S.A. and Canada:

ELSEVIER SCIENCE PUBLISHING COMPANY, INC.
52 VANDERBILT AVENUE
NEW YORK, N.Y. 10017

Library of Congress Cataloging in Publication Data

Main entry under title:

Global international economic models.

    (Contributions to economic analysis ; 147)
    "Eighth IIASA Global Modeling Conference"--Pref.
    Includes index.
    1. International economic relations--Mathematical
models--Congresses. I. Hickman, Bert G., 1924-
II. International Institute for Applied Systems
Analysis. III. IIASA Global Modeling Conference (8th :
1980 : Laxenburg, Austria) IV. Series.
HF1410.5.G57 1983   337'.0724   83-11594
ISBN 0-444-86718-X

PRINTED IN THE NETHERLANDS

INTRODUCTION TO THE SERIES

This series consists of a number of hitherto unpublished studies, which are introduced by the editors in the belief that they represent fresh contributions to economic science.

The term "economic analysis" as used in the title of the series has been adopted because it covers both the activities of the theoretical economist and the research worker.

Although the analytical methods used by the various contributors are not the same, they are nevertheless conditioned by the common origin of their studies, namely theoretical problems encountered in practical research. Since for this reason, business cycle research and national accounting, research work on behalf of economic policy, and problems of planning are the main sources of the subjects dealt with, they necessarily determine the manner of approach adopted by the authors. Their methods tend to be "practical" in the sense of not being too far remote from application to actual economic conditions. In addition they are quantitative rather than qualitative.

It is the hope of the editors that the publication of these studies will help to stimulate the exchange of scientific information and to reinforce international cooperation in the field of economics.

The Editors

PREFACE

The Eighth IIASA Global Modeling Conference marked an increased emphasis on econometric and general equilibrium approaches to modeling and focused on economic interactions among nations through trade, price, capital flow, interest rate, and exchange rate linkages. It was planned by the System and Decision Sciences Area of IIASA in collaboration with the Seminar on Global Modeling of the US National Science Foundation's Conference on Econometrics and Mathematical Economics. The organizing committee was chaired by Bert G. Hickman of Stanford University, who heads the CEME Seminar on Global Modeling. He was assisted at IIASA by Robert M. Coen of the System and Decision Sciences Area and Northwestern University. Other members of the organizing committee were Lawrence R. Klein, University of Pennsylvania, András Nagy, Hungarian National Academy of Sciences, and Stefan Schleicher, University of Graz.

CONTENTS

Part Four: Input—Output Models

Part Five: Hybrid Models

Part Six: Trade and Exchange Rate Models

Part One

Survey of the Models

GLOBAL INTERNATIONAL ECONOMIC MODELS
B.G. Hickman (editor)
Elsevier Science Publishers B.V. (North-Holland)
© IIASA, 1983

A CROSS SECTION OF GLOBAL INTERNATIONAL ECONOMIC MODELS

Bert G. Hickman
Department of Economics, Stanford University, Stanford, California (USA)

The purpose of this volume is to survey the state of the art of global international economic modeling. This is a new and flourishing field as witnessed by the fact that the pioneering Project LINK model is little more than a decade old and most other models reviewed in this volume date from the late 1970s. The models all feature national or regional disaggregation of the world economy and linkages and interactions among the regions, but they emphasize different aspects of the world economic system. Macroeconometric, input—output, general equilibrium, and trade and exchange-rate models are included, as well as several hybrid systems. A few of the models are constructed for short-run forecasting, but the primary focus is on long-run models and applications.

1   OVERVIEW OF THE MODELS

A summary of the principal features of the models is presented in Table 1. For the most part the models are sizable systems, usually covering ten or more regions and containing hundreds or thousands of endogenous variables. A few, however, were constructed for specific analytical purposes — for example, the study of commodity price indexation (REMPIS), oil supplies and North—South development (Manne), and tariff policies (Whalley) — and hence these are smaller and less disaggregated regionally than are the more general systems.

Most of the models are designed to explain regional production as well as interregional trade, but DAMIT deals only with trade flows and the Warner model explains exchange rates and trade flows for given regional paths of potential GNP. The Manne model is intermediate in this respect, with potential GNP exogenous and actual GNP endogenous in the developed and oil-importing developing regions. Similarly, the Brussels model takes GDP as exogenous in the developed world but it is endogenous in the various developing regions.

Nominal prices and inflation rates are endogenous in the four macroeconometric models and three of the macro-hybrids (COMLINK, REMPIS, and FUGI). Only relative prices are determinate in the general equilibrium systems (Brussels, Manne, Whalley), the DYNAMICO programming model, the World (Input—Output) Model, and in Warner's model of exchange rates and trade flows. Relative prices are exogenous in the present version of the INFORUM System and in Nagy's trade matrix model.

TABLE 1 Summary of principal features of the models.

Model (authors of paper)	Type of model (number of variables)	Principal endogenous variables	Principal exogenous variables (number of regions)	Purposes of model
Macroeconometric models				
Project LINK (Filatov, Hickman, and Klein)	Macroeconometric (6,000)	Trade flows and prices, exchange rates, regional macro variables (GNP, prices, employment, trade balances)	Population, oil prices, regional policy variables (32)	1. Ex-ante forecasting of world trade, GNP, inflation, balance of trade. 2. Simulation studies of international transmission mechanism and policies. 3. Long-run simulations of the world economy.
Tsukuba-FAIS (Shishido)	Macroeconometric (800)	Trade flows, exchange rates, interest rates, regional macro variables (GDP, trade balances, prices)	Oil prices, government spending, official discount rate, foreign aid (15)	1. Short- and medium-term projection and policy analysis. 2. Comparative studies of macroeconomic behavior.
Federal Reserve Multicountry Model (Kwack, Berner, Clark, Hernandez, Howe, and Stevens)	Macroeconometric (950)	Trade and capital flows, interest and exchange rates, national accounts, capital accounts, balance of payments	Oil prices, population, regional policy variables (6)	1. To model international influences on US economy. 2. To model US shock effects on other economies. 3. Forecasting.
Multicountry Econometric Model (Fair)	Macroeconometric (900)	Trade and capital flows, exchange and interest rates, regional macro variables (GNP, prices, balance of payments, money supply)	Population, government spending (42)	1. To explain economic linkages among countries.
General equilibrium models				
Brussels Global Development Model (Carrin, Gunning, and Waelbroeck)	General equilibrium (500)	Trade flows, relative prices, national accounts, sectoral composition	Capital flows, population, government expenditures, sectoral allocations of investment policies (10)	1. Sensitivity analysis of policy measures affecting developing countries.

Model	Method (size)	(endogenous variables)	(exogenous variables)	Objectives
General Equilibrium Model of World Trade (Whalley)	General equilibrium (250)	Trade and capital flows, relative prices	(4)	1. Applied welfare analysis of Tokyo Round policy issues. 2. Numerical analog of Heckscher–Ohlin trade model.
Three-Region Model of Energy, Trade, and Growth (Manne)	General equilibrium (16)	Trade flows, relative prices, real GNP	Capital flows, oil prices, potential GNP (3)	1. To estimate trade balance constraints on oil imports of developing countries and provide global background to energy supply–demand problems in individual nations.
Input–output models				
World Model (Duchin)	Input–output (3,000)	Trade and capital flows, regional input–output detail	Pollution-abatement levels, population (15)	1. To investigate alternative future paths of the world economy.
INFORUM System (Nyhus and Almon)	Input–output (300–1500 per country)	Trade flows, regional input–output detail, employment, prices	Personal disposable income, labor force, government expenditures, exchange rates (16)	1. Forecasting. 2. Policy simulation.
Hybrid models				
COMLINK (Adams and Marquez)	1. Macroeconometric (6,000) 2. Commodity models (200)	Project LINK variables, world prices of 23 commodities	Project LINK variables, weather, government regulations in commodity models (33)	1. To provide an endogenous explanation of individual commodity prices. 2. Simulations of effects of changes in commodity market conditions on trade, production, and prices in the regional economies.
REMPIS (Weinberg, Nadiri, and Choi)	1. Macroeconometric (175) 2. Commodity models (225)	Trade flows, primary commodity prices, regional macro variables (GDP, employment, prices)	Oil prices, regional policy variables (5)	1. To study commodity price indexation.

TABLE 1 *Continued.*

Model (authors of paper)	Type of model (number of variables)	Principal endogenous variables	Principal exogenous variables (number of regions)	Purposes of model
Project FUGI (Kaya, Onishi, and Suzuki)	1. Macroeconometric 2. Input–output 3. Commodity (3400)	Trade and capital flows, interest and exchange rates, regional macro variables (GNP, prices, trade balances), input–output detail	Population and manpower (28)	1. To provide long-term scenarios of world economy and industry. 2. To project alternative paths for developed and developing countries in the eighties.
DYNAMICO (Costa)	1. Input–output 2. Econometric 3. Optimizing (800)	Trade and capital flows, regional macro variables (GNP, balance of payments), input–output detail, labor supplies, shadow prices	Population (10)	1. To study the interaction of trade and production structures. 2. To study disequilibrium in commodity markets. 3. To study externalities.
Trade and exchange-rate models				
DAMIT (Nagy)	Trade matrix (1000)	Trade flows	Total exports and imports of regions by commodity groups (12)	1. To study changes in international trade flows in response to different policy regimes.
Trade and Exchange Rate Model (Warner)	Econometric (1000)	Trade and capital flows, exchange rates	Oil prices, potential GNP (26)	1. To test effect on trade flows of different exchange-rate regimes.

2   THE INDIVIDUAL PAPERS

The authors were given wide latitude to decide the contents of their papers, since the models differ substantially in purpose, scope, methodology, and stage of development. Generally speaking, theoretical specifications are emphasized by the authors of newer models and applications are stressed in the papers on older models for which documentation already exists in the literature. The references included in each paper will guide the interested reader to additional sources on the models. In this section we briefly summarize each paper before turning to cross-sectional comparisons of the models.

Project LINK is a cooperative international activity linking 32 individual national and regional models from research centers around the world into a global model. In "Long-Run Simulations With the Project LINK System, 1978–1985," V. Filatov, B. Hickman, and L. Klein project the world economy over a seven-year horizon, analyze fiscal policy and oil price scenarios, and present own- and cross-country dynamic income multipliers for demand shocks in the seven largest OECD countries. The appropriateness of using a system which attempts to model the transmission of business cycles for intermediate-term projections is discussed and the statistical methodology described. In his comment on the paper, E. Ershov raises several important methodological issues concerning long-term policy simulations with multicountry models.

In a similar paper entitled "Long-Term Forecast and Policy Implications: Simulations with a World Econometric Model," S. Shishido uses the Tsukuba–FAIS system of linked models for 15 countries or regions for long-run projections and scenarios. This is the first such application of the model and the resulting projections presented in this interim report should be regarded as preliminary. The author stresses that these are primarily demand-side projections and that the supply side must be taken more fully into account in future work. Forecasts for 1980–2000 are presented and interpreted for three scenarios:

(1)   fixed exchange rates as of 1980 for all developed countries,
(2)   gradually rising exchange rates for Japan and the FRG,
(3)   slower growth of manufacturing imports in the "other developed and socialist countries" region.

In his comment, R. Coen calls for a model specification in which long-term GNP growth is determined essentially by growth of labor supply and technical progress and in which endogenous mechanisms accommodate actual to potential growth, unlike the present version of the Tsukuba–FAIS model.

The paper on "The Structure and Properties of the Multi-Country Model" by S. Kwack et al. surveys the theoretical structure and simulation properties of the model developed at the Federal Reserve Board (FRB). The system links national models for Canada, the FRG, Japan, the United Kingdom, and the United States together with an abbreviated model for the rest of the world. The specification features detailed modeling of financial markets and international linkages through capital flows, international reserves, and exchange rates, although trade and price linkages are not neglected. It is a short-run model and simulation results are limited to an eight-quarter horizon. Dynamic multipliers are presented for a fiscal shock originating in each of the five countries in prelinkage and postlinkage mode — i.e., respectively, without and with feedbacks from the other countries.

A less exhaustive review of monetary multipliers is also included for the United States, Japan, and the FRG.

The new model being developed by R. Fair is similar to that of the Federal Reserve in its emphasis on financial linkages through exchange and interest rates. It has much greater country detail, however — 42 countries versus six for the FRB model — because each national model is small and undifferentiated, in contrast to the large structural models of the FRB. In an "Outline of a Multicountry Econometric Model," Fair presents a qualitative description of the model and its multiplier properties and concludes from the results thus far that price, exchange-rate, and interest-rate linkages are quantitatively important and that any model based primarily on trade linkages is not likely to be a very good approximation to the world economy. His discussant, W. Krelle, finds the general approach very useful but stresses that the interest rate effects stemming from US disturbances are overstated in the model and calls for expanded treatment of the real side of the economies.

The Brussels Global Development Model is presented for the first time in "A General Equilibrium Model For the World Economy: Some Preliminary Results," by G. Carrin, J. Gunning, and J. Waelbroeck. Its theoretical structure is depicted in a compact and elegant exposition and simulations of the impact of higher oil prices are provided to illustrate its uses. The global system contains structural models for nine groups of developing countries and is closed by a single rudimentary model for the developed countries in which regional GDP is exogenous. The model can be solved either on the assumption of flexible, market-clearing prices (except for the world price of energy) or of rigid, non-clearing prices in the urban sectors of the developing regions. In the simulations it is found that most effects of oil-price increases are small if all prices can adjust, whereas there are substantial losses in oil-importing regions if domestic prices are rigid in the face of excess supply. In his comment, L. Bergman emphasizes the usefulness of the extension of the usual general equilibrium framework to incorporate price rigidity and quantity adjustment, although questioning the application of the basic assumptions of general equilibrium theory to developing countries.

"General Equilibrium Modeling of Trade Liberalization Issues Among Major World Trade Blocs" summarizes a series of recent studies by J. Whalley on the structure and application of a numerical general equilibrium model of international production and trade for 33 commodities and four regions. All prices and quantities are determined on the assumption of perfectly competitive markets in zero-profit equilibrium. The model is used for "counterfactual" comparative statics analyses of alternative trade policies rather than for forecasting. An evaluation of various tariff-cutting proposals from the Tokyo Round led to the striking conclusion that the negotiating position of each country appeared from the model results to be counter to its own national interest. A subsequent model evaluation of the Tokyo Round Agreement indicated a resulting overall welfare gain of only 0.1% of world GNP from the tariff cuts, together with a finding that under certain assumptions the developing countries would suffer under the reductions due to adverse movements in the terms of trade. Commenting also on the Whalley paper, Bergman notes that the assumption of general competitive equilibrium may be a reasonable approximation to the actual allocation of resources where well-functioning markets exist, but that the counterfactual comparison with a hypothetical equilibrium for new exogenous trading conditions cannot tell us anything about the duration of the adjustment process or its disequilibrium characteristics. The second discussant, W. Trzeciakowski, observes that the underlying assumptions are less relevant for developing and centrally planned economies, where nonmarket considerations and supply constraints are heavily involved in decision-making, and advances a number of suggestions for modifying the model for future work on the new international economic order.

Professor A. Manne's paper concerns "A Three-Region Model of Energy, International Trade and Economic Growth." This is a small model constructed for the specific purpose of estimating the effects of trade-balance constraints on oil imports and economic growth in the industrialized and developing regions. It is a static general equilibrium model benchmarked in 1976 (prior to the Iranian Revolution), and is solved for 1990. According to the baseline simulation, with a 2.0% growth rate of energy supplies, the real international price of energy would nearly triple between 1976 and 1990, dramatically shifting the terms of trade between the oil exporting and importing regions, and inducing a decrease in the annual growth rate of GNP in the oil importing LDCs from an estimated potential of 5.7% to a realized rate of 4.8%. This region's growth is depressed not only by high oil prices as they affect its ability to import but also by the deceleration of realized GNP growth in the traditional developed-region markets for its export products. Additional scenarios investigate the influence of alternative energy supply—demand scenarios on trade and growth in the three regions and the sensitivity of the projections to variations in the assumed elasticities of substitution between domestic and imported nonenergy inputs and between energy and other inputs. The comment by S. Schleicher stresses that changes in efficiency of energy use could importantly affect the quantitative predictions of the model, which allows only for energy substitution within the given technology, and also that recycling of OPEC surpluses may affect the international distribution of factor endowments, and hence the potential GNP of the various regions, in the long run.

"The World Model: Inter-Regional Input—Output Model of the World Economy," by Faye Duchin, describes the structure of the model constructed by Leontief, Carter, and Petri under United Nations auspices and subsequently maintained and operated by the Institute for Economic Analysis at New York University. As examples of recent applications, the author summarizes the more important results of three disarmament scenarios in which the growth rate of worldwide military expenditure is reduced, accompanied in two cases by a transfer of part of the savings to four poor regions. In his comment, H. Chenery notes the strengths and limitations of the input—output approach to world modeling and criticizes its application to the analysis of international assistance and capital flows whether generated by disarmament or other sources.

The INFORUM system of linked national input—output models, as categorized in Table 1, is as yet incomplete. Sixteen models are in existence or under construction, but only three of these are included in "Linked Input—Output Models for France, the Federal Republic of Germany and Belgium," by D. Nyhus and C. Almon. The models will eventually be linked by methods similar to those used in multicountry macroeconomic models. In the present paper, however, the authors describe an experimental, short-cut method utilizing reduced-form equations for exports as functions of domestic demands in receiving countries and exogenous relative price terms. The linked models are then simulated to estimate the direct and indirect effects of an exogenous increase in personal consumption expenditures in one country on the (industrially disaggregated) exports of the partner countries. The invited discussant, W. Welfe, outlines a more structural approach to the linkage problem even when one is constrained to use exogenous relative prices and suggests that sample period simulations would be less arbitrary and easier to interpret, but nevertheless congratulates the authors for their demonstration that large input—output models can be linked operationally.

"The Impact of Petroleum and Commodity Prices in a Model of the World Economy," by F. Adams and J. Marquez, approaches its subject from two points of view. A simple theoretical model of the same three regions as in the Manne paper is presented and its qualitative short-run responses to exogenous increases in the price of oil or other primary commodities are obtained by differentiation in the first section. The exercise highlights the indirect effects of such price increases through the recycling of the resulting earnings by the primary producing countries and the induced increases in the prices of manufacturers as well as the direct effects from the altered terms of trade. In the second half of the paper, the elaborate COMLINK system of linked commodity and macroeconomic models is described and some simulation results for responses to commodity-price shocks are summarized. In his comment, I. Fabinc argues for a broader historical and theoretical perspective along Marxian lines for dealing with the long-run consequences of changes in oil commodity prices and questions whether macroeconomic or general equilibrium models are properly equipped to overcome the analytical difficulties.

Another hybrid system combining macroeconomic and commodity models is represented in "An Evaluation of the Effects of Commodity Price Indexation on Developed and Developing Economies: An Application of the REMPIS Model," by C. Weinberg, M. Nadiri, and J. Choi. Whereas COMLINK was a marriage between the 32 existing national and regional models of Project LINK and 23 commodity models, the macroeconomic side of REMPIS consists of four newly constructed regional models — for developed market economies, the centrally planned economies, the OPEC countries, and the oil importing developing market economies — and is linked to seven commodity models. The system is then used to examine the impacts of a particular indexing rule for primary commodities on commodity prices and stockpiles, on the inflation and growth rates of the various regions, and on the volume and distribution of world trade. The general conclusion of the authors is that the benefits of an indexation program are modest and its potential cost is unbounded, so that other forms of transfer aid may be preferable. The invited discussant, L. Ohlsson, offers alternative interpretations of some of the findings and raises substantive questions about various aspects of the model specification.

Project FUGI merges three different models: a dynamic global macroeconomic model with 28 nations or regions, a static global input—output model, and a set of global metal-resource models. In "Project FUGI and the Future of ESCAP Developing Countries," Y. Kaya, A. Onishi, and Y. Suzuki present simulation results concerning alternative scenarios for economic growth and industrialization policies in the 1980s. The macro module is used to forecast per capita income growth, inflation rates, and current account balances under both a standard and a high-development scenario, whereas the input—output module is used in linear programming mode to investigate agricultural-oriented and manufacturing-oriented development strategies, within the constraint of the gross regional product projections from the macro model. Professor S. Ichimura raises questions about the specification of the macro model and the methodology of the linear programming analysis of development strategies and closes his comment with some sobering thoughts on the prospects for Asian economic development.

The United Nations model DYNAMICO combines input—output, econometric and activity-analysis techniques in a normative model covering ten regions of the world and ten production sectors. The paper by A. Costa entitled "DYNAMICO: A Multi-Level Programming Model of World Trade and Development" describes the structure and solution algorithm of the system and illustrates its use in a normative analysis of the imputed effective contributions of each region to gross world product in 1980. The imputed contributions reflect regional externalities and may exceed or fall short of regional GNP, with the excesses or shortfalls summing to zero for the world as a whole. In general, regions which supply scarce commodities to the rest of the world make a contribution to world production in excess of their own GNP, whereas the reverse is true for those areas selling commodities which are in excess supply. The discussant, D. Snower, is impressed by DYNAMICO but points out that there is no descriptive counterpart to its normative content, since no price system exists in the model to induce the regions to generate the global optimum and hence the latter must be imposed on the regions by a benevolent dictator.

The DAMIT project described in A. Nagy's paper on "Structural Changes and Development Alternatives of International Trade" represents an application of trade matrix modeling to ensure international consistency among bilateral trade flows for exogenously given vectors of total regional exports and imports by commodity groups. It is not intended to model within DAMIT the domestic economies of the various regions in a linked system of national models, but rather to examine total trade vectors as projected in scenarios from other global systems for international consistency of bilateral flows. In the present paper, space limitations permitted only a brief outline of the model and methodology, together with an historical analysis of the principal changes in international trade patterns occurring during the period 1955—1977 in primary goods and manufactures among the centrally planned, developed market, and developing regions of the world.

In "A Model of Trade and Exchange Rates," D. Warner combines an empirical trade model similar to that embedded in most multinational systems with a simplified version of W. Branson's asset-market model of exchange-rate determination. The model is driven by exogenous trends in the growth rates of potential output in the OECD countries and the effects of money-supply growth on price levels and exchange rates are missing since the growth rate of money stocks is set to zero. The model is simulated over the period 1979—1990 to compare a fixed and flexible exchange-rate regime and two flexible regimes differing only in the assumed growth rate of West German GNP. In his comment, H. Abele questions various aspects of the specification and simulations and recommends an alternative approach examining more limited questions but with more economic content to the model.

3   LINKAGE MECHANISMS

A summary of the linkages among regional models in the various world systems is presented in Table 2. They may include trade flows, foreign and domestic price linkages, exchange rates, and monetary linkages. The specialized trade and exchange-rate models described in the papers by Nagy and Warner are included in the table even though they

TABLE 2 Summary of endogenous linkages among regional models.

Model (authors of paper)	Trade flows	Foreign and domestic prices	Exchange rates	Monetary linkages
Macroeconometric models				
Project LINK (Filatov, Hickman, and Klein)	Imports determined by domestic income, domestic and foreign prices. Endogenous share matrix distributes imports as exports.	Export and domestic prices are markups over factor costs including oil, unit labor costs, and imports. Prices also affected by money supply.	Developed countries: determined by relative prices, current accounts, and interest-rate differentials.	
Tsukuba-FAIS (Shishido)	Manufactured goods: imports determined by income, import, and domestic prices and exchange rates. Endogenous share matrix distributes imports as exports. Primary commodities: global supply and demand models determine exports and imports for each region.	Manufactured goods: export and domestic prices determined by import prices, capacity utilization, and money supply. Primary commodities: world market-clearing prices.	Developed countries: determined by relative prices, current accounts, interest rates, and central bank intervention.	Money supply is affected by changes in foreign reserves to extent determined by intervention and sterilization policies in reduced-form equation.
Federal Reserve Multicountry Model (Kwack, Berner, Clark, Hernandez, Howe, and Stevens)	Bilateral goods and service flows determined by income, prices, and exchange rates.	Export and domestic prices are markups over wages, changes in labor productivity, and import prices.	Exchange rate equilibrates balance of payments.	Net foreign assets of central bank affect monetary base to extent determined by intervention and sterilization policies.
Multicountry Econometric Model (Fair)	Imports determined by prices, income, interest rates, and wealth. Exogenous share matrix distributes imports as exports.	Export and domestic prices determined by income, import prices, and interest rates.	The spot rate is determined by own-country and US interest rates, incomes, and prices.	Interest rates determined by central bank reaction function which includes US interest rate in some national models.

General equilibrium models

Brussels Global Development Model (Carrin, Gunning, and Waelbroeck)	For each good, regional imports determined by domestic demand and the ratio of domestic to world trade prices. Exports determined by ratio of producer to world trade prices and level of world imports.	Export and domestic prices determined by value added and import prices.
General Equilibrium Model of World Trade (Whalley)	Supply and demand functions exist in all regions for all tradeables and quantities are determined under market-clearing prices.	All prices are world market clearing.
Three Region Model of Energy, Trade, and Growth (Manne)	World market-clearing import and export quantities given maximization of GNP in each region.	All prices are world market clearing.

Input–output models

World Model (Duchin)	In each region imports equal a fraction of total demand for each good. Exogenous share matrix distributes imports as exports.	
INFORUM System (Nyhus and Almon)	Imports determined by domestic demand and relative domestic and foreign prices. Endogenous share matrix distributes imports as exports.	Export and domestic prices depend on value-added determinants and import prices.

TABLE 2 Continued.

Model (authors of paper)	Trade flows	Foreign and domestic prices	Exchange rates	Monetary linkages
Hybrid models				
COMLINK (Adams and Marquez)	Same as Project LINK.	Market clearing prices of primary commodities are translated into LINK SITC export and import price indexes. Other linkages same as in Project LINK.		
REMPIS (Weinberg, Nadiri, and Choi)	Developed countries: imports of goods and services determined by income; exogenous share matrix distributes imports as exports. Primary commodities: regional supply and demand functions determine world trade.	Market clearing commodity prices affect export and import price indexes and domestic price levels.		
Project FUGI (Kaya, Onishi, and Suzuki)	Bilateral imports determined by income and price competitiveness or importing capacity adjusted by terms of trade.	Export and domestic prices directly determined by unit labor cost, profit rate on capital, real money balances, and import prices.	Determined by own-country and US export prices, interest rates, and current account balances.	Money supply affected by balance of trade in reduced-form money equation. US discount rate affects official discount rate in reaction function.
DYNAMICO (Costa)	Exports and imports determined by domestic income and the interaction between domestic prices and terms of trade.	Terms of trade for nine commodity groups determine world market-clearing conditions.		

Trade and exchange-rate models

| DAMIT (Nagy) | Interregional trade flows determined bilaterally from exogenous regional total trade vectors as a function of trade policy and economic-distance factors. | | |
| Trade and Exchange Rate Model (Warner) | Regional imports determined by (exogenous) income and by relative prices. Endogenous share matrix distributes imports as exports. | Domestic prices determined by import prices in truncated model. Export prices determined by domestic and competitor's prices. | Determined by capital flows (defined to offset the current account) in truncated model without money stocks. |

are not presently embedded in systems of linked regional models. Similarly the INFORUM System is included with the linkages planned, even though the present version is not yet completely built and linked. Except where otherwise noted, the following comparisons will be confined to the dozen remaining complete multicountry or multiregional models.

The common feature of all these models is linkage through trade flows, so that domestic shocks may be transmitted abroad through the resulting changes in import demands and export prices of the initiating country. Regional import demands are usually functions of income and the relative price of domestic and imported goods, although the relative price is omitted from the REMPIS and World models and the import demand functions are implicit rather than explicit in the Manne model.

The macroeconometric models, including the COMLINK and REMPIS hybrids, usually determine exports from a central trade-share matrix that allocates each region's imports to the various exporting regions.* In this way the world trade identity — that the sum of all exports must equal the sum of all imports — is satisfied in the simultaneous postlinkage solution of the global model. As a further, important extension, the LINK, Tsukuba, and COMLINK models endogenize the trade shares as functions of relative prices, whereas the shares are exogenous in the Fair, REMPIS, and World models.

Exports are handled somewhat differently in DYNAMICO and the general equilibrium models. In the DYNAMICO, Brussels, Whalley, and Manne models, the prices of tradeables move to clear world markets and thereby satisfy the world trade identity.** The difference in approach between the general equilibrium and macro models is more apparent than real, however, since the latter contain equations to determine the export price of each region endogenously. These are generally markup equations rather than competitive supply functions, but they do represent supply-side conditions. Moreover, the regional import price indexes are consistently weighted averages of the export prices of the various supplying regions and employ as weights elements of the same market-share matrix as used for the trade flows. Thus market-clearing conditions are implicitly imposed in the trade-share linkage mechanisms of the macroeconometric models.

Direct linkages between foreign and domestic prices may also serve as international transmission channels. Such direct linkages appear in the form of import-price arguments in the equations determining domestic and export price levels in all the macro and most of the hybrid models, plus the Brussels general equilibrium model. The direct price links are particularly relevant in those macro and hybrid models in which nominal prices are determined, since they contribute importantly to the propagation of "imported inflation" and to the analysis of the inflationary effects of exchange-rate depreciation. Although a similar link appears in the Brussels model, its role is necessarily confined to allocational effects, since only real prices are determined in the model. Finally, only world market-clearing (real) prices appear in DYNAMICO and in the Manne and Whalley general equilibrium models.

Exchange rates are explained endogenously in the four macro systems, FUGI, and Warner's trade and exchange-rate model, although it should be noted that they were made

---

* The exceptions are the Federal Reserve and FUGI models, which employ bilateral import equations.
**In the Brussels model only the import side is exactly satisfied, since the quantity of world trade is defined as a CES aggregate on the export side.

exogenous for the purposes of the long-run simulations presented in this volume for the LINK, Tsukuba, and FUGI models. Since nominal prices are indeterminate in the general equilibrium, input—output, and DYNAMICO programming models, so also are exchange rates.

A direct reduced-form equation for the exchange rate is included for the major developed countries in the LINK, Tsukuba, and FUGI models. The LINK equation includes as arguments the relative price of own and US exports, the differential between own and US interest rates, and the own current-account balance. The Tsukuba equation is similar, except that it is expressed in effective exchange-rate form and also includes the change in official foreign exchange reserves as a proxy for central bank intervention in the foreign exchange market and corrects the nominal interest rate differential for the (expected) change in the exchange rate. In FUGI, the arguments are the relative price of own and US exports, the ratio of own and US interest rates, and the own and US current-account balance. It will be recognized that these various reduced forms incorporate elements of the purchasing power parity (PPP) and asset market approaches to exchange-rate determination and provide linkages between the current accounts, interest rates, and price levels or inflation rates of the various national models in the endogenization of floating exchange rates.

In the Fair model, the spot exchange rate is explained directly as a function of the forward exchange rate and the foreign and domestic interest rates. This is a stochastic equation in order to allow for capital market imperfections which prevent full realization of interest parity through arbitrage. Another stochastic equation determines the forward exchange rate as a function of the relative price of own and US exports and own and US per capita GNP. Taken together, the two equations explain the spot rate by relative domestic and foreign prices, interest rates, and real incomes. Again, the specification combines elements of the PPP and asset-market approaches.

The Warner trade and exchange-rate model incorporates Branson's asset-market model of exchange-rate determination. The exchange rate is specified as a function of the current-account balances in the own country and one (principal) trading partner and the changes in the money stocks of the same two countries. In the present empirical version the money stocks are not modeled and hence the only arguments in the exchange-rate equation are the current balances which, on the assumption of a noninterventionist floating rate regime, are equated with the change in net foreign assets.

The Federal Reserve Multi-Country Model employs a structural balance-of-payments approach to exchange-rate determination. Along with the current balance, private capital flows are explicitly modeled in a portfolio balance framework and changes in official foreign exchange reserves are explained by an intervention function. Thus the exchange rate clears the balance of payments after allowance for central bank intervention in a managed flexible-rate regime.

The Federal Reserve model also contains the richest structural specification of international monetary linkages. The money stock and short-term interest rate are determined by the demand and supply for money, given the monetary base. The foreign asset component of the base will change if a surplus or deficit exists in the balance of payments. To the extent that exchange rates are managed in a particular country, intervention assumptions or functions will determine the change in net foreign assets of the central bank, and sterilization assumptions or functions will determine the extent to which the change is offset by corresponding changes in the domestic component of the base. In the absence of sterilization, the domestic money stock and interest rates, and hence domestic prices and outputs, may be affected by external disturbances and feedbacks.

The money stock is also made endogenous in the Tsukuba model through a reduced-form equation which includes the current account balance and the monetary policies of the central bank, but the capital flow component of the balance of payments is exogenous.

In the foregoing models international monetary linkages operate through induced changes in the monetary base and affect interest rates by affecting money supply. In the Fair system, however, the monetary base and the money-supply process are not modeled. Instead, interest rates are predicted by central bank reaction functions including as arguments the inflation rate, the growth rates of the money supply and real GNP, and, in some cases, the US interest rate. This means that an increase in the US interest rate may directly affect interest rates in some countries, although the response is weak and statistically insignificant during the flexible-exchange regime. Since only the US interest rate appears in the reaction functions, increases originating in other countries have no direct effect on interest rates abroad.

The FUGI model has elements in common with both the Fair and the Tsukuba approaches. Thus a reduced-form equation contains the trade balance and the central bank discount rate as determinants of the money stock, the US discount rate enters a policy reaction function for the own discount rate, and both the money stock and discount rate affect market interest rates.

Finally, it should be noted that the foregoing discussion has been concerned with direct international monetary linkages through either externally induced changes in the monetary base or a policy response of foreign interest rates to the US rate. Interest rates, money stocks, or both are also indirectly affected by external shocks to incomes and prices in all models with domestic monetary sectors, including many of the national models in Project LINK in addition to the other macro systems under discussion.

4   METHODOLOGICAL OBSERVATIONS

All the models in the volume rely on economic theory to provide their basic structures and behavioral hypotheses, with resultant emphasis on substitution possibilities in demand, production, and trade. There is plenty of diversity within the family of economic models, however, and it is interesting to compare their similarities and differences and their strengths and weaknesses.

General equilibrium models are the newest entry into the field of economy-wide empirical modeling. In the purest form they are static resource allocation models assuming utility-maximizing households and profit-maximizing firms operating in a perfectly-competitive market-clearing environment under full-employment conditions.

The econometric models also generally assume optimizing behavior, but in an environment of imperfectly competitive product markets and disequilibrium or lagged wage adjustments in the labor market. They also incorporate a monetary sector, determine nominal price levels and interest rates, and allow for departures from full employment. Finally, they are dynamic models incorporating lagged endogenous variables and generating explicit time paths from given initial conditions and assumptions on exogenous variables and disturbances.

The input—output models resemble the general equilibrium systems in their emphasis on microeconomic resource allocation, with particular reference to linear production technologies and interindustry flows. The input—output specification is less complete than the analogous general equilibrium systems, however. Fixed coefficients in production and trade limit substitution possibilities and real demands for final consumer products are independent of relative prices, and of the equilibrium of utility-maximizing households.

Apart from the central characteristics just summarized, various modifications are possible within each category of model and hybrid systems may readily be formed, as in the examples of the fix-price variant of the Brussels general equilibrium model and the merger of input—output and macroeconometric models in Project FUGI. Under the circumstances, it is virtually impossible to draw hard and fast distinctions among the three basic approaches and care must be taken to avoid stereotyped conceptions in categorizing individual models. Nevertheless, it is worth noting some differences among the approaches in specific attributes before summarizing their respective strengths and weaknesses for particular applications.

4.1 Equilibrium Assumptions

There is no distinction between short-run and long-run market equilibrium in the pure general equilibrium model. It is a static model of long-run competitive equilibrium in all markets for goods and productive services, yielding a full-employment Walrasian general equilibrium with market-clearing prices everywhere and all agents on their demand or supply functions at the equilibrium prices. It is therefore primarily designed for comparative static analyses of alternative equilibria corresponding to alternative policy configurations, factor endowments, or other shifts in exogenous variables or parameters.

Econometric models also recognize interdependencies among markets in the economy and in that sense possess "general equilibrium" as opposed to "particular equilibrium" properties. They are not necessarily, and not usually, in long-run equilibrium in a given period, however, for one or both of the following reasons. First, they may assume disequilibrium in one or more markets such that price does not clear the market and agents are not on their demand or supply curves, as in the most common interpretation of the Phillips curve as a wage adjustment equation for excess demands or supplies of labor. Second, they may assume market-clearing prices in each period, but distinguish between short-run and long-run demand and supply functions because of adjustment costs, expectation errors or gestation lags, so the long-term equilibrium is approached (in a stable model) through a succession of short-term market-clearing equilibria. Since these assumptions involve time lags in an essential way, econometric models become dynamic simultaneous difference equation systems for the analysis of transient or "disequilibrium" responses to shocks relative to the long-term equilibrium path, including systematic departures from full employment.

A static long-run competitive equilibrium is implicit in the price equations for sectoral outputs in input—output models since they constrain the price of gross output to equal value added plus the costs of intermediate inputs. In many applications, factor markets also clear for given endowments and hence full employment prevails. They share with general equilibrium models the inability to track transitions between long-term equilibria.

4.2   Sectoral Disaggregation

The degree of disaggregation by economic activity or sector can vary widely within each model category, so that the size of a given model is not constrained by its formal structure, as is evident from the second column of Table 1. When industrial or product detail is of primary interest, however, the input—output and general equilibrium frameworks have a comparative advantage in ease of specification and parameterization. Where disaggregation by type of economic activity rather than product detail is of prime importance, in contrast, econometric models have an edge, since they deal directly with the determination of macroeconomic variables such as GNP, the price level and inflation rate, and unemployment, in an interdependent system of goods, labor, and money (or financial) markets. The approaches are not mutually exclusive, of course. The hybrid systems combining econometric and input—output specifications are examples of modeling strategies to realize the advantages of each approach in a complementary synthesis.

4.3   Regional Disaggregation

This is again a characteristic which is independent of model type (see Table 1, fourth column). The number of regions can be large or small for any of the approaches, depending on the purposes for which a particular model is built. As Chenery emphasizes in his comment on the Leontief World Model, another crucial aspect of modeling strategy is the choice of nations or regions as the basic geographical unit, for this will bear importantly on the kinds of policy questions that may be addressed.

4.4   Parameter Estimation

Wide disparities are found among the various approaches in this key aspect of model building. The econometric models specify theoretical behavioral functions and typically estimate the parameters from time-series observations using methods of statistical inference to account for random errors. The functional specifications allow for disequilibrium conditions or for divergence between short- and long-run equilibria instead of assuming that all observations are on the long-run supply and demand functions. Objective measures are available to judge such characteristics as the statistical significance of individual coefficients or sets of coefficients, goodness of fit, existence of serial correlation, and other indicators of the reliability of the estimates.

The general equilibrium models combine certain extraneous parameter values with a single observation on the variables to "calibrate" the model. The extraneous parameters may be taken from other studies or chosen a priori. The remaining parameters of the demand and supply functions are obtained nonstochastically on the assumption that the observed prices and quantities in the calibration year were on the functions and satisfied the market-clearing zero profit conditions of long-term competitive equilibrium. Significance bounds are naturally unavailable on the imposed or calibrated parameters, but their values can be altered in simulation tests of the model's sensitivity to parametric variations.

Technological input—output coefficients for a given country are usually inferred nonstochastically from a single cross-section observation on interindustry transactions, assuming a linear technology, and perhaps incorporating specific engineering data for particular coefficients. In multiregional input—output models, however, extrapolative procedures of one kind or another must usually be used to impute observed coefficients from a sample of countries with data-based tables to regional groupings with similar attributes. Open input—output models have many excess variables and may be closed in a variety of ways, so that it is difficult to generalize about methods of parameter determination for the final demand vectors or labor and capital coefficients.

4.5 Solution Modes

Most of the models described in the volume are operated as simulation systems irrespective of their formal structures. The typical application involves comparison of two solutions which differ because of some variation in parameter values or exogenous variables. This is the most feasible procedure for investigating the predicted outcomes of alternative policy actions affecting controllable parameters or variables. Solving for values of policy instruments in terms of specified values for target variables is computationally difficult and expensive in large nonlinear systems and explicit optimization of an objective function even more so, and hence these methods are seldom used in multiregional models.

The outstanding exception to the generalization here is DYNAMICO, a large-scale programming model solved by optimization of a specific worldwide objective function. In the particular example given in Costa's paper, the objective is to maximize world GNP as a weighted sum of the ten regional GNPs. Future simulations will test the stability of economic development paths under alternative global objective functions.

Two other applications involving optimizing solution procedures are also included. In Manne's three-region model, each region chooses its mix of energy and of nonenergy imports so as to maximize its own GNP, subject to its individual balance-of-payments constraint. In Project FUGI, the input—output module is used in linear programming mode to maximize either manufacturing or agricultural development over the developing regions as a group for given values of regional GDP and export and import aggregates from the macro module.

5   APPLICATIONS OF GLOBAL MODELS

The inherent characteristics of the various modeling approaches delimit a range of problems which each is capable of handling or in which it has at least a comparative advantage. In some connections, the several approaches may be able independently to illuminate different facets of the same general problem. Finally, hybrid approaches may be required for certain investigations. This section serves both to survey the wide range of applications of global models and to relate specific applications to the strengths and weaknesses of the various approaches.

5.1   Inherently Macroeconomic Problems

These are the problems of simultaneous determination of aggregate employment, output, and the price level in open economies, and of policies for improving performance in these respects. Linked systems of national macroeconometric models may be used to study the generation and transmission of economic fluctuations and inflation in the world economy. Specific examples in this volume include: (a) the LINK simulations of the effects of coordinated policies to stimulate investment in the major Western countries and of oil-price increases by OPEC, (b) the own- and cross-country income response multipliers from government expenditure shocks in individual countries in the LINK system, (c) the comparison of prelinkage and postlinkage own multiplier responses for major macro-economic variables to independent fiscal and monetary shocks in various countries in the FRB Multicountry model, and (d) the qualitative description of own- and cross-country multipliers on prices, incomes, and interest rates from independent US and West German shocks and under fixed and flexible exchange-rate regimes in the Fair model.

The general equilibrium and input—output approaches are not equipped to deal with distinctions between short- and long-term adjustments in goods and factor markets, with the determination of nominal prices, interest rates, or exchange rates, or with stabilization policies. This is the exclusive territory of the macroeconometric models.

5.2   Inherently Microeconomic Problems

The general equilibrium and input—output models are particularly suited for analyses of resource allocation and income distribution problems and the provision of industrial or product detail. An excellent example is Whalley's counterfactual equilibrium analysis of the effects of reductions in tariffs and nontariff barriers on the level and distribution of world production and trade for 33 product groupings in four regions. Another is the detail for 15 geographical regions on 8 pollution and 5 pollution-abatement activities, 9 resource outputs, and 34 industrial sectors in the Leontief World Model projections. Finally, there is the promise of detailed industrial trading linkages among national input—output models in the INFORUM System.

These techniques may also be applied to international resource allocation and income distribution problems of smaller dimension, as in the example of the analysis of the impact of real oil-price increases on the real incomes of the developed and developing regions in the Manne and Brussels general equilibrium models. As compared with macro-econometric models, their advantages in such applications consist primarily of smaller data bases and easier parameterization techniques.

The macroeconometric models cannot provide detailed structural modeling of numerous product markets even on a national basis, let alone on the multinational level, without becoming cumbersome. This explains the popularity of merged macroeconomic and input—output systems such as Project FUGI and DYNAMICO, where sectoral detail is needed for specific purposes along with consistent predictions of macroeconomic variables.

5.3   Growth Projections

These can be made with any of the techniques. The present volume contains projections to 1985 with the LINK system, to 1990 with the Manne and FUGI models, and to 2000 with the Tsukuba and Leontief models. The Brussels model is also used for long-term projections, although a baseline solution to 1990 is not reported in the present paper. There are interesting differences in the various approaches despite the common concern with growth.

The growth path of regional and world GDP is endogenous in the macroeconometric model projections, including FUGI-Macro. Nominal prices and inflation rates are also endogenous in these models given assumptions on monetary policies and exchange rates.

Growth is partly exogenous in the general equilibrium applications, although this is a question of modeling strategy rather than an inherent limitation of the methodology. In the Brussels model, the growth rate of the OECD countries is exogenous but those of the developing regions are not, whereas potential GNP of the three regions in the Manne model is exogenous but realized GNP is not. The Manne model includes an additional simplification in that capital formation is exogenous, whereas in the Brussels model growth of capital stock and GDP is endogenous in the developing regions.

The Brussels system is made dynamic by adding a model of labor-force growth and capital accumulation to the static general equilibrium model which is the heart of the system. The growth specification is strictly neoclassical in the flex-price version, although unemployment can exist in the fix-price variant. Unemployment slows capital formation and growth by depressing income and saving when prices are inflexible, but ex-ante savings continue to be invested despite excess capacity, as Bergman notes in his comment. This is a striking departure from the most common specification in models of developing economies, which usually assume that capital is the constraining factor and omit labor supply and unemployment as variables of interest in the growth process.

Perhaps the primary use of global input—output models in growth analysis is to achieve consistency checks on the microeconomic feasibility of alternative growth programs with exogenously specified regional growth rates, as in the original application of the Leontief World Model cited in Duchin's paper.

5.4   Other Problems

A contemporary question of great interest is the impact of supply-side shocks from scarcities of primary energy, food supplies, or raw materials. The effects of oil-price increases are investigated in multiplier simulations of the LINK, Brussels, Manne, and COMLINK models in the present set of papers. In addition, the long-term projections discussed in the previous section of necessity incorporate assumptions about the trajectory of the nominal or real price of oil over the forecast horizon. A basic difference between the macroeconometric and general equilibrium approach to the question is that only the real income effects of increases in real oil prices can be studied in the latter models, whereas the inflationary consequences of increasing energy prices can also be analyzed in the macro systems for given assumptions on policy reactions by monetary and fiscal authorities. The containment of the inflationary impact of energy shocks may affect real growth over the medium term in addition to the lasting effects from gains or losses in terms of trade and from the impact of higher real energy prices on the growth of potential GDP.

The COMLINK and REMPIS hybrids are designed for investigation of similar issues with regard to commodity prices more generally, by linking regional macroeconomic and commodity models. The real-income and price-level responses to exogenous increases in selected commodity prices are reported for the COMLINK simulations whereas the effects of commodity-price formula indexation on the developed and developing regions is the focus of the REMPIS paper.

6   FUTURE RESEARCH

It may be useful to close with some speculations on prospective research trends in the field of global international economic modeling as gleaned from the papers and comments in this volume and from personal reflection.

6.1   International Linkages

Few new developments can be expected concerning trade and price linkages, since the basic methodologies are well established (see Table 2). For models using an exogenous trade-share matrix for linkage of trade prices and flows, it is a recommended and relatively simple step to endogenize the share coefficients as functions of relative prices by any of several well-known procedures.

As we have seen, endogenous determination of exchange rates in multinational econometric models is being actively pursued from a variety of theoretical perspectives. For short-run forecasts and simulations, asset market variables must be included among exchange-rate determinants, either in direct reduced-form equations or in a structural balance-of-payments approach. Over longer periods exchange rates appear to follow purchasing power parity (PPP) to a close approximation and some version of PPP should be incorporated in long-run models with nominal domestic price level determination but lacking full financial sectors. Conversely, the structures of models incorporating the financial factors should be consistent with PPP in the long run if not in the short run. Because of differential productivity trends among tradeable and nontradeable goods and services, PPP is probably best specified in terms of export price indexes rather than domestic price levels.

Further work on direct interest rate and monetary linkages in multicountry models, including intervention and sterilization policies, is also highly desirable. Again, under present monetary arrangements this is of importance primarily for short-run applications, since for long-run analyses it is reasonable to assume that independent monetary policies may be conducted in a flexible exchange-rate regime.

6.2   Modeling Improvements

The most promising improvements for the short-term macroeconometric systems include structural modeling of the monetary and balance-of-payment sectors of the constituent models. This includes the endogenous formulation of exchange market intervention and sterilization functions to the extent that systematic policy rules can be identified.

Insofar as long-run projections are concerned, the principal need is to embed supply-side constraints more centrally in macroeconometric models, as Coen stresses in his comment. The underlying growth rate depends essentially on labor-force growth and technical progress, and a viable macroeconometric model for growth analysis should converge to the natural growth path in long-term simulations.

With regard to input—output models, the most exciting contemporary development is the INFORUM project for international linkage of individually built and operated national models. This conception parallels the philosophy of Project LINK, namely that national modelers know their own economies best, especially as regards institutional peculiarities and contemporary developments crucial for short-term forecasting and policy analysis. As compared with LINK, however, the INFORUM project lacks the benefit of a large number of pre-existing national models for which trade linkages could be readily developed on a uniform data base at a low level of disaggregation. Moreover, the open structure of input—output systems implies considerably less uniformity in the modeling of their macroeconomic components than is found in typical econometric models. Progress is apt to be slow for these reasons, but the very lack of a relatively uniform theoretical specification for the national models makes this a promising vehicle for cooperative international research among economists in Western, Socialist, and Third World countries.

It is apparent from the papers in this volume that the new general equilibrium techniques can be used to build elegant and viable empirical multiregional models yielding interesting conclusions in a variety of applications. Those who are skeptical that the usually maintained hypothesis of long-run competitive equilibrium is a sufficiently close approximation to reality will be pleased with the development of the fix-price variant of the Brussels model. On a more general level, the reliability of parameters established by the calibration method in a given year cannot be tested against the data, although extraneous parameter values can be supported by appeal to published econometric research. It would be desirable to develop methods for establishing the credibility and stability of the calibrated parameters, for example, by comparing the values obtained from the same specification in different years under different macroeconomic conditions.

6.3   Applications

A principal application of the global macroeconometric models is to the study of the international propagation of economic fluctuations and inflation. Included are such aspects as short-term forecasting of the level and distribution of world production, trade, payments balances, and prices; multiplier studies of the transmission mechanism; the role of energy- and commodity-price shocks in synchronizing international fluctuations; and policy simulations for independent or coordinated fiscal and monetary actions. In addition to the short-term models represented in the present volume, similar systems have been built for investigation of this range of problems at the European Economic Community (COMET and EUROLINK), the Organization for Economic Cooperation and Development (INTERLINK), the Free University of Brussels (DESMOS), the Netherlands

Central Planning Bureau (METEOR), and the Economic Planning Agency of Japan (EPA World Econometric Model). Proprietary systems have also been constructed by Data Resources, Inc. and Wharton Econometric Forecasting Associates. It appears that the widespread recognition of international interdependence and the desire for better coordination of forecasting activities and economic policies among national entities will continue to motivate attempts to build, improve, and operate linked multicountry models.

Another class of models has been constructed primarily for analysis of long-run developments and projections of the world economy, with particular reference to the North—South income gap and proposals for its reduction. This class is well represented in this volume in the papers on the Brussels, Leontief, FUGI, and DYNAMICO models.

Other models and studies presented here are also concerned with particular aspects of the North—South problem. Thus the Manne model is addressed specifically to the adverse effects of real resource transfers to the OPEC nations on the growth rate of the world economy in general and of the developing countries in particular. The REMPIS model was constructed for the purpose of evaluating proposals for nonoil commodity-price indexation as one way of narrowing the income gap. Finally, Whalley has used his general equilibrium model partly to estimate the gains or losses for the developed and developing regions under the Tokyo Round Agreement on reductions of tariffs and other trade barriers, and he has research underway to augment the model to distinguish between groups of developing countries as a prelude to examining alternative measures to redistribute income in favor of less developed countries under the new international order.

As part of continuing research on this range of questions, some of the modeling groups represented at the IIASA conference have undertaken a subsequent round of comparative simulations under the sponsorship of the Seminar on Global Modelling of the NSF—NBER Conference on Mathematical Economics and Econometrics. The simulations include both baseline projections through 1990 and multiplier studies of the responses to a 25% increase in the real price of oil in the LINK, Tsukuba, FUGI-Macro, and Manne models. It is planned to publish the individual simulations and a comparative analysis of the results on growth, inflation, trade, and other macroeconomic variables for the world economy as a whole and separately for the developed and developing regions. A followup conference on model simulations of other aspects of the North—South problem can hopefully be undertaken for an enlarged group of models. Such cooperative projects should enlarge the pool of information on the feasibility and potential costs and benefits of alternative policies for the new international order and provide a firmer basis for appraising individual model outcomes and accounting for their differences.

Part Two

Macroeconometric Models

GLOBAL INTERNATIONAL ECONOMIC MODELS
B.G. Hickman (editor)
Elsevier Science Publishers B.V. (North-Holland)
© IIASA, 1983

LONG-TERM SIMULATIONS WITH THE PROJECT LINK SYSTEM, 1978–1985

Victor Filatov
Department of Economics, University of Pennsylvania, Philadelphia, Pennsylvania (USA)

Bert G. Hickman
Department of Economics, Stanford University, Stanford, California (USA)

Lawrence R. Klein
Department of Economics, University of Pennsylvania, Philadelphia, Pennsylvania (USA)

1   INTRODUCTION

In this paper we present new long-term simulations of the Project LINK system through 1985. We first describe the system, its appropriateness for medium- or long-term applications, and the methodology of the simulations. Next we present a baseline solution from realistic initial conditions in 1978/1979 and trend extrapolations of exogenous variables through 1985. The following sections include scenarios for investment promotion through coordinated fiscal policies in 13 OECD countries and the response to changes in world oil prices. The paper concludes with an analysis of own (intracountry) and cross-country (intercountry) seven-year dynamic multipliers for government expenditure increases in each of the seven largest OECD countries participating in the LINK system.

2   WHAT IS THE LINK SYSTEM?

Project LINK is a cooperative, international research activity linking structural econometric models of 13 developed market economies, 7 centrally planned socialist countries, and 4 developing regions into a world model closed by rudimentary models for the rest of the world. The individual models and research institutions involved in the project are listed in Table 1. LINK Central, located at the Department of Economics, University of Pennsylvania, serves as the central computer repository for the associated models and databank and bears primary responsibility for forecasts and simulations of the system.

TABLE 1   National and regional models in the Project LINK system, 1980.

Country or region modeled	Institute	Model name	Time unit	Number of variables[a]	
				Endogenous	Exogenous
Australia	University of Melbourne[b]	RBF1	Quarterly	232	160
Austria	Institute for Advanced Study, Vienna	Austrian LINK Model	Quarterly	196	84
Belgium	Free University of Brussels	Quarterly Model of the Belgian Economy	Quarterly	92	71
Canada	University of Toronto	Econometric Model of the Canadian Economy	Annual	330	400
Finland	Bank of Finland	Bank of Finland Quarterly Model	Quarterly	178	143
France[c]	Free University of Brussels	Pompom	Annual	75	68
FRG	University of Bonn	Bonner Model 5.5	Annual	257	103
Italy	Istituto di Scienze Economiche, Bologna	Quarterly Model of the Italian Economy	Quarterly	219	194
Japan	Kyoto University	KYQ79 Forecasting Model of Japan	Quarterly	172	104
Netherlands	Central Planning Bureau	Netherlands LINK Model	Annual	164	133
Soviet Union	Wharton Econometric Forecasting Associates, Philadelphia	SOVMOD II	Annual	275	147
Sweden	Stockholm School of Economics	STEP1	Quarterly	307	302
United Kingdom	London Business School	LBS Quarterly Econometric Model of the UK Economy	Quarterly	359	180
United States	Wharton Econometric Forecasting Associates, Philadelphia	Wharton Quarterly Model, Mark 5.5	Quarterly	698	244
Developing countries	UNCTAD, Geneva	Regional Models of Developing Countries[d]	Annual	461	164
CMEA countries	UN Department for International Economic and Social Affairs, New York	Short-term Forecasting Models for the Centrally Planned Economies of Eastern Europe[e]	Annual	462	463

[a]Including linkage variables.
[b]Formerly located at the Reserve Bank of Australia.
[c]During 1981 the Metric Model of the French economy was substituted for the Pompom Model used in the simulations reported here.
[d]Includes the following regional models: Developing America, South and East Asia, Middle East, Africa.
[e]Includes the following national models: Bulgaria, Czechoslovakia, GDR, Hungary, Poland, Romania.

The LINK center at Stanford University undertakes research on linkage methodologies and dynamic properties of the system, and is also the home of a new model of the People's Republic of China to be incorporated into the system in the near future*.

The 13 national models of developed market economies vary considerably in size and specification but they are typically large, dynamic, disaggregated models of Keynesian (income–expenditure) character on the demand side. The supply side is typically represented by labor-supply and production functions of varying degrees of complexity and by capacity-utilization constraints. Monetary wages are usually explained by a structural labor-market Phillips curve and domestic prices by a mark-up hypothesis coupled with allowance for the direct and indirect effects of oil and other foreign prices. In most of the models money is important because interest rates or real balances affect aggregate demand. The principal institutional fiscal and monetary instruments of the country concerned are included in each national model to facilitate quantitative policy analyses.

The regional models for developing countries emphasize the essential features that differentiate these economies from those of the developed nations. Real GDP is supply-determined by production functions incorporating capital stock and nonfuel imports in the countries that do not export oil. Similarly, fixed investment is partly determined by imports in these models. Imports themselves are constrained by foreign-exchange reserves except for the oil-exporting countries. The domestic price level is a function of real monetary balances and import prices, with the nominal money stock exogenous.

The models of the centrally planned socialist countries are basically supply oriented, with production functions relating real net material product to available capital and labor resources and imported materials. Consumption and fixed investment are explained by demand functions and inventory investment is the residual buffer equating supply and demand ex post. Domestic prices are primarily determined by unit labor costs and import prices.

The various national and regional models are linked into a world system primarily through their trade accounts. Commodity trade is disaggregated into four classes: food and agricultural products, raw materials, fuels, and manufactured products. In the pre-linkage mode, each country's (or region's) real imports are endogenous functions of domestic activity and prices, with import prices exogenous. Conversely, export prices are endogenous and real export demands exogenous before linkage. The postlinkage solution endogenizes all trade prices and quantities through a central trade model, in which import prices are consistently-weighted averages of export prices, the geographical distribution of trade is fully determined, and the world trade identity is satisfied in the simultaneous solution of the complete set of national models.

Since the models for developed market economies incorporate the Keynesian aggregate-demand framework, disturbances at home may be transmitted abroad through induced changes in import demands and export prices, and disturbances may be received from abroad through external changes in export demands or import prices. Domestic prices will respond to externally induced changes in aggregate demand through the traditional foreign trade multiplier and wage–price interactions, but in addition prices are

---

*During 1981 the China model and new models for Denmark, Norway, Spain, Greece, and Switzerland were added to the LINK system, and the Metric model for France (built at INSEE) was substituted for the Pompom model. Also, a quarterly model was implemented for Canada (FOCUS) in place of the annual model (TRACE). Several new versions of other models were introduced during the year.

directly linked, either since import prices enter the domestic-price equations of the national models as cost factors or because the imports compete with domestically produced substitutes.

Analogous linking mechanisms are present in the models of developing and socialist countries even though GDP is supply-determined, since real imports are present as arguments in production and investment functions and import prices directly affect domestic prices. Principal channels for the transmission of shocks from the developing to the developed countries are exogenous changes in the prices of oil or other exports of the developing countries.

Exchange rates and capital flows among the developed countries are determined endogenously by cross-sectional equations in short-term forecasting applications of the LINK system, but these variables are exogenous in the long-run simulations reported in the present paper. It is therefore implicitly assumed in the simulations that induced changes in foreign reserves are "sterilized" by domestic monetary authorities and that incipient induced changes in interest rates through international capital markets are similarly offset*.

3   THE APPROPRIATENESS OF INTERMEDIATE-TERM PROJECTIONS

The initial aim when modeling the international economic system in Project LINK was to study the transmission mechanism, i.e., to examine the way in which economic events in one country or area affect economies elsewhere that trade with the affected economy. It was clearly an attempt to model the transmission of short-term business-cycle activities. In fact, the US component of LINK, the Wharton Quarterly Model, is primarily a short-term model that is used for business-cycle projections. A different Wharton model, based on annual data and incorporating a large input—output system of production-flow relationships, is used in the Wharton group for intermediate-term modeling in annual units, projected for time horizons of a decade or more; however, this Wharton annual model is *not* used directly in the LINK system.

Nevertheless, the Wharton Quarterly Model has been projected for periods as far as 10 years ahead. On one occasion, it was even projected for some 25—30 years ahead, and it was decided that there is a "plausible" solution for such a distant period. In this context, "plausibility" means that:

(i)   The mathematical—statistical system has solutions for more than 20 consecutive years, without there being lack of convergence or serious solution drift. Labor's income share, the velocity of money, capital-output ratios and other similar long-term concepts remain steady in this analysis. Before the LINK team became so interested in longer-term solutions, several individual models had been separately projected to 1985. These were the formative solutions on which the later linked intermediate-term analysis was based.

---

*The LINK system and its attributes are extensively documented in the references. See especially Ball (1973), Waelbroeck (1976), and Sawyer (1979).

(ii) Many conventional economic tendencies can be discerned in the prelinkage solutions of individual country or regional models. The slower overall rate of growth, long-term inflation, and several balance-of-payment problems can all be observed in the collection of intermediate-term projections.

(iii) Several time-honored aspects of economic balance can be found in these projections; for example, the real interest rates approximate the real growth rates of the individual systems, and some key ratios approach long-term equilibrium values. (See also point i.)

Many model proprietors have sent 10-year projections for their own systems to LINK Central. The Wharton Annual Model, with a complete input–output module, is used for basic projections in the intermediate term, and this has served as a pacemaker for 10-year projections of the Wharton Quarterly Model. Against this background, the LINK team was confident, in advance, that an intermediate-term simulation could readily be prepared.

The linked projections made in Spring 1979 were extended to 1985; therefore, in addition to the conventional short-term projections for 1979–1981, we merely added four more years. This did not tax the viability of either the individual models or the linked world system. The LINK team is now preparing for a longer projection — this time to 1990*.

4   THE STATISTICAL METHODOLOGY

It is by no means straightforward and obvious how to prepare a fully linked world simulation solution to 1985 or 1990. The first step is to extrapolate exogenous inputs — including population growth, harvest conditions, duty rates, domestic tax rates, public spending, monetary aggregates, and some other specialized variables that are peculiar to one or more of the systems.

Each exogenous variable in every LINK model is automatically examined for its past growth rate by estimation of semilog-linear time trends. These fitted trends are then extrapolated to 1985, and input values for the LINK solution are taken directly from the regression calculations.

Some models do not report all data necessary for each extrapolated variable. In some cases we can recognize that certain trends have changed and that the variable in question is being held steady or placed on a new path with a different time gradient. The mechanically constructed projections are either semilogarithmic or arithmetic. Usually, a semilog function of time with a constant growth rate is used.

Each exogenous input in every LINK model is examined on its own merits. Does the new trend reflect the historical trend in a plausible way? Is there any a priori evidence to suggest changes for the extrapolated input? Do the suggested changes agree with other independent estimates? (For example, do the new inputs for the Wharton *Quarterly* Model agree with the established trends for comparable statistical series from the Wharton *Annual* Model?)

Listings of the intended inputs are sent back to each LINK-model operator for approval. Then, prelinkage simulation projections are made for each model, based on

---

*Since this paper was prepared, the extension to 1990 has been completed and successfully applied in many scenario analyses.

prevailing initial conditions. Each solution is then examined on its own merits, and the solutions are discussed by the participants at the next semiannual LINK meeting.

After a prelinkage projection to 1985 has been tentatively accepted by the LINK Central staff and their own model operator, attempts are made at regular fully linked solutions, encompassing all the models together. Year-by-year, a fully linked solution is extended to 1985. These projections take into account the configuration of the world trading system. The solutions will of course be different from the unlinked projections of each individual model, yet they must not blatantly contradict the tentatively approved prelinkage projections, and any deviations must be capable of being explained by the workings of the linkage mechanism.

In establishing the fully linked projections, two procedures are used. In the first place, for the initial 2—3 years of the projection, a "believable" cyclical profile must be established, model by model. Each system's inputs will vary cyclically, causing some non-trend movements in economic activity. At present, for example, both the world cyclical slowdown in 1980 and the modest recovery found in regular short-term LINK projections must be fully discernible. Secondly, adjustments are introduced for each model, in addition to exogenous inputs, so that each solution starts out close to recent reality. There is fine tuning of the contemporary business-cycle situation. This is done in an independent computer solution file, but it should be made to agree with the basic LINK short-term solution file.

The adjustments to individual relationships in each model, or in the network of world trading relationships, are retained for the entire extended projection, but the exogenous inputs are not finely tuned to move in specific year-to-year cyclical patterns. Beyond a three-year horizon, it is assumed that only trend knowledge is available for each model. A typical GDP—time profile is shown in Figure 1.

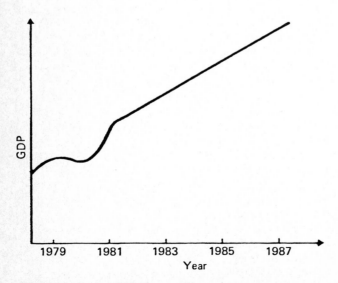

FIGURE 1   Typical GDP—time profile.

The LINK projections with near-term cyclical input, extended trend input, and constant adjustments to "calibrate" the system at the start of the projection period are shown again to all the individual model operators. One more iteration for adjustment and solution is carried out and once again the projection is completed. The projection at this stage, resulting from a combination of cycle and trend, is referred to as the baseline projection.

5   THE BASELINE CASE, 1978–1985

The LINK system, having been subjected to this iterative process of tentative projection, criticism, and reconsideration, and after being run in unlinked and fully linked modes, will now be described in more quantitative terms in the accompanying tables, which show both world totals and some of the main results for individual models.

Two indicators of world totals in Table 2 show significant cyclical fluctuations, followed by general expansion. Real GDP growth among the 13 OECD countries participating in LINK falls to less than 1% for 1980, although there is a positive change from 1979 to 1980. Even 1979 shows a low value, in the sense that 2.6% is a fairly slow growth rate for the OECD countries in the conditions prevailing in that year. The recovery in 1981 is not very vigorous as a result of continued restraint in a number of countries and the beginning of a slowdown in the FRG, Japan, and various economies closely linked to them. After this cyclical episode, however, the world industrial economy appears to be returning to a steady growth rate of somewhat above 3% per annum.

The cyclical fluctuations in trade volume (*TWX*) are sharper. A small absolute decline is estimated for 1980. By 1985 trade volume has returned to an annual rate of expansion of about 6%. At first sight this 6% seems to be a high figure, suggesting genuine recovery, but it is in fact a great deal smaller than the corresponding rates recorded during the trade expansion of the late 1960s – about 9 or 10% per annum. Both production and trade volume, therefore, are headed for a pattern of moderation, in which one or more percentage points have been shaved from the normal historical growth-rate patterns.

In addition to the modest recovery in production shown in this baseline projection, a definite reduction in the rate of inflation (% *PC*) is shown to be attainable. The basic rate of 10%, at the consumer level, falls to about 5 or 6% by the middle of the 1980s.

It should be noted that this is not a "dream" scenario; it presents a highly possible set of circumstances. However, it is based on the assumption of a benign environment – no wars, no other military disturbances, and no "acts of God".

With the steadily rising oil price index (*TWPX3*), the OPEC surplus grows and grows; this is shown in the large increase of the total DEVE surplus from $27.9 billion in 1978 to $239.1 billion in 1985 (these figures include both the oil-exporting and the oil-importing countries in the developing world). The implied OPEC surplus will pose an economic recycling problem, but this is not discussed in detail here.

The overall effect on the developing countries of cyclical fluctuations plus restrained trend expansion is a continuation of their present sluggish growth rates. For the developing countries as a whole (the penultimate group of entries in Table 3) – including both oil exporters and oil importers – annual GDP growth is expected to slow to a figure of less than 4% for 1980, and even this estimate may be on the high side. There is a longer-term

TABLE 2   Baseline projection, 1978–1985. Apart from percentage changes, all variables are expressed in units of 10⁹ US *current* dollars, except for *TWX*, *TWX3*, and *GDP* which are given in 10⁹ US *constant* dollars.

Variable[a]	Value for each year and percentage change (%CH) over previous year's value														
	1978	1979	%CH	1980	%CH	1981	%CH	1982	%CH	1983	%CH	1984	%CH	1985	%CH
13 LINK OECD countries															
X	791.6	938.1	18.5	1061.9	13.2	1179.2	11.0	1326.3	12.5	1505.5	13.5	1704.9	13.2	1936.2	13.6
M	769.8	936.6	21.7	1110.3	18.5	1226.4	10.5	1379.7	12.5	1570.3	13.8	1797.1	14.4	2067.1	15.0
B	21.8	1.4		−48.4		−47.1		−53.4		−64.8		−92.2		−131.0	
GDP	2530.3	2595.6	2.6	2612.9	0.7	2659.5	1.8	2741.4	3.1	2827.2	3.1	2918.9	3.2	3024.1	3.6
%PGDP			9.2		8.5		7.0		6.4		5.8		5.1		4.9
%PC			10.2		9.9		7.3		6.8		6.1		5.7		5.3
Developing countries															
X	302.9	414.0	36.7	547.1	32.2	632.3	15.6	737.5	16.6	883.3	19.8	1053.0	19.2	1270.4	20.6
M	275.0	359.0	30.5	439.4	22.4	518.2	18.0	606.4	17.0	728.4	20.1	863.8	18.6	1031.2	19.4
B	27.9	55.0		107.8		114.0		131.1		154.9		189.2		239.1	
CMEA countries															
X	112.8	128.6	14.0	143.3	11.4	160.6	12.1	182.5	13.6	204.3	11.9	232.6	13.8	262.8	13.0
M	124.6	139.2	11.7	153.0	10.0	172.4	12.7	192.8	11.8	216.5	12.3	236.1	9.0	258.7	9.6
B	−11.8	−10.6		−9.7		−11.8		−10.3		−12.2		−3.5		4.2	
Rest of the World															
X	94.9	120.7	27.2	140.9	16.8	158.1	12.2	172.1	8.8	195.5	13.6	215.9	10.4	238.7	10.6
M	132.8	166.5	25.4	190.6	14.5	213.2	11.9	239.5	12.3	273.5	14.2	309.4	13.1	351.0	13.5
B	−37.9	−45.8		−49.6		−55.1		−67.4		−78.0		−93.5		−112.3	
World totals															
TWVX	1302.2	1601.3	23.0	1893.3	18.2	2130.3	12.5	2418.4	13.5	2788.7	15.3	3206.3	15.0	3708.1	15.6
TWPX	2.6	3.0	17.0	3.6	18.4	3.9	9.2	4.3	9.4	4.6	8.5	5.1	9.4	5.6	9.2
TWX	503.6	529.3	5.1	528.6	−0.1	544.8	3.1	565.2	3.7	600.7	6.3	631.1	5.1	668.1	5.9
TWPX3	6.1	8.6	41.5	13.3	54.2	15.9	19.6	18.9	18.6	22.3	18.4	26.7	19.4	31.9	19.4
TWX3	37.3	38.8	4.1	37.5	−3.3	37.3	−0.5	38.9	2.5	39.6	3.5	40.8	2.9	42.6	4.4

[a]Variables are defined as follows: X, exports; M, imports; B, trade balance; GDP, GDP for the 13 LINK OECD countries; %PGDP, percentage change in the implicit price deflator of GDP for the 13 LINK OECD countries; %PC, percentage change in the personal consumption deflator for the 13 LINK OECD countries; TWVX, value of world trade; TWPX, price of world trade (the implicit price deflator for world trade); TWX, volume of world trade; TWPX3, price index for world imports of oil and other fuels; TWX3, volume index for world exports of oil and other fuels.

TABLE 3   Real GDP growth in local currency units (%), 1979–1985: fiscal-stimulus (Fiscal) and baseline (Base) scenarios, and the difference between them.

	Year						
	1979	1980	1981	1982	1983	1984	1985
Australia							
Fiscal	3.8	2.5	2.2	1.5	1.5	2.4	2.8
Base	3.6	1.8	1.9	2.2	2.2	2.4	2.4
Difference	0.2	0.7	0.3	−0.7	−0.7	0.0	0.4
Austria							
Fiscal	6.7	1.8	2.2	4.3	4.8	4.3	3.6
Base	5.2	1.0	1.9	4.2	4.7	4.1	3.5
Difference	1.5	0.8	0.3	0.1	0.1	0.2	0.1
Belgium							
Fiscal	4.6	2.1	3.0	3.7	3.1	3.3	2.7
Base	3.8	1.5	2.9	3.4	3.1	3.3	2.6
Difference	0.8	0.6	0.1	0.3	0.0	0.0	0.1
Canada							
Fiscal	3.3	1.8	1.6	2.5	3.1	3.8	5.2
Base	3.1	1.4	1.3	2.4	3.0	3.5	5.0
Difference	0.2	0.4	0.3	0.1	0.1	0.3	0.2
Finland							
Fiscal	8.1	4.8	2.9	3.6	4.5	4.4	2.8
Base	7.3	3.9	2.2	3.2	4.2	4.0	2.9
Difference	0.8	0.9	0.7	0.4	0.3	0.4	−0.1
France							
Fiscal	3.4	1.7	3.4	4.3	4.7	4.0	4.4
Base	3.3	1.0	3.4	4.3	4.7	4.0	4.4
Difference	0.1	0.7	0.0	0.0	0.0	0.0	0.0
FRG							
Fiscal	5.2	2.1	4.7	4.4	4.0	4.7	5.5
Base	4.5	1.5	3.8	3.7	3.4	4.4	5.8
Difference	0.7	0.6	0.9	0.7	0.6	0.3	−0.3
Italy							
Fiscal	4.7	3.3	2.6	3.2	2.8	4.0	2.2
Base	4.4	2.9	2.3	3.0	2.6	3.9	2.2
Difference	0.3	0.4	0.3	0.2	0.2	0.1	0.0
Japan							
Fiscal	6.6	3.6	3.7	4.9	5.2	4.7	5.6
Base	6.0	3.1	3.3	4.7	5.0	4.5	5.5
Difference	0.6	0.5	0.4	0.2	0.2	0.2	0.1
Netherlands							
Fiscal	3.2	1.6	2.9	3.5	2.6	1.8	2.5
Base	2.8	0.7	1.9	3.0	2.3	1.8	2.7
Difference	0.4	0.9	1.0	0.5	0.3	0.0	−0.2
Sweden							
Fiscal	5.8	3.6	3.6	2.5	3.0	2.2	1.6
Base	4.8	2.6	3.3	2.8	3.2	2.1	1.5
Difference	1.0	1.0	0.3	−0.3	−0.2	0.1	0.1

TABLE 3   *Continued.*

	Year						
	1979	1980	1981	1982	1983	1984	1985
United Kingdom							
Fiscal	1.2	−0.9	1.5	3.5	1.9	1.8	1.8
Base	0.9	−1.4	1.3	3.7	2.2	1.7	1.8
Difference	0.3	0.5	0.2	−0.2	−0.3	0.1	0.0
United States							
Fiscal	2.4	0.3	1.4	2.8	2.7	3.0	2.6
Base	2.2	−0.4	0.7	2.4	2.6	2.8	2.5
Difference	0.2	0.7	0.7	0.4	0.1	0.2	0.1
Developing countries[a]							
Fiscal	4.7	4.0	5.3	5.1	5.4	4.8	4.2
Base	4.7	3.9	5.2	5.0	5.4	4.7	4.2
Difference	0.0	0.1	0.1	0.1	0.0	0.1	0.0
13 LINK OECD countries							
Fiscal	2.9	1.3	2.3	3.3	3.3	3.4	3.7
Base	2.6	0.7	1.8	3.1	3.1	3.2	3.6
Difference	0.3	0.6	0.5	0.2	0.2	0.2	0.1

[a]Expressed in 1960 US dollars and percentage changes computed.

recovery to about 5% per annum up to 1984. This is below the targets of the UN "development decade" of the 1980s, and even more markedly so when it is remembered that OPEC countries will grow at above-average rates, thus implying that other developing countries will have correspondingly below-average growth rates. Black Africa is expected to experience particularly low rates.

Although not shown explicitly in Table 2, the growth rate of the CMEA group is included in the world GDP total. With the exceptions of Bulgaria and Romania, the Eastern European nations and the Soviet Union are all expanding at rates of about 2–4% per annum. The rate for the Soviet Union sometimes rises above 5% for individual years but the average rate is below that observed in recent historical trends. Romania and Bulgaria show many individual years in which the growth of net material product is around 8%; this is a respectable figure, reminiscent of a significant expansion that formerly took place in Eastern Europe. However, most of the other CMEA countries are faced with large debts outstanding, causing a domestic slowdown. The Soviet Union performs better than the other CMEA countries, on average, but still below Soviet aspirations.

Tables 3 and 4 show individual country (or region) performance for real GDP growth and the inflation rate, respectively. The baseline entries in these tables are compared with values that would arise from specific policy decisions (as will be explained in the next section). Meanwhile, let us consider details of the performance of each country (or region) for the baseline scenario.

It is evident that all countries exhibit a common cyclical slowdown in GDP growth during 1980. The figures are still only modest for 1981, but indicate some recovery from the 1980 values. The respective expansion paths projected for 1981 reinforce earlier conclusions about growth prospects and lead into sustained improvement of performance during the later years of this forecast.

TABLE 4   Inflation rates (consumption deflator, %), 1979–1985: fiscal-stimulus (Fiscal) and base-line (Base) scenarios, and the difference between them.

	Year						
	1979	1980	1981	1982	1983	1984	1985
Australia							
Fiscal	9.9	9.9	8.8	9.6	7.7	7.8	7.8
Base	9.9	9.8	8.7	9.5	7.6	7.8	7.8
Difference	0.0	0.1	0.1	0.1	0.1	0.0	0.0
Austria							
Fiscal	4.2	4.8	3.2	4.0	3.6	4.5	4.2
Base	4.3	4.8	2.9	3.8	3.4	4.4	4.2
Difference	−0.1	0.0	0.3	0.2	·0.2	0.1	0.0
Belgium							
Fiscal	4.0	8.4	7.2	6.3	6.4	6.2	6.1
Base	4.0	8.4	7.1	6.2	6.3	6.1	6.1
Difference	0.0	0.0	0.1	0.1	0.1	0.1	0.0
Canada							
Fiscal	11.5	12.5	11.2	9.2	8.2	7.1	6.0
Base	11.6	12.3	10.7	8.7	7.7	6.8	5.7
Difference	−0.1	0.2	0.5	0.5	0.5	0.3	0.3
Finland							
Fiscal	9.5	6.7	6.3	5.5	6.0	6.8	5.5
Base	9.4	6.7	6.2	5.3	5.7	6.3	4.9
Difference	0.1	0.0	0.1	0.2	0.3	0.5	0.6
France							
Fiscal	12.0	12.7	7.6	8.7	7.6	7.3	6.5
Base	12.0	12.5	7.4	8.6	7.5	7.2	6.4
Difference	0.0	0.2	0.2	0.1	0.1	0.1	0.1
FRG[a]							
Fiscal	4.3	3.8	3.7	3.2	3.3	3.6	3.7
Base	3.9	3.3	3.1	2.6	2.9	3.3	3.6
Difference	0.4	0.5	0.6	0.6	0.4	0.3	0.1
Italy							
Fiscal	16.1	11.8	10.0	7.4	7.2	6.8	7.3
Base	16.1	11.8	10.1	7.4	7.2	6.8	7.3
Difference	0.0	0.0	−0.1	0.0	0.0	0.0	0.0
Japan							
Fiscal	10.2	9.8	7.3	5.9	4.9	4.9	4.5
Base	10.1	9.5	7.1	5.8	4.8	4.8	4.5
Difference	0.1	0.3	0.2	0.1	0.1	0.1	0.0
Netherlands							
Fiscal	6.1	8.9	4.6	5.1	7.6	6.9	7.0
Base	6.2	9.1	4.9	5.3	7.7	6.8	6.8
Difference	−0.1	−0.2	−0.3	−0.2	−0.1	0.1	0.2
Sweden							
Fiscal	7.5	6.4	5.5	5.8	5.5	5.8	5.8
Base	7.7	7.1	5.7	5.6	5.2	5.7	5.8
Difference	−0.2	−0.7	−0.2	0.2	0.3	0.1	0.0

TABLE 4 *Continued.*

	Year						
	1979	1980	1981	1982	1983	1984	1985
United Kingdom							
Fiscal	12.7	17.4	10.0	9.7	9.1	9.7	9.4
Base	12.7	17.4	10.0	9.6	9.0	9.7	9.5
Difference	0.0	0.0	0.0	0.1	0.1	0.0	−0.1
United States							
Fiscal	10.6	9.5	7.1	7.0	6.2	5.4	5.0
Base	10.7	10.0	7.5	7.3	6.4	5.6	5.0
Difference	−0.1	−0.5	−0.4	−0.3	−0.2	−0.2	0.0
13 LINK OECD countries							
Fiscal	10.2	9.7	7.2	6.8	6.1	5.7	5.3
Base	10.2	9.9	7.3	6.8	6.1	5.7	5.3
Difference	0.0	−0.2	−0.1	0.0	0.0	0.0	0.0

[a]The price measure is the GDP deflator.

The forecasted 1980 inflation rates in the OECD countries are mixed (Table 4), with some experiencing increases and others decreases, and with little change in the average rate. A general diminution is projected thereafter, with inflation dropping to more manageable levels, even in those countries that have experienced chronic, more severe (double-digit) inflation in the recent past.

6   FISCAL POLICY SCENARIO

As mentioned previously, Tables 3 and 4 also include values derived from a "fiscal-stimulus" scenario. This case examined the effect on the world economy of a synchronized policy stimulus for investment that improved the rate of return on capital. In models incorporating fiscal parameters related to investment decisions, the policy-instrument variables were changed; examples include investment tax credits, depreciation write-off procedures, corporate tax rates, and similar mechanisms. The overall result of these changes, amounting to investment increases of about 2%, raised the growth rate of most industrialized countries and reduced their rates of inflation. On average, the GDP growth rate was raised by about one-half of a percentage point in the early years of the simulation, but later settled down to an increment of only 0.1−0.2 percentage points in the GDP growth rate. The spillover to growth in the developing world is noticeable, but the absolute values are not large, amounting to an increase of only 0.1 percentage points on average.

Initially, the inflation rate is generally lowered in the fiscal stimulus scenario, showing a fall of 0.1 or 0.2 percentage points as a result of these policies. Eventually, however, the inflation rate ceases to be different in the two scenarios. The fall in US inflation is fairly marked, but only during the first half of the simulation period.

The reason why inflation falls as the economy expands is that the fiscal stimulus introduced is not of the ordinary variety. It is aimed specifically at promoting capital formation − which it does − and the expansion of capital for the short-term production function helps to induce higher productivity gains. This is an important policy alternative to model since capital formation has never properly recovered from the last recession and it is felt to be badly in need of encouragement. Business costs are reduced in the fiscal-stimulus scenario and in the real world this could in turn help restrain prices, at least initially.

The productivity gains arising from the fiscal stimulus can be seen in Table 5. As stated earlier, the fiscal-stimulus scenario devotes a fair amount of attention to the revival

TABLE 5   Productivity gains (% change in output per man-hour), 1979–1985: fiscal-stimulus (Fiscal) and baseline (Base) scenarios, and the difference between them.

	Year							Average,
	1979	1980	1981	1982	1983	1984	1985	1979–1985
Australia								
Fiscal	1.4	0.2	0.1	−1.6	0.7	1.0	1.0	0.3
Base	1.3	−0.2	0.4	−0.7	1.0	0.5	0.5	0.4
Difference	0.1	0.4	−0.3	−0.9	−0.3	0.5	0.5	−0.1
Belgium								
Fiscal	7.2	3.5	2.6	3.8	2.9	3.3	2.6	3.7
Base	6.3	3.1	2.6	3.5	3.0	3.4	2.7	3.5
Difference	0.9	0.4	0.0	0.3	−0.1	−0.1	−0.1	0.2
Canada								
Fiscal	−0.1	1.2	2.7	3.7	3.8	4.4	5.0	2.9
Base	−0.3	0.9	2.6	3.6	3.7	4.2	4.8	2.8
Difference	0.2	0.3	0.1	0.1	0.1	0.2	0.2	0.1
Finland								
Fiscal	4.6	1.5	0.7	1.3	1.7	1.8	1.5	1.9
Base	4.0	1.2	0.3	1.2	1.6	1.6	1.4	1.6
Difference	0.6	0.3	0.4	0.1	0.1	0.2	0.1	0.3
France								
Fiscal	3.5	2.5	2.7	4.3	4.6	4.2	4.5	3.8
Base	3.5	3.4	1.4	4.3	4.6	4.2	4.5	3.7
Difference	0.0	−0.9	1.3	0.0	0.0	0.0	0.0	0.1
FRG								
Fiscal	5.2	3.8	4.6	4.2	4.3	4.4	4.6	4.4
Base	5.0	3.8	4.4	4.3	4.5	4.7	5.0	4.5
Difference	0.2	0.0	0.2	−0.1	−0.2	−0.3	−0.4	−0.1
Italy								
Fiscal	5.5	4.3	3.0	3.2	3.7	3.6	2.8	3.7
Base	5.4	3.9	2.7	3.0	3.6	3.4	2.8	3.5
Difference	0.1	0.4	0.3	0.2	0.1	0.2	0.0	0.2
Japan								
Fiscal	7.3	3.5	5.2	5.0	6.8	4.6	4.8	5.3
Base	6.1	2.4	4.2	4.7	6.8	4.4	4.8	4.8
Difference	1.2	1.1	1.0	0.3	0.0	0.2	0.0	0.5
Netherlands								
Fiscal	2.0	1.5	3.2	2.2	2.0	1.0	1.3	1.9
Base	1.6	1.0	2.7	2.0	1.9	0.2	1.7	1.6
Difference	0.4	0.5	0.5	0.2	0.1	0.8	−0.4	0.3

TABLE 5 *Continued.*

	Year							Average,
	1979	1980	1981	1982	1983	1984	1985	1979–1985
Sweden								
Fiscal	4.8	3.3	3.6	2.2	2.4	1.8	1.5	2.8
Base	4.1	2.7	3.5	2.4	2.5	1.7	1.5	2.6
Difference	0.7	0.6	0.1	−0.2	−0.1	0.1	0.0	0.2
United Kingdom								
Fiscal	2.1	−0.2	2.5	4.6	2.8	2.6	2.6	2.4
Base	1.8	−0.8	2.3	4.9	3.1	2.5	2.6	2.4
Difference	0.3	0.6	0.2	−0.3	−0.3	0.1	0.0	0.0
United States								
Fiscal	1.1	0.1	1.6	1.9	1.5	1.7	1.3	1.3
Base	0.7	−0.4	1.4	1.9	1.6	1.7	1.3	1.2
Difference	0.4	0.5	0.2	0.0	−0.1	0.0	0.0	0.1
12 LINK OECD countries								
Fiscal	3.2	1.6	2.7	3.1	3.3	2.6	2.9	2.8
Base	2.9	1.2	2.4	3.1	3.3	2.9	3.0	2.7
Difference	0.3	0.4	0.3	0.0	0.0	−0.3	−0.1	0.1

of capital formation. The production functions of the model indicate output expansion at a rate that exceeds labor input; therefore, productivity rises. This is likely to remain the case as long as the fixed capital-expansion program is in effect. The new and modernized capital stock paves the way for productivity gains, and these in turn help to bring down the rate of inflation.

The maximum impact on productivity occurs during the second or third year of the projection. Over the longer term, productivity growth is not much better in one scenario than in the other.

7   OIL-PRICE SCENARIOS

A key assumption for the baseline projection, and one that also affects every other LINK scenario, concerns the future path assumed for the world oil price. The movement of an index of this price, *TWPX3*, is shown in Table 2.

Two large annual rises are assumed for 1979 and 1980, and these seem to be realistic. For the intermediate term, the annual price rise is set at just below 20%. Allowing for world inflation (affecting the prices of goods purchased by OPEC countries) of 10% per annum, this still leaves a 10% gain which is a net benefit for the oil exporters.

What would be the outcome if oil prices were to develop quite differently — for example, showing increases higher than those anticipated above? To answer this question we now present results from a LINK simulation with alternative assumptions about oil prices, just to determine the sensitivity of the US and world economies to changes in world oil prices.

TABLE 6   Effects of oil-price increases (changes from baseline values), 1979–1985.

Parameter	Year						
	1979	1980	1981	1982	1983	1984	1985
Change in trade balance (10^9 US dollars)							
13 LINK OECD countries	−15.6	−23.6	−38.9	−55.4	−74.2	−98.0	−124.5
Developing countries	13.4	20.7	35.3	50.8	68.9	91.3	117.4
CMEA countries	1.9	2.4	3.4	4.8	5.9	7.6	9.0
Rest of the World	0.3	0.4	0.1	−0.2	−0.5	−1.0	−1.9
Change in growth and inflation rates (%)							
World export price	1.8	0.9	1.7	1.3	1.5	1.2	1.5
World export volume	−1.5	−0.7	−0.6	−0.9	−0.7	−0.2	−0.3
World export price for oil	8.5	3.2	6.5	5.2	4.6	5.2	4.8
GDP (13 LINK OECD countries)	−0.5	−0.4	−0.5	−0.4	−0.4	−0.4	−0.4
Consumption deflator (13 LINK OECD countries)	0.3	0.3	0.5	0.4	0.4	0.4	0.4

The baseline case actually used for this part of the study antedates the one used elsewhere in the paper; therefore, in order not to confuse the issue, the oil-price simulation results will be presented in terms of *deviations* from this earlier baseline case. Table 6 presents a summary of the projected changes in a number of key indicators resulting from a change in world oil prices. In the oil-price-change scenario, the world oil export price is increased by 8.5 percentage points over the baseline case for 1979, by about three points for 1980, and by approximately five percentage points for subsequent years, as may be seen in Table 6.

A familiar and expected effect is observed. The higher world oil price tends to lower the GDP growth rate and raise the consumer price inflation rate. The 13 OECD countries participating in LINK account for most of the economic activity in the OECD group, and their GDP growth is reduced by about 0.4% per annum throughout the whole projection period. The increase in the domestic inflation rate also averages about 0.4% per annum. The reduction in the annual growth rate of world trade volume is somewhat higher, averaging about 1% during the first half of the simulation period but falling to about 0.2% or 0.3% by the end of the simulation horizon.

The growing trade surplus for the developing countries reflects the large OPEC surplus resulting from the oil price rises. The main offset to the OPEC surplus is the OECD deficit.

8   DYNAMIC INTERNATIONAL INCOME MULTIPLIERS

In this section own (intracountry) and cross-country (intercountry) income multipliers are presented for unsynchronized real-demand shocks in the seven largest OECD countries. These are dynamic multipliers covering a span of seven years a.:d computed relative to the same postlinkage baseline solution for 1978–1985 as used in the preceding scenarios. Each major model was shocked in turn by a sustained exogenous increase of government expenditure over the 1978–1985 period and the new postlinkage solution was compared with the baseline solution to measure the induced changes in real GDP in the 13 OECD countries participating in LINK.

The elasticity multipliers are calculated from the formula

$$M_{ij} = [(Y_j^s - Y_j^b)/Y_j^b]/[(G_i^s - G_i^b)/Y_i^b] \tag{1}$$

where M_{ij} measures the income response in country j to an increase in government expenditure in country i, and the superscripts s and b refer to the shocked and baseline solutions, respectively.

Instead of computing conventional absolute multipliers as in the expression

$$m_{ij} = (Y_j^s - Y_j^b)/(G_i^s - G_i^b) \tag{2}$$

in eqn. (1) the shock is expressed as a percentage of real income in the originating country and the response is similarly measured relative to income in the receiving country. This form is preferable because it is dimensionless and allows for differences in the size of the two countries

$$M_{ij} = m_{ij}(Y_i^b/Y_j^b) \tag{3}$$

Thus the elasticity cross-country multiplier for income is greater or smaller than the absolute multiplier according to whether the originating country is the larger or smaller. An apparently small absolute multiplier from a large country may actually imply a large relative income shock to a small country, and vice-versa, but the elasticity form automatically allows for this factor. The own-country multipliers, of course, have the same magnitude whether measured in absolute or in elasticity units.

The multipliers are shown in matrix form in Table 7. The own multipliers for the seven largest countries appear on the main diagonal in the first seven columns. They exhibit substantial stability over time in all the countries, and range in size from slightly over unity for France and the United Kingdom to peak values of 2.9 for the FRG and 2.8 for the United States. The time paths vary according to the response mechanisms of the individual models, with cumulative increases to approximate plateaus in the later years for Canada, France, Italy, Japan, and the United States as the most typical pattern. The multipliers for the FRG and the United Kingdom peak in the third year, with the former declining sharply and continuously thereafter and the latter stabilizing on a plateau during the last three years. With the exception of the FRG, there is little evidence from any of the models of structural response mechanisms capable of converting demand shocks into endogenous business cycles, except possibly for highly damped minor inventory fluctuations.

The multipliers also imply a high degree of international stability. The destabilizing influence of a shock at home is distributed over many trading partners abroad, so that the cross multipliers are generally small. This is not to deny that disturbances, especially those originating in the FRG or the United States, can have a substantial impact on other countries and particularly on close trading partners which are "small" and open. Even in these cases, however, the countries most affected generally exhibit cross multipliers from West

German or US shocks that are considerably smaller than the responses to their own internal shocks. (Own multipliers for the six smaller OECD countries are not available in the present set of simulations but they were found to be substantially larger than the West German and US cross multipliers for the same countries in similar calculations for 1973–1975 (Hickman, 1974).)

The overall strength of the responses at home and abroad to unsynchronized shocks in the larger countries are summarized from two perspectives in Table 7. The elasticity multipliers for the combined GDP of the 13 OECD countries are given in the penultimate column. These are no greater than 0.2 for shocks originating in Canada, France, Italy, Japan, and the United Kingdom. They exceed unity only for a shock originating from the United States, which has a large own multiplier and also accounts for close to half of the total GDP for the 13 countries together. Even the FRG exhibits a relatively small overall impact on the combined GDP of the 13 countries.

The last column in Table 7 lists the unweighted sums of the percentage responses in the originating and receiving countries. Although these totals differ markedly from the multipliers calculated from the relative increase of the aggregate GDP of the 13 countries, they are more meaningful for most purposes. This is because a 10% increase in, for example, Austrian GNP is as important to the Austrian economy as the same percentage increase in a large country such as the United States, even though world GNP will increase only slightly in the former case. It will be seen that, except for the FRG, there is a general tendency for these total response multipliers to rise over time as the effects accumulate both within and between countries.

Finally, we obtain an index of the effects of simultaneous shocks in the seven larger OECD countries by summing down the columns. This is an approximate measure because the models are nonlinear and not strictly additive, but the results are unlikely to differ much from those for postlinkage simulations with simultaneous shocks. It is again both interesting and encouraging that the overall multipliers even for simultaneous shocks are generally moderate in size, ranging between 1.3 and 2.3 in the first year, 1.5 and 4.0 in the fourth year, and 1.6 and 3.3 in the seventh year.

The magnitude of the cross multipliers depends basically on three factors: (a) the size of the own responses of incomes and prices to the domestic shock in the originating country; (b) the magnitude of the resulting induced changes in its import demands and export prices; and (c) the responses of prices and incomes in the receiving countries to the resulting changes in their export demands and import prices. We may control for the first factor by dividing the cross multipliers in each row by the corresponding own multiplier. The resulting matrix of normalized multipliers is presented in Table 8.

Reading across a row in Table 8 shows the response in country *j* per unit of total increase of income in country *i*, rather than per unit of autonomous income increase alone as in Table 7. Scaling the cross multipliers in this way more nearly isolates the importance of the trade flows between the "disturbing" and "disturbed" countries from the effects of the internal multiplier in the disturbing country. As noted above, however, the cross effects are also influenced by the response mechanism of the receiving country. One may hold this last factor roughly constant by reading down a given column of Table 8, thereby isolating the strength of the external ties between the given country and its trading partners.

TABLE 7   International elasticity multipliers for real income (percentage income change of country in column induced per unit percentage income shock from country in row), 1979–1985.

Country	Year	Canada	France	FRG	Italy	Japan	UK	USA	Australia	Austria	Belgium	Finland	Netherlands	Sweden	13 LINK OECD countries GDP	13 LINK OECD countries Total
Canada	1979	1.38	0.00	0.01	0.01	0.01	0.01	0.02	0.00	0.01	0.01	0.01	0.01	0.01	0.07	1.49
	1980	1.36	0.00	0.02	0.02	0.01	0.01	0.04	0.01	0.01	0.01	0.02	0.02	0.01	0.08	1.54
	1981	1.37	0.01	0.02	0.02	0.01	0.01	0.05	0.01	0.01	0.01	0.03	0.02	0.01	0.09	1.58
	1982	1.40	0.01	0.03	0.03	0.01	0.01	0.05	0.01	0.02	0.02	0.03	0.03	0.01	0.09	1.66
	1983	1.26	0.01	0.03	0.02	0.01	0.01	0.04	0.01	0.02	0.02	0.04	0.03	0.01	0.08	1.51
	1984	1.54	0.01	0.05	0.03	0.02	0.02	0.05	0.01	0.02	0.02	0.05	0.04	0.01	0.10	1.87
	1985	1.58	0.01	0.04	0.04	0.02	0.02	0.06	0.01	0.03	0.02	0.06	0.04	0.01	0.10	1.94
France	1979	0.03	1.07	0.09	0.09	0.03	0.03	0.02	0.01	0.04	0.12	0.05	0.08	0.03	0.10	1.69
	1980	0.04	1.07	0.12	0.11	0.04	0.04	0.03	0.02	0.06	0.14	0.09	0.15	0.05	0.12	1.96
	1981	0.05	1.07	0.19	0.14	0.05	0.06	0.04	0.02	0.08	0.16	0.14	0.21	0.07	0.14	2.28
	1982	0.05	1.07	0.22	0.15	0.05	0.06	0.05	0.02	0.08	0.16	0.18	0.23	0.05	0.15	2.37
	1983	0.05	1.08	0.26	0.16	0.06	0.06	0.05	0.03	0.09	0.17	0.20	0.25	0.05	0.15	2.51
	1984	0.05	1.08	0.25	0.16	0.07	0.06	0.05	0.03	0.09	0.16	0.21	0.27	0.04	0.16	2.52
	1985	0.04	1.09	0.21	0.16	0.06	0.06	0.04	0.03	0.09	0.16	0.21	0.29	0.03	0.15	2.47
FRG	1979	0.06	0.11	1.83	0.28	0.06	0.09	0.04	0.03	0.24	0.34	0.18	0.37	0.11	0.25	3.74
	1980	0.09	0.12	1.87	0.35	0.11	0.12	0.10	0.05	0.34	0.46	0.39	0.63	0.17	0.30	4.80
	1981	0.13	0.17	2.91	0.52	0.17	0.19	0.16	0.08	0.50	0.63	0.66	0.99	0.25	0.47	7.36
	1982	0.14	0.18	2.73	0.57	0.19	0.20	0.18	0.08	0.53	0.65	0.81	1.09	0.25	0.48	7.60
	1983	0.13	0.18	2.37	0.54	0.19	0.18	0.16	0.08	0.47	0.58	0.83	1.11	0.19	0.43	7.01
	1984	0.12	0.17	1.88	0.48	0.18	0.16	0.13	0.07	0.39	0.49	0.83	1.06	0.11	0.36	6.07
	1985	0.09	0.15	1.28	0.40	0.15	0.13	0.08	0.05	0.30	0.41	0.70	0.99	0.03	0.26	4.76
Italy	1979	0.02	0.03	0.07	1.61	0.02	0.02	0.01	0.01	0.05	0.06	0.04	0.06	0.02	0.09	2.02
	1980	0.05	0.06	0.17	1.83	0.05	0.06	0.04	0.02	0.13	0.14	0.11	0.16	0.06	0.14	2.88
	1981	0.05	0.06	0.22	1.94	0.05	0.06	0.06	0.03	0.14	0.15	0.16	0.22	0.07	0.16	3.22
	1982	0.06	0.08	0.30	2.07	0.06	0.07	0.07	0.03	0.15	0.16	0.21	0.26	0.08	0.18	3.60
	1983	0.06	0.09	0.32	2.08	0.07	0.08	0.06	0.04	0.15	0.16	0.23	0.29	0.06	0.18	3.69
	1984	0.06	0.10	0.32	2.09	0.08	0.08	0.06	0.04	0.14	0.16	0.25	0.32	0.05	0.18	3.75
	1985	0.05	0.09	0.24	2.04	0.07	0.07	0.04	0.03	0.12	0.14	0.23	0.32	0.02	0.17	3.46

Japan	1979	0.02	0.01	0.03	0.02	1.08	0.01	0.01	0.01	0.01	0.02	0.02	0.01	0.02	0.14	1.27
	1980	0.03	0.01	0.04	0.04	1.15	0.02	0.03	0.02	0.03	0.03	0.04	0.04	0.04	0.17	1.52
	1981	0.04	0.02	0.06	0.05	1.22	0.03	0.03	0.03	0.03	0.03	0.05	0.05	0.05	0.19	1.69
	1982	0.04	0.02	0.07	0.05	1.26	0.03	0.03	0.03	0.03	0.03	0.06	0.06	0.03	0.19	1.74
	1983	0.03	0.02	0.07	0.05	1.27	0.03	0.03	0.03	0.03	0.04	0.06	0.06	0.02	0.20	1.74
	1984	0.03	0.02	0.07	0.05	1.28	0.03	0.02	0.03	0.02	0.03	0.07	0.07	0.00	0.20	1.72
	1985	0.03	0.02	0.05	0.05	1.25	0.03	0.01	0.03	0.02	0.03	0.06	0.06	0.00	0.19	1.64
United Kingdom	1979	0.05	0.03	0.08	0.08	0.03	1.07	0.02	0.02	0.05	0.08	0.13	0.09	0.06	0.08	1.79
	1980	0.07	0.04	0.11	0.11	0.05	1.14	0.03	0.03	0.08	0.11	0.23	0.17	0.10	0.10	2.28
	1981	0.08	0.05	0.17	0.13	0.05	1.16	0.03	0.03	0.10	0.13	0.32	0.23	0.11	0.12	2.62
	1982	0.08	0.05	0.21	0.15	0.06	1.11	0.04	0.04	0.10	0.14	0.38	0.26	0.08	0.13	2.72
	1983	0.09	0.06	0.25	0.16	0.07	1.08	0.04	0.04	0.11	0.15	0.42	0.30	0.07	0.13	2.86
	1984	0.10	0.07	0.26	0.17	0.08	1.09	0.04	0.04	0.12	0.16	0.48	0.34	0.06	0.14	3.03
	1985	0.10	0.07	0.22	0.17	0.07	1.08	0.04	0.04	0.12	0.16	0.49	0.37	0.05	0.13	2.99
United States	1979	0.53	0.05	0.13	0.14	0.13	0.08	1.60	0.03	0.08	0.10	0.10	0.10	0.07	0.87	3.14
	1980	0.63	0.06	0.21	0.21	0.20	0.12	2.39	0.06	0.14	0.17	0.22	0.20	0.12	1.29	4.73
	1981	0.63	0.07	0.33	0.26	0.22	0.13	2.73	0.08	0.19	0.21	0.35	0.29	0.15	1.47	5.64
	1982	0.68	0.08	0.44	0.31	0.25	0.14	2.74	0.09	0.22	0.24	0.45	0.34	0.15	1.49	6.13
	1983	0.83	0.10	0.55	0.37	0.32	0.17	2.78	0.10	0.26	0.27	0.54	0.43	0.16	1.54	6.88
	1984	0.97	0.12	0.61	0.42	0.37	0.20	2.75	0.11	0.30	0.31	0.64	0.53	0.17	1.54	7.50
	1985	1.15	0.14	0.62	0.48	0.41	0.23	2.81	0.12	0.34	0.34	0.73	0.63	0.17	1.58	8.17
Total	1979	2.09	1.31	2.24	2.23	1.36	1.31	1.72								
	1980	2.27	1.35	2.54	2.67	1.61	1.51	2.67								
	1981	2.35	1.45	3.80	3.06	1.77	1.64	3.13								
	1982	2.45	1.49	4.00	3.33	1.88	1.62	3.18								
	1983	2.45	1.54	3.85	3.38	1.99	1.61	3.18								
	1984	2.87	1.57	3.44	3.40	2.08	1.64	3.12								
	1985	3.04	1.57	2.66	3.34	2.03	1.62	3.09								

TABLE 8   Normalized real income multipliers (ratio of cross to own multipliers in each row of Table 7)[a], 1979–1985.

Country	Year	Country													13 LINK OECD countries	
		Canada	France	FRG	Italy	Japan	UK	USA	Australia	Austria	Belgium	Finland	Netherlands	Sweden	GDP	Total
Canada	1979	1.00	0.00	0.01	0.01	0.01	0.01	0.01	0.00	0.01	0.01	0.01	0.01	0.01	0.05	1.10
	1980	1.00	0.00	0.01	0.01	0.01	0.01	0.03	0.01	0.01	0.01	0.01	0.01	0.01	0.06	1.13
	1981	1.00	0.01	0.01	0.01	0.01	0.01	0.04	0.01	0.01	0.01	0.02	0.01	0.01	0.07	1.16
	1982	1.00	0.01	0.02	0.02	0.01	0.01	0.04	0.01	0.01	0.01	0.02	0.02	0.01	0.06	1.19
	1983	1.00	0.01	0.02	0.02	0.01	0.01	0.03	0.01	0.02	0.02	0.03	0.02	0.01	0.06	1.21
	1984	1.00	0.01	0.03	0.02	0.01	0.01	0.03	0.01	0.01	0.01	0.03	0.03	0.01	0.06	1.21
	1985	1.00	0.01	0.03	0.03	0.01	0.01	0.04	0.01	0.02	0.01	0.04	0.03	0.01	0.06	1.25
France	1979	0.03	1.00	0.08	0.08	0.03	0.03	0.02	0.01	0.04	0.11	0.05	0.07	0.03	0.09	1.58
	1980	0.04	1.00	0.11	0.10	0.04	0.04	0.03	0.02	0.06	0.13	0.08	0.14	0.05	0.11	1.84
	1981	0.05	1.00	0.18	0.13	0.05	0.06	0.04	0.02	0.07	0.15	0.13	0.20	0.07	0.13	2.15
	1982	0.05	1.00	0.21	0.14	0.05	0.06	0.05	0.02	0.07	0.15	0.17	0.21	0.05	0.14	2.23
	1983	0.05	1.00	0.24	0.15	0.06	0.06	0.05	0.03	0.08	0.16	0.19	0.23	0.05	0.14	2.35
	1984	0.05	1.00	0.23	0.15	0.06	0.06	0.05	0.03	0.08	0.15	0.19	0.25	0.04	0.15	2.34
	1985	0.04	1.00	0.19	0.15	0.06	0.06	0.04	0.03	0.08	0.15	0.19	0.28	0.03	0.14	2.30
FRG	1979	0.03	0.06	1.00	0.15	0.04	0.05	0.02	0.02	0.12	0.18	0.10	0.20	0.06	0.13	2.03
	1980	0.05	0.06	1.00	0.19	0.06	0.06	0.05	0.03	0.18	0.25	0.21	0.34	0.09	0.16	2.57
	1981	0.04	0.06	1.00	0.18	0.06	0.07	0.05	0.03	0.17	0.22	0.23	0.34	0.09	0.16	2.54
	1982	0.05	0.07	1.00	0.21	0.07	0.07	0.07	0.03	0.19	0.24	0.30	0.40	0.09	0.18	2.79
	1983	0.05	0.08	1.00	0.23	0.08	0.08	0.07	0.03	0.20	0.24	0.35	0.47	0.08	0.18	2.96
	1984	0.06	0.09	1.00	0.26	0.10	0.09	0.07	0.04	0.21	0.26	0.44	0.56	0.06	0.19	3.24
	1985	0.07	0.12	1.00	0.31	0.12	0.10	0.06	0.04	0.23	0.32	0.55	0.77	0.02	0.20	3.71
Italy	1979	0.01	0.02	0.04	1.00	0.01	0.01	0.01	0.01	0.03	0.04	0.02	0.04	0.01	0.06	1.25
	1980	0.03	0.03	0.09	1.00	0.03	0.03	0.02	0.01	0.07	0.08	0.06	0.09	0.03	0.08	1.57
	1981	0.03	0.03	0.11	1.00	0.03	0.03	0.03	0.02	0.07	0.08	0.08	0.11	0.04	0.08	1.66
	1982	0.03	0.04	0.14	1.00	0.03	0.03	0.03	0.01	0.07	0.08	0.10	0.13	0.04	0.09	1.73
	1983	0.03	0.04	0.15	1.00	0.03	0.04	0.03	0.02	0.07	0.08	0.11	0.14	0.03	0.09	1.77
	1984	0.03	0.05	0.15	1.00	0.04	0.04	0.03	0.02	0.07	0.08	0.12	0.15	0.02	0.09	1.80
	1985	0.02	0.04	0.12	1.00	0.03	0.03	0.02	0.01	0.06	0.07	0.11	0.16	0.01	0.08	1.68

Japan	1979	0.02	0.01	0.03	0.02	1.00	0.01	0.01	0.01	0.02	0.02	0.01	0.02	0.13	1.19
	1980	0.03	0.01	0.03	0.03	1.00	0.03	0.02	0.03	0.03	0.03	0.03	0.03	0.15	1.32
	1981	0.03	0.02	0.05	0.04	1.00	0.02	0.02	0.02	0.02	0.04	0.04	0.04	0.16	1.36
	1982	0.02	0.02	0.06	0.04	1.00	0.02	0.02	0.02	0.03	0.05	0.05	0.02	0.15	1.37
	1983	0.02	0.02	0.05	0.04	1.00	0.02	0.02	0.02	0.02	0.05	0.05	0.02	0.16	1.37
	1984	0.02	0.02	0.05	0.04	1.00	0.02	0.02	0.02	0.02	0.05	0.05	0.00	0.16	1.33
	1985	0.02	0.02	0.04	0.04	1.00	0.01	0.02	0.02	0.02	0.05	0.05	0.00	0.15	1.31
United Kingdom	1979	0.05	0.03	0.07	0.07	0.03	1.00	0.02	0.05	0.07	0.12	0.08	0.06	0.07	1.67
	1980	0.06	0.04	0.10	0.10	0.04	1.00	0.03	0.07	0.10	0.20	0.15	0.09	0.09	2.02
	1981	0.07	0.04	0.15	0.11	0.04	1.00	0.03	0.09	0.11	0.28	0.20	0.09	0.10	2.26
	1982	0.07	0.05	0.19	0.14	0.05	1.00	0.04	0.09	0.13	0.34	0.23	0.07	0.12	2.45
	1983	0.08	0.06	0.23	0.15	0.06	1.00	0.04	0.10	0.14	0.39	0.28	0.06	0.12	2.65
	1984	0.09	0.06	0.24	0.16	0.07	1.00	0.04	0.11	0.15	0.44	0.31	0.06	0.13	2.79
	1985	0.09	0.06	0.20	0.16	0.06	1.00	0.04	0.11	0.15	0.45	0.34	0.05	0.12	2.76
United States	1979	0.33	0.03	0.08	0.09	0.08	0.05	1.00	0.05	0.06	0.06	0.06	0.04	0.54	1.95
	1980	0.26	0.03	0.09	0.09	0.08	0.05	1.00	0.06	0.07	0.09	0.08	0.05	0.54	1.98
	1981	0.23	0.03	0.12	0.10	0.08	0.05	1.00	0.07	0.08	0.13	0.11	0.05	0.54	2.08
	1982	0.25	0.03	0.16	0.11	0.09	0.05	1.00	0.08	0.09	0.16	0.12	0.05	0.54	2.22
	1983	0.30	0.04	0.20	0.13	0.12	0.06	1.00	0.09	0.10	0.19	0.15	0.06	0.55	2.48
	1984	0.35	0.04	0.22	0.15	0.13	0.07	1.00	0.11	0.11	0.23	0.19	0.06	0.56	2.70
	1985	0.41	0.05	0.22	0.17	0.15	0.08	1.00	0.12	0.12	0.26	0.22	0.06	0.56	2.90
Total	1979	1.51	1.22	1.22	1.39	1.26	1.22	1.08							
	1980	1.67	1.26	1.36	1.46	1.40	1.32	1.12							
	1981	1.72	1.36	1.31	1.58	1.45	1.41	1.15							
	1982	1.75	1.39	1.47	1.61	1.49	1.46	1.16							
	1983	1.94	1.43	1.62	1.63	1.57	1.49	1.14							
	1984	1.86	1.47	1.83	1.63	1.63	1.50	1.13							
	1985	1.92	1.44	2.08	1.64	1.62	1.50	1.10							

[a] The last seven rows are normalized by own multipliers from corresponding columns.

Table 8 reveals that the FRG is an important trading partner of most countries in the group, with especially close ties with its European neighbors. The United Kingdom and the United States come next in importance as overall "presences" in foreign markets, with France not far behind. Japan's role in the world economy is understated in these comparisons, since the Southeast-Asian nations with which it trades heavily are not included in the sample.

In Table 8 the column sums from the original multiplier matrix are normalized by the own multipliers from the corresponding columns of Table 7. These figures are an index of the extent to which the effects of individual shocks at home would be amplified by simultaneous shocks of similar magnitude from abroad. The amplification ratios range between 1.08 and 1.51 in the first year and rise moderately for all seven countries for three to four years. The spurt in the West German ratio during the last four years of the projection stems from the cyclical decline in its internal multiplier and that decline serves also to moderate the amplification ratios for the other countries during the same period. The generally low values of the amplification ratios are another index of the overall stability of the international economy, since even simultaneous shocks do not induce explosive or high-amplitude responses in the various countries*.

REFERENCES

Adams, F.G. (1978). Primary commodity markets in a world model system. In F.G. Adams and S.A. Klein (Editors), Stabilizing World Commodity Markets. Lexington Books, Lexington, Massachusetts, pp. 83–104.

Ball, R.J. (Editor) (1973). The International Linkage of National Economic Models: Contributions to Economic Analysis. North-Holland, Amsterdam.

Beaumont, P., Prucha, I., and Filatov, V. (1979). Performance of the LINK system: 1970 versus 1975 base year trade share matrix. Empirical Economics, 4:11–42.

Helliwell, J.F. (1978). Discussion of "Disturbances to the International Economy". In R.M. Solow (Editor), After the Phillips Curve: Persistence of High Inflation and High Unemployment. Federal Reserve Bank of Boston, Boston, Massachusetts, pp. 104–116.

Hickman, B.G. (1974). International transmission of economic fluctuations and inflation. In A. Ando, R. Herring, and R. Marston (Editors), International Aspects of Stabilization Policies. Federal Reserve Bank of Boston, Boston, Massachusetts, pp. 201–231.

Hickman, B.G. (1975). Project LINK in 1972: retrospect and prospect. In G.A. Renton (Editor), Modelling the Economy. Heinemann, London, pp. 657–669.

Hickman, B.G. and Lima, A. (1979). Price determination and transmission of inflation in the LINK system. In J.A. Sawyer (Editor), Modelling the International Transmission Mechanism. North-Holland, Amsterdam, pp. 97–127.

Hickman, B.G. and Schleicher, S. (1978). The interdependence of national economies and the synchronization of economic fluctuations: evidence from the LINK project. Weltwirtschaftliches Archiv, 114(4): 642–708.

Johnson, K.N. and Klein, L.R. (1974). Stability in the international economy: the LINK experience. In A. Ando, R. Herring, and R. Marston (Editors), International Aspects of Stabilization Policies. Federal Reserve Bank of Boston, Boston, Massachusetts, pp. 147–188.

---

*Additional evidence and interpretation of the implications of the LINK system for the international transmission mechanism and the stability of the world economy is presented in Johnson and Klein (1974), Hickman (1974), Hickman and Schleicher (1978), and Hickman and Lima (1979).

Johnson, K.N. and Klein, L.R. (1979). Error analysis of the LINK model. In J.A. Sawyer (Editor), Modelling the International Transmission Mechanism. North-Holland, Amsterdam, pp. 45–71.

Johnson, K.N. and Van Peeterssen, A. (1976). Solving and simulating the LINK system. In J.L. Waelbroeck (Editor), The Models of Project LINK. North-Holland, Amsterdam, pp. 17–41.

Klein, L.R. (1972). Comment in "The Trade Effects of the 1971 Currency Realignment", by W.H. Branson. Brookings Papers on Economic Activity, 1:59–65.

Klein, L.R. (1973). Project LINK: entering a new phase. Items, 27(2):13–16.

Klein, L.R., Moriguchi, C., and Van Peeterssen, A. (1975). The LINK model of world trade with applications to 1972–73. In P. Kenen (Editor), International Trade and Finance. Cambridge University Press, New York, pp. 453–483.

Klein, L.R. and Johnson, K.N. (1974). LINK simulations of international trade: an evaluation of the effects of currency realignment. Journal of Finance, May:617–630.

Klein, L.R. (1976). Five year experience of linking national econometric models and of forecasting international trade. In H. Glejser (Editor), Quantitative Studies of International Economic Relations. North-Holland, Amsterdam, pp. 1–24.

Klein, L.R., Johnson, K.N., Gana, J., Kurose, M., and Weinberg, C. (1976). Applications of the LINK system. In J.L. Waelbroeck (Editor), The Models of Project LINK. North-Holland, Amsterdam, pp. 1–16.

Klein, L.R., Su, V., and Beaumont, P. (1979). Coordination of international fiscal policies and exchange rate revaluations. In J.A. Sawyer (Editor), Modelling the International Transmission Mechanism. North-Holland, Amsterdam, pp. 143–159.

Klein, L.R., Politi, M., and Su, V. (1978). Scenario of a worldwide grain shortage. LINK Memorandum, July. LINK Central, Department of Economics, University of Pennsylvania, Philadelphia, Pennsylvania.

Klein, L.R. and Su, V. (1979). Protectionism: an analysis from Project LINK. Journal of Policy Modeling, 1:5–35.

Sawyer, J.A. (Editor) (1979). Modelling the International Transmission Mechanism. North-Holland, Amsterdam.

Waelbroeck, J.L. (Editor) (1976). The Models of Project LINK. North-Holland, Amsterdam.

COMMENTS*

The LINK project is widely known and has attracted the attention of scientists in numerous countries and experts in a variety of different fields of theoretical and practical economics. For a long time this project has been regarded as an example of global short-term projects (according to its aims) based on cooperation between the creators of individual national, regional, and central models.

The paper presented here describes Project LINK methodology and the results of long-term projections (1978–85), and provides a striking example of the realization of the econometric approach (with multistage simulation) to global modeling problems.

The LINK project itself is rather complicated: it has been described in detail in a number of special publications and is only briefly surveyed in the present paper, so a detailed discussion seems inappropriate here. Therefore, I will comment instead on certain particular characteristics of the project and the simulations mentioned above.

The system links individual models that are mainly macroeconomic and short-term in character; however, these models were separately projected up to 1985 before the post-linkage projection to 1985 was attempted. In the near future, a forecast to 1990 will be prepared.

---

*By E.B. Ershov, Central Economic-Mathematical Institute, Moscow, USSR.

In the long-run simulations the exchange rates, capital flows among the developed countries, and the prices of oil and other exports of the developing countries are all exogenous.

The linking mechanism chosen leads to certain difficulties when the models of different types (including national models of developed market economies, regional models for developing countries, and models of the socialist countries) are actually linked. Some of these models were in fact elaborated by non-native or international organizations. The central model uses the idea of the short-run market equilibrium, which does not seem to be fully adequate.

The analytical power of the system is demonstrated in the example of the income elasticity multipliers, measuring the income response in one country to the increase in government expenditure in another country.

It seems appropriate to raise the following questions about the long-run simulation. What are the realistic possibilities for LINK-system analysis of long-term economic development? Is it possible to model, in this way, the attempts of partners to change particular trends? Is the manipulation of exogenous variables sufficient for these aims?

In my opinion, the consideration of different variants of the dynamics of exogenous variables has a mainly illustrative value. Scenarios themselves should be developed with the help of more flexible, simple, conceptual models and should then be studied with the help of multistage simulation models of the econometric type. For long-term global modeling, the separation of variables into exogenous and endogenous classes may conflict with the appropriate formulation of scenarios.

How can one distinguish the effects of model linking according to the various contributing factors? What is the quantitative role of the central model?

If the transition to completely linked forecasts reveals significant differences from the unlinked forecasts, then it is necessary to analyze the causes of these changes. A fully adequate mathematical framework for this problem has yet to be developed; but in my opinion it is insufficient to emphasize the change in the trade linkage variables between their exogenous prelinkage values and the endogenous postlinkage values. Moreover, the final coordinated values of the linking variables depend also on the linkage and coordinating procedures and the initial assumptions about these exogenous variables. If the effect of linking is negligible, then the whole idea of linking is more elegant than necessary.

In global and long-term modeling efforts it is not so important to obtain quantitative values of model variables. Significant attention should also be paid to the analysis of qualitative properties of the model revealed during experiments using it. Such a complicated and advanced system as LINK should provide the means for such analysis, particularly with respect to the effects of linkage.

In closing, a number of additional questions come to mind. What accounts for the differences among countries in the response of their inflation rates to fiscal stimulus? What are the restrictions on the international trade mechanism induced by the hypothesis of market price equilibrium? What can be said about results of experiments and the model itself if there are sufficiently different projections for similar objects and scenarios?

GLOBAL INTERNATIONAL ECONOMIC MODELS
B.G. Hickman (editor)
Elsevier Science Publishers B.V. (North-Holland)
© IIASA, 1983

LONG-TERM FORECASTS AND POLICY IMPLICATIONS: SIMULATIONS WITH A WORLD ECONOMETRIC MODEL (T-FAIS IV)

Shuntaro Shishido
*University of Tsukuba, Sakura-mura, Ibaragi (Japan),
and Foundation for the Advancement of International Science,
Tokyo (Japan)*

1   INTRODUCTION

The present project was initiated in 1974 under the joint sponsorship of the University of Tsukuba and the Foundation for the Advancement of International Science (FAIS) with the aim of analyzing the world economy by means of a multicountry econometric model (for a detailed discussion of the model, see Shishido, 1980a). The model covers eight developed countries (Japan, the United States, Canada, the United Kingdom, France, the Federal Republic of Germany, Italy, and Australia), five major developing countries (South Korea, Indonesia, India, Iran, and Brazil), and two remaining regions (i.e., the socialist and other developed regions, and the other developing regions). It has been used for various types of international policy simulation, particularly the international coordination of the demand-management policies of developed countries, the assessment of the international impacts of oil-price increases, a comparative study of floating versus fixed exchange-rate regimes, etc. (see for instance Shishido, 1975, 1977, 1979, 1980b; Shishido and Sato, 1981). Although the model is primarily intended for short- or medium-term analysis the present work is an attempt to analyze the long-term structure of the world economy with special reference to growth potentials, trends in international inflation, balances of payments, and currency adjustments in various types of economies such as developed countries and oil-producing and non-oil-producing developing countries.

Since the present long-term analysis is the first such experiment for our model the following projections are of a highly preliminary nature and this should be regarded as an interim report. Only the standard simulations based on the simplified assumptions are discussed here; the other elaborated scenarios will be prepared later.

2   USE OF THE MODEL FOR LONG-TERM ANALYSIS

For developed countries the present model includes major Keynesian-type macroeconomic variables such as the real expenditures on various items, the corresponding price deflators, money incomes including various transfers, money stocks, and interest rates. The supply side of the model includes the potential GNP (based on a production-function approach) which serves as a target for demand management by means of monetary and fiscal policy variables. For developing countries the model includes more supply-oriented variables. For instance, aggregate output is determined mostly by productive investment while imports of primary products are affected by both domestic supply capacity and final consumption.

For both developed and developing countries price levels are important variables which affect international competitiveness in the world market. The rate of inflation, measured by the GNP deflator, is in most cases accounted for by the rate of capacity utilization, the supply of money, import prices, and price expectations.

The money supply is made endogenous in the developed countries but exogenous in the developing countries. In the former case it is determined in a reduced form of supply and demand conditions such as the balance-of-payments surplus (or deficit), government deficits, the business demand for investment, and the monetary policies of the central bank.

The international transmission of economic fluctuations is represented in the model through commodity trade-flow matrices for two commodity groups: (a) primary products and (b) manufactured products. The demand pressures in the model are propagated from importing to exporting countries while the inflationary pressures of prices are in the reverse direction.

Another international bloc includes world commodity models for six types of primary products ((a) coffee and tea, (b) other foods, (c) petroleum, (d) other fuels, (e) metal ores, and (f) nonfood raw materials) for which international prices and output levels are determined by global market conditions. A similar bloc is included for international freight and shipping.

Exchange rates are included in the present model (T-FAIS IV) as endogenous variables for the eight developed countries and as exogenous variables for the developing countries. They are determined by relative prices, current balances, expected real rates of interest, and market intervention by the central bank (see Shishido, 1979). Thus the model allows the analysis of international transmission of economic fluctuations under a floating exchange-rate regime. Various interesting studies have been made in this context, particularly on the comparative analysis of fixed versus floating regimes (see Shishido and Sato, 1981). In the present long-term forecast, however, we temporarily exogenized the exchange rates of all countries to provide consistency with the developing countries.

In using the model for long-term forecasts for the year 2000 the following points need to be considered.

(1) The growth trends of the economies need to be assessed at their normal rates of capacity utilization. Various factors affecting factor inputs and their productivities should be taken into account in our production functions, e.g., environmental investment which is usually considered to be less productive but likely to stimulate the replacement of old polluting facilities, energy-saving investment which tends to be more capital intensive, the reduction of working hours, and demographic trends in the various societies. As shown later, we consider only some of these factors (i.e. working hours and demographic trends) in the preliminary stage of our forecast.

(2) Inflationary tendencies are likely to continue, particularly for the countries with structural balance-of-payments deficits and a falling trend of the exchange rate. Price-determination functions in the model suggest structural imbalances in the rates of inflation in the world economy which are mostly accounted for by differences in productivity growth. For instance, Japan and the FRG show faster rates of technical progress and higher income elasticities in world imports than the other industrial nations (see Shishido, 1980a). Oil-price-induced global inflation tends to enhance these gaps since economies with lower productivity growth rates are in most cases unable to absorb the shock of oil-price increases.

(3) International capital flows are not yet endogenized in the model, and this weakens its stabilizing property since trade gaps in practice tend to be counterbalanced by induced capital flows through international interest-rate arbitrage. In our long-term simulation we have considered this adjustment mechanism to a certain extent by adjusting the assumptions on capital flows.

(4) The supply side of output (particularly sectoral changes in industrial structure, foreign trade, and technical progress) is not taken explicitly into account for each economy in the model except for the distinction between primary and industrial sectors. Since sectoral changes are closely related to long-run productivity growth and international competitiveness, the long-term forecasts using the present model need to be improved in the light of the results of side studies on sectoral analysis.

(5) An alternative forecast for the developed countries could be made by fixing the normal rate of capacity utilization and deriving private consumption as a residual. Although this approach is attractive in obtaining growth trends, fiscal—monetary measures consistent with such trends are likely to become somewhat exaggerated, particularly at times of large external impacts. This approach, however, probably needs to be tested in order to check the present forecasts for developed countries which are based chiefly on the demand side.

3   MAJOR ASSUMPTIONS FOR 1980–2000

Our standard forecast is based on the following major assumptions.

(1) There will be no great wars or great disasters which might affect the trends of demographic factors, output capacities, and policy variables. Thus the public expenditures of each government are assumed to grow at the average growth rate that has been observed in recent years, as shown in Table 1.

(2) The discount rates and money supplies are assumed in principle to reflect recent inflationary trends; i.e. the rates are higher for more-inflationary countries and lower for less-inflationary countries. Short-term fluctuations are occasionally included to smooth the growth path in some cases.

(3) World market conditions for primary products are expected to continue to be tight for energy supplies, particularly crude oil, but to become gradually less restrictive during the 1990s. This tendency will also depend on the rate of inflation in the industrial countries.

(4) The exchange rates for the currencies of Japan and the FRG are assumed either to remain unchanged or to keep rising while those for the other developed countries (except the UK) are assumed to be unchanged. For the developing countries the recent falling

TABLE 1 Major exogenous variables for the developed countries for 1980–2000.

Country	Discount rate[a](%)	Annual rate of change of public investment (%)	Exchange rate (1963 = 1.00)		Annual rate of change of imports (%)
			Case 1	Cases 2 and 3	Case 3
United States	9.0 (10.0)	1.5	1.000	1.000	–
Japan	5.0 (10.0)	5.0	1.570	1.570 → 3.011	–
Canada	10.0	1.5	1.091	1.091	–
UK	9.0 (10.0)	1.0	0.686 → 0.420	0.686 → 0.420	–
France	8.0	2.5	0.985	0.985	–
FRG	4.0 (9.0)	2.5	1.967	1.967 → 2.192	–
Italy	10.0	2.5	0.833	0.833	–
Australia	8.0	2.5	0.974	0.974	–
Other developed and socialist countries	–	–	–	–	6.1[b]

[a]The figures in parentheses denote the upper limit of the discount rates.
[b]Manufacturing imports are assumed to grow exogenously at 6.1% per annum.

trends are extrapolated. These assumptions imply that there will be no significant changes in business and policy behavior in terms of technical progress, international competitiveness, and the management of fiscal and monetary policies.

(5) It is also assumed that the structural relationships between macroeconomic variables, estimated from data for the 1960s and 1970s, will hold for the coming 20 years without significant changes. This rather bold assumption may be subject to criticism. For example, the recent efforts of the US government to stimulate exports may be successful and alter the parameters of US export functions. Similarly, success in an incomes policy to check the rate of inflation might change the values of the parameters in the price-determination functions of the various models. However, in the present preliminary stage we disregard these factors, which can later be included in more elaborate scenarios based on alternative policy variants.

4 THE RESULTS OF STANDARD FORECASTS

We present here only standard forecasts, i.e. standard scenarios based on the highly simplified assumptions discussed in Section 3. Elaborations for alternative scenarios on uncertainties, alternative policies and behavior, etc., remain to be developed later.

For evaluating the alternative impacts of exchange-rate assumptions we prepared two standard scenarios: fixed exchange rates as of 1980 for all the developed countries (case 1); gradually rising exchange rates for Japan and the FRG (case 2). A less-optimistic assumption is also made for the growth of imports of "other developed and socialist countries" (case 3). This is because the original assumption tends to accelerate world imports in an exaggerated way, particularly in the 1990s, in cases 1 and 2. The annual rate of growth of manufactured imports for this region in case 3 is assumed to be about 6% compared with about 9% in the other two cases. The major assumptions for policy variables are summarized in Table 1 and the results of our forecasts are given in Tables 2–9.

TABLE 2 Summary of standard forecasts.

Variable[a]	Case	Year							
		1960	1970	1980	1985	1990	1995	2000	1980–2000
World imports	1	107.0	237.9	443.8	584.3	793.3	1063.9	1547.4	
			8.3	6.5	5.7	6.3	6.0	7.8	6.4
	2			444.9	593.6	831.5	1141.7	1694.9	
			5.0	6.5	5.9	7.0	6.5	8.2	6.9
	3			443.6	586.8	757.7	974.3	1325.5	
				6.4	5.8	5.3	5.2	6.4	5.6
GNP of developed countries	1	1279.5	2092.9	2908.9	3483.8	4576.2	5827.6	8158.9	
			5.0	3.3	3.7	5.6	5.0	7.0	5.3
	2			2900.8	3500.0	4656.4	6040.0	8515.0	
				3.3	3.8	5.9	5.3	7.1	5.5
	3			2899.6	3481.1	4449.1	5466.3	7193.0	
				3.3	3.7	5.0	4.2	5.6	4.6
GNP of developing countries	1	226.0	367.9	670.3	919.6	1321.7	1956.7	2968.4	
			5.0	6.2	6.5	7.5	8.2	8.7	7.7
	2			670.3	921.2	1329.6	1987.3	3048.8	
				6.2	6.6	7.6	8.4	8.9	7.9
	3			670.4	908.6	1276.5	1842.6	2722.1	
				6.2	6.3	7.0	7.6	8.1	7.3

[a]In each case the first row gives the value of the variable and the second row gives its annual growth rate (in percent). The world imports are in billions of US dollars at 1963 prices. The GNPs (or gross domestic products) are in billions of US dollars at 1970 prices based on the purchasing-power parity of Kravis for 1970 (Kravis et al., 1978).

TABLE 3   A comparison of alternative forecasts of annual growth rates for real GNP (in percent).

Forecast	Developed countries[a]	Developing countries[b]	Period
T-FAIS IV			
Case 1	5.3	7.7	1980–2000
Case 2	5.5	7.9	1980–2000
Case 3	4.6	7.3	1980–2000
OECD[c]			
A	4.3	6.5	1975–2000
B$_2$	3.4	6.0	1975–2000
Leontief[d]			
X	4.0	7.2	1970–2000
C	3.6	6.9	1970–2000
WAES[e]			
1	3.7	4.6	1985–2000
2	2.5	3.6	1985–2000

[a]The eight developed countries in T-FAIS IV.
[b]The five major developing countries in T-FAIS IV.
[c]OECD (1979).
[d]Leontief et al. (1977).
[e]WAES (1977).

As shown in Table 2, world trade will tend to grow at about 5.6–6.9% per year in the coming 20 years for cases 1–3 while real GNP for the eight developed countries will tend to rise at about 4.6–5.5% per year. Although their coverage is limited, the five developing countries in the model show a 7.3–7.9% growth rate in real GNP.

In comparing cases 1–3 in Tables 7–9 it is notable that the faster GNP growth rates of Japan, the FRG, Italy, and Australia in cases 1 and 2 are generally reduced in case 3 and the growth gaps between the industrial economies tend to be narrowed. A similar pattern is observed for world imports whose rate of increase is lowest in case 3 (see Table 2).

Generally, however, the results, including case 3, appear to be optimistic compared with other alternative long-term forecasts, as shown in Table 3 (Leontief et al., 1977; OECD, 1979; WAES, 1979). The main reasons for this optimism are that (a) we assume that no significant changes will occur in structural parameters such as those for consumption, investment, exports, and imports, (b) no explicit assumptions are made on a decreasing return to scale in technical progress as a result of increasing costs for antipollution, energy conservation, or other social constraints, and (c) we assume expansionary impacts on world markets by fast-growing nations such as Japan, the FRG, and the Newly Industrialized Countries (NICs)* with higher income elasticities of exports and imports (see Tables 4–6). (The relatively fast growth of Italy and Australia appears to be exaggerated in view of their increasing difficulties in balance of payments and inflation. More-restrictive policies in their demand management would considerably reduce their growth rates.)

Factors (a) and (b) are self-explanatory but factor (c) needs to be explained on a more technical basis. As shown in Tables 4–9, remarkable increases in the exports of the other developed countries to Japan, the FRG, and the NICs are projected as a result of

---

*The NICs included in the present model are Brazil, Indonesia, and South Korea.

TABLE 4   World imports in 1963 prices for case 1: values and average annual growth rates[a].

Country	Year				
	1980	1985	1990	1995	2000
United States	66.1	108.2	127.8	156.0	218.8
		10.4	3.4	4.1	7.0
Japan	23.2	27.3	32.3	43.1	64.1
		3.3	3.4	5.9	8.3
Canada	26.9	41.4	50.9	59.4	78.8
		9.0	4.2	3.1	5.8
UK	34.8	48.1	61.2	77.8	105.6
		6.7	4.9	4.9	6.3
France	27.0	33.6	44.3	57.9	80.7
		4.5	5.7	5.5	6.8
FRG	53.9	54.5	59.0	68.7	98.6
		0.2	3.1	3.1	7.5
Italy	12.0	23.1	32.1	47.8	78.0
		14.0	6.8	8.3	10.3
Australia	6.4	8.6	11.7	15.9	23.7
		6.2	6.4	6.2	8.4
South Korea	4.3	6.4	9.4	13.4	17.9
		8.4	8.0	7.3	6.0
India	3.1	3.5	5.2	7.2	9.7
		2.9	7.9	6.8	6.3
Indonesia	2.6	4.1	5.8	7.9	10.9
		9.3	7.5	6.1	6.7
Iran	9.4	15.6	21.0	26.9	33.9
		10.7	6.2	5.0	4.8
Brazil	4.5	7.5	13.2	23.1	39.8
		10.7	12.0	11.9	11.5
Other developed and socialist countries	103.8	126.5	207.1	303.2	460.1
		4.0	10.4	7.9	8.7
Other developing countries	66.1	76.0	112.4	155.9	226.9
		2.8	8.1	6.8	7.8
Total	443.8	584.3	793.3	1063.9	1547.4
		5.7	6.3	6.0	7.8

[a]For each country the first row of figures gives the value of imports in billions of US dollars and the second row gives the average annual growth rate in percent.

the faster growth of the latter countries; this will in turn increase the growth rates of the former countries. The increasing shares of these fast-growing countries in the world economy will tend to accelerate the average growth rates of total world trade and GNP, particularly in the 1990s (as in cases 1 and 2), partly because of the optimistic assumptions on trade with the socialist countries.

TABLE 5   World imports in 1963 prices for case 2: values and average annual growth rates[a].

Country	Year				
	1980	1985	1990	1995	2000
United States	65.7	107.9	130.9	172.2	261.7
		10.4	3.9	5.6	8.7
Japan	22.9	28.6	34.8	42.9	69.2
		4.6	4.0	4.3	10.0
Canada	26.7	41.1	52.3	65.2	91.8
		9.0	4.9	4.5	7.1
UK	34.8	48.2	62.3	81.1	112.3
		6.7	5.3	5.4	6.7
France	27.1	34.0	45.8	60.9	85.6
		4.6	6.1	5.9	7.0
FRG	53.9	55.0	63.5	75.8	105.4
		0.4	2.9	3.6	6.8
Italy	12.1	23.7	33.5	50.7	83.3
		14.4	7.2	8.7	10.4
Australia	6.4	8.7	12.2	17.7	28.6
		6.5	7.0	7.7	10.0
South Korea	4.3	6.4	9.6	14.2	20.5
		8.5	8.2	8.3	7.6
India	3.0	3.5	5.1	7.0	9.5
		2.8	7.7	6.6	6.3
Indonesia	2.6	4.1	5.9	8.3	12.0
		9.4	7.7	7.0	7.7
Iran	9.4	15.6	21.1	27.1	34.5
		10.7	6.3	5.1	4.9
Brazil	4.5	7.5	13.2	23.3	40.4
		10.7	12.1	12.0	11.6
Other developed and socialist countries	105.1	131.3	222.4	328.0	496.9
		4.6	11.1	8.1	8.7
Other developing countries	66.6	78.1	119.2	167.3	243.5
		3.2	8.8	7.0	7.8
Total	444.9	593.6	831.5	1141.7	1694.9
		5.9	7.0	6.5	8.2

[a]For each country the first row of figures gives the value of imports in billions of US dollars and the second row gives the average annual growth rate in percent.

Although this gradual but accelerating expansion of world trade and income is highly desirable it should be noted that it is based on debatable assumptions of continuous rapid growth of the productivities of the fast-growing countries and growing inflationary pressures on the other developed countries, particularly the United States. This growth-pole hypothesis, which explains an acceleration in world trade and income through the impacts of the fast-growing countries, needs to be further examined by elaborate alternative scenarios.

TABLE 6   World imports in 1963 prices for case 3: values and average annual growth rates[a].

Country	Year				
	1980	1985	1990	1995	2000
United States	65.7	107.7	128.8	154.7	202.8
		10.4	3.6	3.7	5.6
Japan	22.9	28.4	32.2	38.5	51.5
		4.4	2.5	3.6	6.0
Canada	26.7	41.1	51.6	60.7	75.3
		9.0	4.7	3.3	4.4
UK	34.8	48.1	60.7	76.1	99.6
		6.7	4.8	4.6	5.5
France	27.1	33.8	43.2	55.1	73.8
		4.5	5.1	5.0	6.0
FRG	53.9	54.7	59.9	65.1	86.1
		0.3	1.8	1.7	5.8
Italy	12.0	23.3	30.7	44.8	70.9
		14.1	5.7	7.9	9.6
Australia	6.4	8.7	11.7	15.5	21.4
		6.4	6.2	5.8	6.7
South Korea	4.3	6.4	9.3	13.0	16.4
		8.4	7.7	6.8	4.8
India	3.0	3.5	5.1	7.2	9.8
		2.9	7.8	6.9	6.5
Indonesia	2.6	4.1	5.9	7.9	10.5
		9.4	7.5	6.1	5.9
Iran	9.4	15.6	21.1	26.9	33.8
		10.7	6.2	5.0	4.7
Brazil	4.5	6.8	11.2	19.2	32.8
		8.5	10.7	11.3	11.3
Other developed and socialist countries	103.8	127.0	172.7	232.8	316.3
		4.1	6.3	6.2	6.3
Other developing countries	66.6	77.6	113.8	156.9	224.5
		3.1	8.0	6.6	7.4
Total	443.6	586.8	757.7	974.3	1325.5
		5.8	5.3	5.2	6.4

[a]For each country the first row of figures gives the value of imports in billions of US dollars and the second row gives the average annual growth rate in percent.

In view of increasing imbalances in the balance of payments between deficit and surplus nations, case 2 assumes an upward adjustment of exchange rates for Japan (about 3% annually) and the FRG (about 1% annually). At first the two countries suffer a slight decline in the growth rate of their GNP but they tend to recover later, the FRG recovering more quickly because of its smaller adjustment. The other developed countries also accelerate their growth rates owing to an increase in their exports, which further affects

TABLE 7 Real GNPs in 1970 prices[a] for case 1[b].

Country	Year							1980-2000
	1960	1970	1980	1985	1990	1995	2000	
1 United States	662.4	981.3	1317.9	1497.5	1935.1	2295.3	2995.9	
		4.0	3.0	2.6	5.3	3.5	5.5	4.2
2 Japan	102.9	294.0	502.7	670.3	892.6	1202.2	1730.5	
		11.1	5.5	5.9	5.9	6.1	7.6	6.4
3 Canada	48.2	80.2	108.4	116.3	155.3	212.7	267.0	
		5.2	3.1	1.4	6.0	6.5	4.7	4.6
4 UK	128.2	168.7	170.7	176.3	208.2	258.3	338.4	
		2.8	0.1	0.6	3.4	4.4	5.6	3.5
5 France	101.0	177.9	242.3	296.6	381.6	499.9	697.9	
		5.8	3.1	4.1	5.2	5.5	6.9	5.4
6 FRG	140.9	227.2	344.2	419.0	581.9	770.0	1246.9	
		4.9	4.2	4.0	6.8	5.8	10.1	6.6
7 Italy	73.4	126.4	167.6	227.6	308.2	429.4	625.6	
		5.6	2.9	6.3	6.3	6.9	7.8	6.8
8 Australia	22.5	37.2	55.1	80.2	113.3	159.8	256.7	
		5.2	4.0	7.8	7.2	7.1	9.9	8.0
9 South Korea	7.7	18.7	41.7	58.8	82.7	114.5	151.4	
		9.3	8.4	7.1	7.1	6.7	5.7	6.7
10 India	125.1	179.2	208.2	242.6	306.3	405.7	556.4	
		3.7	1.5	3.1	4.8	5.8	6.5	5.0
11 Indonesia	13.7	20.1	43.7	62.0	83.4	108.6	148.7	
		3.9	8.1	7.2	6.1	5.4	6.5	6.3
12 Iran	12.1	28.1	112.0	160.8	211.4	268.0	340.1	
		8.8	14.8	7.5	5.6	4.9	4.9	5.7
13 Brazil	67.0	121.8	264.7	395.4	637.9	1059.9	1771.8	
		6.2	8.1	8.4	10.0	10.7	10.8	10.0
14 Developed countries (1-8)	1279.5	2092.9	2908.9	3483.8	4576.2	5827.6	8158.9	
		5.0	3.3	3.7	5.6	5.0	7.0	5.3
15 Developing countries (9-13)	226.0	367.9	670.3	919.6	1321.7	1956.7	2968.4	
		5.0	6.2	6.5	7.5	8.2	8.7	7.7
16 Total	1505.5	2460.8	3579.2	4403.4	5897.9	7784.3	11127.3	
		5.0	3.8	4.2	6.0	5.7	7.4	5.8

[a]Estimated from the Kravis purchasing-power parity for 1970 (Kravis et al., 1978) and the UN Yearbook of National Accounts, 1976.
[b]For each country the first row of figures gives the GNP in billions of US dollars and the second row gives the annual growth rate in percent.

TABLE 8 Real GNPs in 1970 prices[a] for case 2[b].

Country	1960	1970	1980	1985	1990	1995	2000	1980–2000
1 United States	662.4	981.3	1317.9	1507.3	1979.3	2404.2	3061.7	4.3
		4.0	3.0	2.7	5.6	4.0	5.0	
2 Japan	102.9	294.0	492.5	659.7	859.4	1131.3	1741.4	6.5
		11.1	5.3	6.0	5.4	5.7	9.0	
3 Canada	48.2	80.2	108.8	118.1	157.0	220.3	289.0	5.0
		5.2	3.1	1.7	5.9	7.0	5.6	
4 UK	128.2	168.7	171.1	178.0	212.6	263.3	341.8	3.5
		2.8	0.1	0.8	3.6	4.4	5.4	
5 France	101.0	177.9	242.7	299.2	393.0	528.4	746.3	5.8
		5.8	3.2	4.3	5.6	6.1	7.1	
6 FRG	140.9	227.2	344.7	426.9	621.6	872.4	1377.7	7.2
		4.9	4.3	4.4	7.8	7.0	9.6	
7 Italy	73.4	126.4	167.9	228.9	312.6	438.1	643.2	6.9
		5.6	2.9	6.4	6.4	7.0	8.0	
8 Australia	22.5	37.2	55.2	81.9	120.9	182.0	313.9	9.1
		5.2	4.0	8.2	8.1	8.5	11.5	
9 South Korea	7.7	18.7	41.7	59.0	84.2	121.6	173.0	7.4
		9.3	8.4	7.2	7.4	7.6	7.3	
10 India	125.1	179.2	208.2	242.6	306.3	405.7	557.1	5.0
		3.7	1.5	3.1	4.8	5.8	6.5	
11 Indonesia	13.7	20.1	43.7	62.4	84.9	115.0	165.1	6.9
		3.9	8.1	7.4	6.4	6.3	7.5	
12 Iran	12.1	28.1	112.0	161.1	212.3	271.2	346.8	5.8
		8.8	14.8	7.5	5.7	5.0	5.0	
13 Brazil	67.0	121.8	264.7	396.1	641.9	1073.8	1806.8	10.1
		6.2	8.1	8.4	10.1	10.8	11.0	
14 Developed countries (1–8)	1279.5	2092.9	2900.8	3500.0	4656.4	6040.0	8515.0	5.5
		5.0	3.3	3.8	5.9	5.3	7.1	
15 Developing countries (9–13)	226.0	367.9	670.3	921.2	1329.6	1987.3	3048.8	7.9
		5.0	6.2	6.6	7.6	8.4	8.9	
16 Total	1505.5	2460.8	3571.1	4421.2	5986.0	8027.3	11563.8	6.1
		5.0	3.8	4.4	6.2	6.0	7.6	

[a] See footnote *a* to Table 7.
[b] See footnote *b* to Table 7.

TABLE 9   Real GNPs in 1970 prices[a] for case 3[b].

Country	1960	1970	1980	1985	1990	1995	2000	1980–2000
1 United States	662.4	981.3 / 4.0	1318.1 / 3.0	1502.2 / 2.6	1923.3 / 5.1	2258.3 / 3.3	2873.8 / 4.9	4.0
2 Japan	102.9	294.0 / 11.1	492.1 / 5.3	654.1 / 5.9	798.5 / 4.1	980.7 / 4.2	1233.6 / 4.7	4.7
3 Canada	48.2	80.2 / 5.2	108.7 / 3.1	117.7 / 1.6	151.9 / 5.2	207.7 / 6.5	264.5 / 5.0	4.5
4 UK	128.2	168.7 / 2.8	170.8 / 0.1	177.0 / 0.7	203.4 / 2.8	247.2 / 4.0	317.6 / 5.1	3.1
5 France	101.0	177.9 / 5.8	242.4 / 3.1	297.7 / 4.2	376.8 / 4.8	482.1 / 5.0	646.5 / 6.0	5.0
6 FRG	140.9	227.2 / 4.9	344.6 / 4.3	423.0 / 4.2	577.7 / 6.4	717.6 / 4.4	1032.8 / 7.6	5.6
7 Italy	73.4	126.4 / 5.6	167.7 / 2.9	228.1 / 6.3	304.1 / 5.9	418.9 / 6.6	599.1 / 7.4	6.6
8 Australia	22.5	37.2 / 5.2	55.1 / 4.0	81.3 / 8.1	113.4 / 6.9	153.8 / 6.3	225.2 / 7.9	7.3
9 South Korea	7.7	18.7 / 9.3	41.7 / 8.3	58.9 / 7.2	82.1 / 6.9	110.7 / 6.2	138.0 / 4.5	6.2
10 India	125.1	179.2 / 3.7	208.3 / 1.5	242.7 / 3.1	306.4 / 4.8	406.0 / 5.8	557.4 / 6.5	5.0
11 Indonesia	13.7	20.1 / 3.9	43.7 / 8.1	62.3 / 7.4	83.5 / 6.0	108.1 / 5.3	141.1 / 5.5	6.0
12 Iran	12.1	28.1 / 8.8	112.0 / 14.8	161.0 / 7.5	211.5 / 5.6	267.9 / 4.8	337.6 / 4.7	5.7
13 Brazil	67.0	121.8 / 6.2	264.7 / 8.1	383.7 / 7.7	593.0 / 9.1	950.0 / 9.9	1547.9 / 10.3	9.2
14 Developed countries (1–8)	1279.5	2092.9 / 5.0	2899.6 / 3.3	3481.1 / 3.7	4449.1 / 5.0	5466.3 / 4.2	7193.0 / 5.6	4.6
15 Developing countries (9–13)	226.0	367.9 / 5.0	670.4 / 6.2	908.6 / 6.3	1276.5 / 7.0	1842.6 / 7.6	2722.1 / 8.1	7.3
16 Total	1505.5	2460.8 / 5.0	3570.0 / 3.8	4389.6 / 4.2	5725.5 / 5.5	7308.9 / 5.0	9915.1 / 6.3	5.2

[a]See footnote *a* to Table 7.
[b]See footnote *b* to Table 7.

overall expansion in the developing countries. In this context a gradual long-term adjustment of the Japanese yen seems to be beneficial to all the other nations. However, since current balances in the deficit nations show no significant long-term improvements, faster growth, further import liberalization, or voluntary export restrictions might be preferable on the part of Japan. This again needs to be examined more closely in terms of the competitiveness of related nations, supply restrictions on energy resources, etc.

For the developing countries our standard scenarios also suggest a rather optimistic tendency in growth but are less optimistic about balance of payments except for oil-exporting countries. Because of the limited coverage of the model for the developing countries it can only be stated that NICs such as South Korea and Brazil should perform relatively well, but even a typical non-oil-producing developing country like India should continue to grow at about 5% per year.

Lastly, inflationary pressures can be analyzed in terms of capacity utilization. In cases 1 and 2 the rates tend to keep rising (although they fluctuate in the short term) and to exceed the capacity limits in the 1990s, except for Japan. This might imply that the domestic demand of Japan needs to be stimulated further while the domestic demand of other developed nations, particularly Italy and Australia, should be restrained, if technical progress follows past trends. In case 3, however, most of the developed countries show a fairly balanced growth pattern with modest and nearly normal rates of capacity utilization.

5   ALTERNATIVE SCENARIOS – FURTHER RESEARCH

The standard scenarios presented here indicate a fairly optimistic future for the years 1980–2000. The first two even suggest accelerating expansion in the 1990s as a result of the continued growth of Japan, the FRG, and the NICs regardless of any revaluation of currencies by Japan and the FRG as in case 2. Structural imbalances, however, appear to remain between surplus and deficit developed countries and non-oil-producing developing countries, which suggests the need for continued efforts on economic aid and trade liberalization.

Pessimistic scenarios, which take account of increased trade barriers and more conservative monetary and fiscal policies to deal with stagflation in most of the developed countries and increasingly restricted supplies of energy resources, are now being prepared.

ACKNOWLEDGMENTS

This paper is an interim report on the world econometric forecasting project of the University of Tsukuba and the Foundation for the Advancement of International Science (FAIS). The author is indebted to Kiyo Harada and Fumiko Kimura for research assistance and computer programming, and is also grateful for the valuable comments of Dr. R. Coen during the 8th IIASA Conference on Global Modeling.

REFERENCES

Kravis, I.B., Heston, A., and Summers, R. (1978). International Comparison of Real Product and Purchasing Power, Johns Hopkins University Press, Baltimore, Maryland.

Leontief, W., Carter, A.P., and Petri, P. (1977). The Future of the World Economy. Oxford University Press, New York.

OECD (1979). Facing the Future: Mastering the Probable and Managing the Unpredictable. Organization for Economic Cooperation and Development, Paris.

Shishido, S. (1975). Japan's role in future world economy. In Proceedings of the Tsukuba International Symposium, 2nd. University of Tsukuba, Tsukuba.

Shishido, S. (1977). An econometric approach to the world business recovery. Paper presented at Japan US Forum sponsored by the Brookings Institution and the Foundation for the Advancement of International Science. (Mimeograph.)

Shishido, S. (1979). An Econometric Study on Medium-term Forecasts of the World Economy and International Economic Policy. Foundation for the Advancement of International Science, Tokyo (in Japanese).

Shishido, S. (1980a). A model for the coordination of recovery policies in the OECD region. Journal of Policy Modeling, 2(1):33–55.

Shishido, S. (1980b). Oil price issues and international economic policy alternatives. In Proceedings of the Japan–US Forum on International Issues, 3rd – World Economic Forecast and International Policies after Tokyo Summit. Foundation for the Advancement of International Science, Tokyo.

Shishido, S. and Sato, H. (1981). Multicountry dynamic multipliers under fixed and floating exchange rates: an econometric analysis. Journal of Policy Modeling, 3(3):279–294.

WAES (1977). Energy: global prospect, 1985–2000. Report of the Workshop on Alternative Energy Strategies. Massachusetts Institute of Technology, Cambridge, Massachusetts.

COMMENTS*

Professor Shishido's projections are based on a system of macroeconometric models that was designed for short- to medium-term analysis. The results of these first attempts at simulating the system over a longer horizon illustrate some of the pitfalls of applying a short-run system to long-term analysis.

The projected growth rates of real GNP to 1985 for the major developed nations are reasonable, but thereafter they accelerate to implausibly high levels for several key countries. In Case 1, for example, US growth rises from an average annual rate of 2.6% in 1980–85 to 5.5% in 1995–2000, that of the FRG from 4.0 to 10.1%, and that of the UK from 0.6 to 5.6%. Recent demographic developments in these nations portend declining growth rates of labor supply. With rates of technical progress assumed to be constant, such large increases in GNP growth would therefore require either extraordinary rates of capital formation or sharp increases in utilization rates of available factor inputs.

Shishido reports that capacity utilization rates in Cases 1 and 2 tend to rise over time, reaching excessive levels in the 1990s. In the less optimistic scenario of Case 3, utilization rates remain at normal levels; yet even in this case, growth rates of the nations mentioned above are substantially higher in the last half of the 1990s than they have been over the past two decades.

---

*By Robert M. Coen, Department of Economics, Northwestern University, Evanston, Illinois, USA.

The behavior of utilization rates in Cases 1 and 2 suggests that Shishido's models of the developed nations contain very weak feedbacks, if any, between capacity (or potential) and actual GNP. Growth rates of capacity GNP do not pose effective constraints to actual growth, even in the long run. This is not very surprising given the short-term, demand-oriented character of his models.

Shishido suggests that demand-management policies may need to be modified by nations experiencing excessive or deficient actual growth relative to potential. He overlooks other possibilities for eliminating over- or under-utilization of capacity in the long run. Departures from capacity growth may lead to changes in absolute and relative prices as well as interest rates that stimulate or restrain actual growth. Such self-correcting adjustments are probably not of much importance in the short run and are therefore understandably neglected in Shishido's models, but they are likely to be prominent features of market economies in the long run. Another possibility is the implementation of supply- as opposed to demand-management policies, but here again the short-term orientation of Shishido's models leads to neglect of supply responses to policy or endogenously-generated economic changes.

Another puzzling feature of the projected growth rates is their cyclical character for some nations. In Case 1, for example, GNP growth in the United States rises from 2.6 to 5.3% between 1980–85 and 1985–90, then falls to 3.5% in 1990–95, and rises again to 5.5% in 1995–2000. The corresponding figures for the FRG are 4.0, 6.8, 5.8, and 10.1%. The source of these growth cycles is a mystery, since the projections embody steady growth of government expenditures, fixed exchange rates (except for a falling British pound), and constant central bank discount rates. Macroeconometric models do not typically give rise to such long cycles when simulated with comparable constancy or smoothing of exogenous inputs. It would be interesting to know whether the cycles evident in Shishido's projections result from unstated assumptions about some exogenous inputs, from novel structural characteristics of the national models, or from the influences of trade linkages and lags therein.

Comparisons of Cases 1, 2, and 3 provide insights into the impacts of exchange rate changes and trade growth on world prospects. Case 2 incorporates appreciation of the Japanese yen and the German mark at about 3% and 1% per year, respectively. Case 3 adds an assumption of one-third slower growth of imports of the other developed and socialist regions.

In the revaluation scenario of Case 2, total GNP values of the thirteen countries for which data are reported are somewhat higher throughout the simulation period as compared to Case 1. By the year 2000, total GNP in Case 2 exceeds that in Case 1 by 3.9%. The gains are very unevenly distributed, however. Japan suffers losses through 1995, its GNP being reduced at that point by 5.9%; it then stages a remarkable recovery which raises its GNP in the year 2000 to a level 2.2% above that of Case 1. For the other revaluing country, the FRG, the outcome is entirely different. Its GNP is higher throughout the period, rising 13.3% above that of Case 1 in 1995 and ending the century 10.5% above. While all the other countries (except India) experience increases in GNP, the big winners are Canada, France, Australia, Korea, and Indonesia. Since Japan's losses to 1995 must be traceable to reductions in its export growth, it appears that these five countries, plus the FRG, are the ones that either capture most of the export markets lost by Japan or have the highest export multipliers on their GNPs.

In Case 3, total GNP grows more slowly throughout the period; by the year 2000 it is 14.3% below that of Case 2. All countries except India experience losses, but the most dramatic declines are for Japan, the FRG, Australia, and Korea, whose GNPs are 20–30% below those of Case 2 by the year 2000. The distribution of losses must be determined by the distribution of imports of the other developed and socialist regions, as well as by the national export multipliers; but it is impossible to assess the relative importance of these factors from the information presented in the paper.

The results from these alternative scenarios indicate that long-run GNP developments are highly sensitive to trade. This feature of Shishido's system again seems to me to reflect the short-term, demand orientation of its national and regional models. In such models, an increase in a nation's exports raises aggregate demand and thereby increases real GNP. But capacity constraints may at some point set up forces that reduce or possibly even eliminate the growth-inducing impact of exports, and the reverse should be true for a decline in exports. Thus, while multipliers of exports on GNP may be positive in the short run, we might expect them to decline over time to near zero. Trade expansion should improve growth prospects in the long run only insofar as it raises *potential* GNP, which it might do by promoting either international specialization or domestic rates of capital formation. These supply-side impacts of trade are likely to be small, however, as compared to the conventional demand-side multipliers.

In conclusion, long-term GNP growth ought to be essentially determined by the growth rates of labor supply and labor-augmenting technical progress — Harrod's natural rate. Over brief intervals, economies may expand more or less rapidly than their natural rates, but they should not be able to do so indefinitely. Thus, I regard persistent over-utilization of capacity and close links between trade and growth in the long run to be misleading characteristics of Shishido's system. The constituent models do not contain endogenous mechanisms by which actual growth might be accommodated to potential growth in the long run. Of the three scenarios he presents, I consider Case 3 to be the most probable, for it is apparently the only one that attains rough balance between actual and potential growth rates. Still, I remain skeptical about his underlying estimates of potential growth, which seem unreasonably high in view of projected retardations of labor supply growth and low rates of productivity growth in recent years in the developed countries.

GLOBAL INTERNATIONAL ECONOMIC MODELS
B.G. Hickman (editor)
Elsevier Science Publishers B.V. (North-Holland)
© IIASA, 1983

THE STRUCTURE AND PROPERTIES OF THE MULTICOUNTRY MODEL*

Sung Y. Kwack, Richard Berner, Peter Clark, Ernesto Hernández-Catá, Howard Howe, and Guy Stevens
Board of Governors of the Federal Reserve System, Washington, D.C. 20551 (USA)

1   INTRODUCTION

In this paper we survey the theoretical structure and simulation properties of the Multicountry Model (MCM) that has been developed in the International Finance Division at the Federal Reserve Board. MCM is a system of linked national macroeconomic models at the center of which is a medium-sized model of the US economy. Linked to it, and to each other, are models for Canada, the Federal Republic of Germany (FRG), Japan, the United Kingdom, and an abbreviated model representing the Rest Of the World (ROW).

The country models, which are of roughly similar size, explain the main domestic variables and international transactions of each country. The international linkages between the countries (through trade and capital flows, changes in international reserves, exchange rates, and prices) are specified in considerable detail. The most important instruments of monetary policy (reserve requirements, the discount rate, and net central-bank holdings of domestic and foreign assets) and fiscal policy (government expenditures and tax rates) are integrated into each country model. Since the sample period runs from 1964 to 1975 the country models have been constructed so that they are operational both under a regime of pegged rates (up to 1973 for most of our countries) and under a regime of managed floating (from 1973).

All five models have been simulated in isolation, and they have also been linked with each other and with a small set of equations explaining the merchandise trade of an aggregated ROW sector and short- and long-term Eurodollar interest rates. We present results for dynamic simulations inside and outside the sample period.

One particularly noteworthy result is the ability of our models to track the movements in four bilateral US-dollar exchange rates (vis-à-vis the Canadian dollar, the Deutsche Mark, the pound sterling, and the Japanese yen) during the period of managed floating.

---

*The views expressed here are those of the authors and do not necessarily represent the views of the Federal Reserve System or its staff.

Furthermore, the models perform as well, if not better in many respects, during the period 1973–1975 than during the previous fixed-rate period. These results are particularly gratifying since our project constitutes the first attempt to explain several exchange rates simultaneously in a multicountry setting.

2   THE PROTOTYPE COUNTRY MODEL

There are numerous differences between the five country models, largely reflecting differences in institutional detail. Their basic structures, however, have substantial similarities. This common core reflects the structure of a basic model, called the prototype model, that was built as the point of departure for each country model.

In the prototype model, prices and quantities are determined by the behavior of four classes of economic agents operating in five markets. The agents include the monetary authorities (including the central bank and other holders of official foreign assets), the government, commercial banks, and the private nonbank sector (firms and households).

The five markets in the prototype model are modeled in varying degrees of complexity and with a number of different assumptions concerning whether prices change rapidly enough to ensure market-clearing price changes in the short run (the equating of supply and demand). Each country contains markets for domestically produced goods, labor, money, and short- and long-term bonds. Depending on country-specific institutional factors some models contain markets for a number of other financial assets.

2.1   The Goods Market: Domestic Output and Price Determination

Each country is assumed to produce a different composite consumption–investment commodity; behavior in the market for this good determines the domestic and foreign demand as well as the domestic and export price of the commodity concerned.

There are three key elements in the market: the equations for (a) aggregate demand and expenditure, (b) potential output and capacity utilization, and (c) price determination. As is traditional, aggregate demand (GNP) is broken down into five major components: personal consumption, fixed investment, inventory investment, exports, and imports. The equations explaining these components are related to the underlying theories of the behavior of the four agents and for the most part resemble the corresponding equations in other econometric models. Thus consumption depends on private disposable income and net worth while fixed investment (following the neoclassical approach) is positively related to current and lagged changes in GNP and is negatively related to current and lagged changes in the user cost of capital. Since the long-term rate of interest is an important determinant of the user cost of capital the investment function provides a key link between the monetary and real sectors of the model.

Imports and exports of goods and services are broken down into merchandise trade, investment income, and other services. Because import prices depend on foreign export prices and exchange rates the import equations are crucial in the transmission of external influences to a given country model. The merchandise equations are also noteworthy in that they are bilateral.

The supply side of the goods market is represented by the potential GNP, which is related to the capital stock and potential employment via a Cobb—Douglas production function. Capacity utilization (the ratio of the actual to the potential GNP) is determined via the potential-GNP relationship.

There are three main price variables in the prototype model: the deflator for domestic absorption expenditures (consumption, investment, and government spending), the export unit-value index, and the import unit value. The import prices of a country are determined by the export prices of other countries and the exchange rates, whereas the export price of each country and its domestic price — which need not be equal — are determined by (flexible) markups over wage costs, changes in labor productivity, and the cost of imports. The markups may depend on domestic and foreign capacity-utilization rates and the export prices of competitors.

The price-determination process and the behavior of inventories lead to a picture of a market where price is not sufficiently flexible to equate supply and demand in the short run but where, because of the role of inventories, the demand for GNP is satisfied. Prices adjust only partially to cut off excess demand or supply. However, inventory changes ensure in the short run that supply is adequate to satisfy demand.

2.2 The Labor Market

The rationale behind the equations of the labor market is that, because of the existence of union contracts and minimum-wage laws, wages do not adjust rapidly enough to clear the market. Hence there is typically a disequilibrium in the form of an excess labor supply. The important variables that are determined in this sector are the wage rate in manufacturing and the unemployment rate. The rate of change in nominal wages is primarily a function of the unemployment rate and the expected rate of change in the deflator for aggregate expenditure. Unemployment is of course the difference between the supply and the demand for labor.

2.3 The Monetary Sector: Asset Demand and Interest-Rate Determination

The basic building blocks in the money market are the entries in the balance sheet of the central bank. The balance-sheet identity specifies the link between the main sources of the unborrowed base (net foreign assets, NFA, and the net government position, NGP) and its uses (required reserves, RR, free reserves, FR, and currency, CUR):

$$NFA + NGP = RR + FR + CUR$$

To use this identity as a market-clearing condition one substitutes behavioral functions for the endogenous variables. The required reserves are calculated by multiplying the (policy-determined) reserve-requirement ratios by the corresponding functions for the various deposit stocks. The demand of the commercial banks for free reserves depends on the short-term interest rate and the official discount rate. All these factors, together with the demand for currency, are negatively related to the short-term interest rate. Hence, for a given stock of the unborrowed base the short-term interest rate will adjust so as to equilibrate the existing supply with the direct and indirect demands for base money: *RR*, *FR*, and *CUR*. The short-term interest rate is thus determined implicitly by clearing the market for base money.

Except in the model of the UK, the demand and supply for long-term securities are not explicitly introduced. Instead it is assumed that these securities are close substitutes for short-term money-market instruments; this leads to term-structure equations which express the long-term rate as a weighted average of current and past values of the short-term rate.

2.4   A Substitution for the Bond Market: the Balance-of-Payments Equation

The fifth and final market included in the prototype model is the short-term bond market. For a number of reasons we have decided not to model the bond market directly but to make a substitution for this market which, theoretically at least, leaves unchanged or invariant the model solutions for prices and quantities. (The use of a balance-of-payments equation as a market-clearing condition in place of the short-term bond market is developed at length in Stevens (1976).)

In place of the bond market each model contains a balance-of-payments equation; this is an ex-ante concept, with demand functions substituted for the familiar trade and capital-flow entries in the ex-post balance-of-payments identity.

Stevens (1976) demonstrated that a properly constructed balance-of-payments equation is the summation of the overall budget constraint of a country and all of the equilibrium and disequilibrium conditions for the markets of that country. In particular, one of the market-clearing conditions that is embodied in the balance-of-payments equation is that for the short-term bond market. It can therefore be shown that if the short-term bond market and all other markets are in equilibrium then the balance-of-payments equation must clear; moreover, the clearing of the balance-of-payments equation and the other markets implies that the short-term bond market must also be in equilibrium. By this method one can show that the short-term bond market and the balance-of-payments equation are equivalent and interchangeable in the model.

Of course, to specify a balance-of-payments equation correctly it is necessary to model not only trade and service flows but also capital inflows and outflows. As is the case for equations explaining the demand for domestic assets that appear in the monetary sector, the equations explaining the demand and supply for foreign assets follow the portfolio-balance approach and are specified in stock form. They include private net worth, a transactions variable, and a vector of rates of return as the main explanatory variables. The rates of return are domestic interest rates for domestic assets and, for foreign assets, foreign interest rates plus variables representing the expected change in the exchange rate. The latter variables are the forward rate, future realized exchange rates, or other variables, depending on the country in question and the exchange-rate regime (fixed or flexible).

3   EVALUATION OF MODEL PERFORMANCE

In this section we present evidence on the tracking ability of MCM and its component country models both inside and outside the sample period.

TABLE 1   Within-sample error statistics (1964:4–1975:4)[a].

Variable	USA	Canada	Japan	FRG	UK
GNP (1972 prices)					
Unlinked	2.4	2.4	3.0	4.5	3.4
	(−0.7)	(0.09)	(1.2)	(0.3)	(−1.1)
MCM	2.3	2.0	4.0	3.6	3.9
	(−0.9)	(−0.4)	(−2.5)	(−0.3)	(−1.6)
Absorption deflator					
Unlinked	0.94	2.4	1.3	3.6	5.4
	(−0.6)	(0.1)	(0.4)	(0.3)	(2.9)
MCM	1.0	0.7	2.4	3.5	5.1
	(−0.7)	(0.3)	(−0.8)	(0.04)	(3.1)
Short-term interest rate					
Unlinked	19.3	26.1	9.0	18.5	29.7
	(−15.8)	(8.7)	(2.7)	(6.1)	(8.6)
MCM	20.4	27.7	11.2	10.7	23.1
	(−17.7)	(−1.5)	(1.3)	(−2.9)	(2.2)
Exchange rate (vis-à-vis US\$)[b]					
Unlinked	c	2.5	5.6	9.2	6.2
		(1.0)	(4.7)	(−3.7)	(−5.2)
MCM	c	4.4	12.6	11.5	9.7
		(−3.9)	(9.5)	(−8.7)	(−6.8)
Exports of goods (1972 prices)					
Unlinked	d	1.2	6.2	4.8	3.4
		(−0.2)	(−1.8)	(1.7)	(−0.1)
MCM	5.9	5.2	9.5	2.8	6.2
	(−0.6)	(−1.2)	(−5.5)	(−0.6)	(−1.7)

[a]The first figure reported is the percentage RMSE; the figure in parentheses is the percentage ME or bias.
[b]The statistics are calculated only for the period in which the exchange rate was not fixed, since inclusion of the fixed-rate period would bias the results downward.
[c]No exchange rate is solved when the US model is run alone (see text and footnote d). In MCM the "US" rate is a weighted average of the four bilateral rates that are solved.
[d]When the US model is run alone, because neither the exchange rate nor foreign variables are endogenous, exports are held exogenous.

The individual models and the MCM were simulated dynamically both over their common sample period (from the fourth quarter of 1964 to the fourth quarter of 1975 (1964:4–1975:4)) and outside the sample period (1976:1–1977:1). The statistics for key variables are given in Tables 1 and 2. The Mean Error (ME) is included as an indicator of bias together with the Root Mean Square Error (RMSE). Both statistics are percentage errors so the units of different variables do not hinder comparability. For both the individual country models and the linked MCM there is no evidence of error compounding or accumulation. For the variables that are most commonly compared across country models (i.e. GNP and prices) the magnitudes of the errors are reasonably low considering that the models are simulated dynamically for a period of 45 quarters under a change in exchange-rate regime. The out-of-sample forecasts (Table 2) show that the sizes of the RMSEs for the majority of variables are comparable to those for the in-sample simulation.

TABLE 2   Out-of-sample error statistics (1976:1–1977:1)[a].

Variable	USA	Canada	Japan	FRG	UK
GNP (1972 prices)					
Unlinked	5.5	1.4	0.7	0.9	4.0
	(−5.4)	(0.4)	(0.1)	(−0.6)	(−3.7)
MCM	7.7	0.8	0.9	1.7	6.5
	(−7.5)	(−0.4)	(0.2)	(−1.7)	(−6.2)
Absorption deflator					
Unlinked	0.5	1.4	2.5	1.0	3.4
	(−0.3)	(0.4)	(−2.3)	(−0.4)	(3.0)
MCM	0.5	0.6	2.1	1.0	3.9
	(−0.3)	(−0.1)	(−1.0)	(−0.4)	(3.4)
Short-term interest rate					
Unlinked	9.9	17.4	3.8	11.3	6.9
	(−6.7)	(16.2)	(−0.7)	(7.8)	(2.3)
MCM	25.4	20.4	4.8	11.6	7.9
	(−21.3)	(19.1)	(−1.8)	(7.3)	(−0.7)
Exchange rate (vis-à-vis US$)[b]					
Unlinked	c	10.8	5.8	11.7	24.3
		(−10.1)	(5.5)	(4.1)	(23.2)
MCM	c	13.3	11.2	12.3	20.7
		(−12.4)	(10.2)	(3.0)	(19.6)
Exports of goods (1972 prices)					
Unlinked	d	7.3	4.1	3.6	2.9
		(5.0)	(−2.6)	(0.6)	(0.4)
MCM	3.3	3.7	5.1	2.6	9.6
	(0.9)	(−0.9)	(1.1)	(−2.3)	(−9.5)

[a,b,c,d]See corresponding footnotes to Table 1.

On reviewing the main points of Table 1 concerning the key GNP variable it can be seen that the in-sample RMSEs fall with one minor exception in the 2–4% range. Further, the RMSEs of the domestic-absorption price deflator variables vary from a low of 0.7% (Canada) to a high of 5.4% for the UK. This seems quite satisfactory to us, considering that wide variations in exchange rates and raw commodity prices occurred in the early 1970s. Compared with the other variables in Table 1 the in-sample RMSEs of the short-term interest rates in percentage terms, ranging from 9% for Japan to nearly 30% for the UK, may appear to be quite high. These relatively large errors result from both the nature of the data and the difficulty of models in general in predicting these variables with accuracy. For example, in the Federal Reserve's MPS model of the US economy, the ratio of the RMSE of the short-term rate to its mean is 20.4% while the corresponding statistic in MCM is 28.8%.

The performances of exports are quite remarkable in both the MCM and the country models. The RMSE values range from 1.2% for Canada to 9.5% for Japan. No comparable previous modeling effort has simultaneously endogenized the foreign exchange rates that are present in the MCM. The RMSEs of these variables range from 4.4% for Canada to 12.6% for Japan in the MCM and are slightly less in the country models alone.

Outside the sample period (see Table 2) the results are comparable to and even superior to those for the sample period. However, there are exceptions for the UK and to a smaller extent Canada.

4   FISCAL AND MONETARY MULTIPLIERS

In this section we present and comment upon typical fiscal and monetary multipliers for MCM. Each multiplier can in principle be calculated in two forms: for the unlinked country model simulated in isolation from the rest of the system and for the country model after it has been integrated into MCM. Comparisons of the isolated and the linked results can, with certain qualifications, provide insight into the importance of modeling feedback effects by endogenizing foreign incomes and prices. Such comparisons are made in the following sections, particularly for the fiscal-policy multipliers.

4.1   Fiscal-Policy Multipliers

The fiscal-policy multipliers presented here were computed over the eight-quarter period starting with the second quarter of 1973, the beginning of the floating-rate regime (which, we feel, is of more immediate interest than the fixed-rate period).

The increases in government expenditure were roughly scaled to the GNP magnitude in each country but were held to units of one or ten: US$10 billion in the United States, $C1 billion in Canada, DM10 billion in the FRG, ¥1 trillion in Japan and £1 billion in the UK. Table 3 presents the magnitudes of (real) GNP and government spending in the second quarter of 1973. Relative to the sizes of their economies the increases in government spending are of about the same intensity for Canada and the United States. The increases for the FRG and Japan are slightly larger and relatively equal to each other. The fiscal shock to the UK is markedly larger than the other four shocks and about double the intensity of that for the United States. In all cases the increase is sustained over the full eight-quarter period of the experiment.

The upper portions of Tables 4–8 present the multipliers that are obtained when each country model is operated in isolation (unlinked) and foreign variables are held constant. The lower portions of the tables present the multipliers that are obtained when each country model is integrated into the multicountry system. The tables give responses for

TABLE 3   Relative sizes of fiscal-policy shocks to MCM.

Country	Fiscal-policy shock ΔG	GNP^a	Government spending G^a	$\Delta G/GNP^b$ (%)	$\Delta G/G^b$ (%)
Canada	1	112.0	21.0	0.9	5
FRG	10	862.9	152.3	1.2	7
Japan	1000	99841.9	8630.6	1.0	12
UK	1	57.7	11.7	1.7	9
United States	10	1231.1	253.0	0.8	4

[a]In billions of real units of national currency in the second quarter of 1973.
[b]The figures have been rounded.

TABLE 4   Government-expenditure multipliers for the Canadian model ($C1-billion increase in government expenditure)[a].

Quarter	GNP	P	RS	MG	XG	TBD	E	NFA	M1
Canadian model alone									
1	1.02	0.08	11.5	0.277	−0.002	−0.293	−0.09	−0.010	0.63
2	1.04	0.18	25.6	0.237	0.027	−0.250	−0.47	−0.054	0.75
3	1.08	0.32	37.2	0.257	0.051	−0.273	−0.79	−0.088	0.73
4	1.06	0.45	50.6	0.225	0.048	−0.257	−1.01	−0.110	0.57
5	1.04	0.59	66.3	0.226	0.058	−0.276	−1.24	−0.131	0.38
6	1.01	0.75	77.7	0.176	0.064	−0.222	−1.55	−0.160	0.22
7	1.03	0.92	80.9	0.175	0.081	−0.223	−1.88	−0.189	0.14
8	1.07	1.14	32.8[b]	0.123	0.118	−0.140	−2.59	−0.262	0.78
MCM									
1	1.02	0.08	11.5	0.278	−0.002	−0.294	−0.09	−0.010	0.63
2	1.04	0.18	25.5	0.238	0.027	−0.250	−0.47	−0.053	0.75
3	1.08	0.31	36.5	0.259	0.049	−0.275	−0.78	−0.087	0.74
4	1.06	0.45	50.2	0.227	0.046	−0.260	−0.99	−0.108	0.58
5	1.04	0.58	65.6	0.230	0.054	− 0.283	−1.21	−0.128	0.39
6	1.01	0.74	76.8	0.182	0.058	−0.235	−1.52	−0.156	0.23
7	1.03	0.91	79.7	0.180	0.069	−0.244	−1.85	−0.186	0.15
8	1.06	1.12	32.2[b]	0.125	0.097	−0.174	−2.56	−0.258	0.77

[a]The variables are as follows: *GNP*, gross national product, billions of 1972 Canadian dollars at an annual rate; *P*, absorption deflator, 1972 = 100, percent; *RS*, short-term interest rate (90-day finance-company paper), basis points; *MG* and *XG*, merchandise imports and exports, respectively, billions of 1972 Canadian dollars at an annual rate; *TBD*, trade balance, billions of US dollars at an annual rate; *E*, exchange rate, US dollars per Canadian dollar, percent; *NFA*, stock of foreign-exchange reserves, billions of Canadian dollars; *M1*, stock of currency and time deposits, percent.
[b]This abrupt drop in the interest-rate effect is spurious. It occurs historically at a point where the interest-rate equation experiences a behavioral shift between discount-rate regimes. The drop of 50-odd basis points is a product of the first quarter of 1975 and not the eighth period after a fiscal stimulus.

the major real and financial variables in each domestic economy. Changes in GNP, imports, and exports (in real terms) are reported in units of local currency. Changes in foreign-exchange reserves are reported in current units of local currency. All other changes (domestic prices, the short-term interest rate, the exchange rate, and the money supply) are reported as percentage changes over the respective historical values.

4.1.1 Effects on GNP

The multipliers of the increase in government spending range from a low of 1.1 for Canada to a high of 2.4 for the United States. Between these values lie the FRG with 1.5, the UK at 1.6, and Japan at 2.0. These multipliers fall within the range of results from existing econometric models.

The time patterns of the GNP multipliers also differ appreciably between countries. Canada, the United States, and the UK peak earliest, attaining their maxima between three and five quarters after the shock. The FRG peaks at seven periods, and in Japan the GNP effect continues to rise eight quarters after the shock.

While much of the differences in the GNP multipliers is attributable simply to structural differences between the countries, the directions of the differences are consistent with the economic environment of the simulation period. The sharp falloff in Japanese activity

TABLE 5   Government-expenditure multipliers for the FRG model (DM10-billion increase in government expenditure)[a].

Quarter	GNP	P	RS	MG	XG	TBD	E	NFA	M1
FRG model alone									
1	10.9	0.048	2.2	3.25	0.06	−1.35	−0.27	−0.101	0.44
2	12.7	0.110	6.5	3.41	0.21	−1.80	−0.84	−0.254	0.82
3	13.9	0.200	11.1	4.08	0.46	−2.30	−1.45	−0.280	1.10
4	13.6	0.313	12.4	3.67	0.78	−2.46	−2.14	−0.317	1.22
5	13.9	0.454	13.1	3.95	1.13	−3.15	−2.99	−0.424	1.27
6	14.8	0.628	22.2	4.09	1.53	−3.59	−4.23	−0.558	1.30
7	14.8	0.850	17.8	4.39	2.19	−4.32	−5.48	−0.645	1.36
8	12.9	1.076	14.8	3.49	2.31	−4.22	−6.88	−0.759	1.30
MCM									
1	11.1	0.048	2.2	3.32	0.26	−1.29	−0.24	−0.089	0.45
2	13.1	0.107	6.4	3.60	0.59	−1.65	−0.73	−0.221	0.85
3	14.6	0.190	10.8	4.43	1.03	−2.05	−1.20	−0.224	1.16
4	14.5	0.291	11.5	4.08	1.41	−2.13	−1.72	−0.240	1.31
5	15.0	0.419	12.1	4.49	1.78	−2.73	−2.41	−0.341	1.41
6	16.2	0.580	20.8	4.74	2.18	−3.14	−3.47	−0.467	1.47
7	16.2	0.781	16.6	5.15	2.83	−3.76	−4.55	−0.549	1.56
8	14.2	0.986	13.4	4.21	2.76	−3.64	−5.75	−0.643	1.51

[a]The variables are as follows: *GNP*, gross national product, billions of 1972 Deutsche Marks at an annual rate; *P*, absorption deflator, 1972 = 100, percent; *RS*, short-term interest rate (90-day Frankfurt interbank rate), basis points; *MG* and *XG*, merchandise imports and exports, respectively, billions of 1972 Deutsche Marks at an annual rate; *TBD*, trade balance, billions of US dollars at an annual rate; *E*, exchange rate, US dollars per Deutsche Mark, percent; *NFA*, stock of foreign-exchange reserves, billions of Deutsche Marks; *M1*, stock of currency and demand deposits, percent.

during the 1974 recession provides the slack to account for some of the late strength in the Japanese GNP multiplier. Even though the capacity utilization of the United States drops off almost as rapidly as that in Japan the US multiplier does not show the same late strength as the Japanese multiplier. However, the percentage change in prices is not nearly as great for the United States as for Japan. Whereas the recessionary environment may increase the GNP multiplier in Japan it appears to soften the price impact of the government stimulus in the US model.

4.1.2 Effects on Prices

Except for the United States, the price responses to the fiscal stimulus are of about the same magnitude in all the models — the price levels increase about 1% over what they would otherwise be. In the US model the price level increases by about 0.5%. Strictly on the basis of the relative severities of the shocks, a larger response would have been expected for the UK than for the other countries.

Again, much of the explanation for the pattern lies in the structural differences between the countries. However, as already explained, the relative smallness of the US price response is consistent with the direction of the possible bias induced by cyclical conditions. That the eventual price response of Canada is the largest after eight quarters (1.14%) is consistent with the relatively small degree of slack of Canada in 1975. The steepness of the price rise in the UK late in the simulation period is consistent with the severity of the shock as well as the cyclical activity pattern in which capacity utilization was not as high

TABLE 6   Government-expenditure multipliers for the Japanese model (¥1-trillion increase in government expenditure)[a].

Quarter	GNP	P	RS	MG	XG	TBD	E	NFA	M1
Japanese model alone									
1	1106	−0.03	0.4	82	9	−0.41	−0.07	−5.4	0.43
2	1354	−0.00	3.0	128	23	−0.69	−0.20	−10.8	0.71
3	1513	0.10	7.6	184	42	−1.02	−0.45	−22.8	0.93
4	1573	0.31	11.9	208	50	−1.40	−0.79	−31.5	1.20
5	1687	0.44	15.5	241	80	−1.85	−1.22	−38.7	1.50
6	1828	0.57	18.5	255	117	−1.92	−1.86	−55.0	1.86
7	1961	0.75	20.6	264	161	−2.10	−2.63	−70.0	2.13
8	2082	0.99	23.3	242	159	−2.13	−3.72	−95.7	2.56
MCM									
1	1103	0.02	0.4	75	13	−0.43	−0.07	−5	0.43
2	1344	0.13	2.9	110	33	−0.74	−0.19	−10	0.75
3	1493	0.35	7.1	147	58	− 1.13	−0.43	−22	1.00
4	1511	0.86	10.9	130	68	−1.86	−0.75	−29	1.36
5	1559	1.32	13.6	115	110	−2.67	−1.14	−36	1.78
6	1637	1.73	16.0	111	159	−2.92	−1.85	−60	2.28
7	1687	2.23	18.0	94	218	−3.38	−2.83	−87	2.66
8	1712	2.81	21.6	78	222	−3.79	−4.38	−137	3.17

[a]The variables are as follows: *GNP*, gross national product, billions of 1972 Japanese Yen at an annual rate, *P*, absorption deflator, 1972 = 100, percent; *RS*, short-term interest rate (call-money rate), basis points, *MG* and *XG*, merchandise imports and exports, respectively, billions of 1972 Japanese Yen at an annual rate, *TBD*, trade balance, billions of US dollars at an annual rate; *E*, exchange rate, US dollars per Yen, percent; *NFA*, stock of foreign-exchange reserves, billions of Japanese Yen; *M1*, stock of currency and demand deposits, percent.

as in the other countries initially and then did not decline as much later in the period. The large Japanese price rise (in comparison with the severity of the shock and the sharp activity decline in the control solution) can be partly explained by the strength of the GNP response in Japan. These results suggest that the interaction between economic slack and fiscal stimulus favors reinforcement of the real activity response in the Japanese model whereas it favors an attenuation of the price response in the US model. Although these interpretations are only tentative and suggestive they do point to areas of further research for which MCM is particularly well equipped.

4.1.3 Effects on the Interest Rate

The sizes of the interest-rate responses do not reflect the relative magnitudes of the government-expenditure shocks in all cases. Whereas the eventual rise in the short-term interest rate is in the range 80–100 basis points for Canada, the UK, and the United States, the fiscal shock to the UK model is considerably greater than that to the others. The interest-rate sensitivity to fiscal policy is much lower in the FRG and Japanese models than in the other three. Here the relative increases in government spending (with respect to GNP) are on a par with those for the US and Canadian cases and yet the increases in the short-term interest rate are on the order of 20 basis points.

It is important to emphasize at this point that the fiscal-policy experiments were run without an accomodative monetary policy except in the case of Japan. In all the other countries the net government position of the monetary authorities (net domestic assets),

TABLE 7 Government-expenditure multipliers for the UK model (£1-billion increase in government expenditure)[a].

Quarter	GDP	P	RS	MG	XG	TBD	E	NFA	M1
UK model alone									
1	1.21	0	2.4	0.225	0.002	−0.70	−0.12	−0.01	0.69
2	1.33	0.03	13.3	0.359	0.011	−1.29	−0.50	−0.05	1.22
3	1.42	0.02	28.5	0.440	0.034	−1.81	−1.28	−0.19	1.45
4	1.34	0.07	43.4	0.460	0.065	−2.25	−2.35	−0.35	1.25
5	1.62	0.16	57.9	0.463	0.112	−2.71	−3.28	−0.51	1.11
6	1.58	0.35	67.8	0.404	0.151	−2.54	−4.48	−0.71	1.07
7	1.56	0.60	80.2	0.374	0.206	−2.66	−5.92	−0.94	1.05
8	1.55	0.98	91.9	0.317	0.241	−2.47	−6.82	−1.10	1.11
MCM									
1	1.21	0	2.4	0.225	0.004	−0.83	−0.08	−0.01	0.70
2	1.34	0.025	13.3	0.359	0.016	−1.50	−0.41	−0.07	1.23
3	1.43	0.011	28.4	0.440	0.043	−1.98	−1.12	−0.18	1.47
4	1.35	0.041	43.2	0.461	0.076	−2.28	−2.11	0.33	1.27
5	1.63	0.103	57.5	0.470	0.123	−2.71	−2.98	−0.48	1.14
6	1.60	0.267	67.2	0.415	0.160	−2.45	−4.09	−0.67	1.10
7	1.58	0.483	78.8	0.390	0.211	−2.49	−5.42	−0.88	1.08
8	1.57	0.814	89.4	0.336	0.241	−2.23	−6.25	−1.03	1.12

[a]The variables are as follows: *GDP*, gross domestic product, billions of 1972 pounds sterling at an annual rate; *P*, absorption deflator, 1972 = 100, percent; *RS*, short-term interest rate (91-day Treasury-bill rate), basis points; *MG* and *XG*, merchandise imports and exports, respectively, billions of 1972 pounds sterling at an annual rate; *TBD*, trade balance, billions of US dollars at an annual rate; *E*, exchange rate, US dollars per pound sterling, percent; *NFA*, stock of foreign-exchange reserves, billions of pounds sterling; *M1*, stock of currency and demand deposits, percent.

the discount rate, and reserve requirements were held exogenous at their historical levels. The exogeneity of these variables could very well have different effects on the different models depending on their structural characteristics. In the case of the Japanese model the net government position of the monetary authorities is determined by a reaction function whose arguments include GNP with a positive effect. This accomodative monetary policy which is built into the model is sufficient to explain the small relative increase in Japanese interest rates. There are no cyclical or exogenous factors to explain the low interest-rate sensitivity of the FRG model. While the FRG fiscal stimulus is about two-thirds as intense (as a fraction of GNP) as the UK stimulus the FRG interest-rate response is less than one-quarter as large as the UK response. We are left with the conclusion that the interest-rate responses in these simulations represent different degrees of structural sensitivity in the country models. These are very much the kind of results that we have set out to explore with the structural and disaggregated framework of MCM.

4.1.4 Exchange-Rate Effects

All the countries experience depreciation of their currency in response to the fiscal stimulus. There is no exchange-rate change in the US model alone because it is operated as a fixed-exchange-rate model when it is unlinked. The depreciations range from about 7% in the UK and the FRG to about 2.5% in Canada when the models are operated alone. This range is largely a result of the severities of the shocks. Taking account of the ratio of the increase in government spending to the level of GNP (see Table 3) we can see that the

TABLE 8   Government-expenditure multipliers for the US model (US$10-billion increase in government expenditure)[a].

Quarter	GNP	P	RS	MG	XG	TBD	E	LO	M1
US model alone
1	23.6	−0.049	17.5	0	0.002	0	0	−0.57	0.187
2	21.9	0.011	33.0	1.23	0.101	−1.54		−0.84	0.300
3	20.7	0.077	47.9	2.03	0.049	−2.54		−0.81	0.428
4	23.8	0.134	64.0	2.14	−0.064	−2.89		−0.42	0.546
5	23.4	0.229	78.5	2.36	−0.175	−3.81		0.45	0.658
6	20.1	0.340	88.9	2.50	−0.269	−4.32		1.93	0.753
7	15.4	0.449	94.4	2.52	−0.419	−4.51		3.98	0.782
8	11.5	0.553	91.2	2.02	−0.483	−3.73		6.42	0.728
MCM
1	23.6	−0.050	17.5	0.01	0.002	0	−0.005	0.08	0.19
2	21.9	0.001	32.9	1.28	0.138	−1.49	−0.027	0.50	0.30
3	20.8	0.059	47.7	2.12	0.150	−2.41	−0.040	1.25	0.43
4	24.3	0.115	63.9	2.19	0.123	−2.67	−0.052	2.37	0.55
5	24.3	0.209	78.8	2.43	0.131	−3.47	−0.104	3.89	0.66
6	21.3	0.313	89.7	2.64	0.080	−3.94	−0.215	5.89	0.76
7	17.1	0.416	96.0	2.72	0.058	−3.96	−0.308	8.20	0.79
8	13.3	0.509	93.5	2.26	0.008	−3.17	−0.477	10.61	0.75

[a]The variables are as follows: GNP, gross national product, billions of 1972 dollars at an annual rate; P, absorption deflator, 1972 = 100, percent; RS, short-term interest rate (90-day commercial-paper rate), basis points; MG and XG, merchandise imports and exports, respectively, billions of 1972 US dollars at an annual rate; TBD, trade balance, billions of dollars at an annual rate; E, weighted average of the bilateral exchange rates of the dollar vis-à-vis the Deutsche Mark, the Japanese yen, the pound sterling, and the Canadian dollar, respectively; LO, liabilities to foreign official holders, billions of US dollars; M1, stock of currency and demand deposits, percent.

FRG and the UK have the two most-severe shocks and the largest depreciations. However, the exchange-rate sensitivity of the FRG is appreciably greater than that of the UK. The FRG shock is only 0.7 times as severe as the UK shock and yet produces the same depreciation. The depreciations for Japan and Canada preserve the same order as the severities of the shocks but are not proportional. Whereas the Canadian shock is 0.9 times as severe as the Japanese shock the depreciation of the Canadian dollar is only 0.7 times as great as the yen depreciation.

When the US exchange rate is endogenized by linking the model with the rest of MCM it depreciates less in comparison to the severity of the shock than do the other exchange rates. The US fiscal shock is almost as severe relative to GNP as the Canadian shock but the US dollar depreciates by about 0.5% compared with about 2.6% for the Canadian dollar.

4.2   Monetary Multipliers

In this section we present a somewhat less exhaustive review of the monetary multipliers for MCM. First we analyze the impact of a restrictive open-market operation in the United States, presenting results for both the US model run unlinked and the full MCM. We then focus on the effects of restrictive monetary actions taken abroad: an increase in the Japanese discount rate and a rise in FRG reserve requirements. Although we do not present the results in this paper, typical monetary actions in the other country models follow the same pattern as those in the three cases discussed here.

4.2.1 The Effects of Open-Market Operations in the United States

Table 9 relates to a tightening of US monetary policy: an open-market sale of US$1 billion in government securities is carried out in a period of flexible exchange rates.

TABLE 9   Monetary multipliers for the US model (US$1-billion decrease in monetary base)[a].

Quarter	GNP	P	RS	TBD	E
US model alone					
1	0	−0.001	0.81	0	Exchange
2	−0.075	−0.001	0.72	0	rate
3	−0.225	−0.001	0.68	0.12	exogenous
4	−0.400	−0.001	0.60	0.290	in
5	−0.598	−0.008	0.58	0.689	unlinked
6	−0.669	−0.015	0.40	0.957	US model
7	−0.678	−0.023	0.38	1.375	
8	−0.650	−0.038	0.20	1.250	
MCM					
1	−0.049	−0.013	0.74	−0.07	0.08
2	−0.153	−0.035	0.72	−0.09	1.25
3	−0.329	−0.057	0.69	−0.072	1.65
4	−0.568	−0.083	0.58	−0.001	2.01
5	−0.775	−0.122	0.56	0.275	2.37
6	−0.914	−0.183	0.39	0.690	2.49
7	−0.920	−0.261	0.36	0.90	2.61
8	−0.830	−0.348	0.26	0.765	2.79

[a]The variables are as follows: *GNP*, gross national product, percentage change; *P*, absorption deflator, 1972 = 100, percent; *RS*, short-term interest rate (90-day commercial-paper rate), basis points; *TBD*, trade balance, billions of US dollars at an annual rate; *E*, weighted average of the bilateral exchange rates of the US dollar vis-à-vis the Deutsche Mark, the Japanese yen, the pound sterling, and the Canadian dollar, respectively.

As for the fiscal multipliers, and in order to illustrate the effects that are introduced by MCM which in this case include the endogenization of exchange rates, the results are presented in two stages. First we analyze the effect of the monetary tightening in the context of the model of the US economy taken in isolation.

The results for the unlinked case in Table 9 are generally consistent with those of most existing models of the US economy which, by and large, do not allow foreign variables and exchange rates to vary. There is the expected negative impact on US real GNP; the effect increases gradually, reaching a maximum after seven quarters of about 0.7% below what it would otherwise have been.

This decline is caused largely by the primary impact of the open-market operation, i.e. the rise in the interest rate; the interest rate jumps by 80 basis points initially, and then declines slowly as aggregate demand falls off. In line with the weakening of aggregate demand there is a small decline in the price level and an improvement in the trade balance.

When the US model is linked to the other five models (the other country models and the ROW model) the effects of the same change in US monetary policy are modified significantly. As can be seen in the bottom half of Table 9, the negative impact on GNP is magnified; the maximum effect, which occurs seven quarters after the tightening of monetary policy, is some 0.2% more than when induced changes in external influences on the US economy are ignored. The most dramatic difference between the two sets of results is for the price level; it falls by more than 0.33% after eight quarters. There is also a significant reduction in the trade-balance effect.

The large differences between the results are traceable both to exchange-rate changes, which become endogenous in MCM, and to feedback effects from the foreign economies. The US dollar appreciates with respect to every foreign currency and consequently the weighted-average exchange rate appreciates by almost 3% at the end of two years. Because of this appreciation, the price of imports falls by 1.5% over the period. This decline feeds both directly and indirectly into the US price level. Moreover, the appreciation reduces US exports and increases imports; this relative reduction in the trade balance adds a second depressing effect on US GNP, in addition to the direct effect of the monetary tightening.

A third negative influence on US GNP is the reduction in foreign economic activity. Although not shown in the table, the GNP in each foreign country is affected adversely. This lower level of foreign demand feeds back to the United States, reducing US exports and GNP and diminishing the improvement in the US trade balance.

4.2.2 The Effects of Restrictive Monetary Policies Abroad

The effects of an increase in the discount rate of the Bank of Japan by 1% are shown in the top part of Table 10. The Japanese short-term interest rate increases sharply in the first two quarters and declines gradually thereafter. Although the US short-term rate rises moderately, there is initially a substantial increase in the interest-rate differential in favor of Japan. This increase reduces the relative attractiveness of borrowing from the US and Eurodollar markets, thus leading to an appreciation of the yen against the US dollar. The rise in domestic interest rates also has an adverse impact on fixed investment in Japan, resulting in a contraction of aggregate demand. This leads to an improvement in the Japanese trade balance and to additional upward pressure on the yen. Finally, Japanese prices decline under the combined effects of reduced capacity utilization, increased unemployment, and exchange-rate revaluation.

In the bottom part of Table 10 one can see the effects of a monetary contraction by the FRG. In this experiment, the reserve requirements on demand, time, savings, and foreign deposits were all increased by 1% over their historical values. The results largely follow those of the Japanese monetary contraction. There is a sharp initial increase in the short-term interest rate of about 75 basis points. This increase results in a widening of the interest-rate differential in favor of the FRG, which in turn leads to an inflow of private capital in the first period of about DM2 billion. The interest-rate differential does not increase in the next four periods so there is no incentive for additional portfolio inflows. Moreover, since the Deutsche Mark appreciates in the first period the regressive exchange-rate expectations incorporated in the capital-flow equations lead to capital outflows in subsequent periods. The Deutsche Mark continues to appreciate, however, because of the continued improvement in the current account.

TABLE 10   Monetary multipliers in the FRG and Japanese models[a].

Quarter	*GNP*	*P*	*RS*	*TBD*	*E*
Japanese policy change in MCM[b]					
1	−0.01	−0.107	1.02	0.053	0.45
2	−0.186	−0.327	1.372	0.248	1.29
3	0.412	−0.602	1.321	0.572	2.25
4	−0.617	−1.00	1.24	1.086	3.35
5	−0.778	−1.319	1.163	1.734	4.00
6	−1.041	−1.488	1.104	2.044	4.39
7	−1.265	−1.676	1.063	2.355	4.78
8	−1.476	−1.876	1.011	2.387	5.00
FRG policy change in MCM[c]					
1	−0.100	−0.062	0.743	0.582	1.39
2	−0.207	−0.159	0.739	1.259	3.60
3	−0.297	−0.302	0.752	1.911	5.36
4	−0.361	−0.461	0.764	2.311	6.72
5	−0.395	−0.588	0.769	2.540	6.97
6	−0.485	−0.722	1.037	3.004	8.50
7	−0.514	−0.887	0.790	3.565	9.30
8	−0.380	−0.981	0.670	2.775	8.33

[a]The variables are the same as in Tables 5 and 6. *GNP* is expressed as a percentage change from the control solution.
[b]1% change in the discount rate of the Bank of Japan.
[c]1% change in FRG reserve requirements.

The rise in interest rates has a negative impact on investment, leading to a decline in GNP (about 0.5% at its peak). This decline in GNP leads to a reduction in imports and an improvement in the trade balance which reinforces the upward pressure on the Deutsche Mark. In response to the domestic contraction and the exchange-rate appreciation there is a substantial decline in the FRG import price and a more modest reduction in the domestic expenditure deflator *P*.

5   CONCLUSIONS AND PLANS FOR FUTURE WORK

Although we are somewhat cheered by the dynamic-simulation, forecasting, and multiplier results presented in this paper, we are aware that there is much to be done before MCM can be claimed to be a full-fledged operational model. We are just beginning regular ex-ante forecasting with the model. Moreover, we are investigating a number of problem areas in MCM.

One of the most interesting "problems" that has arisen in simulating MCM is the relatively large exchange-rate changes that one observes in monetary-policy simulations. These large effects can be seen in Tables 9 and 10. For example, the 1% increase in the discount rate of the Bank of Japan leads in MCM to an exchange-rate appreciation that reaches 5% after two years (see Table 10). Most knowledgeable observers feel that this effect is considerably too large. In a recent paper (Stevens et al., 1980) this exchange-rate multiplier was analyzed and its large magnitude was tentatively traced to the capital-flow equations in MCM. We are now considering the merit of alternative solutions to the problem.

Other areas where research is underway on MCM concern the modeling of oil shocks. At present oil imports are separated out only for the US model, but it seems advisable to do this for all oil imports. Moreover, we are seriously considering separating the OPEC countries out of the ROW sector. This is a possibility that must be considered with regard to a number of countries that are now relegated to ROW.

REFERENCES

Stevens, G.V.G. (1976). Balance of payments equations and exchange rate determination. International Finance Discussion Paper No. 95. Board of Governors of the Federal Reserve System, Washington, D.C.

Stevens, G.V.G., Berner, R., Clark, P., Hernández-Catá, E., Hooper, P., Howe, H., Kwack, S.Y., and Tryon, R. (1980). Modeling bilateral exchange rates in a multi-country model. In Proceedings of the Pacific Basin Central Bank Conference on Econometric Modeling, 4th. The Bank of Japan, Tokyo.

GLOBAL INTERNATIONAL ECONOMIC MODELS
B.G. Hickman (editor)
Elsevier Science Publishers B.V. (North-Holland)
© IIASA, 1983

AN OUTLINE OF A MULTICOUNTRY ECONOMETRIC MODEL

Ray C. Fair

Cowles Foundation, Yale University, New Haven, Connecticut 06520 (USA)

1   INTRODUCTION

During the past two years I have been constructing a multicountry econometric model. The first version of this model is described in Fair (1979c), and a revised version is in preparation. This paper presents an outline of the basic structure and properties of the model. Space limitations prevent a complete description of the model here, and the reader is referred to Fair (1979c) for more details.

The theoretical basis of the model is discussed in Fair (1979a, b); the econometric model is an empirical extension of this work. Quarterly data have been collected or constructed for 64 countries, and the model contains estimated equations for 42 countries. For the first version the basic estimation period was from the first quarter of 1958 to the last quarter of 1978 (1958I–1978IV) (84 observations). For the revised version the end of the period has been extended to 1979IV. For equations that are relevant only when exchange rates are flexible the basic estimation period was 1972II–1978IV (27 observations) for the first version and is 1972II–1979IV now. Most of the equations have been estimated by the two-stage least-squares procedure.

The model differs from previous models in a number of ways. First, it accounts for exchange-rate, interest-rate, and price linkages between countries as well as the usual trade linkages. Previous multicountry econometric models have been primarily trade-linkage models. For example, the early LINK model (Ball, 1973) is of this kind, although some recent work has been done on making capital movements endogenous in the model. (See Hickman (1974) for a discussion of this and Berner et al. (1976) for a discussion of a five-country econometric model in which capital flows are endogenous. The current version of the latter model is discussed in Kwack et al. (1983).)

Second, the theory on which the model is based differs somewhat from previous theories. The theoretical model in Fair (1979a) is one in which stock and flow effects are completely integrated. There is no natural distinction in this model between stock-market and flow-market determination of the exchange rate, though this distinction is important in recent discussions of the monetary approach to the balance of payments. (See for example Frenkel and Johnson, 1976; Dornbusch, 1976; Frenkel and Rodriguez, 1975; and

Kouri, 1976). The theoretical model also allows for the possibility of price linkages between countries, something which has generally been missing from previous theoretical work.

Third, the number of countries in the model is larger than usual and the data are all quarterly. Considerable work has gone into the construction of quarterly data bases for all the countries. Some of the quarterly data have had to be interpolated from annual data and a few data points have had to be guessed. The collection and construction of the data bases are discussed in the Appendix in Fair (1979c).

Finally, there is an important difference between the approach taken in this study and an approach like that of Project LINK. I have estimated small models for each country and have then linked them together rather than, as Project LINK has done, take models developed by others and link them together. The advantage of the LINK approach is that larger models for each country can be used. It is clearly not feasible for one person to construct medium- or large-scale models for each country. However, the advantage of the present approach is that the person constructing the individual models knows from the beginning that they are to be linked together, and this may lead to better specification of the linkages. For example, it is unlikely that the specification of the exchange-rate and interest-rate linkages in the present model would develop from the LINK approach. Whether this possible gain in the linkage specification outweighs the loss of having to deal with small models of each country is of course an open question.

The transition from the theoretical model to the econometric model is reviewed in Section 2 and the econometric model is discussed in Section 3. The properties of the model are then discussed in Section 4. Section 5 contains a brief conclusion.

2   THE TRANSITION FROM THE THEORETICAL MODEL TO THE ECONOMETRIC MODEL

One of the important features of the theoretical model is that the decisions of the individual agents are assumed to be derived from the solutions of multiperiod maximization problems: households maximize utility and firms maximize profits. The variables that explain the decision variables are variables that affect these solutions. The demand equations in the econometric model are consistent with this feature in that the explanatory variables in the demand-for-goods equations are goods prices, income, interest rates, and wealth, all variables that one expects from the theory of multiperiod utility maximization to affect demand. Also, as discussed later, the price equations are consistent with the assumption of profit-maximizing behavior on the part of firms.

There are a number of options for determining interest rates in the theoretical model. The option used for the econometric model is the postulation of reaction functions for the monetary authorities of the various countries. These reaction functions are equations in which the monetary authorities are estimated to "lean against the wind". As inflation, real output, or the growth of the money supply increases, the monetary authorities are estimated to allow short-term interest rates to rise. (A reaction function of this type is estimated in Fair (1978) for the US Federal Reserve. This equation for the United States is part of the multicountry model.)

There are also a number of options for determining exchange rates in the theoretical model, depending on what one assumes about the degree of capital mobility. If there is imperfect (but not zero) capital mobility and if one estimates equations explaining the demand of each country for the security of each country (assuming, say, one security per country), then the exchange rates are implicitly determined in the model. Unfortunately very few bilateral financial data are available, and it is not feasible to estimate bilateral financial demands. This means, strictly speaking, that only two polar cases can be considered in empirical work: zero and perfect mobility. For these two cases little is lost by not collecting bilateral data. The in-between case of neither zero nor perfect mobility is of course likely to be the most realistic, and an attempt has been made in the econometric model to approximate this case. This approximation, which will now be described, affects the determination of the spot and forward exchange rates in the flexible exchange-rate regime and the determination of the short-term interest rates in the fixed and flexible exchange-rate regimes. It should be kept in mind in the following discussion that the United States is assumed to be the "leading" country with respect to the determination of interest rates. In particular the reaction function that explains the US interest rate was estimated over the entire sample period; this, as will now be seen, was not done for the other countries.

First note that if there is perfect mobility the following arbitrage condition holds:

$$e_{it} = F_{it}(1 + r_{1t})/(1 + r_{it}) \tag{1}$$

where e_{it} is the exchange rate of country i (units of local currency per US dollar), F_{it} is the three-month forward exchange rate, r_{it} is the three-month interest rate of country i, and r_{1t} is the three-month interest rate of the United States. If, say, r_{it} increases relative to r_{1t} and F_{it} is held constant then e_{it} must decrease (an appreciation of the currency of country i relative to the US dollar).

Consider now the fixed exchange-rate period. If there were zero capital mobility then one could estimate interest-rate reaction functions for each country; the interest rate of each country would be determined by its own reaction function. However, if there were perfect capital mobility then no reaction functions could be estimated (apart from the one for the United States). In this case r_{it} for each country would be determined by the arbitrage condition (1). If the forward and spot exchange rates are always equal to each other in the fixed exchange-rate period — this is approximately true — then the interest rate of each country would always equal the US rate. The approximation that was used in this study was to estimate reaction functions for each country, but to add to these equations the US interest rate as an explanatory variable. If capital is nearly perfectly mobile then the US rate should be the only significant explanatory variable in this equation and should have a coefficient estimate close to 1.0. If capital is nearly immobile then the coefficient estimate of the US rate should be close to zero and the other variables should be significant. The in-between case would correspond to the case in which both the US rate and the other variables were significant.

Consider now the flexible exchange-rate period. In this period, under either polar assumption about capital mobility, one can estimate interest-rate reaction functions, and this was done in the empirical work. The only reason for expecting the US rate to be a significant variable in these equations, under either assumption about capital mobility, is if the US rate is one of the variables that affects the decisions of the monetary authorities. The mobility assumptions in this case affect not the determination of the interest rate but rather the determination of the exchange rate. Under zero mobility equations explaining both e_{it} and F_{it} can be estimated (with perhaps the equation explaining e_{it} being interpreted as an exchange-rate reaction function of the monetary authorities of country i). By contrast, under perfect mobility eqn. (1) holds, and so only one of the two equations can be estimated. The approximation that was used in this case was to estimate an equation that was like the arbitrage condition but which allowed more flexibility between the four variables. The more estimated flexibility there is in this relationship, the further the model will be from the case of perfect mobility. Given this equation for a particular country, one further equation can be estimated – an equation determining either e_{it} or F_{it}.

To summarize, the in-between case of imperfect capital mobility was approximated by (1) estimating separate interest-rate reaction functions in the fixed and flexible exchange-rate periods, (2) adding the US interest rate to the reaction functions in the fixed-rate period, and (3) estimating "flexible" arbitrage conditions in the flexible-rate period.

3   THE ECONOMETRIC MODEL

Each country is assumed in the model to produce one good (its GNP). An equation explaining the demand of the private sector for the domestic good was estimated for each country. Similarly, for each country a demand-for-imports equation was estimated in which an aggregate import index was used as the import variable to be explained. The explanatory variables used in these demand equations have been mentioned earlier (prices, income, interest rates, wealth). The price variables used in the equations were a price index of domestic goods (measured by the price index of exports) and a price index of imports. Both short-term and long-term interest rates were tried in the equations (data permitting).

The export-price index of each country is explained by an estimated equation. The explanatory variables in this equation include import prices, a demand-pressure variable, and interest rates. A number of theoretical arguments can be made for the inclusion of import prices in the export-price equation, and some of these should perhaps be mentioned here. In the discussion of the US model in Fair (1976) it is argued that import prices may affect the expectations of a firm about the pricing behavior of other firms; this may in turn affect its own price decision. This "expectational" justification is consistent with the profit-maximizing model of firm behavior in Fair (1974). On a more practical level, if some wages and prices in a country are indexed and if the index in part includes import prices then import prices may directly or indirectly (through a wage effect on prices) affect domestic prices. The inclusion of the interest rate in the price equation can also be justified on profit-maximization grounds. For example, for the profit-maximization model in Fair (1974) the interest rate affects the optimal-price decision of a firm.

Standard demand-for-money and term-structure equations have been estimated for each country. The demand for money is assumed to be a function of the short-term interest rate and income, and the long-term interest rate is assumed to be a function of current and lagged short-term interest rates and an expected future-inflation term.

The short-term (three-month) interest rate for each country is explained by the aforementioned reaction function. Each equation was estimated twice: once for the fixed exchange-rate period and once for the flexible exchange-rate period. One would expect from the discussion in Section 2 that the US interest rate in these equations would be much more significant in the fixed-rate period than in the flexible rate period. This is in fact the case. For example, the t-ratios for the coefficient estimate of the US rate for the seven countries for which the best short-term interest-rate data exist are as shown in Table 1. Although these results are only suggestive it does seem that the US rate is more significant in influencing the interest rates of other countries in the fixed-rate period than in the flexible-rate period.

TABLE 1   t-Ratios for the coefficient estimate of the US interest rate for seven countries.

Country	Fixed-rate period	Flexible-rate period
Canada	4.29	1.74
Japan	−0.89	0.02
Belgium	4.03	−0.15
France	1.76	0.04
FRG	4.33	0.86
Netherlands	3.98	0.90
United Kingdom	2.30	0.78

The results of estimating the flexible arbitrage condition (of course, only over the flexible exchange-rate period) indicate that for most countries the arbitrage condition (1) nearly holds. Given for each country an estimate of this equation and an estimate of the interest-rate reaction function, an equation explaining either e_{it} or F_{it} can be estimated. For the first version of the model an equation explaining F_{it} was estimated but the results of estimating this equation were not very good. In the revised version of the model e_{it} is explained, and F_{it} is then determined from the estimated arbitrage condition. The equation explaining e_{it} is meant to be an approximation to the (unknown) reduced-form equation that would be obtained by solving the structural model for e_{it}, where if capital were not perfectly mobile the structure would have to include the estimated bilateral demand equations mentioned in Section 2.

4   THE PROPERTIES OF THE MODEL

A useful way of describing the properties of the model is to consider the effects of changing government-expenditure variables. Before discussing these effects, however, it will be useful to list a few of the partial (ceteris paribus) effects in the model. These are as follows:

(1) Interest rates have a negative effect on demand (goods-demand equations).
(2) Interest rates have a positive effect on export prices (price equations).
(3) Import prices have a positive effect on export prices (price equations).
(4) Income has a positive effect on the demand for money (demand-for-money equations).
(5) The rate of inflation, real output growth, and lagged money-supply growth have a positive effect on interest rates (interest-rate reaction functions).

(6) The US interest rate has an important (positive) effect on the interest rates of other countries in the fixed exchange-rate regime (interest-rate reaction functions).

(7) The short-term interest rate of country i has a negative effect on e_{it} (i.e. a positive effect on the value of the currency of country i). In the first version of the model this arises from the estimated arbitrage equation, assuming F_{it} as given. In the revised version the interest rate is an explanatory variable in the equation explaining e_{it}.

(8) A depreciation of the currency of a country (a rise in e_{it}) leads to an increase in the import prices that it faces.

Since I am in the process of revising the model I do not have quantitative multiplier results that I trust available. However, from performing a number of preliminary experiments, I do have a fairly good idea of the qualitative properties of the model, and so the emphasis in the following discussion will be on the qualitative properties.

Consider first an increase in US government spending (on US goods) in the fixed exchange-rate period. This increases US income, which in turn increases the US demand for imports. The increase in the US demand for imports increases the exports of other countries, which in turn increases their income and demand for imports. This is the standard trade-multiplier effect. The increase in US income also leads to an increase in the US price level, which increases the import prices of other countries. This produces an increase in their domestic prices (and thus their export prices), resulting in further increases in import prices of other countries (including the United States). This is what might be called a "price-multiplier" effect. There are thus both trade-multiplier and price-multiplier effects in the model: imports affect exports and vice versa, and import prices affect export prices and vice versa.

The other important effect in this case is the interest-rate effect. The increase in US income and prices leads to an increase in the US interest rate through the reaction function of the US Federal Reserve. This offsets some of the increase in US income that would otherwise have occurred and also leads to an increase in the interest rates of other countries. If capital were assumed to be perfectly mobile in the model then the interest rates in the other countries would go up by the same amount as the US rate. Since, as discussed in Sections 2 and 3, this restriction was not imposed on the model the interest rates in the other countries generally increase less than the US rate. Interest rates do of course rise and this worldwide increase in interest rates offsets some of the increase in world income that would otherwise have occurred. In fact for some experiments that I have run the change in real GNP for some countries is negative, and this is primarily due to the increase in interest rates. The interest-rate effect in the model is thus quantitatively important and over time offsets much of the trade-multiplier effect.

Consider next an increase in government spending in the Federal Republic of Germany (FRG) (on FRG goods) in the fixed-rate period. The trade and price effects are similar to the effects for the US increase in that exports and prices increase. The main difference in the FRG case concerns the interest rate. If capital were perfectly mobile and if the US Federal Reserve were assumed to be the monetary authority setting the (world) interest rate then the only change in interest rates that would occur in response to the FRG income increase would be as a result of the Federal Reserve's responding through its reaction function to the increase in US income and prices induced by the FRG increase. As noted earlier, the assumption of perfect mobility was not imposed on the model, and the FRG interest rate does rise much more than the interest rates of any of the other countries in response to the FRG income increase. The interest rates in the other countries do not rise very much in this case, which is due largely to the fact that the US rate does not rise very much. Even though capital is not assumed to be perfectly mobile the United States is still the leader with respect to interest rates in the fixed exchange-rate regime; therefore, in general, interest rates in other countries will not change very much unless the US rate does. The exception of course is when a large shock occurs in a particular country. Since interest rates do not increase very much in the FRG experiment there is little offset to the increases in output from the trade-multiplier effect.

The properties of the model in the flexible exchange-rate period are more difficult to describe and are more subject to change as the model is revised. One key difference between the fixed- and flexible-rate periods is that the US interest rate has much less effect on the interest rates of the other countries in the flexible-rate period. There is thus less interest-rate offset to the output increases in this period.

The other key difference between the two periods is of course the endogeneity of the spot and forward exchange rates in the flexible-rate period. An increase in US government spending has a number of indirect effects on the US exchange rate, some positive and some negative, and the net effect is ambiguous. An increase in US spending leads to an increase in the US interest rate relative to the rates of other countries, which has a positive effect on the value of the US dollar. However, an increase in US spending leads to an increase in the US rate of inflation relative to the rates of other countries, and this may have a negative effect on the value of the US dollar. In the first version of the model F_{it} was affected for some countries by differential price movements between the particular country and the United States. F_{it} in turn affected e_{it} through the arbitrage equation. In the revised version of the model differential price variables are included directly in the e_{it} equations. Thus in either version an increase in the US inflation rate relative to the rates in other countries has, other things being equal, a negative effect on the value of the US dollar.

Exchange rates also have important effects on prices, and vice versa. For example, an exchange-rate depreciation increases import prices, which in turn increases domestic (export) prices through the price equation. The price-multiplier effects are thus more complicated in the flexible exchange-rate regime, with some currencies appreciating and some depreciating, and there is clearly no unambiguous effect on the inflation rate of a given country from, say, an increase in US government spending.

Finally it should be noted that changes in inflation rates have effects on interest rates through the reaction functions of the monetary authorities, and so changes in exchange rates have effects over time on interest rates (and vice versa).

5 CONCLUSION

I have tried in this paper to give a general idea of the structure and properties of the model without going into very many details. When the revised version is finished there will be multiplier tables available to show the quantitative properties of the model. It does appear from the results so far that price, exchange-rate, and interest-rate linkages between countries are quantitatively quite important, so that any model based primarily on trade linkages is unlikely to be a very good approximation of the world economy.

Finally I should note that although I have not discussed any tests of the model in this paper, these are an important part of my research effort. So far I have compared for each variable the accuracy of the first version of the model to that of a fourth-order autoregressive model, and these results are presented in Fair (1979c). I will also do this for the revised version. I am also interested in trying to apply at least part of the method for comparing models given in Fair (1980) to comparisons using the model.

REFERENCES

Ball, R.J. (Editor) (1973). The International Linkage of National Economic Models. North-Holland, Amsterdam.
Berner, R., Clark, P., Howe, H., Kwack, S., and Stevens, G. (1976). Modeling the international influences on the US economy: a multi-country approach. International Finance Discussion Paper No. 93. Board of Governors of the Federal Reserve System, Washington, D.C.
Dornbusch, R. (1976). Capital mobility, flexible exchange rates and macroeconomic equilibrium. In E. Claassen and P. Salin (Editors), Recent Developments in International Monetary Economics. North-Holland, Amsterdam.
Fair, R.C. (1974). A Model of Macroeconomic Activity. Vol. 1. The Theoretical Model. Ballinger, Cambridge, Massachusetts.
Fair, R.C. (1976). A Model of Macroeconomic Activity. Vol. 2. The Empirical Model. Ballinger, Cambridge, Massachusetts.
Fair, R.C. (1978). The sensitivity of fiscal policy effects to assumptions about the behavior of the Federal Reserve. Econometrica, 46:1165−1180.
Fair, R.C. (1979a). A model of the balance of payments. Journal of International Economics, 9: 25−46.
Fair, R.C. (1979b). On modeling the economic linkages among countries. In R. Dornbusch and J.A. Frenkel (Editors), International Economic Policy: Theory and Evidence. Johns Hopkins University Press, Baltimore, Maryland.
Fair, R.C. (1979c). A multicountry econometric model. Cowles Foundation Discussion Paper No. 541. Yale University, New Haven, Connecticut.
Fair, R.C. (1980). Estimating the expected predictive accuracy of econometric models. International Economic Review, 21:355−378.
Frenkel, J.A. and Johnson, H.G. (Editors) (1976). The Monetary Approach to the Balance of Payments. University of Toronto Press, Toronto.
Frenkel, J.A. and Rodriguez, C.A. (1975). Portfolio equilibrium and the balance of payments: a monetary approach. American Economic Review, 65:674−688.
Hickman, B.G. (1974). International transmission of economic fluctuations and inflation. In A. Ando, R. Herring, and R. Marston (Editors), International Aspects of Stabilization Policies. Federal Reserve Bank of Boston, Boston, Massachusetts, p. 203.
Kouri, P.J.K. (1976). The exchange rate and the balance of payments in the short run and in the long run. Scandinavian Journal of Economics, 2:280−304.
Kwack, S.Y., Berner, R., Clark, P., Hernandez-Catá, E., Howe, H., and Stevens, G. (1983). The structure and properties of the Multicountry Model. In B.G. Hickman (Editor), Global International Economic Models. North-Holland, Amsterdam; this volume, pp. 69−84.

COMMENTS*

This paper outlines the theoretical basis of an econometric model dealing with important parts of the world economy (excluding centrally planned economies and some of the developing countries) and reports on some preliminary results.

The theoretical model connects flows and stocks in an interesting way: there is a rudimentary portfolio model comprising money and bonds. Unfortunately, the most important part, namely, real capital, has not been included. This means that the model may be used only for ex post or very short-term ex ante simulations. In other words, Professor Fair's model concentrates heavily on the monetary side of the economies and only sketches in the real side (out of the nine variables explained by stochastic equations there are only two equations explaining the real side, namely, those referring to real private domestic purchases and merchandise imports). Thus it seems to me that, comparing his approach to that of Project LINK and other models of this kind, Professor Fair errs towards another extreme by more or less skimming over the real side of the economies. To correct this, one should explicitly introduce production, consumption, and investment functions and endogenize the government demand.

However, even within the limitations of the Fair model perhaps something more could have been done to make the model more realistic. For example, it follows from portfolio theory that the demand for money in a country should be a function of the interest rates, the rate of change of the interest rates, the price levels, the rates of inflation, the value of GNP, and the wealth of all countries. Professor Fair retains only the rate of interest and the value of GNP of the country in question as explanatory variables. Similarly, following portfolio theory the price level of a country should be explained by the exchange rates, the rates of change of the exchange rates, the rates of inflation, the interest rates, the rates of changes of the interest rates, the profit rates, the money supplies, the real GNP, and the real wealth of all countries. Professor Fair retains only the price levels of other countries converted to the currency of the country in question by the appropriate exchange rates, the own interest rate, and the own real GNP of the country in question. At the very least, the absence of the money supply is a serious deficiency. Of course, there are other possibilities for deriving a price level function, for example, starting from the cost side. This is perhaps what Professor Fair has in mind. But in this case one needs the wage level, the productivity rate, the rate of indirect taxation, and other variables which are not in the model. Thus, the monetary approach might be more appropriate.

Professor Fair uses reaction functions to determine the Central Bank's decisions on interest rates. This is quite a useful approach in all cases where the average interest rates follow the discount rate (set by the Central Bank) closely. However, this is not always the case. In general, one must explain the short- and long-term rates as functions of the discount rate and other explanatory variables.

The reaction functions used here are based on the assumption that the interest rate of a country is determined by its monetary authorities by considering the US interest rate, the price level, the money supply, the "pressure of demand", and the interest rate one

*By W. Krelle, Institut für Gesellschafts- und Wirtschaftswissenschaften, Rheinische Friedrich Wilhelms Universität, Bonn, FRG. These comments are based on the complete model described at the IIASA Conference in July 1980, and some of the criticisms do not apply to later versions of the model.

quarter before. In the case of the FRG, only the US interest rate, the pressure of demand, and the interest rate of the quarter before are retained. This is, in the case of the FRG, a rather crude description of reality. According to its stated policy, the Bundesbank considers (besides the interest rates) the balance of payments (current account), the rate of inflation, and the unemployment rate. Our group estimated a reaction function for the Bundesbank on this basis, with good results.

Another feature of the model should be mentioned. Professor Fair puts the United States in the center of the world economy by relating all export prices, GNP figures, and other variables to the corresponding variables of the United States. It would be better to relate them to the corresponding world trade figures. In 1978 the total exports of the United States amounted to 11% of world exports, whereas the exports of the EC-countries amounted to 35%, the exports of the FRG to 11%, and the exports of Japan to 7.5%. This seems to indicate that the total volume of world trade is a better indicator of total world economic activity than the figures for the United States taken in isolation.

Summing up, it seems to me that total world trade should be treated more as an interwoven net of trade and capital flows and not (to exaggerate a bit) as an annex to the American economy. The consequences of this asymmetric approach show up in the results. The outcome of the simulation experiments are very different depending on whether a variable of the US economy or that of another country has been shocked (in this particular case, government expenditure in the FRG). The outcome is much more plausible for the German case, because the FRG is treated on an equal footing with all other nations. The results of simulating an autonomous increase in US real income are much less plausible, due to the exaggerated influence of all American data on the total world economy.

The results of the estimations are astonishingly good from the statistical point of view, with the exception of the equation for the forward exchange rate. Since this is, however, a crucial variable in the model, this result is discomforting. There are a lot of speculative effects determining the forward rate. Presumably it would be better to try to get along without this variable by explaining the current exchange rate directly and not from the forward rate, using the arbitrage condition reproduced in the paper. Of course, the best way would be to determine the exchange rate by equalizing supply and demand on the foreign exchange market. But this means estimating the trade and capital flows, which does not seem feasible from the data base available. However, it should be possible to use this approach at least for the most important world market countries.

Professor Fair tried out a lot of different specifications of the behavior functions (along the lines of the theoretical model) and retained those where the parameters had the right sign and were statistically significant (as a rule). But this means that the behavior functions often look quite different for essentially similar countries, and sometimes that important variables are missing. For instance, in the import function for the FRG, prices have no influence. The same is true for other countries, for example, the UK and Switzerland. The price elasticity of imports is unlikely to be zero, not even for commodities like crude oil. Thus it seems as if some more individual treatment of the more important countries would have been rewarding. The relation between the long-term and the short-term interest rate is well captured, but the short-term interest rates themselves (determined by reaction functions) are not so well explained. As already mentioned, the fit of the equation explaining the forward exchange rate is least satisfactory.

Professor Fair tested the model by comparing its fit with an autoregressive model where each endogenous variable was regressed on itself, on time, and on three seasonal dummy variables. The results show that his model performs at least no worse than, and in some cases better than the autoregressive model. This test, as he states himself, is not quite fair since Professor Fair's model uses exogenous variables which are not included in the autoregressive model. A real test would be an ex ante forecast outside of the reference period. This has not yet been done. In order to use the model for questions of practical economic policy, the exogenous variables need to be forecast as well. These include some quite important variables such as government demand. Thus, another model has to be constructed to forecast the exogenous variables.

The simulation experiments with the model are quite interesting. The special position of the US model yields results which, in my opinion, are hard to accept. Take for instance the following example. An *increase* in US real income induces a *fall* in German private demand and a *fall* in real GNP in the FRG. The mechanism behind this result is as follows. An autonomous increase in US income raises the US interest rate. The interest rates of the other countries (including the FRG) are positively correlated with the US interest rate. The negative effect of the higher interest rates on the GNP overrules the positive effect of higher US income for most of the other countries, for example, the FRG. But all these are minor details which may be corrected in later versions of the model. Basically, this is a very useful approach, and Professor Fair is to be congratulated for having completed a model of this size all alone. He uses only a limited set of data for each economy and, in most cases, obtains plausible results. As a model for the world economy as a whole and for the simultaneous determination of interest rates and exchange rates, however, it seems to me that the real side of the economy should not be treated in such a cursory fashion and that the overemphasis on the US economy should be corrected. In future work, real forecasting should be tried and the dynamic properties of the model explored further.

Part Three

General Equilibrium Models

GLOBAL INTERNATIONAL ECONOMIC MODELS
B.G. Hickman (editor)
Elsevier Science Publishers B.V. (North-Holland)
© IIASA, 1983

A GENERAL EQUILIBRIUM MODEL FOR THE WORLD ECONOMY: SOME PRELIMINARY RESULTS

G. Carrin, J.W. Gunning, and J. Waelbroeck
Free University of Brussels, Brussels (Belgium)

1   INTRODUCTION

This paper is a report on the first results that have been obtained with the Global Development Model constructed at the University of Brussels. This modeling effort is part of the World Bank research program and will contribute to the formulation and economic analysis of forecasts for the developing world that are to appear in future World Development Reports from the World Bank. The present model uses the general equilibrium approach to modeling and is therefore building on the research of Ginsburgh and Waelbroeck (1981) on the methodology of general equilibrium.

The basic data framework adopted is the one used in the World Development Report, i.e. the model developed by Gupta et al. (1979). However, we have introduced some new features: the Extended Linear Expenditure System (ELES), migration from rural to urban areas, and elasticities of substitution for import substitution and for competition between exporters. Another important characteristic of our model is that it can be used to study the effects of policy decisions when prices are either rigid or fully flexible.

It should also be noted that the solution algorithm that we have used is basically a Gauss—Seidel procedure in which some variables are adjusted by tâtonnement.

The paper is organized as follows. In Section 2 the model is presented and discussed. In Section 3 we analyze the impact of an increase in oil prices on the less developed countries (LDCs) using the policy simulations that we have carried out. The paper ends with some general conclusions. The equations of the model appear in the Appendix; the notation used and a list of regions are given in Tables 1 and 2.

2   THE MODEL

The model consists of regional models for nine groups of developing countries and a rudimentary model for the rest of the world and the developed and centrally planned countries. International trade and capital flows provide the links between the ten regions.

TABLE 1   The variables used in the model[a].

Variable	Description	Units[b]
C	Private consumption	a
D	Domestic demand	a
E	Exports	a
F	Fertilizer use	e
FC	Deficit on the current account of the balance of payments	b
G	Public consumption	a
I	Investment	a
IC	Investment in current prices	b
K	Capital stock	a
L^d	Cultivated area (dry land)	d
L^i	Cultivated area (irrigated land)	d
M	Imports	a
M^{RU}	Rural-to-urban migration	c
N	Labor force	c
pd	Domestic price (of the CES aggregate of domestic and imported goods)	f
pm	Import price (i.e. the world price of the CES aggregate of exports of all regions)	f
pp	Producer price	f
pr	Price of value added	f
RR	Rural supply (value added)	a
RU	Urban supply (value added)	a
t	Time	g
T	Tax revenue	b
WT	World trade	a
X	Gross output	a
y	Supernumerary income (i.e. income net of taxes and committed expenditures)	b
Y	GDP	a
ζ^d	Share of domestic supply in domestic demand	—
ζ^m	Share of imports in domestic demand	—

[a]Subscripts (*i* or *j* for sectors, *r* for regions) and superscripts (R and U for rural and urban) are suppressed in the table.
[b]The units are as follows: a, millions of US dollars (1975 prices); b, millions of US dollars (current prices) (current prices take into account only relative price changes since 1975, not absolute price changes in developed countries; relative prices are assumed not to have changed between 1975 and 1978); c, thousands; d, millions of hectares; e, thousands of tons; f, index (1978 = 1) of a price, relative to the price level in region 10 (developed countries); g, years.

Each developing region is described by a simple general equilibrium model but there is no intertemporal optimization. The model consists of three parts: (A) the static (general equilibrium) part of the regional model; (B) the equations which determine world trade and prices; and (C) the dynamic part of the regional model which contains the production functions and in which the values of factor supplies are updated for the next period.

We will first describe a version of the model in which all prices are market clearing. However, our simulation results are not based on this version; the world price of energy is fixed in all the runs and in some runs there are additional price rigidities. These modifications will be discussed later.

2.1   Simplified Presentation of the Static Model

The static regional model is best understood by stripping it down to its bare essentials. If (a) there is no public consumption, no taxation, and no intermediate demand,

TABLE 2   The sectors and regions used in the model (with their indexes).

Sectors

$i = 1$	Agriculture (food)	} rural
2	Agriculture (nonfood)	
3	Manufacturing	} urban
4	Energy	
5	Services	

Regions

$r = 1$	AFRICA	(Africa south of the Sahara, excluding South Africa and Nigeria)
2	LEMENA	(North Africa and Middle East, excluding countries in regions 3 and 8)
3	MEMENA	(Bahrain, Iran, Iraq, Lebanon)
4	LASIA	(Asia, excluding Indonesia, Mongolia, China, North Korea, and the countries of region 5)
5	ASIA	(Hong Kong, Singapore, Brunei, Samoa, Guam, New Caledonia, French Polynesia)
6	LAC	(Latin America and the Caribbean, excluding Mexico and Venezuela)
7	SEUROP	(Portugal, Spain, Gibraltar, Malta, Cyprus, Greece, Yugoslavia, Turkey, Israel)
8	OPECME	(Saudi Arabia, Kuwait, Qatar, Libya, United Arab Emirates, Oman)
9	OPECOTH	(Nigeria, Mexico, Venezuela, Indonesia)
10	DEVW	(Rest of the world)

(b) there are only two sectors (1, rural; 2, urban), and (c) the rural and urban consumption functions are identical, then the model reduces to the following 11 equations (see Tables 1 and 2 for the notation; the equations of the full model are given in the Appendix).

$$D_i = C_i + I_i \tag{1}$$

$$X_i = \zeta_i^{\mathrm{d}} D_i + E_i \tag{2}$$

$$M_i = \zeta_i^{\mathrm{m}} D_i \tag{3}$$

$$\zeta_i^{\mathrm{d}} = (d_i^{\mathrm{d}})^{\hat{\sigma}_i}(pd_i/pp_i)^{\sigma_i} \tag{4}$$

$$\zeta_i^{\mathrm{m}} = (d_i^{\mathrm{m}})^{\sigma_i}(pd_i/pm_i)^{\sigma_i} \tag{5}$$

$$(pd_i)^{1-\sigma_i} = (d_i^{\mathrm{d}})^{\sigma_i}(pp_i)^{1-\sigma_i} + (d_i^{\mathrm{m}})^{\sigma_i}(pm_i)^{1-\sigma_i} \tag{6}$$

$$R_i = X_i \tag{7}$$

$$pd_i C_i = pd_i \gamma_i + \beta_i y \tag{8}$$

$$I_i = \lambda_i(1 - \beta_1 - \beta_2)y / \sum_i pd_i \lambda_i \tag{9}$$

$$y = \sum_i (pp_i X_i - pd_i \gamma_i) \tag{10}$$

$$E_i = b_i^{\eta_i}(pm_i/pp_i)^{\eta_i} WT_i \tag{11}$$

The variables which are endogenous in this part of the model are D, X, C, I, E, M, pd, pp, ζ^d, ζ^m, and y. World trade WT and world prices pm are determined in part B while the production functions of part C determine supply R. These variables are here treated as exogenous.

The main elements of the specification are easily recognized. First, we stress (as is natural in a model of world trade) the importance of substitution possibilities in demand between imported and domestic goods. We assume that these substitution possibilities can be described by a constant elasticity of substitution (CES) function:

$$D_i^{-r_i} = d_i^d (X_i - E_i)^{-r_i} + d_i^m M_i^{-r_i}$$

where $\sigma_i = 1/(1 + r_i)$ is the elasticity of substitution between domestic goods $X_i - E_i$ and imports M_i in total domestic demand D_i. Equations (1)–(5) follow from the CES formulation. Hence in each sector i there are three goods: the domestic good (also used for exports), the imported good, and a CES aggregate formed by "mixing" these. The balance equations (1), (2), and (3) and the prices pd, pp, and pm, correspond to these three goods, respectively. It should be noted that the pricing rule (6) is consistent, implying that

$$pd_i D_i = pp_i(X_i - E_i) + pm_i M_i$$

$$pd_i = pp_i \zeta_i^d + pm_i \zeta_i^m$$

Also, the balance equations reduce to the familiar form

$$X_i = C_i + I_i + E_i - M_i$$

only if $\zeta_i^d + \zeta_i^m = 1$, a condition which is in general satisfied only in the base year*. The equation that does hold is the current-price equivalent

$$pp_i X_i = pd_i C_i + pd_i I_i + pp_i E_i - pm_i M_i$$

Substitution elasticities differ between sectors; e.g. in the full model (in which there are five sectors) σ is high for agriculture and low for services and for energy.

Secondly, we use the ELES (see Lluch et al., 1977) to determine private consumption and savings (eqns. (8)–(10)).

Thirdly, investment is endogenous, and therefore static effects (changes in prices and incomes in the current period) affect savings and hence (via investment) factor availability in the next period.

---

*In the base year ($t = 0$), $pd_i = pp_i = pm_i = 1$ and since the parameters d^d and d^m are estimated from

$$(d_i^d)\text{xi} = (X_{i0} - E_{i0})/D_{i0} \qquad (d_i^m)^{\sigma_i} = M_{i0}/D_{i0}$$

the shares ζ do sum to unity.

Fourthly, exports react to changes in the ratio of domestic and world prices; the process of adjustment to equilibrium in the model therefore involves changes in both imports and exports.

The value of the elasticity η is of course a key parameter that determines to what extent LDCs benefit from trade liberalization or growth in the rest of the world. (See Ginsburgh and Waelbroeck (1981, Chapter 12) for a comparison of two extreme cases of elasticity optimism and pessimism.)

Finally, in this version of the model prices are market clearing: we use price tâtonnement iterating on prices pp until the equilibrium condition (7) is satisfied.

2.2   Full Specification of the Static Model

The full model differs from eqns. (1)–(11) in four respects.

(a) There are two groups of consumers and hence two sets of ELES coefficients, one for rural income and one for urban income.

(b) There is intermediate demand and public consumption. Domestic demand is now written as

$$D_i = \sum_j a_{ij} X_j + C_i + I_i + G_i$$

This implies that while input–output coefficients giving the demand for intermediate inputs are fixed in terms of the CES aggregate (a_{ij}) there are (as for final demand) substitution possibilities between domestically produced and imported intermediate inputs. (Use of the former is given by $a_{ij}^d = \zeta_i^d a_{ij}$ and use of the latter by $a_{ij}^m = \zeta_i^m a_{ij}$. Note that $a_{ij}^d + a_{ij}^m \neq a_{ij}$; as noted before the shares ζ^d and ζ^m do not sum to unity.) Public consumption is exogenous. Rural and urban income is taxed at fixed rates.

(c) In addition to household savings and government savings there are now foreign savings. Instead of the equality of imports and exports we now have

$$\sum_i (pm_i M_i - pp_i E_i) = FC$$

where FC is the deficit on the current account of the balance of payments. (That balance-of-payments equilibrium in this sense is implied is shown in the Appendix.) To most regions this foreign capital inflow is exogenous; we ignore the possibility that the adjustment process involves changes in foreign borrowings.

We use an extreme assumption on the distribution of investment (see eqns. (A15) and (A16) in the Appendix): by sector of destination, rural investment is financed only by the savings of rural households, all foreign and government savings go to the urban sector.

(d) There now are five rather than two sectors: two rural sectors (agriculture (food) ($i = 1$) and agriculture (nonfood) ($i = 2$)) and three urban sectors (manufacturing ($i = 3$), energy ($i = 4$), and services ($i = 5$)).

The production functions of part C determine rural supply as a function of labor, dry land, irrigated land, and fertilizer use, and urban supply as a function of capital and labor. In principle we should have five equilibrium conditions. Since supply R is defined in terms of value added, the counterpart of eqn. (7) would be

$$R_i = (1 - \sum_j a_{ij}) X_i \qquad (i = 1, 2, \ldots, 5)$$

In principle this could be done but in this preliminary version of the model we have made two simplifying assumptions which enable us to aggregate so that the equilibrium conditions appear as

$$RR = \sum_{i=1}^{2} (1 - \sum_j a_{ji}) X_i$$

$$RU = \sum_{i=1}^{5} (1 - \sum_j a_{ji}) X_i$$

Hence there are only two "resources": a rural one RR which is used to meet the demand in the two rural sectors and an urban one RU, the supply of which must equal net demand in the three other sectors. (Note that "resources" are not production factors; it is a value-added concept as in "domestic resource cost".) The two assumptions which enable us to aggregate are the following:

(a) The production functions for the two rural sectors ($i = 1, 2$) are identical; similarly there are no differences between the production functions for the urban sectors ($i = 3, 4, 5$).

(b) There is no factor specificity: implicitly it is assumed that capital and labor can shift without cost and instantaneously between the three urban sectors and, within agriculture, that land and labor shift between food and nonfood production. This simplification reduces the dimensions of the space of prices in which we have to iterate: there are now only two value-added prices (pr_1 and pr_2, corresponding to RR and RU). In spite of the five-sector disaggregation of demand and external trade the model remains essentially a two-sector model.

These four extensions define the full version of the regional general equilibrium model (eqns. (A1)–(A18) in the Appendix).

It should be noted that the distribution λ of investment by sector of origin is fixed (and independent of the sector of destination, eqn. (A17)) and that the introduction of intermediate demand leads to a distinction between gross output prices pp and value-added prices pr; also the use of the Leontief pricing equation (A4) implies that gross output in current prices $pp_i X_i$ is exhausted by payments for intermediate inputs $X_i \sum_j a_{ji} pd_j$ and value added in current prices $X_i (1 - \sum_j a_{ji}) pr_k$ all of which ends up as (pretax) household income (eqns. (A12) and (A13)).

This model is clearly rather crude. In interpreting our results it is useful to keep five features of the specification in mind.

(1) The substitution possibilities between domestic goods and imports (summarized by the elasticity σ) are the same whether the source of demand is intermediate demand, consumption, or investment.

(2) As noted earlier, government and foreign savings are used entirely for investment in the urban sector.

(3) There are (in this version of the model) no indirect taxes, subsidies, or tariffs. Also there are no quantitative restrictions, e.g. import controls. Price rigidities, however, play an important role in one variant of the model.

(4) Households receive all value added (there are no retained earnings) and since households are not further disaggregated the functional distribution of income does not appear. What does matter in the model is the distribution of income between rural and urban households.

(5) Regarding trade, the model can be used to study changes in comparative advantage for the rural and urban composites but, with the present aggregation, not for the five individual sectors.

It should be noted that, within the current period, trade flows are determined by demand (the ELES coefficients, the input–output matrix, and the substitution elasticities σ and η in domestic and world demand); there is no movement along the production-possibility frontier which in part A of the model is reduced to a single point since supply R_i is predetermined. Hence in the short run changes in world prices for the two goods have no effect on their production. Over time, however, there is such a movement as rural and urban factor supplies are affected by investment and migration.

2.3   International Trade

The regions are linked in part B of the model (eqns. (A19)–(A22) in the Appendix).

Exports of the same good by different regions are treated as imperfect substitutes. World trade is defined as a CES function of the exports of the ten regions. The world price of this aggregate is defined in a way that is consistent with this CES formulation (see eqn. (A21)). Imports are, however, homogenous; we ignore the direction of trade effects. It is as if (for a given commodity i) all exports are sent to a central pool and are transformed into an aggregate commodity which is used to meet import demand from all regions. The imports of different regions therefore have the same composition in terms of the region of origin. (This implies that world trade WT_i can be written as $\Sigma_r M_{ir}$ (where r denotes the regions) but that the sum $\Sigma_r E_{ir}$ has no meaning. Note that eqn. (A19) is not an independent equation but is implied by eqns. (A18) and (A21).) The import demand of the non-LDC countries (region 10) is related by fixed elasticities to that region's Gross Domestic Product (GDP) (exogenous) and price level (relative to world prices). (While for the other nine regions the price variable is the ratio pd_i/pm_i (eqn. (A2)), for the rest of the world only pm_i appears in eqn. (A22); this is because prices are defined relative to those of region 10.)

There are no quantitative restrictions in the trade model but there is an important price rigidity: in all variants of the model the export price pe_4 of energy is fixed. The difference between this export price and the domestic price defines an (endogenous) tax rate on energy exports:

$$\tau_{oil} = pe_4 - pp_4$$

The revenues $\tau_{oil} E_4$ from this tax appear in the government budget.

2.4   The Dynamic Part of the Regional Model

Part C of the model (eqns. (A23)–(A31) in the Appendix) contains the production functions. For the urban sector this is a Cobb–Douglas function in capital and labor, where (apart from natural growth) the urban labor force grows with migration. The migration function is based on the work of Mundlak (1976). Implicitly there are balance equations for production factors but these are not stated here. Rural supply is a function of the cultivated area (itself a function of rural savings), of fertilizer use (a function of the area under crops and of the rural–urban terms of trade), and of labor supply. (Except for the term in labor this function is based on the specification of Strout (1975) and the estimation results of Choe's cross-country regressions for 78 developing countries used in Verreydt (1977). The function explaining fertilizer use is that of Osterrieth et al. (1980).)

2.5   Fixed-Price Variant

So far we have discussed the flexible-price variant of the model in which the only price rigidity is that of the world price of energy. In the fixed-price variant, however, the resource price pr_2 is fixed as well (to facilitate comparison of the two variants this price is fixed at the level of the flexible-price base run). The equilibrium condition (eqn. (A8)) is no longer satisfied: pr_2 no longer clears the market. For the regions which are net exporters of energy there is excess demand in the urban sector. The excess demand is eliminated by raising the tax rate on urban incomes. The extra tax revenues do not appear as in the government budget; they are invested abroad. There is therefore a capital outflow FCE and balance-of-payments equilibrium now appears as

$$\sum_i (pm_i M_i - pe_i E) = FC - FCE$$

where $pe = pp$, except for the energy sector.

The nonoil regions are in an excess-supply regime in this variant $(RU > \sum_{i=3}^{5} (1 - \sum_j a_{ji}) X_i)$. No further adjustment occurs for these regions: urban factors of production are partly unemployed.

2.6   Data and Computation

We have used the World Bank's data base for 1978 which underlies the projections in the Bank's World Development Report. When possible we have based the values of the ELES on estimation results (income and price elasticities are taken from Lluch et al. (1977); the coefficients β and γ are derived from these elasticities and the base-year data); however, the elasticities of substitution between domestic and foreign goods (σ) and between exports of different regions (η) are chosen on a priori grounds and indeed we will test the sensitivity of the model to these chosen values by varying them parametrically.

Our computational method is simple. Recent experience (e.g. Adelman and Robinson, 1978; Taylor et al., 1980; Ginsburgh and Waelbroeck, 1981) with what are essentially Gauss–Seidel iterative methods in general equilibrium models has been encouraging and we have used a similar approach in this international model. Prices are changed between each iteration τ on the basis of excess demand; e.g. for the rural sector

$$(pr_{1(\tau+1)} - pr_{1\tau})/pr_{1\tau} = \xi \left[\sum_{i=1}^{2} (1 - \sum_j a_{ji}) X_{i\tau} - RR \right]/RR$$

(Note that here we suppress the subscript τ for RR; supply is predetermined and hence does not change between iterations.) In the simplified model (eqns. (1)–(11)) this iterative method implies that changes in excess demand between iterations can be approximated in the neighborhood of equilibrium by the system of linear difference equations

$$
\begin{pmatrix} Z_{1(\tau+1)} - Z_{1\tau} \\ Z_{2(\tau+1)} - Z_{2\tau} \end{pmatrix} = \xi \begin{pmatrix} C_{11} & C_{12} \\ C_{21} & C_{22} \end{pmatrix} \begin{pmatrix} Z_{1\tau} \\ Z_{2\tau} \end{pmatrix}
$$

where Z_i is the excess demand $X_i - R_i$. It can be shown that if household income net of taxes and committed expenditure is positive ($y^R, y^U > 0$) then (a) the diagonal elements (C_{11}, C_{22}) are negative so that $\partial X_i / \partial pp_i$ is unambiguously negative and that (b) the system is locally asymptotically stable. This condition is sufficient, but not necessary. The method seems to work well; on the CDC computer of the University of Brussels the solution of four variants of the model for six years each (1979, 1980, 1982, 1985, 1987, 1990 (we use exponential interpolation for the intervening years)) requires 357 seconds of CPU time; the solution of the model for a single year requires an average of 45 iterations.

3   SIMULATION RESULTS: THE IMPACT OF HIGHER OIL PRICES

The model has been used for a number of simulation experiments. In some of these we changed our assumptions about variables which are exogenous in the model (e.g. we changed the growth rate of OECD countries to see how important this variable is to the LDCs) while in other experiments we changed the values of parameters (e.g. substitution elasticities or coefficients of the production functions) about which there is considerable uncertainty. In this paper we illustrate the working of the model by considering the impact of an increase in oil prices.

In the base run the oil price (more precisely, the export price of energy) remains constant in real terms from 1980 onwards (but at a level which is some 50% higher than that in 1978). The alternative assumption is that after 1981 the price rises by 4% per year, reaching in the final year (1990) a level which is some 40% higher than that in the base run (prices are defined relative to the OECD price level; hence the nominal difference between the price level of the two runs would be larger). Hence the price increase that we consider is substantial. Tables 3–5 present the results for four LDC regions which are net importers for energy and for the most important exporting region (OPECME). (The bottom parts of the tables give results of the run in which oil prices increase; the upper parts give percentage differences of the results of that run from the results of the corresponding base run.) Consider first the results for the four importing regions when domestic resource prices can adjust (flexible-price version). For these regions the difference between exports and imports in current prices is fixed: it has to be equal to the foreign-capital inflow FC which is the same for the two runs. Adjustment to higher oil import prices therefore requires an increase in exports and a reduction in imports, both in real terms. One obtains an indication of the terms-of-trade loss by calculating the increase of $E - M$ (exports minus imports in 1978 prices) as a percentage of total GDP in the base run. For 1990 this gives 2.0% for AFRICA, 2.6% for LASIA, 2.3% for LAC, and 4.9% for SEUROP. Hence the impact is about twice as large for SEUROP as for the other three regions. This reflects

TABLE 3 The effects of increasing oil prices on the AFRICA and LASIA regions[a].

Variable[b]	AFRICA Flexible-price run		AFRICA Fixed-price run		LASIA Flexible-price run		LASIA Fixed-price run	
	1982	1990	1982	1990	1982	1990	1982	1990
VA^R	n	−0.72	−0.32	−1.67	−0.05	−0.63	−0.53	−2.95
VA^U	n	+0.43	−0.83	−4.04	−0.03	−0.62	−1.26	−7.11
VA	n	n	−0.65	−3.33	−0.04	−0.62	−0.93	−5.54
YD^R	−1.10	−3.23	−1.38	−6.25	−1.04	−3.67	−1.47	−6.95
YD^U	−0.74	−3.58	−1.26	−5.22	−0.64	−4.11	−0.97	−4.61
I	+0.35	+1.09	−0.94	−5.17	−0.88	−4.30	−2.30	−11.48
M_4	−4.89	−15.64	−5.31	−17.67	−2.22	−7.13	−2.80	−10.71
E_4	−3.26	−11.26	−3.62	−12.75	−2.84	−11.60	−3.55	−12.89
pr_1	−1.49	−3.08	−1.59	−6.38	−2.32	−8.65	−1.87	−8.27
pr_2	−0.59	−2.23	F	F	−1.54	−6.93	F	F
M_4^c	4.41	5.39	4.39	5.24	4.58	5.83	4.54	5.60
E_4^c	1.90	2.39	1.89	2.34	0.14	0.17	0.14	0.17
VA^c	81.80	116.94	81.16	112.69	161.71	228.35	159.99	216.82
VA^{Ud}	na	na	99	96	na	na	98	93

[a]The symbols n, F, and na stand for negligible, fixed, and not applicable, respectively.

[b]VA^R, VA^U, rural and urban value added; YD^R, YD^U, rural and urban disposable income; I, investment. These variables are expressed in constant prices. All the figures represent the percentage change from the corresponding base run (in which the oil price remains constant), unless otherwise indicated.

[c]In billions of US dollars at 1978 prices (higher oil prices).

[d]As a percentage of supply RU (higher oil prices).

TABLE 4 The effects of increasing oil prices on the LAC and SEUROP regions[a].

Variable[b]	LAC				SEUROP			
	Flexible-price run		Fixed-price run		Flexible-price run		Fixed-price run	
	1982	1990	1982	1990	1982	1990	1982	1990
VA^R	n	n	-0.40	-2.27	-0.36	-0.84	-1.16	-8.69
VA^U	-0.01	-0.09	-2.00	-8.58	-0.05	-0.05	-2.55	-15.13
VA	n	-0.08	-1.79	-7.88	-0.10	-0.15	-2.32	-16.19
YD^R	-0.09	-0.54	-2.57	-10.79	-0.82	-4.22	-5.57	-15.93
YD^U	-0.79	-3.53	-2.25	-9.68	-1.74	-7.61	-2.58	-17.75
I	-0.06	-0.58	-2.11	-9.88	n	-1.32	-4.39	-28.89
M_4	-3.94	-11.64	-5.28	-17.43	-1.30	-4.01	-3.24	-16.70
E_4	-3.26	-11.30	-3.53	-12.76	-3.35	-11.18	-3.50	-12.81
pr_1	-0.71	-2.65	-2.25	-8.24	-2.05	-8.82	-5.33	-8.76
pr_2	-1.35	-5.79		F	-2.97	-10.73		F
M_4^c	9.47	12.42	9.27	11.50	15.41	18.23	15.05	15.48
E_4^c	1.10	1.38	1.09	1.36	0.66	0.83	0.66	0.82
VA^c	323.44	465.02	315.42	424.80	319.03	385.03	311.11	323.18
VA^{Ud}	na	na	97	92	na	na	97	85

a, b, c, d See corresponding footnotes to Table 3.

TABLE 5   The effects of increasing oil prices on the OPECME region[a].

Variable[b]	Flexible-price run		Fixed-price run	
	1982	1990	1982	1990
VA^R	−0.03	+1.66	+0.06	+1.60
VA^U	+0.49	+8.45	+0.92	+6.98
VA	+0.48	+8.36	+0.91	+6.92
YD^R	+0.05	+13.31	−0.19	+12.70
YD^U	+0.03	+14.03	−1.93	−2.16
I	+9.63	+34.96	+9.45	+26.39
M_4	−1.63	+0.86	−2.09	−4.93
E_4	−3.29	−11.24	−3.58	−12.75
pr_1	+1.26	+19.37	−0.23	+11.40
pr_2	+2.97	+15.63	F	F
$M_4{}^c$	0.42	0.82	0.42	0.77
$E_4{}^c$	57.64	72.47	57.42	71.10
VA^c	144.40	302.31	145.02	298.17
Capital exports[c]	17.20	10.17	18.82	32.59

a, b, c See corresponding footnotes to Table 3.

the greater importance of energy imports for that region; as a percentage of GDP (base run, 1990) net energy imports (in constant prices) are 4.7% for SEUROP but only 3.2% for AFRICA, 2.7% for LASIA, and 2.7% for LAC. There is a second difference between the regions: two regions (AFRICA and LAC) are themselves significant exporters of energy. As a result the required adjustments in exports and imports are much smaller than those for LASIA and SEUROP (Table 6).

The effect on production (VA^R, VA^U, and total value added VA) is small: in all regions GDP falls by less than 1%. In the absence of price rigidities this should come as no surprise. Disposable income (YD^R and YD^U) falls by considerably more as a result of the terms-of-trade loss. It is this fall in consumption and investment which causes the fall in both rural and urban prices (pr_1 and pr_2). We find again that these effects are weaker for AFRICA and for LAC. There are two reasons for this, a static and a dynamic effect.

First, the terms-of-trade loss is much smaller for these two regions because higher export prices partly compensate the higher oil import bill. Secondly, as the difference between the export price and the domestic price of energy widens, the government's revenues from the oil tax rise enormously: from US$1.3 billion to US$2.5 billion for AFRICA (in 1990) and from US$1.0 billion to US$2.0 billion for LAC. Government savings therefore rise; in LAC this partly offsets the fall in other sources of savings while

TABLE 6   Percentage changes in exports and imports of energy (at constant prices) from the base run.

Region	Exports	Imports
AFRICA	+3.2	−3.5
LASIA	+12.0	−9.8
LAC	+8.8	−7.6
SEUROP	+17.7	−10.7

in AFRICA investment even increases slightly. The dynamic effect is that, with a smaller decrease (or even an increase) in investment, supply is higher. That prices fall less in AFRICA and LAC is therefore the result of a smaller fall in both supply and demand.

The effect on disposable incomes is again strongest in SEUROP: there the price increase results in a fall in rural income of 4% while urban incomes fall by almost 8% (in 1990). We have seen that one useful way of understanding the differences between the results for the various regions is by classifying them according to the relative importance of imports and exports of energy. A second useful distinction is between relatively closed regions (AFRICA, LASIA) and economies which are more open to foreign trade (LAC, SEUROP). The difference is clearest for the rural sector: external trade is of little importance in, say, India (included in LASIA). In the open economies the rural price pr_1 falls relatively little; in the closed economies it has to fall quite far before the induced increase in exports is sufficient to clear the market. This is reflected in what happens to the rural–urban terms of trade (the ratio of pr_1 and pr_2): these deteriorate in AFRICA and LASIA (where rural prices fall more than urban prices) but improve in LAC and SEUROP.

So far we have considered the flexible-price version of the model. While both versions of the model are extreme – one would not expect prices to remain rigid for a decade* – price rigidities are important and we suspect that the truth is probably closer to the fixed-price results. Compared to the flexible-price version the impact of the increase in oil price is now much stronger; with urban prices fixed there is less scope for substitution effects, and adjustment therefore requires larger changes in real incomes.

The price rigidity leads to excess supply in the urban sector; by 1990 demand is 4% below urban supply in AFRICA, 7% below in LASIA, and 9% below in LAC. The model suggests again that the impact would be most serious in SEUROP: there the difference eventually becomes 15%.

Real incomes fall markedly in LAC (rural disposable income falls by 11% and urban disposable income by 10%) and SEUROP (16%, 18%) but by much less in AFRICA (6%, 5%) and LASIA (7%, 5%). In addition to the importance of energy exports in the last two regions, the reason for this difference is that it is the urban price which is fixed and the urban sector is of course relatively unimportant in AFRICA and LASIA.

We noted that in the flexible-price runs the effect on output is quite small. In the fixed-price version, however, the GDP loss is quite substantial: 3.3% for AFRICA, 5.5% for LASIA, 7.9% for LAC, and even 14.3% for SEUROP. Since the price effect is now complemented by a much stronger income effect, energy imports fall much more (e.g. for LAC, 17.4% as opposed to 11.6% in the flexible-price run).

One point applies to both sets of results: effects become stronger over time. There are two reasons for this. First, what we are studying is not a once-and-for-all price increase; oil prices continue to grow after 1982. Secondly, there is an important dynamic effect: as investment falls in the short run (an effect which is especially strong in the fixed-price case where investment is reduced by 5% in AFRICA, 11% in LASIA, 10% in LAC, and 29% in SEUROP) the effects for 1990 are the result not only of the direct influence of higher oil prices but also of reduced factor availability.

---

*It is important to remember that pr_2 is not constant in the fixed-price version; it is fixed at the value obtained in the flexible-price run for the same year.

Table 5 gives the results for the OPECME region. In the flexible-price case the increase in imports is large (US$38 billion or 40% in 1982), reflecting an enormous terms-of-trade gain: 17.25% of GDP (calculated as shown earlier). The increase would be even larger if taxation of urban income had not increased. This tax (needed to eliminate excess demand) shows up in the table as an increase of US$10 billion (current prices) in capital exports. While this tax does not affect the government budget — we assume that all proceeds are invested abroad — the increase in the revenues of the oil tax does. This increase (US$44 billion in 1990) explains the enormous rise in investment.

This is the only region for which there is a large change in GDP (+8.4%) in the flexible-price run; the explanation lies of course in the rise in investment. The investment largely bypasses the rural sector; rural GDP increases very little but (with inelastic supply and a strong income effect) rural households do benefit from large increases in agricultural prices. For the urban sector the shift of the demand curve has more effect on imports than for the insulated rural sector; as a result rural households gain from a terms-of-trade effect.

When we consider the corresponding results for the fixed-price version it is interesting to note that for this region the effects are now weaker rather than stronger: rural disposable income increases less and urban income actually falls. Oil exports fall somewhat more than in the flexible-price version because of the income losses in the importing regions.

In the flexible-price case market clearing required a 16% increase in urban prices. With that possibility now blocked the burden of adjustment rests heavily on taxing urban incomes to eliminate excess demand. This mechanism, which leads to the US$22 billion increase in capital exports, is strongly deflationary. For rural households the gain in disposable income is, however, approximately the same in the two versions, first because they are not affected by the excess-demand tax and secondly because with the urban price fixed the rise in rural prices is no longer eroded; there is a large improvement in the rural—urban terms of trade (the mirror image of the deterioration in the first four regions; there the fall in rural prices is accompanied by a fall in urban prices in the flexible-price run but not in the fixed-price case).

Finally, we give an illustration of the second kind of simulation experiment in Table 7. Here we performed the same experiment as in Tables 3—5, except that all substitution elasticities are now 30% higher (the values assumed in the experiments for Tables 3—5 are given in Table 8). For LASIA the differences between the two tables are small, but the 30% increase is very modest. Oil imports now fall more (8% rather than 7% in the flexible-price case) and GDP falls less (5.1% rather than 5.5% in the fixed-price case). For a region which depends more on oil imports (e.g. SEUROP) or for a larger increase in elasticities the differences would of course be larger.

4   CONCLUSION

This paper presents preliminary results and is meant to illustrate how the model works rather than to make predictions. As an example we have chosen to simulate the effect of an oil-price increase but this is of course only one of many questions we could address with the aid of the model. The results suggest that there are important differences

TABLE 7   The effects of increasing oil prices and higher elasticities of substitution on the LASIA region[a].

Variable[b]	Flexible-price run		Fixed-price run	
	1982	1990	1982	1990
VA^R	−0.15	−0.62	−0.36	−2.33
VA^U	−0.04	−0.07	−1.19	−6.72
VA	−0.09	−0.27	−0.81	−5.08
YD^R	−0.81	−2.94	−1.57	−6.52
YD^U	−0.81	−4.76	−0.80	−4.24
I	−0.72	−3.09	−2.31	−11.20
M_4	−2.46	−7.98	−2.96	−11.40
E_4	−4.35	−14.29	−3.65	−15.34
pr_1	−1.48	−5.62	−2.05	−8.45
pr_2	−1.26	−6.08	F	F
M_4^c	4.56	5.82	4.52	5.60
E_4^c	0.13	0.16	0.13	0.16
VA^c	161.61	229.17	159.96	218.11
$VA^{U\,d}$	na	na	98	94

a, b, c, d See corresponding footnotes to Table 3.

TABLE 8   Trade substitution elasticities.

Type of product	σ	η
Food	1.2[a]	1.8
Agricultural (nonfood)	1.2	1.8
Manufacturing	2.0	1.8
Energy	0.3	0.2
Services	0.8	1.8

[a]Except for LASIA where the value is 2.0.

in the impact between regions and that, while most effects are small if all prices can adjust, there are substantial losses in importing regions if there is price rigidity.

REFERENCES

Adelman, L. and Robinson, S. (1978). Income Distribution Policy in Developing Countries: A Case Study of Korea. Oxford University Press, Oxford.

Ginsburgh, V.A. and Waelbroeck, J. (1976). Computational experience with a large general equilibrium model. In J. Los and M. Los (Editors), Computing Equilibria: How and Why. North-Holland, Amsterdam.

Ginsburgh, V.A. and Waelbroeck, J.L. (1981). Activity Analysis and General Equilibrium Modelling. North-Holland, Amsterdam.

Gupta, S., Schwartz, A., and Padula, R. (1979). The World Bank model for global interdependence: a quantitative framework for the World Development Report. Journal of Policy Modeling, 1(2): 179–200.

Lluch, C., Powell, A.A., and Williams, R.A. (1977). Patterns in Household Demand and Savings. Oxford University Press, New York.

Mundlak, Y. (1976). Migration in and out of agriculture: empirical analysis based on country data. (Discussion draft.)

Osterrieth, M., Verreydt, E., and Waelbroeck, J. (1980). The impact of agricultural price policies on demand, supply, incomes, and imports: an experimental model for South Asia. In C. Bliss and M. Boserup (Editors), Economic Growth and Resources, Volume 3. Proceedings of the World Congress of the International Economic Association, 5th. Macmillan, London.

Strout, A. (1975). World agricultural potential: evidence from the recent past. (Discussion draft.)

Taylor, L., Bacha, L., Cardoso, E.A., and Lysy, F. (1980). Models of Growth and Distribution for Brazil. Oxford University Press, New York.

Verreydt, E. (1977). An experimental two-gap requirement model of agricultural and nonagricultural growth in South Asia (1975–1985). Paper presented at Economic Forecasting Seminar, University of Brussels, Brussels.

APPENDIX

A1 Regional Model (Static) (Part A)

$$\zeta_i^d = (d_i^d)^{\sigma_i}(pd_i/pp_i)^{\sigma_i} \qquad \text{(share of domestic supply in domestic demand)} \qquad \text{(A1)}$$

$$\zeta_i^m = (d_i^m)^{\sigma_i}(pd_i/pm_i)^{\sigma_i} \qquad \text{(share of imports in domestic demand)} \qquad \text{(A2)}$$

$$(pd_i)^{1-\sigma_i} = (d_i^d)^{\sigma_i}(pp_i)^{1-\sigma_i} + (d_i^m)^{\sigma_i}(pm_i)^{1-\sigma_i} \qquad \text{(A3)}$$

$$pp_i = \sum_j a_{ji}pd_j + (1 - \sum_j a_{ji})pr_k \qquad \begin{array}{l}(k = 1 \text{ for } i = 1, 2 \text{ (rural)}; k = 2 \text{ for} \\ i = 3, 4, 5 \text{ (urban)})\end{array} \qquad \text{(A4)}$$

$$X_i = \zeta_i^d (\sum_j a_{ij}X_j + C_i + G_i + I_i) + E_i \qquad \text{(production)} \qquad \text{(A5)}$$

$$M_i = \zeta_i^m (\sum_j a_{ij}X_j + C_i + G_i + I_i) \qquad \text{(imports)} \qquad \text{(A6)}$$

$$RR = \sum_{i=1}^{2} (1 - \sum_j a_{ji})X_i \qquad \text{(price of } RR \text{ is } pr_1) \qquad \text{(A7)}$$

$$RU = \sum_{i=3}^{5} (1 - \sum_j a_{ji})X_i \qquad \text{(price of } RU \text{ is } pr_2) \qquad \text{(A8)}$$

$$G_i = g_i G \qquad \text{(} G \text{ exogenous, shares } g_i \text{ fixed)} \qquad \text{(A9)}$$

$$T^R = (\sum_i pd_i g_i)\tau^R \sum_{i=1}^{2} (1 - \sum_j a_{ji})X_i \qquad \begin{array}{l}\text{(taxes on rural income in current} \\ \text{prices)}\end{array} \qquad \text{(A10)}$$

$$T^U = (\sum_i pd_i g_i)\tau^U \sum_{i=3}^{5} (1 - \sum_j a_{ji})X_i \qquad \begin{array}{l}\text{(taxes on urban income in current} \\ \text{prices)}\end{array} \qquad \text{(A11)}$$

$$y^R = \sum_{i=1}^{2} (pp_i - \sum_j a_{ji}pd_j)X_i - T^R - \sum_i pd_i\gamma_i^R$$

$$\begin{array}{l}\text{(rural supernumerary income, net of taxes} \\ \text{and committed expenditures)}\end{array} \qquad \text{(A12)}$$

$$y^U = \sum_{i=3}^{5} (pp_i - \sum_j a_{ji}pd_j)X_i - T^U - \sum_i pd_i\gamma_i^U$$

(urban supernumerary income, net of taxes and committed expenditures) (A13)

$$pd_iC_i = (\gamma_i^R + \gamma_i^U)pd_i + (\beta_i^R y^R + \beta_i^U y^U)$$

(private consumption in current prices) (A14)

$$IC^R = (1 - \sum_i \beta_i^R)y^R$$

(rural investment in current prices) (A15)

$$IC^U = (1 - \sum_i \beta_i^U)y^U + (T^R + T^U - \sum_i pd_iG_i) + FC$$

(urban investment in current prices) (A16)

$$I_i = \lambda_i(IC^R + IC^U)/\sum_i pd_i\lambda_i$$

(distribution of total investment by sector of origin (λ_i) fixed and independent of composition by sector of destination) (A17)

$$E_{ir} = b_{ir}{}^{\eta_i}(pm_i/pp_{ir})^{\eta_i}WT_i$$

(the subscript r (suppressed in eqns. (A1)– (A17)) denotes the region) (A18)

The following points should be noted.

(a) Within a regional model the endogenous variables are ζ^d, ζ^m, pd, pp, pr (determined by eqns. (A7) and (A8)), X_i, C_i, I_i, G_i, E_i, M_i, T^R, T^U, y^R, y^U, IC^R, and IC^U. Total public consumption G is exogenous, the supplies RR and RU are predetermined, and world trade WT and world prices pm are determined in the trade model.

(b) Given the shares g_i and λ_i in eqns. (A9) and (A17), the tax rates τ in eqns. (A10) and (A11), and the input–output coefficients a_{ij}, the parameters of the regional model are the substitution elasticities σ and η and the ELES coefficients γ and β.

(c) Except for the base year the shares ζ_i^d and ζ_i^m will in general not sum to unity. Hence the commodity balance in constant prices cannot be written in its usual form

$$X_i = \sum_j a_{ij}X_j + C_i + G_i + I_i + E_i - M_i$$

(d) The balance holds in current prices. Writing D_i for $\sum_j a_{ij}X_j + C_i + G_i + I_i$ one finds from eqns. (A1)–(A6) that

$$pp_i(X_i - E_i) + pm_iM_i = D_i(\zeta_i^d pp_i + \zeta_i^m pm_i)$$

$$= D_i[(d_i^d)^{\sigma_i}(pp_i)^{1-\sigma_i} + (d_i^m)^{\sigma_i}(pm_i)^{1-\sigma_i}](pd_i)^{\sigma_i}$$

$$= D_i(pd_i)^{1-\sigma_i}(pd_i)^{\sigma_i} = pd_iD_i$$

hence

$$pp_iX_i = \sum_j pd_i a_{ij}X_j + pd_i(C_i + G_i + I_i) + pp_iE_i - pm_iM_i$$

(e) This result may be used to check that balance-of-payments equilibrium is satisfied. Summing over all sectors i one obtains

$$\sum_i (pp_i X_i - \sum_j pd_i a_{ij} X_j) = \sum_i (pp_i - \sum_j a_{ji} pd_j) X_i$$

$$= \sum_i [pd_i(C_i + G_i + I_i) + (pp_i E_i - pm_i M_i)]$$

which is the GDP identity at current prices. From eqns. (A12)–(A17),

$$\sum_i (pp_i - \sum_j a_{ji} pd_j) X_i = y^R + y^U + T^R + T^U + \sum_i pd_i(\gamma_i^R + \gamma_i^U)$$

$$= \sum_i pd_i(C_i + G_i + I_i) - FC$$

Hence

$$\sum_i (pm_i M_i - pp_i E_i) = FC$$

i.e. the deficit on the current account of the balance of payments is equal to the net inflow of foreign capital.

A2   Trade Model (Part B)

$$(WT_i)^{-\rho_i} = \sum_r b_{ir} E_{ir}^{-\rho_i}$$

(i denotes a sector, r a region; world trade is a CES aggregate of the exports of the various regions, where the substitution elasticity is $\eta_i = 1/(1 + \rho_i)$)   (A19)

$$WT_i = \sum_r M_{ir}$$

(world markets clear; the composition of imports in terms of the regions of origin is the same for all regions)   (A20)

$$(pm_i)^{1-\eta_i} = \sum_r (b_{ir})^{\eta_i}(pp_{ir})^{1-\eta_i}$$

(A21)

$$M_{ir} = \bar{M}_{ir} Y_r^{\mu_i}(pm_i)^{-\nu_i}$$

(only for $r = 10$, i.e. for developed countries; for that region GDP (Y_r) is exogenous; exports of developed countries are determined in the same way as for other regions, i.e. by eqn. (A18))   (A22)

A3   Regional Model (Dynamic) (Part C)

$$N^R = N_{t-1}^R (1 + n^R) - M_{t-1}^{RU}$$

(natural growth and rural-to-urban migration determine the growth of the rural labor force)   (A23)

$$N^U = N^U_{t-1}(1 + n^U) + M^{RU}_{t-1}$$

(natural growth and rural-to-urban migration determine the growth of the urban labor force) (A24)

$$K^U = K^U_{t-1}(1 - \delta) + (IC^U / \sum_i pd_i \lambda_i)_{t-1}$$

(exponential depreciation of the urban capital stock and one-year gestation lag) (A25)

$$RU = A^U(K^U)^{\phi_1}(N^U)^{\phi_2} e^{\phi_3 t}$$

(Cobb–Douglas production function) (A26)

$$L^d = L^d_{t-1} + l^d(IC^R / \sum_i pd_i \lambda_i)_{t-1}$$

(increases in the cultivated area of dry land require rural investment) (A27)

$$L^i = L^i_{t-1} + l^i(IC^R / \sum_i pd_i \lambda_i)_{t-1}$$

(increases in the cultivated area of irrigated land require rural investment) (A28)

$$F = f(L^d)^{\psi_1}(L^i)^{\psi_2}(pd_3 / pr_1)^{\psi_3}_{t-1} e^{\psi_4 t}$$

(fertilizer use) (A29)

$$RR = A^R F^{\pi_1}(L^d + L^i)^{\pi_2}(L^i)^{\pi_3}[F^2/(L^d + L^i)]^{\pi_4}(N^R)^{\pi_5} e^{\pi_6 t}$$

(production function in agriculture) (A30)

$$M^{RU} = m_1 \{[(y^U + \sum_i pd_i \gamma^U_i)/N^U][(y^R + \sum_i pd_i \gamma^R_i)/N^R]^{-1} - m_2\}^{\alpha_1}$$

$$\times (N^U/N^R)^{\alpha_2}(1 + n^R)^{\alpha_3}(N^R)^{\alpha_4}$$

(migration) (A31)

The following points should be noted.

(a) RR and RU can both be written as functions of lagged variables only; they are therefore treated as predetermined in the static model.

(b) Except for the effect of relative price changes on fertilizer use and the (weak) effect of rural savings on the cultivated area, RR is determined by time trends (ψ_4 and π_6 in eqns. (A29) and (A30) respectively) and by the growth of the rural labor force.

COMMENTS*

In my opinion the model presented here is an impressive piece of work. In particular, I find the incorporation of rigid prices, and thus quantity adjustment, within the general equilibrium framework very interesting. The usefulness of this extension of the usual general equilibrium model is clearly demonstrated by the results presented in the paper.

Although the simulations of the impact of an oil-price increase have primarily illustrative purposes, the results help to explain part of the inconsistency between model simulation results and public beliefs in this field. In spite of the sometimes rather strong public conviction that oil-price increases have significant negative effects on the economy,

---

*By Lars Bergman, Stockholm School of Economics, Stockholm, Sweden.

many model simulations carried out during the last few years have failed to confirm such effects. According to the results presented here, oil-price increases are likely to significantly affect the economic system only if factor and product prices have a limited flexibility. In many other model analyses of this topic, not least my own, more or less perfectly flexible factor and product prices are assumed.

There are many similarities between this model and the one presented elsewhere in this volume by Whalley, but there are also differences. For instance, Whalley's model is not an econometric model in the usual sense. Instead of testing the specification of the model against actual data, the equilibrium conditions of the model are imposed on a data set for an individual year. By adding some exogenous parameter estimates, a solution for the rest of the models' parameters can be obtained. The basic rational for this procedure is that the model is intended to be a numerical representation of a theoretical model rather than a condensed representation of the actual behavior of the economic system. In Whalley's paper, this approach is adopted throughout; all behavioral equations are derived from constrained optimization behavior assumptions, and there are no constraints on factor mobility; i.e., the model contains the basic elements of the standard neoclassical general equilibrium model.

However, in the present model there are constraints on factor mobility; all savings generated in the agricultural sectors are invested in these sectors, while the savings generated in the urban sectors, together with net foreign borrowing, are invested in the urban sectors. Consequently, the rates of return on capital may very well differ between the urban and rural sectors, and these differences are reduced only in a rather indirect way through labor migration.

I can understand that this is a very reasonable way of representing the dual nature of many less-developed countries. However, the whole modeling exercise involves many drastic simplifications of real world conditions, and, except for one practical reason, it is not obvious to me why these capital market imperfections could not also have been disregarded. The "practical reason" I can see is that the isolation of rural savings from the rest of the capital market simplifies the specification of the investment expenditure functions significantly.

A related question concerns the field of application of the model. In general, one would expect the basic assumptions of general equilibrium theory to be fairly well satisfied in developed market economies, but less so in developing countries with relatively large rural sectors and institutional frameworks quite different from the one inherent in the standard general equilibrium model. However, in this paper the model is primarily applied to groups of less developed countries.

As mentioned earlier, the calculated impact of an oil-price increase is significantly stronger when prices are rigid than when prices are flexible. Nevertheless, I think that the results in the "fixed price" case could be biased downwards. This is due to the specifications of the investment expenditure functions: all savings are invested in new real capital, even if the existing capacity is not fully utilized. That leads me to the following question. The model yields year-by-year projections of the economy's development, and it contains some of the most important rigidities in the economy's adjustment to changing exogenous conditions. However, it does not contain money or other financial assets. How and to what extent is that likely to affect the results?

Finally, I have a couple of comments on technical details of the model. The first concerns the trade model. That part of the model is very simplified, but to me it seems to be a reasonable first version of a trade model. However, the specification of the trade model implies that the imports to the different groups of countries do not differ in terms of the regions of origin. That, in turn, implies that each region imports part of its own exports, which is highly implausible in the real world. The second technical comment concerns the aggregation of the production sectors. By aggregating the rural sectors and the urban sector, respectively, the model is transformed into a two-sector model on the production side. That has computational advantages, but requires some very strong assumptions. Thus, the aggregation is consistent only if the energy sector and the service sector have identical production functions! Again, that is hardly a plausible assumption.

GLOBAL INTERNATIONAL ECONOMIC MODELS
B.G. Hickman (editor)
Elsevier Science Publishers B.V. (North-Holland)
© IIASA, 1983

GENERAL EQUILIBRIUM MODELING OF TRADE-LIBERALIZATION ISSUES AMONG MAJOR WORLD TRADE BLOCS*

John Whalley

Department of Economics, University of Western Ontario, London, Ontario (Canada)

1   INTRODUCTION

In this paper a numerical general equilibrium model of international trade involving four major trading areas (the United States, Japan, the nine-member European Economic Community (EEC), and the rest of the world) is described. The model has been used to analyze the effects of various trade-liberalization proposals and other trade-policy changes involving major participants in negotiations under the General Agreement on Tariffs and Trade (GATT). The model is presently undergoing further development to allow general equilibrium assessments of policy issues in the North—South debate between developed and developing countries. The model-building exercise is motivated by a desire to provide a policy-appraisal tool as an input into policy decision making which is consistent with the dominant model appearing in the literature on the pure theory of international trade. No forecasting has been attempted with the model; instead the focus has been on counterfactual static equilibrium analysis. The model has been described in more detail elsewhere (Whalley, 1980a, b, c; Brown and Whalley, 1980) and in this paper a nonmathematical summary only is given.

The model is most easily thought of as an empirical counterpart to Heckscher—Ohlin-type trade models. The major departure from Heckscher—Ohlin character is the use of the Armington (1969) assumption of product heterogeneity by trading area. The model assumes constant-returns-to-scale production, and no scale economies are introduced. In each trading area 33 products are considered, four of which are treated as nontraded goods. A number of household groups in each trading area are incorporated; this yields the capability of analyzing the effects on income distribution between various domestic groups that stem from trade-policy changes. The dimensionality in terms of products represents a tradeoff between the constraints of data availability, ease of computational

*This paper draws heavily on work for a project on trade liberalization which has been supported by the Ford Foundation under its research program on International Economic Order.

solution, and the concerns dictated by the policy analyses desired. The model is solved numerically for alternative world trade equilibria associated with different policy regimes. The variations in terms-of-trade effects associated with different trade-policy regimes are captured since a price-endogenous general equilibrium framework is used.

In previous literature on international trade Heckscher—Ohlin trade models have not been extensively used in empirical work. This is partly due to difficulties in the assembly and computational solution of such models but also reflects the surprisingly limited efforts made towards numerical investigation within this framework. The present model attempts to stay within the theoretical framework suggested by the pure theory of international trade and to expand this framework in a numerical manner. Given the orientation in the theoretical literature towards analysis of static equilibria and the way in which these equilibria change as a result of alterations in trade-distorting policies, the same approach of counterfactual static equilibrium analysis has been used. In contrast to the way many other global models have been used, no forecasting has been attempted with this model. The scenarios examined do not unfold over time but are counterfactual scenarios which represent attempts to simulate the way the international economy would have behaved had alternative policy variations been adopted. This limitation in use is not absolute since forward projections under alternative policy regimes could be attempted; however, the applications of the model so far have not required this.

As is true with most simulation models, there are certain parameters in the model which turn out to be critical. Within the general equilibrium framework these are elasticity parameters and are discussed later. The Armington variant of the Heckscher—Ohlin model used allows the modeler to accommodate the perplexing empirical phenomenon of cross-hauling* in the trade statistics; it also enables the parametric specification procedures in the model to integrate empirical estimates of import-price elasticities by trading area and is important in the later discussion of elasticity.

In contrast to traditional trade models, with the Armington assumption no autarky solution exists (with conventional preferences) since domestic production of foreign goods is not possible. Also trade does not simply arise from differences in factor endowments (as in a pure Heckscher—Ohlin model) since differences in preferences arise. The implicit complete specialization in Armington models may result in a stronger terms-of-trade effect than in a comparable model with incomplete specialization; this observation is important in evaluating model findings.

The model also incorporates a rich specification of trade-distorting policies by trading area. The effects of tariff policies are captured together with the important nontariff barriers which are quantified in ad valorem equivalent form (some nontariff barriers are difficult to quantify and are excluded). In addition the trade-distorting effects of domestic taxes are captured; a complete representation of the domestic tax system of the three major industrialized trading areas is included in the model.

So far the applications of the model have involved the analysis of trade-policy alternatives. One application was the evaluation of alternative tariff-cutting proposals made in the Tokyo Round trade negotiations under the GATT. A portion of the negotiations involved multilateral tariff reductions under which a general formula for tariff cuts would apply to all the countries participating in the trade negotiations. Another application was the evaluation of the agreement which came out of the Tokyo Round negotiations. This involves tariff cuts together with certain changes in nontariff barriers and moves toward

---

*Trade in both directions in the same product.

the establishment of a new international economic order. The agreement was represented in model equivalent form and an analysis of possible effects was performed. A third area of application was the analysis of the trade-distorting effects of domestic tax policies. In this case there are no policy proposals currently under consideration which will limit the structure of domestic taxes because of international trade impacts but the results indicate the substantial importance of domestic taxes in affecting the structure of international trade. Lastly, we are currently investigating the effects of various kinds of policy changes connected with the debate on the new international economic order involving the North—South dialogue; however, no results have as yet been obtained from this exercise.

2   THE STRUCTURE OF THE MODEL*

The general equilibrium model incorporates four trading blocs reflecting major participants in world trade; the (nine-member) EEC, the United States, Japan, and the rest of the world. The sizes of these blocs in the model reflect the relative GNP for these areas for 1973 (the GNP for the rest of the world is obtained from the World Bank Atlas, 1975). The EEC, the United States, and Japan between them account for some 60% of world production and a substantial fraction of world trade**. In setting their trade policies each of these areas can therefore be expected to have some impact on the terms of trade which they face.

The model considers a number of products, with each traded good being treated as if it is produced in all the trading blocs with an assumed heterogeneity by trading area prevailing across production sources. Products are differentiated on the basis of geographical point of production as well as their physical characteristics, with "similar" products being close substitutes in demand; thus Japanese cars are treated as qualitatively different products from US or EEC cars. This "Armington-type" Heckscher—Ohlin model is used to accommodate the statistical phenomenon of cross-hauling in international trade and to exclude complete specialization in the production of commodities (as conventionally defined) as a model solution. This structure also allows empirically based import-demand elasticities to be incorporated into the model specification.

The products considered are listed in Table 1 while the household classification used for the demand side in each trading area is given in Table 2. Even the 33-product classification considers broad groups of commodities which are much coarser than the finely divided categories which are the subject of GATT trade-policy negotiations. For instance, tariff negotiations under the Tokyo Round involved negotiations on a tariff-line

---

*A more detailed description of the model appears in Whalley (1980a). An appendix describing the model in equation form appears in Whalley (1980b). The differences in structure between the various model versions are that the earlier version (Whalley, 1980a) uses a fixed-coefficient technology to describe intermediate production while the later version (Whalley, 1980c) embodies substitutability between intermediate products.
**For each of the trading blocs there is a trading area that is considered in the model as a part of the rest of the world which is important for that bloc but relatively unimportant for the others. For the United States, Canada fills this role; for the EEC, the European Free Trade Association fills the role; for Japan, the role is played by Taiwan, Hong Kong, and South Korea. Tariff and other trade policies towards each of these areas are important for the major blocs concerned but relatively unimportant for the others. These additional areas are not separately identified in the model.

TABLE 1   Product and industrial classification used in the general equilibrium trade model.

Agriculture	*Manufacturing (durable goods)*
(1) Meats and dairy products	(18) Lumber, wood and furniture
(2) Cereals	(19) Primary and fabricated metals, stone, glass
(3) Other agricultural products	(20) Machinery except electrical
(4) Forestry and fisheries	(21) Electrical machinery
	(22) Transport vehicles
Mining	(23) Scientific and precision instruments
(5) Coal	(24) Miscellaneous manufacturing
(6) Oil, natural gas	
(7) Metallic, nonmetallic, and other	*Services*
	(25) Construction[a]
Manufacturing (nondurable goods)	(26) Water transportation
Prepared food and kindred products	(27) Other transportation and communications
(8) Tea, sugar, coffee, spices, cocoa	(28) Housing services[a]
(9) Alcoholic drinks	(29) Electricity and sanitary services
(10) Other foods	(30) Wholesale and retail trade[a]
(11) Tobacco	(31) Finance, insurance, and real estate
(12) Apparel and textile products	(32) Other services
(13) Paper, printing, publishing	(33) Government[a]
(14) Pharmaceuticals and toiletries	
(15) Other chemical and allied products	
(16) Petroleum and coal products	
(17) Rubber and plastics	

[a]Denotes a nontraded good.

TABLE 2   Classification of households in each trading area on the demand side of the model.

USA

Ten households classified by annual gross income in 1973 expenditure-survey data:
   $0–999; $1,000–1,999; $2,000–2,999; $3,000–3,999; $4,000–4,999; $5,000–5,999; $6,000–7,499; $7,500–9,999; $10,000–14,999; $15,000+

Japan

16 households classified by annual gross income in 1973 expenditure-survey data:
   ¥0–4 million; ¥4–6 million; ¥6–8 million; ¥8–10 million; ¥10–12 million; ¥12–14 million; ¥14–16 million; ¥16–18 million; ¥18–20 million; ¥20–25 million; ¥25–30 million; ¥30–35 million; ¥35–40 million; ¥40–45 million; ¥45–50 million; ¥50+ million

EEC

Six major national groups[a]:
   the Federal Republic of Germany; France; Italy; the Netherlands; Belgium; the United Kingdom

[a]Ireland, Denmark, and Luxembourg are not separately identified on the demand side of the model but the production side of the activity of these economies is incorporated in the single EEC economy. The incomes of these economies (with a population of approximately 8 million from a community total of 250 million) are to be considered as distributed across the groups included.

basis which included as many as 20,000 commodity items in certain cases, and it is clearly not possible to use a tariff-line basis in the model since this produces a general equilibrium structure which can be neither formulated nor solved. The model therefore gives indications of general equilibrium impacts in terms of the broad product categories which characterize GATT trade-liberalization negotiations. The detail by household gives a capability of exploring income distribution and other household effects of trade-policy changes;

since the effects of the changes in GATT agreements are relatively small this feature has not been exploited to any significant extent in the use of the model so far.

An outline of the model is given in Figure 1. Production and demand patterns in each of the trading blocs revolve around the domestic and world price system. Producers maximize profits and competitive forces operate such that in equilibrium all supernormal profits are "competed away". Explicit demand functions which are derived from utility maximization are used.

For each product the market price is the price at the point of production. Sellers receive these prices, and purchasers (of both intermediate and final products) pay these prices gross of tariffs and domestic taxes; no transportation costs are considered. Financial investment flows enter the world market system and are treated as components of foreign trade. They are treated as purchases of capital goods by agents located in the country of source of the capital funds. The difference between investment flows and merchandise trade is that the capital goods acquired are not repatriated to the country of location of the purchaser but remain in the source country to generate income in future periods.

An equilibrium in the model is a situation where demands equal supplies for all products and in each industry a zero-profit condition is satisfied, representing the absence of supernormal profits. A condition of zero foreign trade balance (including investment flows, dividends, interest, and transfers) applies for each country. The effect of a trade-policy change in any country is to alter the relative prices of imported and domestically produced goods and to affect the volume of imports. This in turn changes the pattern of domestic demands and, indirectly, the prices of products. Alterations in trade policies affect the equilibrium achieved, resulting in new equilibrium prices and quantities. Measures of worldwide gains or losses and their distribution by trading bloc resulting from trade-policy variations are obtained through a comparison of equilibria using Hicksian compensating and equivalent variations.

2.1   The Production Side of the Model

On the production side of the model each industry in each trading bloc has available a number of possible methods of production. Each production process uses two different sets of inputs. The first are substitutable capital and labor inputs located in that country, and the second are intermediate products produced by other industries.

Each industry has a value-added production function of constant elasticity of substitution (CES) form which specifies the substitution possibilities between the primary factor inputs, capital services, and labor services. No technical change is incorporated and it is thus assumed that no changes in technology will result from the adoption of alternative trade policies. This specification also excludes the possibility of relocation by industries in response to trade-policy changes.

In addition to the CES value-added functions each industry uses the outputs of other industries (both domestic and imported) as inputs into its own production process. In an earlier version of the model described by Whalley (1980a) it is assumed that the input—output coefficients are fixed and are unable to change. This is somewhat unrealistic in that it specifies, for example, that fixed amounts of both Japanese and US steel are required to produce a car in the United States. These intermediate requirements operate

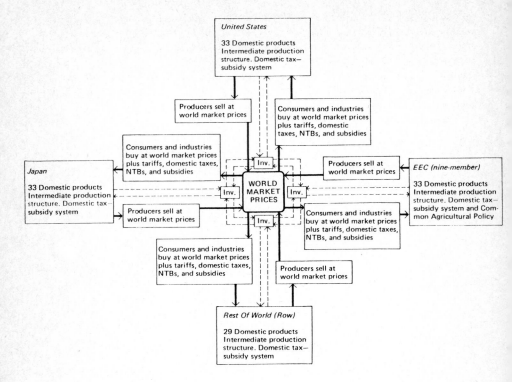

FIGURE 1   A structural outline of the general equilibrium model of United States–EEC–Japanese trade.

Intermediate production incorporates intermediate substitution between similar inputs differentiated by country of origin; e.g. a fixed steel requirement per car produced in the USA might be specified but this can be met by a substitutable mix of domestically produced steel and steel imported from the various trading blocs.

The rest of the world is specified schematically and no strong claims to realism are made. An arithmetic average of comparable parameters in the three major trading areas is used. This also applies to policy parameters in the rest of the world. The factor endowments in the rest of the world are, however, selected to reflect the relative capital abundance of the three major trading areas. The capital-to-labor ratio in the rest of the world is considered to be in aggregate one-fifth of that in the combination of the three major trading areas with a ratio of 1/10 for manufacturing.

In the figure, NTB stands for nontariff barrier and Inv. denotes investment flows.

independently of the relative prices of Japanese and US steel. In the later version of the model (Whalley, 1980c), substitution between intermediate products is considered and fixed coefficients in terms of composite goods only are assumed. Thus the fixed amount of steel required to make a car can be met by a substitutable mix of Japanese and US steel. Each fixed coefficient in terms of composite goods is a CES function with elements of the composite (products identified by geographical point of production) entering as arguments.

2.2   The Demand Side of the Model

On the demand side of the model a number of household consumer groups appear in each of the trading blocs. Ten household groups, stratified by income range, are considered in the United States; 16 such groups in Japan; in the EEC six separate nationality groups are considered. Each of these groups has demand functions that are defined over the various products available. Government and business (investment) are separately treated with each having price-endogenous demand patterns.

These demand functions for each agent are obtained by maximizing a nested CES utility function. Within this functional form a fixed elasticity of substitution is assumed between products that are imported from the various trading areas and domestic products of a similar type, together with a different elasticity of substitution between the composite products. This approach allows empirical estimates of price elasticities in world trade to be incorporated into the model and these values are used to guide parameter choice for internest elasticity values in the CES functions (i.e. between "similar" products subscripted by location and production).

Since each group generates demands arising from utility maximization the market-demand functions satisfy Walras' law, i.e. the condition that at any set of prices the total value of demands equals the total value of incomes. The incomes of consumer groups are derived from the ownership of the primary factors located in each trading bloc (and which can be sold at the set of factor prices which each consumer faces) plus transfers received from the government. The government in each trading bloc collects taxes from households and also disperses transfer incomes. Government expenditures enter as a separate demand category and are financed by tax collections. A separate demand category is incorporated for investment expenditures.

2.3   Policies Considered in the Model

A number of different components of commercial policy are considered since the model has been constructed to yield a multipurpose capability of analyzing the price-distorting effects of a number of policy interventions in world trade. Tariffs, nontariff barriers, and domestic tax policies are all incorporated in ad valorem form. These change the pattern and structure of world trade between the trade blocs from a no-policy regime.

Tariffs are considered to apply in ad valorem form to imports of products for both final and intermediate uses valued at free on board (f.o.b.) prices. (This approximates the customs-clearance basis in the United States; in Japan and the EEC tariffs apply to valuations much closer to a cost, insurance, and freight (c.i.f.) price.) Tariff collections become part of the general government revenues for financing government expenditures. As is well known, it is very difficult to obtain average tariff rates in ad valorem form for aggregated classifications of the form presented in Table 1. The procedure used in earlier versions of the model was to adopt the averaged rates from the 1974 GATT study for manufactured and mining products which use 1973 MFN ("most favored nation") tariff schedules. The GATT averaging procedure of using world imports for 1970 and 1971 was extended in arriving at estimates consistent with the classifications in Table 1. In more recent work we have used an alternative procedure based on tariff rates for 1976 for all trade areas collected in a special data analysis by the Special Trade Representatives Office in the United States.

Nontariff barriers include an assortment of policies which either deliberately or coincidently affect trading patterns in addition to those effects induced through tariff policy. In recent years they have attracted increasing attention because of the view of many people that they serve in practice as a more severe impediment to trade than conventional tariff policy. A number of studies (Baldwin, 1970; Walter, 1972; UNCTAD, 1969, 1970) have attempted to classify and describe these barriers, although numerical estimates as to their importance are somewhat sparse. A study by Roningen and Yeats (1976) drawing on UNCTAD documentation provides estimates for France, Japan, Sweden, and the United States, and a related study by Yeats (1976) contains estimates of the influence of nontariff barriers on agricultural products in the EEC. A descriptive list of nontariff barriers would include government purchasing policies, quotas, seasonal restrictions, specific licensing regulations, valuation procedures for tariff purposes, voluntary export restraints, special import charges (including such items as variable levies in the EEC agricultural policy), and health and sanitary regulations. Clearly some of these are more important than others and some can be quantified more satisfactorily than others.

Domestic taxation and subsidy policies also enter the model and affect trade patterns. The model incorporates the domestic taxation and subsidy systems of each of the trading blocs by treating corporate and property taxes as taxes on profit-type returns by industry, social and security taxes on labor use by industry, value-added taxes and sales taxes as production-type taxes, specific excises as consumption taxes, and income taxes as charges on income receipts by consumer groups.

Quotas and other nontariff barriers are represented in the model in ad valorem equivalent form rather than as restrictions on quantities imported. A distinguishing characteristic of both quotas and nontariff barriers is that in practice they generate no tax revenue for the government. This is accommodated by returning receipts from these charges in lump-sum form to consumer groups, the lump-sum payments being determined by ratios of consumer incomes in basic data.

The effects of quotas are more realistically captured in a general equilibrium model not as equivalent ad valorem charges but directly as quantity restrictions. From a computational point of view it is straightforward to incorporate the quantity restrictions implied by quotas by considering an additional fictitious commodity which must be purchased when a good involved is imported. The endowment of this commodity can be made equal to the value of the quota involved and its ownership can be assigned to the recipient of the rents which quotas create. If a quota is not binding in equilibrium, the corresponding artificial commodity will have a zero price. While this approach can be implemented in small dimensions the extra dimensions created raise computational difficulties. These are avoided in the model by considering quotas in equivalent ad valorem form.

3 "CALIBRATING" THE MODEL

The model as specified contains a large number of parameter values which must be estimated before the model is used to evaluate the effects of alternative trade policies. A model on such a scale cannot be easily estimated in its entirety using conventional econometric methods and resort is therefore made to a sequence of procedures which have been developed in recent years for "calibration" of large-scale general equilibrium models. The procedure is to assemble a set of data for a given period of time in a form which is consistent with the equilibrium conditions of the model. Once the set of data has been assembled parameter values for equations can be directly estimated from the equilibrium conditions. The data set is termed a benchmark equilibrium data set and has the properties of a worldwide competitive equilibrium that demands and supplies for products will balance, that no profits will be made in any of the domestic industries, and that each country will be in zero balance in its trading relations with all other countries.

The adoption of this overall approach implies the need to construct an equilibrium data set involving both the domestic and the trading activity of each of the trading blocs. Many divergent source materials need to be assembled and corrected for inconsistent classifications and definitions, and even when this task is complete further corrections are necessary to adjust the data mutually so that the equilibrium conditions of the model are satisfied. A complete description of the sources used in the assembly of this data set for the year 1973 appears in Appendix B of Whalley (1980a). 1973 was chosen as a recent year for which most of the data were available at the time of data assembly (1977–1978). (The GATT tariff study used was available only for 1973 tariff data; the data used for the United States draw heavily on the data set constructed by Fullerton et al. (1978) for 1973; certain of the data used for Japan and the EEC had 1973 as the latest year of availability.) The disruptions stemming from the Middle East war towards the end of 1973 are largely absent from the data. Even so, there are substantial problems of inconsistent classifications and definitions, gaps in data availability, and differences in the dates of basic sources; the data set produced must therefore be considered only as a first approximation to an ideal data set for the model.

The calibration procedure utilizes the model equilibrium conditions together with the benchmark equilibrium data set. A nonstochastic estimation procedure is used for determining parameter values which are consistent with both benchmark data and the equilibrium conditions. On the demand side, demand functions are solved for parameters consistent with both equilibrium prices and equilibrium quantities. On the supply side, cost functions derived from the production structures assumed are used to solve for parameter values consistent with equilibrium prices and input use by industry. Depending on the complexity of the functional forms, this procedure may require additional information beyond that provided by the benchmark equilibrium data set. This information, where needed, takes the form of the specification of unit-free parameters represented by the elasticities of substitution in the functional forms. (The ease with which the estimation of parameters from the equilibrium data set can proceed depends on the complexity of the behavioral equations used in the model. If Cobb–Douglas functional forms are used for demand functions, the exponents in the Cobb–Douglas functions are given directly by the expenditure shares in the basic data. With CES functions more information is needed and extraneous values of the substitution elasticities are needed prior to the use of this procedure.) On the production side the elasticities of substitution are obtained from a literature search. (The survey by Caddy (1976) provides the main source for these estimates. An average over the estimates reported by Caddy is used for each industry in the model; the same value is used for each trading area.) On the demand side no empirical evidence is directly available and a procedure of relating the substitution elasticities in preference functions to estimates of the price elasticities in world trade is used.

At the benchmark equilibrium given by the consistent data set it is possible to calculate the implied point estimates of the price elasticities of demand for imports in each of the trading blocs. These values can be compared to estimates obtained from literature searches and on that basis modifications can be made to the estimates of the substitution elasticities in preferences.

The substitution elasticities derived from import-price elasticities are critical parameters for the model since their value substantially affects responses to trade-policy changes in the model; not surprisingly changes in the elasticity values used also affect the results. The model specification relies heavily on the recent compendium of elasticity values produced by Stern et al. (1977). These authors suggest that the empirical evidence on price elasticities in world trade is not conclusive and argue that only limited reliance can be placed on the elasticity values that are available for detailed product classifications. They produce "best-guess" estimates for price elasticities for total imports by country and conclude that the majority of these are approximately in the region of −1.0. This is somewhat larger than the region suggested by Houthakker and Magee (1969) in their earlier survey although some authors such as Balassa and Kreinin (1967) have argued for and used higher values on the grounds of a downward bias associated with time-series estimation procedures.

Two alternative specifications of the substitution elasticities are used in the model, each derived from estimates of import-demand functions. One makes the substitution elasticities in demand functions have the same value for substitution between products designated by area. This gives import-price elasticities with limited variation for all products. Different values by product type are also set to calibrate approximately to the best-guess estimate by product of Stern et al. (1977).

When it has been fully specified the model is solved for a general equilibrium by using a Newton method which has been modified from earlier computer programs that were originally designed to refine the approximation obtained from the application of Scarf's algorithm (see Scarf (1973) and the extension to international trade models with tariffs by Shoven and Whalley (1974)). These Newton methods work swiftly and although there is no ex ante facto argument of convergence which is built into the procedures they have been successful in implementation. Because of the complexity of the model no statement of the uniqueness of equilibrium is available although with other variants of the model some experimentation has been done in displacing equilibria once they have been found and then checking that they are returned to and also in approaching equilibria from different points and at different speeds. None of these tests has yet revealed a situation of nonuniqueness of equilibrium in these complex environments, although nonuniqueness is certainly not excluded. The structure of the computer programs used in the set of analyses is outlined in Figure 2 and Table 3.

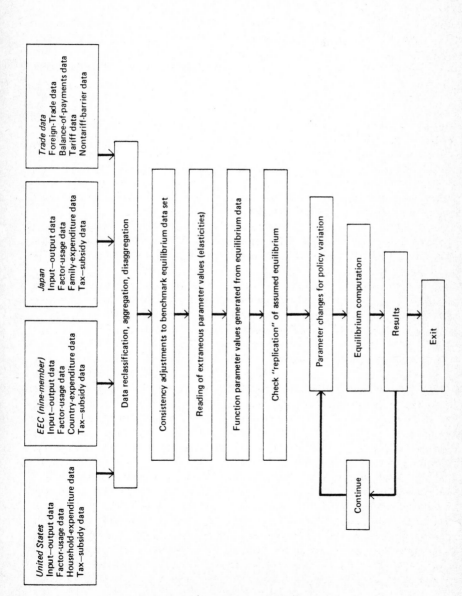

FIGURE 2 The structure of the computer programs used in the general equilibrium model of world trade. (This figure, and also Table 3, are taken from Brown and Whalley, 1980.)

TABLE 3   Features of the machine and program used for the general equilibrium model of world trade.

Machine: Cyber 73 (slower than a CDC 7600 by a factor of perhaps 16; slower than an IBM 370/168 by a factor of perhaps 8)
Program length in (approximate) number of statements: equilibrium computation, 4,000; data classification and adjustments, 3,000; parameter value generation, 2,000; print format and results, 3,000
Execution time: depending on parameter values and nature of policy change, in the region of 0.5 h
Compilation time: approximately 40–50 s for the code of the main program
Space requirement: main frame (49K) plus most of an extended core facility (88K) plus 250K of a mass-storage device; space requirements arise mainly in the work with basic data
Data requirements: "crude" data usage, around 60,000 numbers; "model" data requirement, 1,000 parameter values
Behavioral-function evaluations: a run of 0.5 h would evaluate around 20 excess-demand correspondences

---

4   APPLICATIONS OF THE MODEL

So far a number of applications of the model have been made which center around various trade-policy alternatives.

4.1   Evaluation of the Tariff-Cutting Proposals in the Tokyo Round

This application of the model was reported by Brown and Whalley (1980) who sought to evaluate the different tariff-cutting proposals that were made at an early stage in the Tokyo Round trade negotiations under the GATT. Under this round of negotiations all the countries participating in the negotiations agreed to multilateral tariff cuts to be guided by a general tariff-cutting formula. The various participating countries made proposals at an early stage as to the structure that this formula should follow. The proposed formulas are listed in Table 4. There are substantial differences in the various formulas which are not examined in any detail here. In simple terms the United States proposed a linear cut in tariffs, the EEC proposed a highly nonlinear cut in tariffs, the Canadian proposal involved universal adoption of a common tariff, and the Japanese proposed a tariff cut which would apply to old tariff schedules (since when the Japanese had already made substantial cuts). In effect the Japanese proposal involved cuts in all tariffs but the Japanese. The outcome of the negotiations was the adoption of a compromise Swiss formula proposal.

The different proposals were analyzed by the model and Brown and Whalley came to a number of striking conclusions about them. Using counterfactual equilibrium analysis as a method of appraisal they constructed an aggregate measure of welfare gain and loss for each trading area associated with the alternative proposals. The negotiating position taken by each country appears from the model results to be counter to national interest. For the "central-case" numerical specification considered the EEC gains more from the US proposal than it does from its own and vice versa. The results tend to portray country blocs as negotiating to promote their own proposals whereas in fact each other's proposal is better for them. This theme from the set of results was explored in terms of both the structure of the domestic tariff and the terms-of-trade effects associated with

TABLE 4 Tariff-cutting formulas proposed by country participants in the Tokyo Round[a].

US proposal
(T_N = postcut tariff, T_0 = precut tariff)

$T_N = 0.4T_0$ $\qquad$ if $T_0 > 0.067$

$T_N = 0.5T_0 - 1.5T_0^2$ $\qquad$ if $T_0 \leqslant 0.067$

EEC proposal
(4 iterative cuts)

$T_N = T_0 - 2T_0^2 + 2T_0^3 - T_0^4 - (T_0 - 2T_0^2 + 2T_0^3 - T_0^4)^2$

$\qquad - [T_0 - 2T_0^2 + 2T_0^3 - T_0^4 - (T_0 - 2T_0^2 + 2T_0^3 - T_0^4)^2]^2$

Japanese proposal
(applied to post-Kennedy Round and not to current tariffs)

$T_N = 0.3T_0 + 0.035$ $\qquad$ if $T_0 > 0.05$

$T_N = T_0$ $\qquad$ if $T_0 \leqslant 0.05$

Canadian proposal[b]
(cut on the basis of USA tariffs and all countries adopt reduced USA tariffs)

$T_N = 0.4T_0^{US}$ $\qquad$ if $T_0 > 0.05$

$T_N = 0$ $\qquad$ if $T_0 \leqslant 0.05$

Swiss proposal
(compromise formula)

$T_N = AT_0/(A + T_0)$ $\qquad$ (A is a constant (a realistic value is 0.14))

---

[a]The table is extracted from Brown and Whalley (1980).
[b]This proposal only applied to certain sectors but is considered as a "candidate" general tariff-cutting formula.

the alternative proposals, and trading areas that gain most seem to propose shallow cuts. Brown and Whalley also compared the tariff-cutting proposals with more extensive forms of liberalization of world trade and concluded that only a small portion of the potential gains from trade liberalization are likely to be achieved through the adoption of any one of the proposals.

4.2 Evaluation of the Tokyo Round Agreement

In a subsequent paper Whalley (1980c) evaluated the Tokyo Round agreement with the model. Under the Tokyo Round trade agreement all the GATT participants have agreed to tariff cuts which are guided by a "Swiss" tariff-cutting formula. On average a 25% cut in tariffs over a period of eight years is to take effect and is to be accompanied by certain changes in nontariff barriers. In addition other proposals motivated by changes in the new international economic order accompany the agreement although in quantitative terms these are of relatively limited significance. The structure of the agreement is complex;

it is summarized by Whalley (1980c) and is not discussed here. The results stress four main themes.

(1) The static worldwide welfare gains from the tariff cuts in the Tokyo Round are estimated to be small. The aggregate static welfare gain is in the region of US $2 billion per year using 1973 data and 1976 tariff rates for a world GNP of around US $5 trillion in 1973. This indicates a welfare gain of less than 0.1% of world GNP. This can be dismissed as negligible or alternatively as dominated by known margins of error in the national accounts. The suggestion from this calculation is that, in terms of aggregate microeconomic impacts, tariff-reduction negotiations under the GATT are concerned with relatively minor issues and the detailed discussion of alternative tariff-cutting formulae and similar issues in such agreements may not be worthwhile.

(2) Within the agreement the results indicate that impacts from those changes in nontariff barriers which can be quantified are likely to be larger than impacts from all the agreed tariff cuts. This is a striking finding but involves substantial qualification because of poor data and limited information as to the precise nature of the agreement on nontariff barriers. A suggestion is made that changes in government procurement practices within the agreement are in all likelihood more significant by themselves than the impacts from all the agreed tariff changes over the eight-year period associated with the agreement.

(3) A third conclusion is that while aggregate welfare impacts are small the terms-of-trade impacts can be more significant and the gain or loss for individual trading areas can exceed the aggregate gain. Under certain assumptions less developed and developing countries will be the major losers from tariff cuts under the agreement owing to an adverse movement in the terms of trade. Although the rest of the world is shown in the results as potentially offsetting losses from tariff cuts with gains from reductions in nontariff barriers there are some significant implications of this finding for the position of less developed countries in the trade negotiations.

(4) A fourth conclusion derives from an alternative set of calculations in which attempts were made to compute equilibria characterizing the retaliatory incentives for each of the trading areas in a stylized tariff war; these equilibria were then used as a base point from which to evaluate the agreement. Under this calculation the Tokyo Round trade agreement, viewed in terms of process rather than in terms of piecemeal change, becomes extremely important. When the gains achieved from negotiated reductions in levels of protection to the levels currently prevailing are compared to a noncooperative retaliatory outcome such as under a tariff war they become more significant. It is suggested that the welfare loss to the world from retaliatory trade wars might be around 3% of world GNP assuming full employment were to be maintained. On this basis an argument can be made that the Tokyo Round trade agreement should not be viewed as piecemeal change but as part of an ongoing process of accommodation of a cooperative solution to the game-theoretic structure that characterizes protectional policy between major trading areas. This and other findings are explored in Whalley (1980c).

4.3   Taxes and Foreign Trade

In a further application of the model Whalley (1980b) analyzed the effects of domestic taxes on foreign trade. Although there are no precise policy proposals pending under the GATT or elsewhere on domestic taxes, over the years many policy issues have arisen where the trade implications of taxes have been important. One area of discussion has been border tax adjustments; this question arises especially with the value-added tax in the EEC.

Calculations performed with the model show that there are certain features of domestic taxes which, in effect, operate as export taxes. One striking conclusion is that the US domestic tax on capital income by industry operates indirectly as an export tax because the tax rates are higher on export industries than on industries competing with imports. Abolition of the corporate tax in the United States could, under certain assumptions, inflict a welfare loss on the United States which is contrary to the usual analysis of this tax in which it is viewed as a distorting tax in a closed-economy framework. An implication of the model results in this area is that the effects of domestic taxes on world trade may be far more important in quantitative terms than the effects of tariff policies. Future negotiations on world trade liberalization should therefore be concerned to extend their range of discussion to include taxes.

4.4 The New International Economic Order

A fourth area which is currently being investigated involves the application of the model to certain issues in the new international economic order. This will involve an extension of the current model with a substantial adaptation of the treatment of the rest of the world. Other industrialized countries will be separated from the rest of the world in this treatment and the remaining countries will be broken down into four blocs. The oil producers, the newly industrialized countries, the middle-income Less Developed Countries (LDCs) and the low-income LDCs will all be identified. Once this has been done a number of themes in the new international economic order will be examined. These involve the effect of protection in the industrialized world on the various groups of LDCs and also the effect of protection in LDCs on international trade and, in turn, on industrialized countries. The effect of possible arrangements to write off the foreign debt of LDCs will be evaluated in terms of world trade impacts; the possible effects of commodity-price stabilization agreements will also be evaluated.

The theme of the new international economic order is to distribute income in favor of LDCs in one of two ways: either through direct transfers (through writing-off of debt, relocation of manufacturing industry, and transfers of cash) or by changing the relative prices which LDCs face in their trade with the industrialized world. In this application the relative efficiency of these methods will be explored. In the case of transfers the classical analysis of the transfer problem in the literature on international trade will be explored, with an examination of issues of secondary burden.

5   CONCLUSION

In this paper the main characteristics of an empirically oriented Heckscher–Ohlin-type general equilibrium model of international trade have been summarized. An outline of the model structure has been provided and methods of model calibration have been summarized. A brief description has been given of various applications of the model. Further work on the model in future years is anticipated.

REFERENCES

Armington, P.S. (1969). A theory of demand for products distinguished by place of production. IMF Staff Papers, pp. 159–176.

Balassa, B. and Kreinin, M.E. (1967). Trade liberalization under the "Kennedy Round": the static effects. Review of Economics and Statistics, XLIX:125–137.

Baldwin, R.E. (1970). Non-Tariff Distortions of International Trade. Brookings Institution, Washington, D.C.

Brown, F. and Whalley, J. (1980). General equilibrium evaluations of tariff cutting proposals in the Tokyo Round and comparisons to more extensive liberalization of world trade. Economic Journal, 90:838–866.

Caddy, V. (1976). Empirical estimation of the elasticity of substitution: a review. Industries Assistance Commission, Melbourne, Australia. (Mimeograph.)

Fullerton, D., Shoven, J.B., and Whalley, J. (1978). General equilibrium analysis of US taxation policy. In 1978 Compendium of Tax Research. Office of Tax Analysis, Department of the Treasury, Washington, D.C.

GATT (1974). Basic documentation of the tariff study. General Agreement on Trade and Tariff, Geneva.

Houthakker, H.S. and Magee, S.P. (1969). Income and price elasticities in world trade. Review of Economics and Statistics, LI (May):111–125.

Roningen, V. and Yeats, A.J. (1976). Non-tariff distortions of international trade: some preliminary empirical evidence. Weltwirtschaftliches Archiv, 112:613–625.

Scarf, H.E. (in collaboration with Hansen, T.) (1973). The Computation of Economic Equilibria. Yale University Press, New Haven, Connecticut.

Shoven, J.B. and Whalley, J. (1974). On the computation of competitive equilibria on international markets with tariffs. Journal of International Economics, 4:341–354.

Stern, R.M., Francis, J., and Schumacher, B. (1977). Price Elasticities in International Trade: An Annotated Bibliography. Macmillan, London (for the Trade Policy Research Centre).

UNCTAD (1969, 1970). Liberalization of Tariffs and Non-Tariff Barriers. UNCTAD Documents TD/B/C.2/83, 1969, TD/B/C.2/R.I, 1969, and TD/B/C.2/R.3, 1970. United Nations Conference on Trade and Development, Geneva.

Walter, I. (1972). Non-tariff protection among industrialized countries: some preliminary evidence. Economia Internazionale, XXV:335 et seq.

Whalley, J. (1980a). General equilibrium analysis of US–EEC–Japanese trade and trade distorting policies. Economie Appliqué (symposium issue on international trade general equilibrium models), XXXIII:191–230.

Whalley, J. (1980b). Discriminatory features of domestic taxation policies and their impact on world trade: a general equilibrium approach. Paper presented at the Econometric Society Meeting, Chicago, Illinois. (Revised version in Journal of Political Economy, 88(6):1177–1203.)

Whalley, J. (1980c). An evaluation of the recent Tokyo Round Trade Agreement through a general equilibrium model of world trade involving major trading areas. Working Paper No. 8009. Centre for the Study of International Economic Relations, University of Western Ontario, London, Ontario.

World Bank (1975). World Bank Atlas. World Bank, Washington, D.C.

Yeats, A.J. (1976). Effective protection for processed agricultural commodities: a comparison of industrial countries. Journal of Economics and Business, XX:31–40.

COMMENTS: I*

It seems to me that John Whalley has provided a very useful tool for quantitative analysis within the theoretical framework of the Heckscher—Ohlin model. With the aid of tools like Whalley's model, we can get beyond the qualitative results usually obtained from the Heckscher—Ohlin model, and start to analyze the impact of trade policies in quantitative terms. Moreover, the general equilibrium nature of the model makes it possible to demonstrate that the concept of "trade policy" should not be interpreted too narrowly; Whalley's results show that changes in domestic taxes may have equally significant impacts on international trade as various tariff cuts.

However, although a model of this type is a powerful tool for demonstrating the theorems of trade theory in quantitative terms as well as the interdependencies between different countries through international trade, it is not always easy and straightforward to use a model such as the one presented here for evaluation of actual trade policy proposals. The main reason is as follows. The structure of the model, and especially the assumption about intersectorally mobile capital and labor, implies that the model solutions correspond to situations where the economic agents are well adjusted to prevailing factor and product prices, and these prices are such that no economic activity generates loss or excess profit. Of course, such situations never occur in the real world, but if factor and product markets function reasonably well, and expectations are realized to a large extent, the actual allocation of resources should be fairly close to something like a general equilibrium allocation.

The problem, however, is that if some set of exogenous conditions is changed, there will be a process of adjustment before the new equilibrium is attained. A Heckscher—Ohlin type of general equilibrium model tells us neither anything about the length of the adjustment period, nor about the disequilibrium characteristics of the adjustment process. These are indeed important issues in the formation of trade policies, and consequently the general equilibrium model gives an incomplete picture of the impact of contemplated trade policies.

In the model applications presented in the paper different equilibria are compared on the basis of Hicksian compensating and equivalent variations. This is well in line with the philosophy of the modeling effort as a whole, but it should be pointed out that such exercises, when based on aggregated data, require strong assumptions about individual preference structures. Otherwise distributional effects can make it impossible to draw welfare conclusions on the basis of measures of aggregated economic efficiency.

It would in any case have been interesting to compare the different cases also in terms of measures such as GDP, private consumption, terms of trade, and the sectoral allocation of production and employment. One reason for this is that the formation of economic policy to a large extent seems to be based on observations on, and expectations about, such variables rather than the somewhat esoteric concepts of welfare theory. A second reason is that the changes in the equilibrium values of the sectoral variables in particular could give some indications about adjustment problems in connection with the economy's movement between two equilibria.

---

*By Lars Bergman, Stockholm School of Economics, Stockholm, Sweden.

An interesting problem, touched upon briefly in the paper, is how quotas and other nontariff barriers could be incorporated in a general equilibrium model. I can fully understand that the chosen approach, representation in equivalent ad valorem form rather than in the form of direct quantity restrictions, has computational advantages. However, since barriers of this type are likely to have a significant impact on international trade and domestic resource allocation, I think it would be worthwhile trying to incorporate the nontariff barriers in a somewhat more realistic way. As I understand it, the method adopted implies that many of the inefficiencies typical for quotas and other quantity regulations do not appear in the model. For instance, when an import quota is represented by a uniform, but artificial, tax rate on the imported goods in question, adjusted so that the import restriction is satisfied in equilibrium, the quotas are automatically allocated to the importers which, on the margin, are the most efficient ones. That may not be the case in the real world, and there are also costs associated with the administration of the regulations.

It is pointed out in the paper that the present model, although a numerical one, is primarily intended to be consistent with the dominating international trade theory. Thus it is not an econometric model in the sense that individual equations, on the basis of statistical criteria, capture the actual behavior of the economic system. It follows that in a model such as Whalley's the numerical values of the parameters have to be estimated in a different way than is usual for econometric models. The method used here is a nonstochastic one, and it employs data for essentially one single year, a so-called "benchmark equilibrium data set." When all the equilibrium conditions of the model, together with some elasticity estimates, are imposed on the data set, it is possible to solve for the model's parameters.

However, this method works for any complete data set, and therefore not only for data sets representing something close to an equilibrium. Moreover, the estimation method does not provide measures of the accuracy of the resulting parameter estimates. Consequently it is very important that the "benchmark equilibrium data set" is constructed with great care, in other words that it really represents a situation which is fairly close to an equilibrium.

I have some experience with applications of this estimation method for a general equilibrium model of the Swedish economy. In that work I had problems with significant intersectoral profit differentials in the benchmark data set; it is well known that such differentials could not persist in equilibrium if capital were fully mobile. Against that background, I would like to know whether similar problems arose in the construction of the benchmark data set for the present model, and, if that was indeed the case, what was done to mitigate them.

COMMENTS: II*

Professor Whalley successfully takes up a very complex problem of great practical importance: the analysis of the effects of various trade liberalization proposals and trade policy changes under GATT rules.

---

*By W. Trzeciakowski, Foreign Trade Research Institute, Warsaw, Poland.

The Whalley model is not explicitly described in economic terms in the paper; hence my comments are based only on the general description of the model. The main merit of the model is its policy oriented character. The model is concerned with well-defined questions studying the consequences of strictly-determined policy proposals. Within the strictly-defined questions, the model gives reasonable answers.

The Whalley model creates a coherent analytical framework for the analysis of liberalization proposals for the three main partners in foreign trade: the United States, Japan, and the EEC. All these economies rely on the functioning of the competitive market. The form of the model is not so appropriate for less developed countries and for centrally planned economies, where decision-making is based on nonmarket considerations to a much larger extent, supply possibilities are of primary importance, and exports constrain imports; in other words the model is most suitable for demand-constrained economies, and much less suited to supply-constrained economies. Hence my first tentative conclusion. The model is well suited to the assessment of trade policies among the main parties to the GATT negotiations as they are all basically demand-constrained economies; however, the model would need further adaptation if it were required to analyze North—South relations.

The model takes into acount the variations in terms of trade effects associated with different trade policy regimes, and the scenario approach, simulating the way the international economy would have behaved had alternative policy variations been adopted, seems very useful. The dimensionality of the model in terms of products represents a reasonable tradeoff between the limited data availability and concerns dictated by the policy analysis desired. The assumption of product heterogeneity by trading areas seems useful in many instances, but is not completely convincing as a general rule: the exclusion of domestic production of foreign goods is a strong assumption. On the other hand, the model, in its latest version, takes into account the substitution between intermediate products, which permits the choice of inputs by geographical point of production within the global fixed coefficient in terms of composite goods.

If the objective of the study is to analyze the impact of various trade policy regimes on foreign trade growth, the assumption of constant returns to scale may give rise to some doubts, as economies of scale are often the essence of international specialization. I can see the technical advantages of using constant returns to scale, but various consequences of using this approach depend on the time horizon of the analysis. It is permissible in the short run; however, it is not adequate to evaluate the long-term effects.

The static worldwide effects in welfare gains from tariff cuts in the Tokyo Round are surprisingly small. The author estimates that the loss of world GNP under conditions of a retaliatory tariff war would amount to 3%. This evaluation, based on a static approach, seems to underestimate the dynamic results of a world protectionist system in the long run. Not utilizing the advantages of the international division of labor within the existing productive capacities is only part of the phenomenon; at least as important is the question of not undertaking investments aimed at international specialization in an uncertain protectionist environment. In my opinion, these dynamic long-term consequences are much more harmful than the static short-term consequences. Hence I would conclude that the real importance of the GATT negotiations lies in the avoidance of major trade wars during recessionary periods and in the maintenance of some rules of mutually respected behavior over the long term.

The use of elasticity parameters in the model is critical for the results obtained. These elasticities are derived from reality, and hence are affected by existing trade policies. What will happen to these parameters if we change tariffs, nontariff barriers, and taxes, remain open questions.

The assumption that competitive forces operate and all supernormal profits are competed away can be treated as a general rule; however it seems doubtful for commodity markets (e.g., for oil) where monopolies operate. The results of the model lead to the well-known conclusion that tariffs create less acute impediments to foreign trade than do nontariff barriers, which remain the main tool of protection. However, these nontariff barriers, such as government purchases, quotas, restrictions, licensing regulations, so-called "voluntary" export restraints, sanitary or health regulations, and the like, are typical forms of foreign trade control systems throughout the "rest of the world." They are difficult to represent in an ad valorem equivalent form. At best, only "guesses" can be made, as no statistical data are available.

Whalley's conclusion that the negotiating position taken by each country often appears to be counter to national interests (for example, that the EEC gains more from the US proposal than it does from its own, and vice versa) points to one of two alternative conclusions: either "Alles ist begränzt nur die menschliche Dummheit ist unbegränzt" (everything is limited except man's stupidity), or more plausibly that the model has some invisible weakness, since it seems doubtful to assume that all participants in the negotiations were stupid!

My final comments deal with the proposal to apply the Whalley model to the analysis of taxes and their impact on foreign trade and to the North—South dialog (and consequently to the related question of East—West dialog). I have already mentioned specific methodological problems encountered in the analysis of supply-constrained economies, and I would also opt for a separate treatment of centrally planned economies. Further, the basic characteristics of protection should be clarified at the outset, because even such notions as the rate of exchange, tariffs, subsidies, and taxes, can have very different interpretations and functions in a classical market economy, in a developing economy, and in a centrally planned economy. In developed market economies, we deal with marginal equilibrium rates. In developing and centrally planned economies, we usually encounter nonconvertible currencies with overvalued exchange rates fixed at non-marginal, non-equilibrium levels. Consequently, various corrective measures are applied, which can take the form of directives, quotas, tariffs, or subsidies; however, it is important to realize that these may not necessarily be intended as protectionist measures but may rather be introduced to correct the overvaluation of the exchange rate. Equally, the role of quantitative directives and restrictions is different in the foreign trade control system of each of the groups of countries. Hence, my general conclusion: in order to widen the analysis to deal with North—South problems the actual model should be reformulated.

Finally, I agree with the author that the investigation of world indebtedness would certainly be an interesting subject for model analysis. Here again, the model would have to be specifically adapted for this new task.

My general impression is that Professor Whalley's paper is an inspiring and good piece of work.

GLOBAL INTERNATIONAL ECONOMIC MODELS
B.G. Hickman (editor)
Elsevier Science Publishers B.V. (North-Holland)
© IIASA, 1983

A THREE-REGION MODEL OF ENERGY, INTERNATIONAL TRADE, AND ECONOMIC GROWTH

Alan S. Manne with the assistance of Sehun Kim and Thomas F. Wilson
Department of Operations Research, Stanford University, Stanford, California (USA)

1   GENERAL BACKGROUND

Although the developing countries now consume a relatively small fraction of the world's energy, this fraction could grow rapidly over the coming decades. By comparison with the already industrialized nations, the Less Developed Countries (LDCs) have high population growth rates and high income elasticities of demand for commercial energy. Moreover, if today's North—South income disparities are to be reduced, the LDCs' per capita incomes will have to grow more rapidly. Taken together, these factors imply a substantial increase in the LDC demand for energy. For example, the WAES study (1977, p. 269) projected that the developing countries' share of the world's commercial energy consumption would grow from 15% in 1972 to 25% in the year 2000.

In view of the energy-price increases experienced since 1973 it is quite likely that the oil-exporting LDCs will continue to enjoy a rapid increase in their GNP and will consume ever-increasing amounts of their own energy production. The oil-importing LDCs, however, constitute a far more populous group, and their energy-demand projections appear to be quite uncertain. With sluggish growth in their traditional export markets among the industrialized nations, the oil-importing LDCs are likely to encounter chronic balance-of-payments difficulties. In principle these difficulties could be solved through aid or through private capital flows. In practice, however, official aid allocations are determined primarily by geopolitical factors, and few of the oil-importing LDCs are sufficiently creditworthy to obtain large amounts of foreign capital through commercial channels.

In qualitative terms it is easy enough to arrive at these generalizations, but what about their quantitative impacts? For this purpose it appears to be essential to construct a computable model of international trade. One region's export prospects cannot be assessed without an understanding of the import propensities of its trading partners. International trade may relieve energy constraints on the growth of individual countries, provided that they can expand their exports of nonenergy products to other nations. The ease or difficulty of this process will be governed largely by the elasticities of substitution in energy and in international trade.

Our three-region model is designed so as to emphasize the key role played by these substitution elasticities and the uncertainties over their numerical values. The approach avoids several of the defects that are inherent in "bottom-up" methods of projection such as those employed by WAES (1977) and the World Bank (IBRD, 1979). Price movements are calculated so as to eliminate "gaps" between the supply and demand for energy. Import and export prices of nonenergy products are adjusted so as to limit trade gaps to plausible rates of capital transfers. Despite these advantages of logical consistency there are inherent difficulties in this type of global modeling. With a "top-down" approach, aggregation can lead to serious difficulties. Large-scale models are time consuming, are expensive to construct, and are frequently incomprehensible to outsiders. It is essential that there should be a two-way flow of information between global models and those models that contain sufficient detail so as to be meaningful to individual policy-making units.

2   THE BASIC SIMPLIFICATIONS

These are the general considerations that have led to the specific approach taken in this paper, i.e. a three-region computable general equilibrium model. This is not intended as a general-purpose analysis of international trade and macroeconomic fluctuations, nor is it designed to deal with inflationary processes and with currency movements. Moreover, it is not designed to deal with individual commodities outside the energy sector; hence it is inappropriate for policy issues such as comparative advantage and tariff and nontariff barriers to trade. For these purposes one would need far more disaggregation than that adopted here (see for example Ginsburgh and Waelbroeck, 1975, and Whalley, 1980). Like these more detailed trade analyses, we shall engage in comparative statics for a single point of time, 1990. There will be no attempt to analyze the year-by-year details of the transition from 1976 (the data benchmark year) to 1990.

For benchmark purposes, heavy reliance has been placed on the World Development Report (WDR) 1979 (IBRD, 1979). Following the practice in WDR 1979, the industrialized market economies are aggregated into a single region. Unlike in that report, however, the LDCs are described here in terms of only two regions: oil exporters and importers. This leads to the following three-region classification of the market economies*: region 1, industrialized nations (Organization for Economic Cooperation and Development (OECD) + Israel + South Africa); region 2, oil-exporting LDCs (Organization of Petroleum Exporting Countries (OPEC) + Mexico); region 3, oil-importing LDCs (all other market economies).

Following in the tradition of Armington (1969a, b), Barten (1971), Hickman et al. (1979), and Hickman and Lau (1973), nonenergy tradables are aggregated in dollar terms but are distinguished by their region of origin. Energy forms are expressed in terms of their oil equivalents. Thus there are only four internationally traded goods whose prices

---

*If one were specifically concerned with East—West trade issues this three-region classification would be unusable. Taken literally, it implies that there will be zero net trade in energy and nonenergy products with the centrally planned economies. To improve the realism of these projections, East—West trade flows might be projected exogenously. For practical purposes — aggregate projections of the market economies' trade flows — this might be just as accurate as attempting to include the centrally planned nations endogenously as a fourth region.

are to be determined endogenously: energy and one composite nonenergy export product for each of the three regions. Transport costs are neglected and there is no distinction between cost, insurance, and freight (c.i.f.) and free on board (f.o.b.) prices. Current-account exports include both merchandise trade and nonfactor services (shipping, tourism, etc.). We include a rough allowance for noncommercial energy in region 3. For details on data sources, regional definitions, etc., see Appendix A. Our estimates are based largely on WDR 1979.

Several alternative scenarios will be explored with respect to energy supplies. Within each scenario supplies will be viewed as exogenous for each region in 1990. This approach appears to be more practical than attempting to estimate price-responsive supply curves. For projections within the next decade, OECD domestic supplies appear to be far less dependent on future prices than on institutional and public acceptability factors, e.g. petroleum leasing policies, environmental constraints on air quality, and nuclear safety regulations. For calculations beyond 1990, however, it would appear to be preferable to incorporate rising-cost supply curves.

In order to project each region's demand for energy and nonenergy imports we employ nested Constant-Elasticity-of-Substitution (CES) production functions*. Each region's future endowments of capital and labor are estimated exogenously in accordance with its potential GNP growth under constant prices of energy and nonenergy imports. Each region views these international prices as a datum. To the extent that OPEC exercises monopoly power, this is already incorporated in the scenario assumptions with respect to the quantities of energy supplied by region 2 (OPEC + Mexico).

Prices are adjusted so as to equilibrate supplies and demands. Given the prices of the internationally tradable goods — and given the production functions and capital, labor, and energy endowments — it is supposed that each region will choose a mix of energy and nonenergy imports so as to maximize its GNP. The maximization is subject to region-by-region constraints on the balance of trade. The outcome of this process is termed the realized GNP. This may exceed or fall below the potential GNP depending on whether there is an improvement or a deterioration in the international terms of trade for the individual region.

3   ALGEBRAIC FORMULATION

The following definitions will be adopted here.

Input data (excluding production function parameters):

d_j = domestic energy supplies in 1990, region j;

---

*With a CES production function there are diminishing marginal returns from imports into each region. To this extent the model automatically allows for "absorptive capacity" constraints within the rapidly growing economies of the oil exporters (see Ezzati, 1978).

To improve on our current description of the oil-exporting nations it might be worthwhile to add one refinement, a value assigned to oil resources that are not consumed during 1990. At sufficiently high prices this means that it might pay to produce less oil than the supplies projected exogenously. In this sense we could incorporate a backward-bending supply curve for the oil exporters.

"Target revenue requirements" is another mode of behavior that has been attributed to several of the capital-surplus oil producers. This type of "satisficing" hypothesis may provide a realistic description but appears to be logically inconsistent with the other assumptions that underlie our general equilibrium model.

x_{ii} = potential GNP in 1990, region i; at constant 1976 prices of energy and non-energy imports; can be interpreted as an index number of capital and labor growth.

Quantity variables:

y_i = realized GNP, region i (in 1976 dollars, adjusted for terms of trade);
x_{ij} = nonenergy products of region i imported into region j ($i \neq j$; $i, j = 1, 2, 3$);
x_{4j} = energy consumed by region j.

Price variables:

π_j = price of nonenergy products, region j ($j = 1, 2, 3$);
π_4 = price of energy.

It will be convenient to report all prices as π_j/π_1; i.e. the numéraire is defined as region 1 products in 1976 dollars. For 1980 dollars, add approximately 50%.

The nested CES production functions appear within the first three material balances given later in this section. There will be considerable debate about the magnitudes of the exponents in these CES functions. The ease or difficulty of substituting between domestic and imported nonenergy inputs will be determined by the parameter α. The "elasticity of trade substitution" is defined as $1/(1 - \alpha)$. Similarly, the "elasticity of energy substitution" is $1/(1 - \beta)$.

Given the values of the exponents α and β, we employ 1976 data to estimate the a_{ij} constants that appear in the nested CES functions. (The 1976 benchmark estimates are reproduced in Table 1.) Assuming that the inputs were optimally adjusted to the international prices prevailing in 1976, it is straightforward to determine the a_{ij} coefficients from the first-order optimality conditions; i.e. the marginal productivity of each input must be equal to its 1976 price. For details, see the dissertation by Kim (1981). This also describes our solution algorithm, which is an extension to nonlinear economies of the procedure described by Manne et al. (1980).

In connection with this benchmarking, two observations should be noted. (1) To allow for the incomplete adjustment (approximately 30%) that had taken place by 1976 in response to the energy-price increases of 1973–1974 we assume that the 1976 "reference price" of oil was only $7 barrel^{-1}. This is the price inserted into the first-order optimality equations, and not the actual 1976 price of $12.5 barrel^{-1}. (2) The production functions incorporate institutional as well as technological constraints. In effect our benchmarking procedure ignores the possibility of changes in tariff and nontariff barriers to international trade between 1976 and 1990. Other approaches are required to investigate such issues.

Our model is based on four material-balance equations and one balance-of-trade constraint for each of the three regions. These are as follows.

Material balances for the four tradeable commodities:

GNP + exports of nonenergy ≤ domestic production,
    products   nonenergy

$$y_i + \sum_{j \neq i} x_{ij} \leq \left[\left(\sum_{j=1}^{3} a_{ij} x_{ji}^{\alpha} \right)^{\beta/\alpha} + a_{i4} x_{4i}^{\beta} \right]^{1/\beta} \qquad (i = 1, 2, 3)$$

                                 nonenergy   energy
                                  inputs   inputs

TABLE 1 1976 actual values and 1990 World Bank projections[a, b].

Region i^c		GNP, y_i	Exports to region 1, nonenergy, x_{i1}	Exports to region 2, nonenergy, x_{i2}	Exports to region 3, nonenergy, x_{i3}	Energy consumption, x_{4i}	Domestic energy production available, d_i	Energy/GNP ratio, $1000 x_{4i}/GNP_i$	Trade deficit at current prices
Region 1	1976	4240	—	58	118	71.8	47.0	16.9	58[f]
	1990	7470	—			114.6	72.5	15.3	
	Annual growth (%)	4.1				3.4	3.1	−0.7	
Region 2	1976	350	9	—	3	4.3	33.5[e]	12.3	−76[f]
	1990	720		—		10.1	50.3[e]	14.0	
	Annual growth (%)	5.3				6.3	2.9	0.9	
Region 3	1976	820	112	11	—	15.3[d]	10.9[d]	18.7	18[f]
	1990	1790			—	31.8[d]	21.6[d]	17.8	
	Annual growth (%)	5.7				5.4	5.0	−0.3	
Total, regions 1–3	1976	5410	121	69	121	91.4	91.4	16.9	0
	1990	9980				156.5	144.4	15.7	
	Annual growth (%)	4.5				3.9	3.3	−0.5	

[a] Source: WDR 1979.
[b] Unit for GNP and exports, billions of 1976 US dollars; unit for energy, million barrels daily, oil equivalent.
[c] The regions are defined in Appendix A, Table A1.
[d] Includes 3.5 MBDO of noncommercial energy both in 1976 and 1990. Estimated as 30% of commercial energy consumption in 1976. This provides a rough adjustment for commercial energy–GNP elasticities greater than unity in region 3.
[e] Production net of "bunkers and others". Plus net exports of energy by the centrally planned economies.
[f] Deficit based on 1976 oil price of $12.5 barrel^{-1}, in billions of US dollars.

where subscripts for region i are omitted on exponents α and β;

total energy consumption $\leqslant$ total energy supplies

$$\sum_{j=1}^{3} x_{4j} \qquad \leqslant \qquad \sum_{j=1}^{3} d_j$$

Balance-of-trade constraint for region i:

value of nonenergy $\geqslant$ value of nonenergy + value of energy imports
exports   imports   (exports)

$$\pi_i \sum_{j \neq i} x_{ij} \qquad \geqslant \qquad \sum_{\substack{j \neq i \\ j \neq 4}} \pi_j x_{ji} \qquad + \qquad \pi_4 (x_{4i} - d_i) \qquad\qquad (i = 1, 2, 3)$$

As written here, the three balance-of-trade constraints imply that net capital transfers will be zero in 1990. To allow for future net capital transfers would require only minor changes in the basic model. Perhaps the simplest approach would be to modify the structure of ownership to allow for this possibility. Recall that each region is viewed as the owner of its energy resources and production function. Since the values of x_{ii} (capital and labor) are fixed there will be diminishing returns to scale in terms of the other inputs and hence a positive "rent" on the ownership of each production function. Then suppose that we wish to consider a case in which regions 1 and 2 have agreed to transfer 1% of their net incomes to region 3 in 1990. This would be logically equivalent to assigning region 3 a 1% ownership share of the factor endowments in the other two regions.

4   BASE-CASE ASSUMPTIONS AND RESULTS

Before we consider a base case and alternative scenarios it is useful to take a close look at the underlying numerical estimates on which our three-region model is based (see Table 1). For the most part these calculations will be based on estimates that appeared in WDR 1979, i.e. on both the historical statistics for 1976 and the World Bank's projections for 1990. For 1976 benchmarking purposes the region-by-region statistics include GNP, energy production and consumption, nonenergy imports and exports, and the resulting trade deficit. Note that the deficits of the oil-importing regions add up so as to match the $76 billion trade surplus recorded by the oil exporters in 1976. For our 1990 projections it will be assumed that these trade deficits must be eliminated by one means or another — by changes in the relative prices of energy and nonenergy products, by changes in GNP growth rates, and by changes in the pattern of international trade.

In addition to the 1976 historical statistics, Table 1 contains the World Bank's projections for 1990. Let us first examine the energy projections. Under the assumptions employed in WDR 1979 there is a significant gap between the energy supplies and demands projected independently, i.e. an excess demand of $12.1 = 156.5 - 144.4$ MBDO (million barrels daily, oil equivalent). This type of logical inconsistency is eliminated through a market-equilibrium framework of the type employed here. Prices and incomes are automatically adjusted so as to reduce energy demands to the limited supplies that are available.

Our GNP projections are derived from those that appear in Table 1. The World Bank projections are employed as a guide to selecting the potential GNP growth rates. (Recall that x_{ii} is based on the potential GNP growth rate under constant prices of energy and other terms of trade whereas y_i refers to the realized GNP under changing price conditions.) For the developing nations (regions 2 and 3) our potential GNP growth rates are taken directly from the World Bank projections reproduced in Table 1. For the industrialized nations, however, it is widely believed that WDR 1979 was overly optimistic. Accordingly, we shall take 3.5% instead of 4.1% as the potential annual growth rate in region 1 between 1976 and 1990.

With respect to energy supplies (denoted here by d_i) our base case follows the overall projections described in Pocock (1979), i.e. Royal Dutch—Shell's World of Internal Contradictions (WIC) scenario. Under these circumstances the market economies' total energy supplies will expand at the annual rate of only 2.0% between 1976 and 1990*. This estimate is considerably lower than the 3.3% supply increase estimated in WDR 1979 (recall Table 1). Later we shall see that this relatively minor difference in supply growth rates can lead to large differences in future energy prices.

Table 2 contains our base-case calculations, with the 1990 results given in italics. In this type of model the numerical results depend crucially on what is assumed with respect to the elasticities of substitution (see the rightmost column of Table 2). For international trade we have employed elasticities that are close to but not identical to unity: 1.25 for region 1 but only 0.80 for the developing nations (regions 2 and 3). These are of the same order of magnitude as the empirical estimates of international trade elasticities summarized by Whalley (1980, p. 33).

For the energy elasticities a uniform value was adopted in all three regions. These estimates refer to 1990 and are not necessarily a complete long-term adjustment to the energy-price increases that have occurred since 1973. A 0.25 value for 1990 would therefore be consistent with a long-run elasticity value of 0.30 or possibly higher. They may be compared with the empirical estimates of energy-price elasticities cited in Choe et al. (1980, pp. 30—33).

The three-region model is sufficiently compact so that all numerical assumptions and results appear on a single page in Table 2. Perhaps the key result is the international price of energy which is shown here as $19.2 barrel^{-1} expressed in 1976 dollars. This implies no major changes in energy prices during the decade of the 1980s. It should be noted, however, that this is a "no surprise" world. Other scenarios could lead to very different results.

In the base case energy prices are nearly three times higher than the "reference price" of $7 barrel^{-1} employed for 1976 benchmarking purposes. This is the principal reason for the dramatic shift in the terms of trade between the oil-exporting and oil-importing regions. This also explains why the realized GNP growth rate exceeds the potential in region 2 and why the converse holds for regions 1 and 3. Note that the GNP shortfall is relatively minor for the OECD nations (region 1). For the oil-importing

---

*For these illustrative projections we applied Royal Dutch—Shell's 2.0% overall growth rate uniformly to all three regions. We also experimented with a more realistic set of region-by-region estimates that add up to the identical total energy supplies for the market economies. It turned out that this affected the GNP growth and trade projections for individual regions but had only a second-order impact on international energy prices.

TABLE 2 Base-case assumptions and results[a].

Region i[b]		GNP Realized, y_i	GNP Potential, x_{ii}	Exports to region 1, nonenergy, x_{i1}	Exports to region 2, nonenergy, x_{i2}	Exports to region 3, nonenergy, x_{i3}	Energy consumption, x_{4i}	Domestic energy production available, d_i	1990 elasticity Trade	1990 elasticity Energy
Region 1	1976	4240	4240	—	58	118	71.8	47.0	1.25	0.25
	1990	6715	6860	—	220	166.9	89.7	62.0		
	Annual growth (%)	3.3	3.5		10.0	2.5	1.6	2.0		
Region 2	1976	350	350	9	—	3	4.3	33.5	0.80	0.25
	1990	792	720	6.1	—	2.6	9.0	44.1		
	Annual growth (%)	6.0	5.3	-2.7		-1.0	5.4	2.0		
Region 3	1976	820	820	112	11	—	15.3	10.9	0.80	0.25
	1990	1583	1790	264.5	55.2	—	21.8	14.4		
	Annual growth (%)	4.8	5.7	6.3	12.2		2.6	2.0		
Total, regions 1–3	1976	5410	5410	121	69	121	91.4	91.4		
	1990	9090	9370	270.6	275.2	169.5	120.5	120.5		
	Annual growth (%)	3.8	4.0	5.9	10.4	2.4	2.0	2.0		
1990 equilibrium prices π_{ij}/π_1[c]				1.00	1.83	0.70	19.2[d]			

[a] Unit for GNP and exports, billions of 1976 US dollars; unit for energy, million barrels daily, oil equivalent.
[b] The regions are defined in Appendix A, Table A1.
[c] Ratios to 1976 dollars for region 1; energy prices expressed in US dollars per barrel.
[d] Compare with the 1976 "reference price" of $7 barrel^{-1} employed for benchmarking purposes.

LDCs (region 3), however, there is a significant difference between the potential growth rate (5.7%) and the realized rate of 4.8%. This region's growth is depressed by a combination of factors, i.e. not only high oil prices but also slow GNP growth in the traditional markets for its export products.

It is unclear whether further refinements of these calculations would produce a major change in the overall picture on gains and losses from these shifts in the terms of trade. If region 3 were to receive large amounts of untied foreign aid or if it could rapidly expand its domestic energy supplies, its GNP growth prospects would be improved. Offsetting these favorable possibilities is the likelihood that region 3 would be hard pressed to raise its exports as dramatically as is projected here (a 6.3% and 12.2% annual increase for regions 1 and 2, respectively). This export expansion would not occur painlessly. The base case implies major changes in the relative prices of nonenergy products, i.e. an 83% increase in region 2 and a 30% decrease in region 3. These shifts in relative prices are also significant for would-be exporters of nonenergy products from region 2. There could even be an absolute decline in the volume of this region's nonenergy exports (see Table 2). This decline is not an inevitable outcome but it represents one of the many channels through which balance-of-payments equilibrium might be restored by 1990.

5   ALTERNATIVE SUPPLY–DEMAND SCENARIOS

Along with the base case, it is instructive to consider four alternative supply–demand scenarios. In Figure 1 these are labeled A, B, C, and D, respectively (for details see Appendix B). The first three cases represent alternative assumptions on energy supplies; the fourth refers to the possibility of OECD demand reductions induced by oil import quotas.

Cases A and C are identical to case B (the base case) except for the energy-supply parameters d_i. In case A these are taken directly from WDR 1979. This means that case A is based on a 3.3% annual growth in energy supplies for the market economies over the period 1976–1990. By contrast, in cases B and C (base case and low energy supplies, respectively) the energy-supply growth rates are 2.0% and 1.0%, respectively.

These differences between annual growth rates appear to be minor but they compound to a 37% difference between cases A and C by 1990. In turn this leads to a wide range of uncertainty on future energy prices. These supply differences alone could imply price variations between $9.4 and $31.8 barrel^{-1} (all expressed in dollars of 1976 purchasing power).

Figure 1 provides a graphical comparison between the potential and the realized GNP growth rates in each of the three regions. With low global energy supplies the OPEC nations would make substantial gains at the expense of the importers. In relative terms, however, the oil-importing LDCs would be more affected than the OECD nations. There are the direct effects through higher oil prices and indirect effects through balance-of-trade constraints on growth. With low global energy supplies (case C) the oil-importing LDCs would achieve only 84% of their potential GNP in 1990.

Case D analyzes a demand-management scenario in which the OECD nations reach a collective agreement aimed at reducing OPEC prices and revenues. Specifically, it is supposed that the agreement consists of a tariff or quota system designed to limit 1990 imports to the "Tokyo summit" level of 24.8 MBDO. This would represent a 2.9-MBDO reduction from the base-case import levels projected for 1990. Case D is analyzed as though

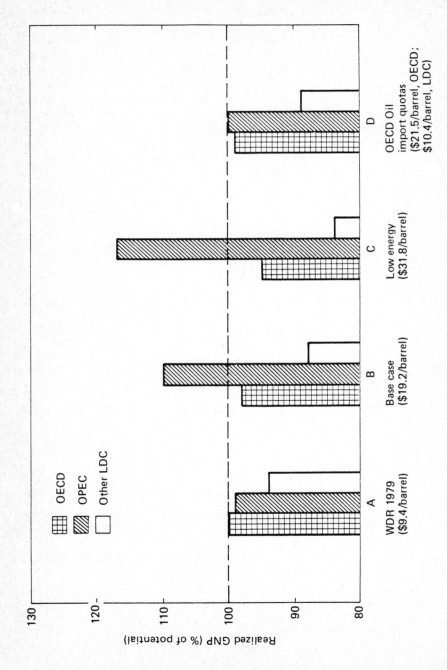

FIGURE 1   Four alternative supply—demand scenarios. For each scenario the oil price, in 1976 dollars per barrel, is shown in parentheses.

OPEC will not respond through further cuts in production. Under this assumption, the quotas or tariffs would drive down OPEC prices to $10.4 barrel^{-1} and hence would raise the 1990 GNP levels realized by the oil-importing nations. Within OECD as a whole the "public benefit" (defined as the increase in GNP per barrel of oil import reduction) would be $75 barrel^{-1}. This is far higher than the internal OECD price of $21.5 faced by domestic producers and consumers. If implemented through a tariff rather than a quota system, this scenario would require an additional import tax of 107% over the international price. It remains an open issue whether the OECD nations could exercise sufficient self-discipline to form a consumers' cartel of this type.

6   ELASTICITY ESTIMATES

In market equilibrium models, elasticity estimates can make a substantial difference; see Energy Modeling Forum (1980). If, for example, the energy elasticities were 0.20 (instead of 0.25), the 1990 oil price projection would increase by 28% over its base-case value (see Case E, Table 3). It is no wonder that so many econometric price forecasts have gone awry. This is also one of the reasons why energy-industry practitioners tend to avoid explicit price forecasts. If the analyses are restricted to supply and demand quantities, there is a much smaller margin for projection error.

Our last two cases explore the impact of variations in trade elasticities. In case F these elasticities are reduced uniformly to 0.80 and in case G they are raised uniformly to 1.50. According to Table 3, these variations would not have a major impact on energy prices. They would, however, affect the relative prices of nonenergy exports. In region 3 the base case required a 30% real price decrease (e.g. through currency devaluation). With higher trade elasticities (case G) the required price (and/or exchange-rate) adjust-

TABLE 3   Key results.

Case	1990 energy exports, region 2 (MBDO)	1990 energy price (1976 $ barrel^{-1})	1990 GNP (trillions of 1976 dollars)			
			Region 1	Region 2	Region 3	Total (regions 1−3)
A. WDR 1979	41.6	9.4	6.87	0.71	1.69	9.27
B. Base case	35.1	19.2	6.72	0.79	1.58	9.09
C. Low energy supplies	29.2	31.8	6.53	0.84	1.50	8.87
D. OECD oil import quotas	35.4	21.5(OECD) 10.4(OPEC)	6.80	0.72	1.60	9.12
E. Energy elasticities of 0.20	34.4	24.6	6.64	0.83	1.54	9.01
F. Trade elasticities of 0.80	34.9	18.2	6.73	0.79	1.55	9.07
G. Trade elasticities of 1.50	35.5	19.3	6.68	0.80	1.65	9.13
Potential GNP		7.0 (reference price)	6.86	0.72	1.79	9.37

ments would be considerably smaller: a 17% decrease for region 3 and a 39% increase for region 2 (see Appendix B, Table B7).

Through future empirical work it may be possible to reduce the margins of uncertainty on the trade and energy elasticities. One possible avenue for improvement would be to allow separately for import share elasticities by region of origin. Here we have not distinguished these share elasticities from the elasticity of substitution between domestic factors versus total imports. If the share elasticities were defined through the exponent γ, our production function for region i might then be rewritten with three levels of nesting as

$$\left\{ \left[a_{ii} x_{ii}^{\alpha} + \left(\sum_{\substack{j=1 \\ j \neq i}}^{3} a_{ij} x_{ji}^{\gamma} \right)^{\alpha/\gamma} \right]^{\beta/\alpha} + a_{i4} x_{4i}^{\beta} \right\}^{1/\beta}$$

With this revised functional form it may be possible to make a closer connection between the earlier empirical work by Hickman et al. (1979) and Hickman and Lau (1973) and the approach to global modeling reported in this paper.

ACKNOWLEDGMENTS

This work was supported by National Science Foundation Grant SOC 78-16811. Helpful suggestions have been received from Bert G. Hickman, Lawrence J. Lau, and Jean Waelbroeck, but they are in no way responsible for any remaining errors.

REFERENCES

Armington, P.S. (1969a). A theory of demand for products distinguished by place of production. International Monetary Fund Staff Papers, XVI (March).

Armington, P.S. (1969b). The geographic pattern of trade and the effects of price changes. International Monetary Fund Staff Papers, XVI (July).

Barten, A.P. (1971). An import allocation model for the Common Market. Cahiers Economiques de Bruxelles, No. 50 (2e. trimestre). Université Libre de Bruxelles, Brussels, Belgium.

BP (1978). BP Statistical Review of the World Oil Industry, 1978. British Petroleum, London.

Choe, B.J., Hughes, H., and Lambertini, A. (1980). Energy Prospects for the Developing Countries. International Bank for Reconstruction and Development, Washington, D.C.

Energy Modeling Forum (1980). Energy Modeling Forum 4: Aggregate Elasticity of Energy Demand. Stanford University, Stanford, California, January.

Ezzati, A. (1978). World Energy Markets and OPEC Stability. Lexington Books, Lexington, Massachusetts.

Ginsburgh, V. and Waelbroeck, J. (1975). A general equilibrium model of world trade: Part I, Full format computation of economic equilibria. Cowles Foundation Discussion Paper No. 412, Yale University, New Haven, Connecticut.

Hickman, B.G., Kuroda, Y., and Lau, L.J. (1979). The Pacific Basin in world trade: an analysis of changing trade patterns, 1955–1975. Empirical Economics, 4(1).

Hickman, B.G. and Lau, L.J. (1973). Elasticities of substitution and export demands in a world trade model. European Economic Review, 4.

IBRD (1978). World Development Report, 1978. International Bank for Reconstruction and Development, Washington, D.C.

IBRD (1979). World Development Report, 1979. International Bank for Reconstruction and Development, Washington, D.C.

IBRD (1980). World Development Report, 1980. International Bank for Reconstruction and Development, Washington, D.C.

IMF (1978). Direction of Trade. International Monetary Fund, Washington, D.C.

Kim, S. (1981). General Equilibrium Models: Formulation and Computation. Ph.D. Dissertation. Department of Operations Research, Stanford University, Stanford, California.

Manne, A.S., Chao, H., and Wilson, R. (1980). Computation of competitive equilibria by a sequence of linear programs. Econometrica, 48(7) (November).

Pocock, C.C. (1979). Oil and Gas in 2000: the Shipping Outlook. Royal Dutch–Shell, London.

Whalley, J. (1980). An Evaluation of the Recent Tokyo Round Trade Agreement Through a General Equilibrium Model of World Trade Involving Major Trading Areas. University of Western Ontario, London, Ontario.

Workshop on Alternative Energy Strategies (WAES) (1977). Energy: Global Prospects 1985–2000. McGraw-Hill, New York.

APPENDIX A: DEFINITION OF REGIONS, BASIC DATA, AND SOURCES

TABLE A1   Definitions of regions (market economies only).

Region	Definition
1	United States, Canada, Japan, European OECD members (excluding Southern Europe), New Zealand, Israel, South Africa, Turkey
2	OPEC, Mexico
3	Other LDCs: all other market economies including Southern Europe (Greece, Portugal, and Spain)

TABLE A2   GNPs (in billions of 1976 US dollars)[a].

Region	Country/group	GNP 1976	GNP 1990	Annual growth rates (%)
1	United States	1697.14	2947.23	4.0 (1976–90)
	Canada	174.23	304.62	3.7 (1976–80), 4.2 (1980–90)
	Japan	553.85	1247.38	5.4 (1976–80), 6.2 (1980–90)
	OECD, Western Europe	1667.77	2711.30	2.9 (1976–80), 3.8 (1980–90)
	Other developed	145.70	257.49	3.5 (1976–80), 4.4 (1980–90)
	Total	4238.68	7468.02	4.1 (1976–90)
2	OPEC	281.21	568.00	5.4 (1976–80), 5.1 (1980–85), 5.0 (1985–90)[b]
	Mexico	67.58	147.05	5.7 (1976–80), 5.8 (1980–85), 5.6 (1985–90)
	Total	348.79	715.05	5.3 (1976–90)
3	Other LDCs	822.34	1794.78	5.7 (1976–90)[c]

[a]Sources: the 1976 GNP figures are from WDR 1978, Table 1, pp. 76–77 (IBRD, 1978); the 1990 GNP projections are calculated using assumptions on real annual growth from a preliminary analysis for WDR 1979 unless otherwise noted.
[b]Judgmentally chosen from preliminary WDR 1980 estimates (IBRD, 1980).
[c]From WDR 1979 assumptions on growth rates for these regions of the world.

TABLE A3   Energy consumption (in million barrels daily of oil equivalent)[a,b].

Region	Country/group	1976	1990
1	United States	36.6	55.0
	Canada	3.9	6.3
	Japan	6.6	15.8
	OECD, Western Europe	21.8	31.8
	Other developed	2.9	5.7
	Total	71.77	114.55
2	OPEC	3.14	7.31
	Mexico	1.21	2.75
	Total	4.35	10.06
3	Other LDCs, commercial	11.76	28.25
	Other LDCs, noncommercial	3.5	3.5
	Total	15.26	31.75

[a]Sources: the 1976 energy data are from a World Bank analysis of United Nations data series; the consumption figures for several industrialized nations are taken from BP (1978); the 1990 energy-consumption projections are from preliminary work for WDR 1979.
[b]The energy-consumption estimates for region 3 include 3.5 MBDO of noncommercial energy both in 1976 and 1990. Noncommercial energy use is estimated as 30% of commercial energy consumption in 1976. The production and consumption estimates for regions 1 and 2 include only commercial energy.

TABLE A4   Energy production and bunkers (in million barrels daily of oil equivalent)[a,b,c].

Region	Country/group	Production		Bunkers and others	
		1976	1990	1976	1990
1	United States	29.6	41.6	0.37	0.50
	Canada	4.5	6.3	0.06	0.07
	Japan	0.9	3.2	0.35	0.66
	OECD, Western Europe	9.6	17.0	0.81	0.99
	Other developed	2.9	5.7	0.10	0.18
	Total	47.5	73.7	1.69	2.40
	Total less bunkers[d]	47.0	72.5	--	--
2	OPEC	32.6	45.3	0.35	0.76
	Mexico	1.3	5.8	0.00	0.00
	Total	33.9	51.1	0.35	0.77
	Total less bunkers[d]	33.5	50.3	--	--
3	Other LDC	7.6	19.1	0.60	1.34
	Total less bunkers[d,e]	10.9	21.6	--	--

[a]Source: the 1976 production and bunker estimates and the 1990 production estimates are from preliminary work for WDR 1979. Bunkers are assumed to remain a constant proportion of oil consumption for each nation.
[b]Net exports of energy by the centrally planned economies are also included here in "bunkers and others". Production estimates are therefore adjusted upward by 1.2 MBDO in region 1 and by 0.3 MBDO in region 3 both in 1976 and 1990.
[c]The sums of entries in the table may not equal totals because of roundoff.
[d]Including adjustments for net energy imports from the centrally planned economies.
[e]Including noncommercial (see footnote [b] to Table A3).

TABLE A5   Nonenergy trade, 1976: nonenergy merchandise exports (in millions of 1976 US dollars)[a,b].

From	To		
	Region 1	Region 2	Region 3
Region 1	—	47,993.9	97,497.1
Region 2	6,191.2	—	1,643.8
Region 3	77,606.2	7,062.5	—

[a]Source: IMF (1978), which contains a country-by-country breakdown of world merchandise trade.
[b]It is assumed that nonfuel trade has the same pattern as overall trade. Trade is measured at the point of exportation and is valued at f.o.b. prices.

TABLE A6   Nonenergy trade, 1976: exports of goods and nonfactor services (nonenergy) (in millions of 1976 US dollars)[a,b].

From	To		
	Region 1	Region 2	Region 3
Region 1	—	58,022.9	117,850.1
Region 2	9,247.2	—	2,587.8
Region 3	112,606.2	11,062.5	—

[a]Sources: Table A5, WDR 1978, and WDR 1979; WDR 1979 has estimates for exports of goods and nonfactor services (Table 12, p. 12; Figure 3, p. 14) and energy (fuel) exports (Tables 9 and 10, pp. 142–145).
[b]It is assumed that the trade of goods and nonfactor services follows the same pattern as merchandise trade and that nonfuel trade has the same pattern as overall trade. Trade is measured at the point of exportation and is valued at f.o.b. prices.

APPENDIX B: RESULTS FOR CASES A–G

TABLE B1　Case A: WDR 1979 energy supplies and economic growth rates[a]

Region i[b]		GNP		Exports to region 1, nonenergy, x_{i1}	Exports to region 2, nonenergy, x_{i2}	Exports to region 3, nonenergy, x_{i3}	Energy consumption, x_{4i}	Domestic energy production available, d_i	1990 elasticity	
		Realized, y_i	Potential, x_{ii}						Trade	Energy
Region 1	1976	4240	4240	–	58	118	71.8	47.0	1.25	0.25
	1990	6868	6860	–	135.3	193	108.1	72.5		
	Annual growth (%)	3.5	3.5		6.2	3.6	3.0	3.1		
Region 2	1976	350	350	9	–	3	4.3	33.5	0.80	0.25
	1990	714	720	12.2	–	4.4	8.7	50.3		
	Annual growth (%)	5.2	5.3	2.2		2.8	5.2	2.9		
Region 3	1976	820	820	112	11	–	15.3	10.9	0.80	0.25
	1990	1694	1790	255.5	32.5	–	27.6	21.6		
	Annual growth (%)	5.3	5.7	6.1	8.0		4.3	5.0		
Total, regions 1–3	1976	5410	5410	121	69	121	91.4	91.4		
	1990	9276	9370	267.6	167.8	197.4	144.4	144.4		
	Annual growth (%)	3.9	4.0	5.8	6.6	3.6	3.3	3.3		
1990 equilibrium prices, π_j/π_1[c]				1.00	1.14	0.76	9.45			

[a] Unit for GNP and exports, billions of 1976 US dollars; unit for energy, million barrels daily, oil equivalent.
[b] The regions are defined in Appendix A, Table A1.
[c] Ratios to 1976 dollars for region 1; energy prices expressed in US dollars per barrel.

TABLE B2   Case B: Base case, Royal Dutch–Shell (WIC) energy-supply projections[a].

Region i[b]		GNP		Exports to region 1, nonenergy, x_{i1}	Exports to region 2, nonenergy, x_{i2}	Exports to region 3, nonenergy, x_{i3}	Energy consumption, x_{4i}	Domestic energy production available, d_i	1990 elasticity	
		Realized, y_i	Potential, x_{ii}						Trade	Energy
Region 1	1976	4240	4240	—	58	118	71.8	47.0	1.25	0.25
	1990	6715	6860	—	220	166.9	89.7	62.0		
	Annual growth (%)	3.3	3.5	—	10.0	2.5	1.6	2.0		
Region 2	1976	350	350	9	—	3	4.3	33.5	0.80	0.25
	1990	792	720	6.1	—	2.6	9.0	44.1		
	Annual growth (%)	6.0	5.3	−2.7	—	−1.0	5.4	2.0		
Region 3	1976	820	820	112	11	—	15.3	10.9	0.80	0.25
	1990	1583	1790	264.5	55.2	—	21.8	14.4		
	Annual growth (%)	4.8	5.7	6.3	12.2		2.6	2.0		
Total, regions 1–3	1976	5410	5410	121	69	121	91.4	91.4		
	1990	9090	9370	270.6	275.2	169.5	120.5	120.5		
	Annual growth (%)	3.8	4.0	5.9	10.4	2.4	2.0	2.0		
1990 equilibrium prices, π_i/π_1[c]				1.00	1.83	0.70	19.2			

[a],[b],[c]See corresponding footnotes to Table B1.

TABLE B3   Case C: Low energy supplies[a].

Region i [b]		GNP		Export to region 1, nonenergy, x_{i1}	Exports to region 2, nonenergy, x_{i2}	Exports to region 3, nonenergy, x_{i3}	Energy consumption, x_{4i}	Domestic energy production available, d_i	1990 elasticity	
		Realized, y_i	Potential, x_{ii}						Trade	Energy
Region 1	1976	4240	4240	—	58	118	71.8	47.0	1.25	0.25
	1990	6529	6860	—	298.6	149	77.5	54		
	Annual growth (%)	3.1	3.5	—	12.4	1.7	0.5	1.0		
Region 2	1976	350	350	9	—	3	4.3	33.5	0.80	0.25
	1990	839	720	4.0	—	1.8	9.3	38.5		
	Annual growth (%)	6.4	5.3	-5.6	—	-3.6	5.7	1.0		
Region 3	1976	820	820	112	11	—	15.3	10.9	0.80	0.25
	1990	1501	1790	250.7	76.2	—	18.3	12.5		
	Annual growth (%)	4.4	5.7	5.9	14.8	—	1.3	1.0		
Total, regions 1–3	1976	5410	5410	121	69	121	91.4	91.4		
	1990	8869	9370	254.7	374.8	150.8	105.1	105.1		
	Annual growth (%)	3.6	4.0	5.5	12.8	1.6	1.0	1.0		
1990 equilibrium prices, π_j/π_1 [c]				1.00	2.59	0.68	31.8			

[a],[b],[c] See corresponding footnotes to Table B1.

TABLE B4　Case D: OECD oil import quotas[a].

Region i[b]	GNP Realized, y_i	GNP Potential, x_{ii}	Exports to region 1, nonenergy, x_{i1}	Exports to region 2, nonenergy, x_{i2}	Exports to region 3, nonenergy, x_{i3}	Energy consumption, x_{4i}	Domestic energy production available, d_i	1990 elasticity Trade	1990 elasticity Energy
Region 1									
1976	4240	4240	—	58	118	71.8	47.0		
1990	6796	6860	—	140.0	160.6	86.8	62.0	1.25	0.25
Annual growth (%)	3.4	3.5		6.5	2.2	1.4	2.0		
Region 2									
1976	350	350	9		3	4.3	33.5		
1990	724	720	10.8	—	3.6	8.7	44.1	0.80	0.25
Annual growth (%)	5.3	5.3	1.3		1.3	5.2	2.0		
Region 3									
1976	820	820	112	11	—	15.3	10.9		
1990	1603	1790	280.0	38.0	—	25.0	14.4	0.80	0.25
Annual growth (%)	4.9	5.7	6.8	9.3		3.6	2.0		
Total, regions 1–3									
1976	5410	5410	121	69	121	91.4	91.4		
1990	9123	9370	290.8	178.0	164.2	120.5	120.5		
Annual growth (%)	3.8	4.0	6.5	7.0	2.2	2.0	2.0		
1990 equilibrium prices π_j/π_1[c]			1.00	1.19	0.66	21.5 (OECD) 10.4 (OPEC)			

a,b,cSee corresponding footnotes to Table B1.

TABLE B5 Case E: Energy elasticities of 0.20[a].

Region i[b]		GNP		Exports to region 1, nonenergy, x_{i1}	Exports to region 2, nonenergy, x_{i2}	Exports to region 3, nonenergy, x_{i3}	Energy consumption, x_{4i}	Domestic energy production available, d_i	1990 elasticity	
		Realized, y_i	Potential, x_{ii}						Trade	Energy
Region 1	1976	4240	4240	—	58	118	71.8	47.0	1.25	0.20
	1990	6637	6860	—	279.3	156.7	89.1	62.0		
	Annual growth (%)	3.3	3.5		11.9	2.0	1.6	2.0		
Region 2	1976	350	350	9	—	3	4.3	33.5	0.80	0.20
	1990	831	720	4.5	—	2.0	9.7	44.1		
	Annual growth (%)	6.4	5.3	−4.8		−2.9	6.0	2.0		
Region 3	1976	820	820	112	11	—	15.3	10.9	0.80	0.20
	1990	1541	1790	261.1	71.9	—	21.7	14.4		
	Annual growth (%)	4.6	5.7	6.2	14.4		2.5	2.0		
Total, regions 1–3	1976	5410	5410	121	69	121	91.4	91.4		
	1990	9009	9370	265.6	351.2	158.7	120.5	120.5		
	Annual growth (%)	3.7	4.0	5.8	12.3	2.0	2.0	2.0		
1990 equilibrium prices, π_f/π_1[c]				1.00	2.39	0.69	24.6			

[a],[b],[c]See corresponding footnotes to Table B1.

TABLE B6   Case F: trade elasticities of 0.80[a].

Region i[b]		GNP		Exports to region 1, nonenergy, x_{i1}	Exports to region 2, nonenergy, x_{i2}	Exports to region 3, nonenergy, x_{i3}	Energy consumption, x_{4i}	Domestic energy production available, d_i	1990 elasticity	
		Realized, y_i	Potential, x_{ii}						Trade	Energy
Region 1	1976	4240	4240	—	58	118	71.8	47.0	0.80	0.25
	1990	6731	6860	—	219.6	148.9	90.4	62.0		
	Annual growth (%)	3.4	3.5	—	10.0	1.7	1.7	2.0		
Region 2	1976	350	350	9	—	3	4.3	33.5	0.80	0.25
	1990	792	720	8.6	—	2.3	9.2	44.1		
	Annual growth (%)	6.0	5.3	-0.3	—	-1.9	5.6	2.0		
Region 3	1976	820	820	112	11	—	15.3	10.9	0.80	0.25
	1990	1550	1790	254.7	60.7	—	20.9	14.4		
	Annual growth (%)	4.7	5.7	6.0	13.0	—	2.3	2.0		
Total, regions 1–3	1976	5410	5410	121	69	121	91.4	91.4		
	1990	9073	9370	263.3	280.3	151.2	120.5	120.5		
	Annual growth (%)	3.8	4.0	5.7	10.5	1.6	2.0	2.0		
1990 equilibrium prices, π_i/π_1[c]				1.00	1.83	0.62	18.2			

a,b,cSee corresponding footnotes to Table B1.

TABLE B7 Case G: trade elasticities of 1.5^a.

| Region i^b | | GNP | | Exports to region 1, nonenergy, x_{i1} | Exports to region 2, nonenergy, x_{i2} | Exports to region 3, nonenergy, x_{i3} | Energy consumption, x_{4i} | Domestic energy production available, d_i | 1990 elasticity | |
		Realized, y_i	Potential, x_{ii}						Trade	Energy
Region 1	1976	4240	4240	—	58	118	71.8	47.0	1.5	0.25
	1990	6681	6860	—	218.2	162.2	88.9	62.0		
	Annual growth (%)	3.3	3.5		9.9	2.3	1.5	2.0		
Region 2	1976	350	350	9	—	3	4.3	33.5	1.5	0.25
	1990	803	720	8.0	—	2.5	8.6	44.1		
	Annual growth (%)	6.1	5.3	−0.8		−1.3	5.1	2.0		
Region 3	1976	820	820	112	11	—	15.3	10.9	1.5	0.25
	1990	1652	1790	213.3	54.4	—	23.0	14.4		
	Annual growth (%)	5.1	5.7	4.7	12.1		3.0	2.0		
Total, regions 1–3	1976	5410	5410	121	69	121	91.4	91.4		
	1990	9136	9370	221.3	272.6	164.7	120.5	120.5		
	Annual growth (%)	3.8	4.0	4.4	10.3	2.2	2.0	2.0		
1990 equilibrium prices, π_j/π_1^c				1.0	1.39	0.83	19.3			

^{a,b,c} See corresponding footnotes to Table B1.

COMMENTS*

This paper is an elegant exercise in comparative statics in the context of North–South disparities. The mathematical model employed is of the general equilibrium type, investigating the effect of energy supplies on trade flows, GNP, and prices for tradables.

The model used splits the global economy into three regions (industrialized nations, oil-exporting LDCs, and oil-importing LDCs) which are linked via nonenergy and energy tradables. CES production functions with nonenergy and energy inputs determine regional nonenergy supply, which is used for domestic absorption or exports. Balance equations match both global energy consumption and supplies and regional balance of trade. Given regional energy supplies and capital and labor endowments (summarized in potential GNP estimates), equilibrium prices for both types of tradables and the corresponding realized GNP levels and trade flows are calculated.

The following remarks attempt to evaluate the numerical results of the various scenarios in the light of the assumptions that had to be introduced to make the model operational.

1. The specified production functions emphasize substitution among factor inputs but do not allow for changes in efficiency. Recent energy studies of all industrial countries indicate, however, the vast potential for increasing the efficiency of energy inputs, thus providing the same energy services with smaller energy flows.

2. Switching to more energy-efficient economies — a recommendation strongly supported by the theory of exhaustible resources — would require explicit modeling of the capital-stock adjustment process, distinguishing between investments which increase production capacity and investments which increase energy efficiency.

3. A comparative static analysis may not be justified at all if we allow for disequilibria and spillover effects between various markets in the adjustment process. These phenomena seem to be evident in the experience since the 1973 oil shock.

4. The problem of recycling the "petrodollars" indicates the importance of financial elements, especially in a global energy perspective. Since the oil producers seem to be unable to absorb domestically the financial wealth obtained from their oil exports, a global redistribution of property rights can be observed which, in the long run, will affect the implicit assumption in the model about unchanged factor distributions.

5. The challenge of the energy problem reveals serious gaps in the economic theory used to handle this issue. It seems necessary not only to integrate general equilibrium theory with the theory of exhaustible resources but also to fundamentally rethink the valuation of energy systems, observing the quality loss of available energy after every application as measured by an entropy increase. Research along these lines could provide better criteria to determine the allocation of capital between the use of exhaustible energy resources and improvements of energy efficiency to obtain the desired energy services.

---

*By Stefan Schleicher, Department of Economics, University of Graz, A-8010 Graz, Austria.

Part Four

Input—Output Models

GLOBAL INTERNATIONAL ECONOMIC MODELS
B.G. Hickman (editor)
Elsevier Science Publishers B.V. (North-Holland)
© IIASA, 1983

THE WORLD MODEL: AN INTERREGIONAL INPUT–OUTPUT MODEL OF THE WORLD ECONOMY

Faye Duchin

Institute for Economic Analysis, New York University, New York, NY 10003 (USA)

1   INTRODUCTION

The purpose of this paper is to describe the World Model, an interregional input–output model of the world economy developed under the direction of Professor Wassily Leontief that has been operational for about five years. It should be clear, but is nonetheless worth repeating, that the model is a first step and a research tool, not a finished polished product. The World Model involves a detailed representation of production technologies and changes in technologies in the various economies. While the methodology requires detailed factual information about the structural characteristics of all the sectors of a particular economy, the present data base contains a great many rough judgmental approximations. The model requires for its closure an explanation of individual consumption and savings behavior, corporate investment decisions, patterns in world trade, etc. Yet, at the present state of concrete understanding of these phenomena, only the simplest representations seem to be justified. No attempt is made within the model either to forecast population, the size of the labor force, and interest rates or exchange rates or to specify the undoubted feedback effects of variables within the model (e.g. changes in relative prices) on technology; these are represented instead in alternative scenarios. In short, many simplifying assumptions have been made at all stages of design, implementation, and application.

Yet only a model that can track the detailed flows of commodities throughout the world economy can address some of the most crucial issues of our times, such as the evaluation of alternatives for global resource management or international patterns of specialization, from the points of view both of international strategy and of national economic policy formation. Because of this conviction, work on the model continues.

A number of directions are currently being pursued to improve the World Model. These include special-purpose empirical studies which yield substantive results at the same time that the model as a tool is refined and systematic improvement of parts of the data base including efforts to replace the representation of individual economies with first-hand data.

2   THE STRUCTURE OF THE MODEL

The World Model was constructed to investigate the impact of prospective economic issues and policies on international development for the Second United Nations Development Decade. For this purpose the world was divided into 15 regional economies, each described in considerable detail, and the model was used to project eight alternative development paths that might be followed by each regional economy from the base year 1970 through 1980 and 1990 to 2000 (Leontief et al., 1977). At the Institute for Economic Analysis the model has since been used to investigate the impacts of population growth (Leontief, 1979a) and of the growth of maritime traffic (Leontief, 1979b), and in several studies of the worldwide implications of changes in military spending (Leontief et al., 1978; Leontief and Duchin, 1980a,b; 1982). For the last studies the model was expanded to represent explicitly the military sectors of the economy.

For each of the 15 geographical regions (identified in Appendix A, Table A1) and for each of four points in time (1970, 1980, 1990, and 2000) the economy of each region is represented by an input—output matrix describing the structure of production and consumption in terms of the use of labor, capital, raw materials, and intermediate and finished goods in that economy in that year.

The input—output tables of the different regions are interconnected by trade flows representing each region's imports and exports of commodities and capital. The tables of a given region from one decade to the next are interconnected through the accumulation of capital and the depletion of reserves of raw materials.

The basic structure of the World Model can perhaps be presented most clearly by first examining the properties of a model of a single economy in a given year. This economy will be described in terms of n productive sectors: the number n and the identity of the sectors actually used in empirical analysis will depend on a number of considerations including the particular issues to be addressed by the analysis and access to input—output tables and other, particularly engineering, data. In the year in question each of these sectors produces a certain amount of output and requires for its operation a particular combination of the outputs of the other sectors and of labor and the use of plant, equipment, and other capital goods. A technological relationship determines the particular mix of inputs and the quantity of each required per unit of output by each sector.

Within the economy, the total amounts of each type of good that are produced and used must be in balance. The output of each production sector will be entirely absorbed by the requirements of the other sectors (on both current and capital accounts), by private and public consumption, and by net exports to the rest of the world.

There is also an interdependence between the prices of sectoral outputs and the value added that is paid out by each sector per unit of its output. The price must be in balance with the cost of inputs plus value added.

The relationships just described involve the square n-order interindustry matrix of technical coefficients, A, and four n-order vectors, X, Y, P, and V, corresponding to levels of total output, final demand, prices, and values added, respectively; they can be described by the following two matrix equations (where I is the n-order identity matrix, and the prime ($'$) represents the matrix transpose).

$$(I - A)X = Y \tag{1a}$$

$$(I - A)'P = V \tag{2a}$$

The equations implied for the ith sector are

$$X_i - a_{i1}X_1 - \ldots - a_{ii}X_i - \ldots - a_{in}X_n = Y_i \qquad (i = 1, 2, \ldots, n) \tag{1b}$$

$$P_i - a_{1i}P_1 - \ldots - a_{ii}P_i - \ldots - a_{ni}P_n = V_i \qquad (i = 1, 2, \ldots, n) \tag{2b}$$

where a_{ij} (the entry in the ith row and jth column of A) measures the units of input from sector i required to produce one unit of output of sector j, X_i is the total output of the ith sector, Y_i is the final demand for the output of the ith sector, etc.

Typically the value-added row vector is separated into labor inputs and other components of value added, and the constituents of the final-demand column vector — which include investment, public and private consumption, and net exports — are represented separately. The resulting rectangular input—output matrix, which will be called M, can be partitioned as shown in eqn. (3) where the block F corresponds to value-added rows and C corresponds to final-demand columns:

$$M = \begin{bmatrix} I - A & -C \\ \hline -F & \end{bmatrix} \tag{3}$$

The right-hand sides of eqns. (1b) and (2b) can now be rewritten as

$$Y_i = c_{i1}Z_1 + \ldots + c_{ik}Z_k \qquad (i = 1, 2, \ldots, n) \tag{1c}$$

where Z_j is the level of activity of the jth category (out of k categories) of final demand, and

$$V_i = f_{1i}w_1 + \ldots + f_{li}w_l \qquad (i = 1, 2, \ldots, n) \tag{2c}$$

where f_{1i} is the labor coefficient for the ith sector, w_1 is the wage rate, f_{ji} is the level for the jth category (out of l categories) of other values added, and w_j is its unit cost. ("Other values added" include capital services and other payments already in value terms. The unit cost w_j is in this case equal to one.)

M contains the parameters of the system and can be viewed as a collection of columns or of rows. Each column represents the technology of a particular sector, and the corresponding row describes that sector's deliveries to other sectors and to final demand. A final-demand column describes the structure of the corresponding category of consumption and a value-added row shows the distribution of the corresponding factor to the productive sectors.

The variables of the system are the components of the vectors X, Y, P, and V ($4n$ in number) or, in the more typical case, X, Z, P, and W (for a total of $2n + k + l$) while there is a total of $2n$ physical plus price equations. A necessary condition to ensure a unique solution for the system is that the values of $k + l$ variables must be specified from outside the model. The selection of exogenous variables will depend in part on the availability of data and on the issues that are addressed in a particular analysis.

The final paragraphs of this section describe the conceptual extensions of the basic model of a single economy at one point in time to the World Model, which is a set of balance equations describing the interrelatedness of 15 regional economies at four points in time.

The one-region model developed earlier includes a single final-demand column (say the jth column in the matrix block C) describing the structure of net exports: c_{ij} is the proportion out of total net exports (measured in value units) of the output of sector i. The representation of trade is different in the World Model, which requires balance equations that ensure that one region's net exports correspond to other regions' net imports for each productive sector.

The World Model uses a separate "trade pool" to represent international flows of each category of goods and services (and capital). Each region's imports of a particular good are assumed to be equal to a given proportion, called the import coefficient, of the corresponding domestic production. (Import levels of raw materials, which are often non-competitive imports at World Model levels of disaggregation, must be specified for some regions.) The level of the trade pool is the sum of all regions' imports. Finally, export shares specify the proportion of each pool provided by each region. The 15 export shares for each pool naturally add up to one.

In the one-region one-period model described earlier the composition of investment goods, averaged over all using sectors, is described by a single investment column vector (in the C block of the matrix) while the total level of expenditure for capital services of each using sector per unit of sector output appears in a value-added row. In the four-decade World Model the simplifying assumption is made that all capital goods required during a given decade can be produced during the decade. Capital coefficients for each of five types of capital and for each sector of the economy specify capital stock requirements per unit of sector output.

Investment levels in a given year cover expansion and replacement capital. In the World Model the replacement rate is specific to each capital good while the growth rate is the actual rate of growth of the capital stock computed over the preceding decade. Investment levels for, say, 1990 are determined endogenously as a linearized function of the capital stock required in 1990 and the stock existing in 1980.

The emissions of eight different pollutants and the operation of five pollution-abatement activities are represented in the World Model. The input structure (column vector) corresponding to each production sector includes parameters describing tons of gross emissions of each pollutant per unit of sectoral output (in complete analogy to the representation of its input requirements). The columns describing the abatement activities include three sets of coefficients: one describes input requirements on current and capital accounts per ton of pollutant abated; the other two describe the total amount of emissions treated and the nonabatable residual, both per unit abated. The amount of pollutant subject to abatement is treated as a variable.

3   ENUMERATION OF EQUATIONS AND VARIABLES

The classification and counting of the equations and variables in a large model is indispensable as an organizing device for the users of the model and facilitates comparisons

TABLE 1 Classification and enumeration of the equations (rows) and variables (columns) in a regional model of the World Model.

Type	Equations	Variables
Production	54	55
Historic and cumulative production	9	27
Trade	97	108
Capital	16	24
Pollution	21	26
Consumption and population	6	10
Identities	4	4
Total	207	254

among models. Table 1 identifies the equations and variables of the World Model: there are over 200 equations and over 250 variables for each of 15 regions at each of four points in time. The table indicates that the typical matrix **M** is partitioned on roughly the following scale:

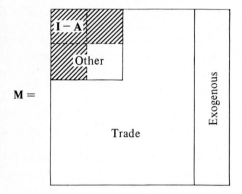

$$\mathbf{M} =$$

The density of the matrix **M** (the proportion of nonzero elements) is very uneven; in particular the numerous rows and columns describing world trade are very sparse*. The densest block of the matrix is the square interindustry portion $\mathbf{I} - \mathbf{A}$. There are also many nonzeros in the extension of the interindustry columns showing the use of other inputs in the production process, and in the extension of the interindustry rows showing the use of goods and services in final demand and other sectors. (These are the hatched areas of the diagram.) The production sectors, i.e. the production technologies, are the core of the World Model.

---

*The computer programs used to solve the entire World Model system repeatedly for different scenarios have been designed to exploit both the block structure and the zero—nonzero structure of the matrices (Duchin and Szyld, 1979).

4   DATA

The World Model requires a great deal of information to describe each regional economy in each year: over 200 balance equations in over 250 variables involving over 3000
(nonzero) parameters and 50 exogenous variables. The estimation of these parameters
and variables is subject to three constraints: input structures represented by column vectors must be technologically sound; output (supply) and consumption (demand) must be
in balance within a sector, an economy, and the world economy as a whole; and prices
must cover costs plus value added.

Assembly of the World Model data base was begun in the early 1970s. 1970 was
selected as the base year for which historical data were collected; constant 1970 US dollars are the unit for all quantities expressed in value terms (the exception is the balance
of payments which is measured in current-year US dollars). At that time official input—
output tables were published at varying time intervals for about 50 countries. However,
even though a very significant amount of effort was expended to compile the World
Model data base, the full use of national input—output tables in a world model is an
even more ambitious project which remains to be implemented. The World Model serves
as a framework for efforts like that now underway at the University of Venice to incorporate an interregional model of the Italian economy based on direct survey data as a
separate region of the World Model. New national models will be required to match World
Model sectors for traded goods only.

The principal data sources for the World Model data base were the official input—
output table of the 1967 US economy published by the Bureau of Economic Analysis
(BEA), ten other national input—output tables including those (for one or more years)
for Colombia, France, Hungary, India, Italy, Japan, and the Federal Republic of Germany,
and aggregate control totals for all regions generally obtained from United Nations accounting data. In addition a number of special studies were carried out by researchers
or consultants to the project to gather and organize existing information on particular
subjects.

Control totals include, for example, national commodity-consumption figures for
1970 which are generally available and can be aggregated to World Model regions. These
figures are not directly incorporated in the World Model. Instead entries in the row
corresponding to each sectoral output – say, copper – specify the amount of copper
absorbed by each using sector per unit of the using sector's output on the basis of assumptions about the using sector's technology. It is these coefficients that determine consumption levels. Once these have been estimated, a preliminary World Model solution is obtained
for each region. A region's total production plus imports minus exports of copper shown
in this solution for 1970 must be approximately equal to the control total for consumption. Discrepancies during the stage of model development require that one or more
row coefficients be adjusted.

For each block of data (e.g. the interindustry portion of the regional matrix **M**)
the usual procedure was first to establish a reference matrix for 1970 for North America
based on the 1967 BEA table for the United States. Adjustment factors were then estimated to convert the reference matrix into coefficient matrices for the other 14 regions
of the world in 1970. This was typically done by regressing specific coefficients and

groups of coefficients on GDP per capita using data from the other input—output tables (adjusted for classification scheme, international differences in relative prices, and some accounting conventions). Projections of coefficients to 1980, 1990, and 2000 were based both on anticipated rates of increase of regional GDP per capita and on anticipated world-wide changes in technology. Eleven volumes of unpublished documentation describe the assembly of this data base and are drawn on for the discussion in this section (Petri et al., 1974—1979). In subsequent work mentioned earlier, historical data from the late 1970s were used to update estimates of population and employment and to represent specifi-cally the production, use, and trade of 11 categories of military goods and services.

In all cases, additional information was incorporated where available and, overall, a great deal of subjective judgment was exercised. Independent aggregate control totals for 1970 and the balance constraints of the system imposed discipline on the procedure.

Two special studies by outside consultants were concerned with forecasting techno-logical change over the model horizon in terms of anticipated substitution of materials, production processes, and products in World Model sectors.

Two other special studies considered the extraction and use of minerals. For each mineral, data were collected on the grade of ore being mined over time and in different countries, and the cost of extraction was assumed to be inversely proportional to the metal content of the ore (British-thermal-unit (Btu) content in the case of coal; petroleum and natural-gas cost structures were estimated using other procedures). On the basis of this information region-specific input coefficients were estimated for 1970. 1970 coeffi-cients were projected to future years using step multipliers based on projected levels of exhaustion of the richer layers of reserves in each region.

Metal and energy consumption coefficients were estimated on a region-specific basis to take account of different usage patterns associated with differences in regional per capita income and in regional endowments.

The composition of personal consumption was assumed to be region specific only with regard to the use of agricultural products and to be related to per capita income otherwise.

5   USE OF THE MODEL

While the World Model data base is itself a significant resource, the principal use of the model lies of course in the possibility it affords for carrying out experiments, or computing scenarios, where each experiment (or scenario) describes one possible path that could be followed by the world economy from the year 1970 to the year 2000. The approach taken at the Institute for Economic Analysis has been to revise portions of the model and to expand and improve the data base in the process of using the model to analyze specific issues. This has been done in two recent studies of the worldwide economic implications of changes in military spending and in another, nearing completion, on the future production and consumption of nonfuel minerals.

The future of the world economy obviously cannot be summarized in a handful of numbers. Full outcomes for several scenarios showing all variables, all regions, and all years are generally included in empirical publications involving the World Model. However, the outcome for even a single scenario exceeds the number of pages to which this paper must be limited. A compromise solution has been to include as Appendix B the detailed outcome for the baseline scenario (called Base) which has been aggregated (after solution) from 15 regions to the world as a whole*. (Appendix A includes a description of the regions in the model and of units appearing in Appendix B.) To help in interpreting this scenario, those variables which are exogenous in the Base scenario are indicated in Table 2.

TABLE 2   Exogenous variables in the Base scenario.

Region[a]	Variables
All	Historic (i.e. lagged) levels of capital stock and resources
	Levels of pollution abatement
	Fish catch
	Population
Some	Levels of output or trade for particular resources
Developed countries	Employment
Less developed resource-poor countries	Balance of payments (set equal to zero)
Southern Africa	GDP
Oil-rich Middle East	Consumption
Centrally planned Asia	Investment
Resource-rich Latin America	Balance of payments

[a]The regions are described in Appendix A, Table A1.

Since projections about the future and the assumptions on which they are based are fundamentally unverifiable until after the fact, an important use of the model lies in the comparison of alternative projections incorporating alternative assumptions but made within a common framework that permits comparisons. The promise of this approach can be indicated by a brief summary of the more important results of a comparison of the baseline scenario and three disarmament scenarios (Leontief and Duchin, 1980b). Some of the baseline scenario results can be seen in Appendix B while others are lost due to the aggregation.

According to the baseline scenario, worldwide military purchases can be expected to increase very substantially between 1980 and the end of the century, as can be seen in the aggregate outcome in Appendix B, especially for the oil-rich Middle East and for Japan. Even under the "disarmament" scenarios the real level of military spending continues to grow, although less steeply. (In the disarmament scenarios it is assumed that the proportion of GDP devoted to military spending is reduced relative to the Base scenario by 25% in 1990 and 40% in 2000. For North America and the Soviet Union parity of spending is maintained for these years but at two-thirds of the baseline level.)

The rate of growth of real per capita consumption between 1970 and 2000 varies considerably over the 15 regions in the baseline scenario and for Arid Africa and Medium-

---

*A complete baseline solution with detail for all 15 regions is available on microfiche on request from the Publications Department, IIASA, A-2361 Laxenburg, Austria.

Income Latin America it actually falls. With disarmament, per capita consumption improves in all regions relative to the baseline, but most in Arid Africa (the region including Egypt and Israel) and next most in the Soviet Union and Eastern Europe.

In two scenarios disarmament is assumed to be accompanied by a transfer of part of the savings (relative to the baseline scenario) of rich regions to four poor ones (Arid Africa, Tropical Africa, Low-Income Asia, and Medium-Income Latin America). This results in a significant improvement in per capita consumption in the four recipient regions (receiving between them a total of some 55 billion 1970 US dollars in 2000), but these regions show the lowest per capita consumption in the world both before and even after receiving this aid. Each billion dollars of aid has the largest positive impact on GDP and total consumption in Arid Africa and the smallest in Tropical Africa. On a per capita basis the impact is also greatest in Arid Africa but very slight indeed for Low-Income Asia (which includes India).

Most production and virtually all export of military goods takes place in four of the developed regions of the world (as can be seen in the aggregate in Appendix B). In some scenarios import dependence for military goods is reduced (by lowering the corresponding import coefficients). The direct impact is of course to stimulate domestic production in current client regions and to reduce the output of current suppliers. Overall, many economies of both types appear to benefit from this reduction in worldwide military trade (both at high and at low levels of military spending).

REFERENCES

Duchin, F. and Szyld, D. (1979). Application of sparse matrix techniques to inter-regional input—output analysis. Series 1, Preprint 1. Institute for Economic Analysis, New York University, New York.

Leontief, W. (1979a). Population growth and the future of the world economy. In Economic and Demographic Change: Issues for the 1980s. Proceedings of the 1978 Helsinki Conference. International Union for the Scientific Study of Population, Liège, Belgium, pp. 183—211.

Leontief, W. (1979b). The future of world ports. Ports and Harbors, September. (Reprinted as "The growth of maritime traffic and the future of world ports" in International Journal of Transport Economics, VI(3).)

Leontief, W., Carter, A.P., and Petri, P. (1977). The Future of the World Economy. Oxford University Press, New York.

Leontief, W. and Duchin, F. (1980a). Worldwide implications of hypothetical changes in military spending (an input—output approach). Draft Final Report for the US Arms Control and Disarmament Agency.

Leontief, W. and Duchin, F. (1980b). Worldwide economic implications of a limitation on military spending. Report prepared for the United Nations Center for Disarmament.

Leontief, W. and Duchin, F. (1982). Military Spending: An Examination of the Worldwide Economic Implications of Some Policy Alternatives for the Future. Oxford University Press, New York.

Leontief, W., Dresch, S., Duchin, F., Fischer, D., and Sohn, I. (1978). Preliminary study of worldwide economic and social implications of a limitation on military spending (an input—output approach). Report to the United Nations Center for Disarmament. Department of Economics, New York University, New York.

Petri, P., et al. (1974—1979). United Nations World Model Data Documentation (4 Technical Reports and 11 volumes of documentation), Brandeis University, unpublished.

APPENDIX A: THE WORLD MODEL REGIONS AND UNITS USED IN APPENDIX B

TABLE A1   Regional groupings in the World Model.

Code	Grouping	Region
DC	Developed countries	Eastern Europe (EEM)
		Japan (JAP)
		North America (NAH)
		Oceania (OCH)
		USSR (RUH)
		Southern Africa (SAF)
		Western Europe, high income (WEH)
		Western Europe, medium income (WEM)
LDC I	Less developed countries, resource rich	Latin America, resource rich (LAL)
		Middle East and Africa, oil rich (OIL)
		Tropical Africa (TAF)
LDC II	Less developed countries, resource poor	Arid Africa (AAF)
		Asia, centrally planned (ASC)
		Asia, low income (ASL)
		Latin America, medium income (LAM)

TABLE A2   World Model units.

Unit[a]	Description
Mt	Millions (10^6) of metric tons
Mt(ce)	Millions of metric tons, coal (Btu) equivalent
kt	Thousands of metric tons
B$	Billions (10^9) of 1970 US dollars; current dollars for balance of payments
MMY	Millions of person-years
Mha	Millions of hectares
g	Grams
M	millions

[a]These unit abbreviations appear in Appendix B.

APPENDIX B: THE BASE SCENARIO WITH MILITARY VARIABLES AGGREGATED TO THE WHOLE WORLD

TABLE B1   Consumption and population, investment and capital, international transactions, and level of abatement activities.

Variable	Unit	1970	1980	1990	2000
Consumption and population					
GDP	B$	3,220.8	4,873.0	7,454.7	10,389.3
Personal consumption	B$	2,128.1	3.216.5	4,796.2	6,711.7
Government (civilian)	B$	322.1	487.3	745.5	1,038.9
Government (military)	B$	214.6	291.3	452.8	646.0
Population	M	3,620.4	4,370.5	5,276.3	6,248.5
Urban population	M	1,322.7	1,824.3	2,446.0	3,233.7
Employment	MMY	711.0	880.8	1,123.9	1,365.6
GDP per head	$	889.6	1,115.0	1,412.9	1,662.7
Consumption per head	$	587.8	736.0	909.0	1,074.1
Calories per day per head		2,391.0	2,400.7	2,427.8	2,490.1
Proteins per day per head	g	67.0	68.5	70.8	74.1
Investment and capital					
Investment	B$	508.1	828.9	1,388.6	1,902.0
Equipment	B$	229.2	321.4	536.4	727.6
Plant	B$	274.1	504.4	848.0	1,170.2
Irrigation (area)	Mha	3.4	2.1	3.1	3.1
Land (area)	Mha	11.6	8.0	9.6	9.6
Inventory change	B$	40.2	38.9	61.6	78.6
Capital stock	B$	5,777.3	9.506.1	15,792.2	24,291.4
Equipment	B$	2,020.5	3,061.2	4,896.9	7,225.4
Plant	B$	3,756.8	6,444.9	10,895.2	17,066.0
Inventory stock	B$	723.5	1,033.7	1,510.3	2,137.0
Surplus savings	B$	13.8	30.5	−27.3	15.1
International transactions					
Imports	B$	352	578	1,025	1,577
Exports	B$	351	577	1,023	1,575
Payments surplus	B$	−1	−6	−0	7
Foreign investments	B$	0	−31	−33	0
Foreign income	B$	0	−3	−3	0
Level of abatement activities					
Air	Mt	54.28	96.89	117.77	153.85
Primary water	Mt	11.02	21.82	36.31	48.60
Secondary water	Mt	0.65	1.24	3.24	4.41
Tertiary water	Mt	0.13	0.55	0.71	0.96
Solid waste	Mt	534.94	902.06	1,208.55	1,977.21

TABLE B2   Net total emissions, resource outputs, and cumulative resource output at end of period.

Variable	Unit	1970	1980	1990	2000
Net total emissions					
Pesticides	Mt	2.6	5.5	13.8	15.9
Particulates	Mt	14.8	12.8	23.7	17.9
Biological oxygen	Mt	30.9	38.1	49.9	63.6
Nitrogen (water)	Mt	0.7	0.9	1.4	1.7
Phosphates	Mt	0.4	0.6	0.8	1.0
Suspended solids	Mt	18.6	21.3	26.6	32.9
Dissolved solids	Mt	129.2	180.3	261.6	339.5
Solid waste	Mt	312.4	353.4	653.0	727.5
Resource outputs					
Copper	Mt	6.4	9.4	16.0	22.0
Bauxite	Mt	11.4	16.8	26.9	35.8
Nickel	kt	668.0	975.5	1,570.8	1,998.8
Zinc	Mt	5.4	7.5	12.0	16.7
Lead	Mt	3.5	5.3	9.2	13.6
Iron	Mt	424.7	650.5	1,047.2	1,475.6
Petroleum	Mt(ce)	3,003.7	5,571.1	10,049.4	14,757.4
Natural gas	Mt(ce)	1,426.8	2,410.7	4,304.2	5,556.4
Coal	Mt(ce)	2,165.3	3,236.6	4,926.9	7,712.9
Cumulative resource output at end of period					
Copper	Mt	0	79	206	396
Bauxite	Mt	0	141	360	674
Nickel	kt	0	8,218	20,949	38,797
Zinc	Mt	0	64	162	305
Lead	Mt	0	44	117	231
Iron	Mt	0	5,376	12,150	24,764
Petroleum	Mt(ce)	0	42,874	112,955	236,989
Natural gas	Mt(ce)	0	19,187	52,707	102,011
Coal	Mt(ce)	0	27,009	67,827	131,026

TABLE B3 Output levels and military output levels.

Variable	Unit	1970	1980	1990	2000
Output levels					
Animal products	Mt	210.4	277.2	368.7	480.6
High-protein crops	Mt	137.5	182.0	254.7	347.9
Grains	Mt	1,221.1	1,525.9	2,128.3	2,871.6
Roots	Mt	462.6	550.1	714.6	901.2
Other agriculture	B$	209.1	258.9	299.2	438.4
Other resources	B$	15.7	25.6	42.8	61.8
Food processing	B$	174.1	302.2	425.1	581.5
Petroleum refining	B$	45.7	70.5	117.9	167.7
Primary metals	B$	104.4	172.0	296.7	434.0
Textiles, apparel	B$	183.6	260.1	350.0	514.3
Wood and cork	B$	42.4	64.5	92.2	121.5
Furniture, fixtures	B$	84.1	116.1	107.9	161.7
Paper	B$	53.9	87.8	143.6	205.5
Printing	B$	53.7	92.1	162.9	243.4
Rubber	B$	35.8	60.2	106.7	157.1
Industrial chemicals	B$	76.3	114.8	178.4	266.9
Fertilizers	Mt	67.6	106.9	172.2	234.3
Other chemicals	B$	60.2	93.6	154.4	215.3
Cement	B$	5.6	9.8	17.3	26.5
Glass	B$	53.3	91.2	154.7	226.3
Motor vehicles	B$	96.8	157.8	288.8	418.7
Aircraft	B$	34.7	51.4	90.1	128.1
Shipbuilding	B$	20.2	29.2	45.2	66.9
Metal products	B$	132.8	218.1	381.2	547.9
Machinery	B$	162.7	233.9	384.4	554.3
Electrical machinery	B$	105.6	166.4	289.6	416.2
Instruments	B$	26.4	39.5	66.6	94.2
Other manufactures	B$	40.7	60.5	89.7	133.3
Utilities	B$	77.6	149.2	282.8	399.8
Construction	B$	367.2	645.5	1,083.8	1,537.0
Trade	B$	571.4	906.4	1,448.0	2,026.1
Transportation	B$	187.2	281.9	416.6	591.1
Communications	B$	59.1	93.8	166.1	233.7
Services	B$	829.0	1,354.9	2,362.6	3,535.6
Military output levels					
Aircraft	B$	30.276	43.057	66.121	94.021
Ships	B$	7.434	10.684	16.084	22.084
Electronics equipment	B$	15.008	20.561	31.658	44.696
New construction	B$	5.446	7.982	12.077	18.079
Maintenance	B$	3.982	5.836	8.831	13.219
Missiles	B$	11.236	15.173	23.025	31.273
Ammunition, n.e.c.[a]	B$	4.336	5.992	9.227	13.055
Tanks	B$	5.829	9.575	14.323	21.486
Small arms	B$	0.300	0.429	0.667	0.936
Small arms ammunition	B$	0.695	0.968	1.498	2.109
Other ordnance	B$	1.498	2.071	3.196	4.509
Total output	B$	86.040	112.329	186.706	265.466

[a]Not elsewhere classified.

TABLE B4   Fish, exports, and military exports.

Variable	Unit	1970	1980	1990	2000
Fish					
Fish catch	Mt	66.0	66.0	66.0	66.0
Nonhuman use	Mt	22.0	22.0	22.0	22.0
Fish imports	Mt	4.0	4.0	4.0	4.0
Fish exports	Mt	4.1	4.1	4.1	4.1
Exports					
Livestock	Mt	10.0	12.7	16.7	20.5
High-protein crops	Mt	25.7	34.0	48.1	61.5
Grains	Mt	104.8	126.9	184.0	242.1
Roots	Mt	13.4	15.3	19.1	22.6
Other agriculture	B$	28.0	31.2	36.1	50.3
Food processing	B$	13.4	16.1	21.0	29.1
Textiles, apparel	B$	24.0	51.8	106.1	204.7
Wood and cork	B$	4.8	9.2	16.9	26.9
Furniture, fixtures	B$	1.5	2.6	2.9	4.1
Paper	B$	8.5	18.0	38.8	69.1
Printing	B$	1.8	4.2	9.8	17.9
Rubber	B$	2.1	4.1	9.1	18.1
Industrial chemicals	B$	15.1	24.6	42.9	67.1
Fertilizers	Mt	6.7	11.8	23.8	29.4
Other chemicals	B$	6.9	14.2	29.3	52.1
Cement	B$	0.3	0.6	1.5	3.9
Glass	B$	3.8	8.8	19.9	36.9
Motor vehicles	B$	27.1	43.2	82.8	144.5
Shipbuilding	B$	4.6	6.4	10.5	15.5
Aircraft	B$	6.1	9.6	18.5	26.4
Metal products	B$	6.8	11.2	18.1	24.4
Machinery	B$	36.2	64.0	112.6	171.1
Electrical machinery	B$	16.7	33.8	67.6	125.2
Instruments	B$	6.2	11.1	21.3	33.5
Other manufactures	B$	8.8	14.1	22.7	33.2
Services	B$	19.8	28.3	42.1	55.7
Transportation	B$	27.1	42.3	71.0	103.5
Aid inflow	B$	27.0	41.3	65.4	96.9
Capital inflow	B$	26.5	49.5	88.3	132.6
Military exports					
Aircraft	B$	2.558	5.743	8.732	15.616
Ships	B$	0.266	0.804	1.275	2.231
Electronics equipment	B$	1.098	2.469	3.761	6.799
Missiles	B$	0.600	1.188	1.841	3.185
Ammunition, n.e.c.[a]	B$	0.317	0.700	1.066	1.912
Tanks	B$	0.845	2.111	3.167	5.985
Small arms	B$	0.020	0.044	0.068	0.119
Small arms ammunition	B$	0.052	0.120	0.184	0.332
Other ordnance	B$	0.110	0.250	0.382	0.688
Total exports	B$	5.867	13.428	20.476	36.868
Military grants inflow	B$	2.197	0.313	0.479	0.654

[a]Not elsewhere classified.

COMMENTS*

This paper summarizes the basic structure of the interregional input—output model developed by Leontief, Carter, and Petri (1977). While the purpose of the paper is mainly expository, the final section gives some indication of recent applications of the model to the effects of shifting resources from military expenditure to foreign assistance programs under alternative assumptions. These effects are illustrated by reference to a new "Baseline Scenario."

The Leontief World Model (LWM) takes several extreme methodological positions in comparison to other attempts at long-term world modeling. Since this is a relatively new field, there has been little methodological discussion of the appropriateness of different types of assumption for the analysis of different policy questions. I will comment briefly on some of these issues and then turn to the Leontief World Model itself.

Model Design

For a given analytical and empirical effort, a global analyst can choose to elaborate his model in one or more directions:

(1) By adding to the number of economic units (regions or countries) considered;
(2) By increasing the number of economic activities or sectors included;
(3) By refining the specification of each relationship — for example, by introducing both supply and demand conditions and prices.

The Leontief input—output approach to world modeling puts its main efforts into disaggregating by sector (54) and by region (15). Conversely, there is relatively little modeling of aggregate relations, such as the effects of exchange rates on imports or exports.

Another significant methodological choice is between the use of regions or countries as the basic units of analysis. The regional or "top-down" approach provides a complete accounting for world production and trade in specified commodities. Conversely, a country-based or "bottom-up" approach would lay much greater stress on modeling individual countries, treating the rest of the world in a more aggregated way. The Leontief World Model — and most world trade models — provide illustrations of the first approach, while the Link model and its derivatives are examples of the second.

These two aspects of model design — the choice of geographical units and the form of disaggregation and analytical emphasis within each unit — determine the appropriateness of each type of model for different applications.

Strengths and Limitations of the Leontief World Model

The strength of the input—output approach is its differentiation of individual sectors or industries, which allows for changes in the composition of demand and illustrates the

---

*By H.B. Chenery, Vice-President for Development Policy, World Bank, Washington, D.C., USA.

consequences of these changes for trade and investment. However, the linkages among regions are specified in a rather primitive form of fixed import coefficients and export shares, so that the projections of trade flows and growth tend to be unrealistic.

There are two serious flaws in the present version of the LWM for policy analysis:

(1) The "regions" do not correspond to political units (except for the USSR and Japan), and hence the policy implications of different scenarios are hard to evaluate.

(2) There are no endogenous behavioral relations to constrain the choice of exogenous variables. The specification of the exogenous elements (savings and investment rates, trade policies, etc.) therefore becomes as important as the analysis incorporated in the model.

Given these characteristics, the LWM should be useful for analyzing the effects of resource limitations in agriculture, minerals or energy or of technological changes in the coefficients that reflect their use. Conversely, the model is less useful for the analysis of problems where the policy choices of individual countries are crucial, as in the case of trade and development strategies.

On these grounds, I doubt that the use of the LWM adds much to the analysis of international assistance and capital flows, whether generated by disarmament or other sources. The policy assumptions used in making these projections — both in the original study by Leontief, Carter, and Petri (1977) and in the present paper — do not seem to be derived from any consideration of likely LDC reactions to the changes specified; and some of the results seem rather farfetched.

More generally, I would suggest that greater attention should be given to the selection of models for given problems, and vice versa.

GLOBAL INTERNATIONAL ECONOMIC MODELS
B.G. Hickman (editor)
Elsevier Science Publishers B.V. (North-Holland)
© IIASA, 1983

LINKED INPUT–OUTPUT MODELS FOR FRANCE, THE FEDERAL REPUBLIC OF GERMANY, AND BELGIUM

Douglas E. Nyhus and Clopper Almon
Department of Economics, University of Maryland, College Park, Maryland 20742 (USA)

In the course of the last two years there has been rapid development of an international consortium of input–output models and their builders. The consortium now includes models or model-building groups for the United Kingdom, Portugal, France, Belgium, the Netherlands, the Federal Republic of Germany (FRG), Norway, Sweden, Finland, Austria, Hungary, Bulgaria, India, South Korea, Japan, Canada, and the United States. All these countries except the Netherlands, Canada, and Japan are presently represented by one or more active groups. In addition, there are strong signs of interest in Mexico and Italy.

The models are built with a package of programs designed to take the drudgery out of input–output modeling. The programs provide for behavioral equations for household consumption, exports, imports, investment, inventory changes, input–output coefficient changes, and the determination of wages, profits, and prices. From an initial input–output table a model can be made in an hour or so. The model built will have very flexible easy-to-use facilities for imposing scenarios, making pretty tables, and drawing graphs. However, its behavioral equations will be totally naive. This is where the national partner groups come in. They develop the behavioral equations, and much originality, ingenuity, and judgment is hoped for from them. The programs impose no constraints on the behavioral functions, save those inherent in the accounting system.

One of the principal attractions of this family of models to groups interested in building models of their own countries has been the possibility of linking the models through international trade. In many of the countries modeled, exports are a major source of income. For these countries it makes little sense to develop an elaborate model of the domestic economy and then to take exports as exogenous. Within the consortium this linking is facilitated by the fact that all the models are built on the same "skeleton" program "fleshed out" by the national model builders. The common skeleton means that all the models have not only essentially the same operating manual — so that one person can operate them all — but also the same format for their output files. Both these features simplify the task of linking.

Most of the resources available at the International Institute for Applied Systems Analysis (IIASA) over the last two years for work on this project have been used in helping national partners to get started. The linking will be largely carried out by Economics Research International, a nonprofit Belgian institution organized for the purpose of furthering this cooperation. The shortcut linking that is reported in the present paper, however, has been done at IIASA. The full linking task remains a major challenge.

A linking mechanism has long been planned, and equations for it were estimated several years ago (Nyhus, 1975). This mechanism involves considerable sensitivity to prices, both in determining the share of imports in the total domestic use of a product by a nation and in determining the share of each source country in the nation's imports. A full bilateral trade-flow model was envisaged for each commodity. The problem with this approach arises from the fact that the price forecasts are usually developed only after the "real" constant-price part of the model has been working for some time. However, export projections are needed from the very outset. We have therefore sought a shortcut method in which prices are not used. Instead, the exports of a particular product by one country in real terms are related directly to the domestic consumption of that product in other countries. In this paper we report on the first efforts to use this shortcut method.

The full-blown linking mechanism will work in two steps. In the first step exports (by commodity) of one country will be related to imports (by commodity) of its customer countries. In the second step imports of a commodity by a country will be related to that country's use of the commodity and to relative foreign and domestic prices for that commodity. There is a full description of the linking mechanism in Nyhus (1975) and a description of the operation of the whole linked system in Nyhus (1980).

In the shortcut link, to be used where forecast prices are not available, we have omitted the first step and half of the second and have related the exports of one country directly to the domestic demands for the product in the customer countries. Imports are still related to domestic demands and relative international prices but now the distinction between imports and domestic production in domestic demand is not used in forecasting the exports of other countries. More precisely, we estimate the equation

$$X(t) = [a + b \sum_k w_k D_k(t)/D_k(0)] (d/f)^n \tag{1}$$

where X is one country's exports of a particular commodity, w_k is the fraction of these exports which went to country k in the base year, D_k is the domestic demand for the product in country k, f and d are moving averages of foreign and domestic prices, respectively, and n is the price elasticity. Domestic demand is defined statistically as domestic output plus imports minus exports. In the foreign price index f, foreign domestic prices of the customer countries are combined with weights proportional to the share of each country in the exports of the given country. Of course not all countries are covered in these indexes but we have indexes for the major countries with industrial market economies. By taking moving averages of prices we allow for delay in the response of exports to change in relative prices. The estimation of the weights in these moving averages is taken from Nyhus (1975). Since products seldom have the same definition in the input—output tables of different countries, the D_k do not in fact match X perfectly in definition. In some cases several sectors in a customer country will be combined to give a single D_k; in other cases the domestic demand in a single input—output sector in the buying country has to serve as the D_k for several sectors in the table for the exporting country.

In fact we estimated eqn. (1) using production in country k in place of D_k simply because at the time we did not have the consistent series on output, exports, and imports necessary to create the domestic-demand series. When we obtain the necessary data on more countries we will reestimate eqn. (1) with domestic-demand data. Further, for the forecasts we made projections of the historical d/f ratio by extrapolating past trends.

One might think — as we once thought — that if eqn. (1) has been estimated with gross outputs in place of D then it should also be simulated with gross outputs in place of D. However, this procedure leads to error magnification. Suppose that from an equilibrium position we add a positive "error" or "perturbation" to French automobile exports. Then French automobile production will increase. Automobile exports from the FRG, since they are affected by French production, will also rise. French exports, affected by FRG production, will then rise further. Such positive feedback is obviously undesirable in a linked system. When we use domestic demand this particular positive feedback (or error magnification) does not occur. We have therefore used indexes of domestic demand for linking the models. (Because D_k enters eqn. (1) in index form, the units do not change when we change from production to domestic demand.)

The results of fitting eqn. (1) have been described in Lee (1978) for France and in Almon and Nyhus (1977) for Belgium. Tables 1–3 show the relevant demand and price elasticities of the estimated export equations.

The three models that have been linked so far are those for France, the FRG, and Belgium. They have 78, 49, and 51 sectors respectively. The D_k values for other countries in eqn. (1) are exogenous and remain fixed in the experiment described below.

In order to observe the linking mechanism at work we needed a base case and a variation. The base case was a fairly conservative estimate of potential growth. The annual growth rates of gross national product (or some similar measure) between 1980 and 1987 were as follows: France, 2.6%; Belgium, 2.2%; the FRG, 2.2%. The growth rates of exports from individual industries are shown in Tables 4–8 in the column labeled "base". The variation was to add 1% per year to the growth rate of French expenditure on personal consumption throughout the period 1980–1987. This is clearly a fairly large variation. First the French model was run with this variation and then the FRG and Belgian models were run to observe their reaction to the French good fortune. The overall growth rate of exports from the FRG increased from 1.74% per year to 1.85% per year while Belgian exports accelerated from 2.40% per year to 2.64% per year. These are growth rates for all exports, not just exports to France. Table 4 shows in the columns labeled "1st" and "Full" the impacts of this variation on individual industries in the FRG. The greatest impact is in consumer goods despite the fact that the French model includes investment functions which translate the accelerated growth of output into demands for capital goods. The columns labeled "2–1" and "3–1" show the changes in the rates of growth for the exports of various industries. For the FRG the largest changes are for clothing (sector 30) (0.48% per year), textiles (29) (0.34% per year), and meat (33) (0.30% per year).

The first-round effects do not include any effects of the French prosperity on the simulation of other economies. As a second round we reran the French model with the higher output levels in the FRG and Belgium. We did not allow any Keynesian multiplier however. Because the Belgian and FRG models were already considered to be running at or near the potential of the corresponding economies, we assumed in effect that the income

TABLE 1   Elasticities of French export equations.

Sector	Demand elasticity	Price elasticity
1 Agriculture and forestry	1.94	−0.50
2 Fish and fish products	0.55	−0.50
3 Meat	0.58	−0.50
4 Cereal products	1.69	−0.50
5 Dairy products	1.76	−0.50
6 Sugar	1.44	−0.50
7 Animal feed	2.13	−0.50
8 Miscellaneous food products	1.67	−0.50
9 Beverages	1.70	−1.00
10 Fats and oils	1.31	−1.00
11 Tobacco and matches	2.36	−1.00
14 Coking	1.66	−0.50
16 Electricity	1.66	−0.50
18 Crude oil	1.44	−0.50
19 Natural gas	2.04	−0.50
20 Refined oil	0.66	−1.00
21 Building materials	4.78	−2.00
22 Glass	1.44	−2.00
24 Scrap iron	0.18	−1.60
25 Iron and steel	0.78	−0.60
26 Nonferrous minerals	0.94	−0.20
27 Nonferrous metals (scrap)	1.80	−1.40
28 Nonferrous metals (primary)	1.54	−2.00
29 Nonferrous cables, pipe	1.60	−1.80
30 Steel forgings, pipes, structural units	1.04	−0.20
31 Foundries	1.47	−2.00
32 Hardware, metal furniture	1.75	−2.00
33 Industrial machinery	1.18	−3.00
34 Instruments and computers	1.42	−3.00
35 Domestic appliances	0.38	−0.20
37 Industrial electrical equipment	1.52	−3.00
38 Radio, television, and communications equipment	1.49	−3.00
39 Electric appliances	1.06	−3.00
40 Automobiles, motorcycles, etc.	1.56	−3.00
41 Shipbuilding	1.39	−3.00
42 Aircraft construction	1.11	−3.00
43 Armaments and munitions	1.15	−3.00
45 Inorganic chemicals	1.24	−2.00
46 Organic chemicals	1.08	−2.00
47 Parachemicals	0.72	−2.00
48 Pharmaceuticals	0.93	−2.00
49 Rubber and synthetic rubber	2.20	−2.00
50 Rubber and asbestos products	1.63	−2.00
51 Natural fibers	0.33	−2.00
52 Artificial fibers	0.96	−2.00
53 Yarns and thread	1.21	0.00
54 Textiles	1.10	0.00
55 Knitted products	2.60	−2.00
56 Clothing	2.51	−1.50
57 Crude leather and skins	1.26	0.00
58 Leather and fur products	1.76	−0.30

TABLE 1 *Continued.*

Sector	Demand elasticity	Price elasticity
59 Shoes and related items	2.10	−1.40
60 Wood and lumber	0.26	0.00
61 Plywood and millwork	1.07	−1.00
62 Furniture and bedding	1.42	−1.50
63 Wood pulp and wastepaper	1.51	−1.00
64 Paper and cardboard	1.60	−1.20
65 Printing and publishing	1.10	−0.40
66 Paper products	1.23	−3.00
67 Miscellaneous industries	1.36	−3.00

TABLE 2 Elasticities of FRG export equations.

Sector	Demand elasticity	Price elasticity
1 Agriculture	2.48	−0.50
2 Electricity	1.02	−0.75
5 Coal mining	0.76	0.00
6 Other mining	0.39	−0.50
7 Oil	3.18	−0.50
8 Chemicals	1.35	−2.00
9 Mineral oil	0.69	−1.00
10 Plastics	2.03	0.00
11 Stone and earth	1.25	−1.00
12 Glass	1.05	−1.00
13 Iron and steel	0.72	−1.80
14 Nonferrous metals	1.46	−0.40
15 Foundries	1.42	−1.40
16 Steel making	0.98	−1.60
17 Nonroad vehicles	1.05	0.00
18 Mechanical engineering	0.98	−0.40
19 Automobiles	1.33	−2.50
20 Repairs of automobiles	0.28	−0.60
21 Data processing machinery	2.08	−2.00
22 Electrical engineering	1.48	−2.00
23 Precision engineering	1.04	−1.20
24 Small consumer durables	1.24	−2.00
25 Wood	1.65	−1.00
26 Paper and cardboard	1.96	−1.50
27 Printing and publishing	1.50	−1.50
28 Leather	2.55	−0.70
29 Textiles	3.72	−1.00
30 Clothing	2.95	−1.00
31 Food	3.23	−0.50
32 Milk products	3.11	−0.50
33 Meat	3.06	−0.50
34 Drink	1.56	−0.50
35 Tobacco	1.70	−0.50

TABLE 3   Elasticities of Belgian export equations.

Sector	Demand elasticity	Price elasticity
1 Agricultural products	2.08	−0.50
2 Fish products	1.57	−0.80
5 Crude oil and gasoline	1.24	−1.75
6 Electric power	1.59	−1.75
9 Iron and steel	0.92	−1.80
10 Nonferrous metals	1.22	−1.40
11 Glass	1.20	−0.60
12 Cement, lime, gypsum	1.00	−1.80
13 Other nonmetals	1.59	−1.80
14 Chemical products	1.41	−2.00
15 Metal products	1.52	−2.50
16 Machines	1.50	−0.80
17 Office machines, precision engineering	2.17	0.00
18 Electrical engineering	1.55	−0.80
19 Automobiles and motorcycles	2.15	−3.00
20 Other means of transport	0.47	−0.40
21 Meat	3.06	−1.40
22 Milk	2.81	−1.50
23 Other foodstuffs	2.42	−0.30
24 Drinks	2.04	−1.00
25 Tobacco products	1.70	−1.50
26 Knitted goods and clothing	4.35	−1.50
27 Other textile products	1.85	−1.70
28 Leather, skins, shoes	2.93	0.00
29 Wood and wooden furniture	2.24	−3.00
30 Paper, paper products	2.28	−3.00
31 Printing	1.34	−1.40
32 Rubber products	1.63	−1.00
33 Plastic products	1.43	−2.00
34 Other industries (diamonds)	1.29	−1.80
35 Building, roads, water	1.61	−2.00

stimulus provided by the increased exports would be neutralized either by inflation or by tax policy. Consequently real personal-consumption expenditure does not change in any of the countries as we go from round 1 to round 2; only the increase in intermediate consumption makes round 2 differ from round 1. The difference between the two rounds is small; however, we ran a third round which differed only minutely from the second. The growth rates of exports in this third round are shown in the column labeled "Full" in the tables. They are virtually identical to the first-round growth rates. Table 5 contains the results for France. There are of course no first-round effects. The indirect effects can be seen in the column labeled "Full".

Far from being a disappointment, this virtual congruence of the first and third rounds is reassuring because one of our concerns had been how much computing would be necessary to make the system converge. The answer appears to be, as far as the present linking method is concerned, not more than two rounds, and the first round shows nearly everything.

TABLE 4   Annual growth rates (in percent) of FRG exports in 1980–1987 for the French expansion alternative.

Sector	Base	1st	Full	2−1	3−1
1 Agriculture	2.47	2.54	2.55	0.07	0.08
2 Electricity	2.95	3.27	3.29	0.32	0.34
3 Gas distribution	−4.34	−4.34	−4.34	0.00	0.00
4 Water	−5.77	−5.77	−5.77	0.00	0.00
5 Coal mining	1.30	1.35	1.36	0.05	0.06
6 Other mining	1.10	1.11	1.11	0.01	0.01
7 Oil	5.17	5.17	5.17	0.00	0.00
8 Chemicals	5.85	5.91	5.92	0.06	0.07
9 Mineral oil	1.52	1.61	1.61	0.09	0.09
10 Plastics	2.84	3.00	3.01	0.16	0.17
11 Stone and earth	0.21	0.32	0.32	0.11	0.11
12 Glass	0.24	0.33	0.34	0.09	0.10
13 Iron and steel	2.19	2.28	2.28	0.09	0.09
14 Nonferrous metals	−0.03	0.06	0.07	0.09	0.10
15 Foundries	−2.73	−2.63	−2.63	0.10	0.10
16 Steel making	−1.85	−1.74	−1.73	0.11	0.12
17 Nonroad vehicles	1.40	1.43	1.44	0.03	0.04
18 Mechanical engineering	0.49	0.59	0.59	0.10	0.10
19 Automobiles	−0.37	−0.24	−0.21	0.13	0.16
20 Repairs of automobiles	−3.21	−3.19	−3.19	0.02	0.02
21 Data processing machinery	4.31	4.55	4.56	0.24	0.25
22 Electrical engineering	−0.72	−0.58	−0.57	0.14	0.15
23 Precision engineering	−2.52	−2.42	−2.40	0.10	0.12
24 Small consumer durables	−1.91	−1.83	−1.82	0.08	0.09
25 Wood	−0.60	−0.36	−0.35	0.24	0.25
26 Paper and cardboard	−0.83	−0.59	−0.56	0.24	0.27
27 Printing and publishing	2.36	2.56	2.57	0.20	0.21
28 Leather	−5.90	−5.66	−5.66	0.24	0.24
29 Textiles	1.99	2.31	2.33	0.32	0.34
30 Clothing	0.50	0.97	0.98	0.47	0.48
31 Food	1.54	1.67	1.69	0.13	0.15
32 Milk products	2.30	2.36	2.36	0.06	0.06
33 Meat	2.84	3.14	3.14	0.30	0.30
34 Drink	3.41	3.52	3.52	0.11	0.11
35 Tobacco	0.16	0.35	0.35	0.19	0.19
36 Building	1.16	1.24	1.25	0.08	0.09
37 Wholesale trade	1.76	1.87	1.88	0.11	0.12
39 Railways	0.15	0.18	0.18	0.03	0.03
40 Shipping	0.81	0.87	0.87	0.06	0.06
41 Other transport	2.27	2.39	2.40	0.12	0.13
42 Federal postal service	2.45	2.59	2.60	0.14	0.15
43 Banks and bank charges	2.39	2.52	2.53	0.13	0.14
44 Insurance	3.09	3.25	3.26	0.16	0.17
46 Publishing	1.80	1.91	1.92	0.11	0.12
47 Other services	1.50	1.59	1.60	0.09	0.10
100 Total	1.74	1.85	1.86	0.11	0.12

TABLE 5   Annual growth rates (in percent) of French exports in 1980–1987 for the French expansion alternative.

Sector	Base	1st	Full	2—1	3—1
1 Agriculture	1.22	1.22	1.23	0.00	0.01
2 Fish and fish products	—0.11	—0.11	—0.11	0.00	0.00
3 Meat	—0.44	—0.44	—0.44	0.00	0.00
4 Cereal products	1.27	1.27	1.27	0.00	0.00
5 Dairy products	2.34	2.34	2.34	0.00	0.00
6 Sugar	2.67	2.67	2.67	0.00	0.00
7 Animal feed	1.19	1.19	1.19	0.00	0.00
8 Miscellaneous food products	3.23	3.23	3.23	0.00	0.00
9 Beverages	—0.03	—0.03	—0.03	0.00	0.00
10 Fats and oils	—0.04	0.04	—0.04	0.00	0.00
14 Coking	0.09	0.09	0.09	0.00	0.00
16 Electricity	1.91	1.91	1.92	0.00	0.01
20 Refined oil	1.49	1.49	1.49	0.00	0.00
21 Building materials	2.45	2.45	2.46	0.00	0.01
22 Glass	1.22	1.22	1.23	0.00	0.01
23 Iron ore	—5.39	—5.39	—5.39	0.00	0.00
24 Scrap iron	8.10	8.10	8.10	0.00	0.00
25 Iron and steel	1.40	1.40	1.41	0.00	0.01
26 Nonferrous minerals	2.11	2.11	2.13	0.00	0.02
27 Nonferrous metals (scrap)	—2.66	—2.66	—2.65	0.00	0.01
28 Nonferrous metals (primary)	6.22	6.22	6.24	0.00	0.02
29 Nonferrous cables, pipe	2.70	2.70	2.72	0.00	0.02
30 Steel forgings, pipes, and structural units	0.83	0.83	0.84	0.00	0.01
31 Foundries	—0.06	—0.06	—0.06	0.00	0.00
32 Hardware, metal furniture	—0.49	—0.49	—0.49	0.00	0.00
33 Industrial machinery	4.60	4.60	4.60	0.00	0.00
34 Instruments and computers	3.18	3.18	3.19	0.00	0.01
37 Industrial electrical equipment	0.69	0.69	0.70	0.00	0.01
38 Radio, television, and communications equipment	8.01 12.78	8.01	8.01	0.00	0.00
39 Electric appliances		12.78	12.78	0.00	0.00
40 Automobiles, motorcycles, etc.	1.32	1.32	1.33	0.00	0.01
41 Shipbuilding	5.24	5.24	5.24	0.00	0.00
42 Aircraft construction	5.49	5.49	5.50	0.00	0.01
43 Armaments and munitions	0.91	0.91	0.91	0.00	0.00
44 Miscellaneous minerals	—0.88	—0.88	—0.88	0.00	0.00
45 Inorganic chemicals	—1.06	—1.06	—1.06	0.00	0.00
46 Organic chemicals	9.91	9.91	9.92	0.00	0.01
47 Parachemicals	5.62	5.62	5.63	0.00	0.01
48 Pharmaceuticals	1.29	1.29	0.00	0.00	—1.29
49 Rubber and synthetic rubber	1.88	1.88	1.90	0.00	0.02
50 Rubber and asbestos products	0.58	0.58	0.59	0.00	0.01
51 Natural fibers	4.58	4.58	4.59	0.00	0.01
52 Artificial fibers	7.55	7.55	7.56	0.00	0.01
53 Yarns and thread	0.93	0.93	0.94	0.00	0.01
54 Textiles	0.76	0.76	0.78	0.00	0.02
55 Knitted products	1.96	1.96	1.99	0.00	0.03
56 Clothing	2.25	2.25	2.25	0.00	0.00
57 Crude leather and skins	0.72	0.72	0.72	0.00	0.00
58 Leather and fur products	—0.73	—0.73	—0.73	0.00	0.00

TABLE 5   *Continued.*

Sector	Base	1st	Full	2–1	3–1
59 Shoes and related items	0.26	0.26	0.27	0.00	0.01
60 Wood and lumber	0.25	0.25	0.25	0.00	0.00
61 Plywood and millwork	−1.21	−1.21	−1.21	0.00	0.00
62 Furniture and bedding	2.10	2.10	2.10	0.00	0.00
63 Wood pulp and wastepaper	0.21	0.21	0.22	0.00	0.01
64 Paper and cardboard	1.59	1.59	1.61	0.00	0.02
65 Printing and publishing	0.56	0.56	0.56	0.00	0.00
66 Paper products	7.40	7.40	7.42	0.00	0.02
67 Miscellaneous industries	−0.10	−0.10	−0.09	0.00	0.01
100 Total	3.16	3.16	3.17	0.00	0.01

A second variation, a kind of reverse of the first, was tried. Personal-consumption expenditures were increased in the FRG model by 1% per year throughout the period. The impact on France is shown in Table 6 and the impact on the FRG in Table 7. The total impact on French exports is only slightly higher than the reverse impact for the FRG. As was true for the FRG under the French consumption increase, the largest sectoral changes in French exports because of the German good fortune are found in consumer-goods industries: clothing (sector 56) (an increase of 0.58% per year), semimanufactured wood products (61) (an increase of 0.50% per year), electricity (16) (an increase of 0.43% per year), and shoes (59) (an increase of 0.41% per year). Figure 1 compares for selected goods the impact of the French prosperity on the FRG with the impact of the FRG prosperity on France.

A comparison of the two alternatives is presented in Table 8 for the third linked country, Belgium. The first column shows the base-case growth rates; the second, the first-round effects with the French expansion alternative (1F); the third, the first-round effects of the FRG good fortune (1G); the fourth and fifth, the full effects of the French and FRG expansion alternatives; the sixth and seventh, the increments to the growth rates under the French expansion alternative; columns eight and nine, the increments for the FRG expansion alternative; the last column, the difference between the fourth and fifth columns. Here we pay most attention to columns seven, nine, and ten.

Comparing column seven with column five of Tables 4 and 6 we see that Belgium is far more affected by its partners than are the FRG or France. The five sectors showing the largest increases due to the French good fortune are meat (sector 21) (0.77% per year), clothing (26) (0.76% per year), fisheries (2) (0.59% per year), printing (31) (0.56% per year), and beverages (24) (0.53% per year). Figure 2 shows some of the largest impacts on Belgium of faster growth in France and the FRG.

Column nine showing the full impact of the FRG good fortune on Belgium can be compared to column five of Tables 5 and 7. The five largest impacts are for meat (sector 21) (0.95%), clothing (26) (0.81%), shoes (28) (0.77%), automobiles (19) (0.41%), and wood and furniture (29) (0.36%).

Column ten shows the differences by sector in the growth rates generated by the two alternatives. Positive numbers indicate that the FRG expansion alternative had more effect and negative numbers show that the effect of the French expansion alternative was

TABLE 6   Annual growth rates (in percent) of French exports in 1980–1987 for the FRG expansion alternative.

Sector	Base	1st	Full	2−1	3−1
1 Agriculture and forestry	1.22	1.40	1.41	0.18	0.19
2 Fish and fish products	−0.11	−0.07	−0.07	0.04	0.04
3 Meat	−0.44	−0.30	−0.30	0.14	0.14
4 Cereal products	1.27	1.48	1.48	0.21	0.21
5 Dairy products	2.34	2.50	2.50	0.16	0.16
6 Sugar	2.67	2.77	2.77	0.10	0.10
7 Animal feed	1.19	1.27	1.27	0.08	0.08
8 Miscellaneous food products	3.23	3.42	3.42	0.19	0.19
9 Beverages	−0.03	0.27	0.26	0.30	0.29
10 Fats and oils	−0.04	0.01	0.01	0.05	0.05
14 Coking	0.09	0.18	0.18	0.09	0.09
16 Electricity	1.91	2.33	2.34	0.42	0.43
20 Refined oil	1.49	1.64	1.64	0.15	0.15
21 Building materials	2.45	2.89	2.89	0.44	0.44
22 Glass	1.22	1.35	1.35	0.13	0.13
23 Iron ore	−5.39	−5.39	−5.39	0.00	0.00
24 Scrap iron	8.10	8.12	8.12	0.02	0.02
25 Iron and steel	1.40	1.45	1.45	0.05	0.05
26 Nonferrous minerals	2.11	2.19	2.19	0.08	0.08
27 Nonferrous metals (scrap)	−2.66	−2.57	−2.57	0.09	0.09
28 Nonferrous metals (primary)	6.22	6.34	6.34	0.12	0.12
29 Nonferrous cables, pipe	2.70	2.80	2.80	0.10	0.10
30 Steel forgings, pipes, and structural units	0.83	0.89	0.89	0.06	0.06
31 Foundries	−0.06	0.10	0.10	0.16	0.16
32 Hardware, metal furniture	−0.49	−0.31	−0.31	0.18	0.18
33 Industrial machinery	4.60	4.72	4.72	0.12	0.12
34 Instruments and computers	3.18	3.43	3.43	0.25	0.25
37 Industrial electrical equipment	0.69	0.90	0.90	0.21	0.21
38 Radio, television, and communications equipment	8.01	8.22	8.22	0.21	0.21
39 Electric appliances	12.78	12.93	12.94	0.15	0.16
40 Automobiles, motorcycles, etc.	1.32	1.57	1.57	0.25	0.25
41 Shipbuilding	5.24	5.30	5.30	0.06	0.06
42 Aircraft construction	5.49	5.65	5.65	0.16	0.16
43 Armaments and munitions	0.91	0.95	0.95	0.04	0.04
44 Miscellaneous minerals	−0.88	−0.88	−0.88	0.00	0.00
45 Inorganic chemicals	−1.06	−1.00	−0.99	0.06	0.07
46 Organic chemicals	9.91	10.00	10.00	0.09	0.09
47 Parachemicals	5.62	5.69	5.69	0.07	0.07
48 Pharmaceuticals	1.29	1.34	1.34	0.05	0.05
49 Rubber and synthetic rubber	1.88	2.07	2.07	0.19	0.19
50 Rubber and asbestos products	0.58	0.73	0.73	0.15	0.15
51 Natural fibers	4.58	4.62	4.63	0.04	0.05
52 Artificial fibers	7.55	7.68	7.68	0.13	0.13
53 Yarns and thread	0.93	1.03	1.03	0.10	0.10
54 Textiles	0.76	0.91	0.92	0.15	0.16
55 Knitted products	1.96	2.23	2.24	0.27	0.28
56 Clothing	2.25	2.83	2.83	0.58	0.58
57 Crude leather and skins	0.72	1.06	1.06	0.34	0.34
58 Leather and fur products	−0.73	−0.43	−0.43	0.30	0.30
59 Shoes and related items	0.26	0.66	0.67	0.40	0.41
60 Wood and lumber	0.25	0.32	0.32	0.07	0.07

TABLE 6   *Continued.*

Sector	Base	1st	Full	2—1	3—1
61 Plywood and millwork	--1.21	—0.71	—0.71	0.50	0.50
62 Furniture and bedding	2.10	2.29	2.29	0.19	0.19
63 Wood pulp and wastepaper	0.21	0.40	0.40	0.19	0.19
64 Paper and cardboard	1.59	1.83	1.83	0.24	0.24
65 Printing and publishing	0.56	0.69	0.69	0.13	0.13
66 Paper products	7.40	7.60	7.60	0.20	0.20
67 Miscellaneous industries	--0.10	0.06	0.07	0.16	0.17
100 Total	3.16	3.32	3.32	0.16	0.16

TABLE 7   Annual growth rates (in percent) of FRG exports in 1980—1987 for the FRG expansion alternative.

Sector	Base	1st	Full	2—1	3—1
1 Agriculture	2.47	2.47	2.48	0.00	0.01
2 Electricity	2.95	2.95	2.98	0.00	0.03
3 Gas distribution	-4.34	- 4.34	—4.34	0.00	0.00
4 Water	—5.77	—5.77	-5.77	0.00	0.00
5 Coal mining	1.30	1.30	1.32	0.00	0.02
6 Other mining	1.10	1.10	1.10	0.00	0.00
7 Oil	5.17	5.17	5.17	0.00	0.00
8 Chemicals	5.85	5.85	5.87	0.00	0.02
9 Mineral oil	1.52	1.52	1.53	0.00	0.01
10 Plastics	2.84	2.84	2.87	0.00	0.03
11 Stone and earth	0.21	0.21	0.22	0.00	0.01
12 Glass	0.24	0.24	0.26	0.00	0.02
13 Iron and steel	2.19	2.19	2.20	0.00	0.01
14 Nonferrous metals	—0.03	—0.03	—0.01	0.00	0.02
15 Foundries	--2.73	—2.73	—2.72	0.00	0.01
16 Steel making	—1.85	—1.85	--1.83	0.00	0.02
17 Nonroad vehicles	1.40	1.40	1.41	0.00	0.01
18 Mechanical engineering	0.49	0.49	0.50	0.00	0.01
19 Automobiles	---0.37	---0.37	—0.33	0.00	0.04
20 Repairs of automobiles	—3.21	- -3.21	--3.21	0.00	0.00
21 Data processing machinery	4.31	4.31	4.33	0.00	0.02
22 Electrical engineering	—0.72	—0.72	—0.70	0.00	0.02
23 Precision engineering	--2.52	—2.52	—2.50	0.00	0.02
24 Small consumer durables	—1.91	—1.91	—1.90	0.00	0.01
25 Wood	—0.60	—0.60	—0.59	0.00	0.01
26 Paper and cardboard	--0.83	--0.83	--0.79	0.00	0.04
27 Printing and publishing	2.36	2.36	2.38	0.00	0.02
28 Leather	—5.90	-- 5.90	—5.88	0.00	0.02
29 Textiles	1.99	1.99	2.02	0.00	0.03
30 Clothing	0.50	0.50	0.51	0.00	0.01
31 Food	1.54	1.54	1.56	0.00	0.02
32 Milk products	2.30	2.30	2.31	0.00	0.01
33 Meat	2.84	2.84	2.84	0.00	0.00
34 Drink	3.41	3.41	3.41	0.00	0.00
35 Tobacco	0.16	0.16	0.16	0.00	0.00
36 Building	1.16	1.16	1.18	0.00	0.02
37 Wholesale trade	1.76	1.76	1.78	0.00	0.02

TABLE 7   *Continued.*

Sector	Base	1st	Full	2–1	3–1
39 Railways	0.15	0.15	0.16	0.00	0.01
40 Shipping	0.81	0.81	0.82	0.00	0.01
41 Other transport	2.27	2.27	2.29	0.00	0.02
42 Federal postal service	2.45	2.45	2.48	0.00	0.03
43 Banks and bank charges	2.39	2.39	2.41	0.00	0.02
44 Insurance	3.09	3.09	3.11	0.00	0.02
46 Publishing	1.80	1.80	1.82	0.00	0.02
47 Other services	1.50	1.50	1.51	0.00	0.01
100 Total	1.74	1.74	1.75	0.00	0.01

larger. The total effect (shown on the bottom row of the table) is virtually the same in each case. Although the total effects are similar, the sectoral breakdowns are very different. The French effect exceeded the FRG effect by more than 0.30% in four sectors: −0.51% in fisheries (2), −0.48% in printing (31), −0.40% in beverages (24), and −0.30% for tobacco (25). The largest differences where the influence of the FRG was higher were in shoes (28) (0.29%), meat (21) (0.18%), electrical goods (18) (0.15%), and automobiles (19) (0.13%). The French expansion alternative affected some relatively small export sectors more than the FRG alternative. In 17 sectors the French expansion had more effect, in ten sectors the FRG expansion had more effect, and in 18 sectors the effects were approximately the same.

The present linking mechanism will be used to make the initial system of "real-side" models work together. When one model is given a price side we can incorporate the results into the d/f ratio of eqn. (1). Equations of this type are currently used in the US model.

The present system of linking using the d/f ratio may prove adequate until we want to study bilateral trade flows; then we will have to use the more complicated mechanism originally planned. Also the present system lacks consistency checks; it cannot tell whether France's agricultural exports are consistent with the agricultural imports of France's trading partners. This simple mechanism, however, has the decided advantage that it expands easily as more models are added. Instead of using exogenous values for D_k in eqn. (1) we can simply substitute the values that are produced by the model when the model for country k joins the system.

The shortcut method is in some ways akin to our method of developing the national models themselves. That method is to start with a very simple model (needing only an input–output table for one year) and to add the various submodules to it as they are developed. At each stage we have a working model. This process may seem pedestrian but experience is a powerful teacher. We feel that a working model, even with deficiencies, is often of more use than an elaborate theoretical model that cannot be implemented.

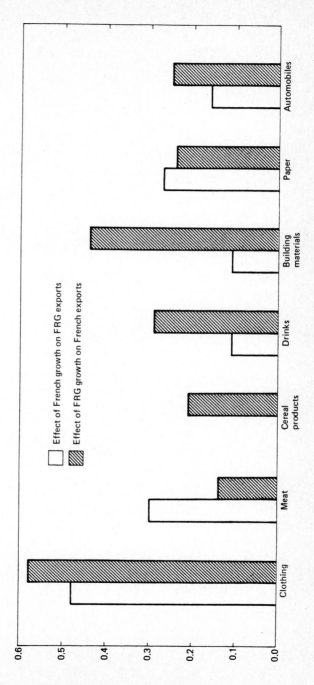

FIGURE 1   Reciprocal effects of growth in personal-consumption expenditure on the FRG and France.

TABLE 8   Annual growth rates (in percent) of Belgian exports in 1980–1987 for the French and FRG expansion alternatives[a].

Sector	Base (1)	1F (2)	1G (3)	Full F (4)	Full G (5)	2–1 (6)	4–1 (7)	3–1 (8)	5–1 (9)	5–4 (10)
1 Agricultural products	0.90	1.26	1.13	1.26	1.14	0.36	0.36	0.23	0.24	-0.12
2 Fish products	2.31	2.89	2.39	2.90	2.39	0.58	0.59	0.08	0.08	-0.51
3 Coal mines, brown coal	2.59	2.59	2.59	2.59	2.59	0.00	0.00	0.00	0.00	0.00
4 Coke	4.11	4.11	4.11	4.11	4.11	0.00	0.00	0.00	0.00	0.00
5 Crude oil and gasoline	2.14	2.17	2.31	2.17	2.31	0.03	0.03	0.17	0.17	0.14
6 Electric power	1.44	1.64	1.63	1.64	1.64	0.20	0.20	0.19	0.20	0.00
7 Gas distribution	-5.51	-5.51	-5.51	-5.51	-5.51	0.00	0.00	0.00	0.00	0.00
9 Iron ore and iron	2.72	2.76	2.75	2.76	2.75	0.04	0.04	0.03	0.03	-0.01
10 Nonferrous metals	1.11	1.26	1.20	1.28	1.23	0.15	0.17	0.09	0.12	-0.05
11 Glass	2.55	2.71	2.64	2.72	2.65	0.16	0.17	0.09	0.10	-0.07
12 Cement, lime, gypsum	0.93	1.12	0.96	1.12	0.97	0.19	0.19	0.03	0.04	-0.15
13 Other nonmetals	0.68	0.80	0.76	0.80	0.77	0.12	0.12	0.08	0.09	-0.03
14 Chemical products	1.50	1.64	1.61	1.65	1.62	0.14	0.15	0.11	0.12	-0.03
15 Metal products	2.30	2.49	2.47	2.49	2.49	0.19	0.19	0.17	0.19	0.00
16 Machines	0.68	0.92	0.82	0.92	0.84	0.24	0.24	0.14	0.16	-0.08
17 Office machines, precision engineering	4.81	5.03	5.09	5.03	5.10	0.22	0.22	0.28	0.29	0.07
18 Electrical engineering	0.02	0.16	0.31	0.17	0.32	0.14	0.15	0.29	0.30	0.15
19 Automobiles and motorcycles	3.71	3.98	4.11	3.99	4.12	0.27	0.28	0.40	0.41	0.13
20 Other means of transport	-0.55	-0.50	-0.49	-0.50	-0.49	0.05	0.05	0.06	0.06	0.01
21 Meat	3.64	4.41	4.59	4.41	4.59	0.77	0.77	0.95	0.95	0.18
22 Milk	1.63	1.72	1.79	1.73	1.79	0.09	0.10	0.16	0.16	0.06
23 Other foodstuffs	0.96	1.19	1.14	1.19	1.15	0.23	0.23	0.18	0.19	-0.04
24 Drinks	2.28	2.81	2.40	2.81	2.41	0.53	0.53	0.12	0.13	-0.40
25 Tobacco products	2.86	3.18	2.88	3.18	2.88	0.32	0.32	0.02	0.02	-0.30
26 Knitted goods and clothing	3.18	3.94	3.99	3.94	3.99	0.76	0.76	0.81	0.81	0.05
27 Other textile products	3.62	3.87	3.84	3.89	3.86	0.25	0.27	0.22	0.24	-0.03
28 Leather, skins, shoes	-1.17	-0.70	-0.42	-0.69	-0.40	0.47	0.48	0.75	0.77	0.29
29 Wood and wooden furniture	4.82	5.31	5.17	5.31	5.18	0.49	0.49	0.35	0.36	-0.13
30 Paper, paper products	1.08	1.50	1.27	1.51	1.29	0.42	0.43	0.19	0.21	-0.22
31 Printed matter	0.69	1.25	0.75	1.25	0.77	0.56	0.56	0.06	0.08	-0.48
32 Rubber products	2.53	2.67	2.77	2.68	2.78	0.14	0.15	0.24	0.25	0.10

33 Plastic products	4.77	5.00	4.96	5.01	4.97	0.23	0.24	0.19	0.20	−0.04
34 Other industries (diamonds)	5.08	5.40	5.23	5.40	5.23	0.32	0.32	0.15	0.15	−0.17
35 Building, roads, water	2.39	2.64	2.63	2.64	2.64	0.25	0.25	0.24	0.25	0.00
37 Scrap	2.39	2.64	2.63	2.64	2.64	0.25	0.25	0.24	0.25	0.00
38 Commerce	2.39	2.64	2.63	2.64	2.64	0.25	0.25	0.24	0.25	0.00
39 Hotels, restaurants	2.39	2.64	2.63	2.64	2.64	0.25	0.25	0.24	0.25	0.00
40 Railways, trams	2.39	2.64	2.63	2.64	2.64	0.25	0.25	0.24	0.25	0.00
41 Road transport	2.39	2.64	2.63	2.64	2.64	0.25	0.25	0.24	0.25	0.00
42 Inland navigation	2.39	2.64	2.63	2.64	2.64	0.25	0.25	0.24	0.25	0.00
43 Sea and coastal transport	2.39	2.64	2.63	2.64	2.64	0.25	0.25	0.24	0.25	0.00
44 Air transport	2.39	2.64	2.63	2.64	2.64	0.25	0.25	0.24	0.25	0.00
45 Storage and distribution	2.39	2.64	2.63	2.64	2.64	0.25	0.25	0.24	0.25	0.00
46 Communications	2.39	2.64	2.63	2.64	2.64	0.25	0.25	0.24	0.25	0.00
47 Credit banking	2.39	2.64	2.63	2.64	2.64	0.25	0.25	0.24	0.25	0.00
48 Commercial services	2.39	2.64	2.63	2.64	2.64	0.25	0.25	0.24	0.25	0.00
100 Total	2.40	2.64	2.63	2.65	2.64	0.24	0.25	0.23	0.24	−0.01

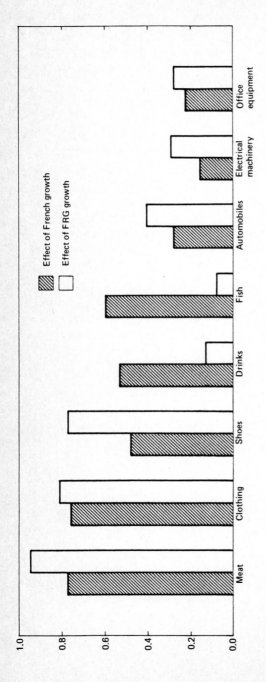

FIGURE 2   Effects on Belgian exports of a 1% annual increase in personal-consumption expenditure in France and the FRG.

REFERENCES

Almon, C. and Nyhus, D. (1977). The INFORUM international system of input–output models and bilateral trade flows. INFORUM Research Report No. 21, September. Department of Economics, University of Maryland, College Park, Maryland.

Lee, Y.S. (1978). An input–output model of France. INFORUM Research Report No. 25, July. Department of Economics, University of Maryland, College Park, Maryland.

Nyhus, D. (1975). The trade model of a dynamic world input–output system. INFORUM Research Report No. 14, July. Department of Economics, University of Maryland, College Park, Maryland.

Nyhus, D. (1980). The INFORUM–IIASA system of national economic models. Paper presented at the IFAC–IFORs Conference on Dynamic Modeling and Control of National Economies, 3rd, Warsaw, Poland, June. IFAC, Warsaw.

COMMENTS*

The development over the last few years of the INFORUM family of national input–output models advocated by Almon and Nyhus was from the very beginning accompanied by the hope that the models would eventually be linked through bilateral trade flows. The present paper surveys the first "operational" attempt at "short-cut" linking applied to the input–output models of three countries, France, the FRG, and Belgium, for which a simulation exercise has been performed and analyzed.

The introduction of a short-cut linking procedure instead of a comprehensive mechanism is explained by the absence of price equations in the national input–output models. It seems, however, that this argument does not fully justify the simplifications made by the authors. The linking element in the chain of relationships is the export demand function of a given commodity group defined for each country. The exports depend on a weighted index of "domestic demands" of importing countries, the weights being the allocation shares of exports in the base year, and on the ratio of domestic and foreign prices. The notion of the domestic demand is used in the paper with two different meanings. In the estimation process gross or net output indexes were used as proxies, whereas in the simulation exercises they were substituted by indexes of domestic demand (defined as output plus imports and exports) to reduce, as the authors state, the positive feedbacks of the linked system. But why?

It is not obvious why, in the export functions, the domestic demands of the importing countries have not been directly represented by their imports (volume indexes) and why, in each country model, import equations were not explicitly introduced. The "short-cut" relationships represent in fact the reduced forms of a system of export and import equations. These forms were obtained using rather severe restrictions. It was assumed that over the long term there is no substitution between imported and domestic products (raw materials, energy, etc.) due to changes in relative prices or technologies, or to policy constraints. It can easily be seen that the construction of import equations does not assume the existence of price equation systems in input–output models. The forecasting problem of domestic and import prices can be solved in the same inconsistent manner as was used for the export prices, i.e., by extrapolation of their time trends.

---

*By Władysław Welfe, Institute of Econometrics and Statistics, University of Łódź, Łódź, Poland.

The simulation exercise is confined to three country models linked together — for France, the FRG, and Belgium. Two similar experiments were conducted, involving increasing by 1% per year the personal consumption either in France or (separately) in the FRG. This change affected the domestic output of these countries, increasing their own imports and the exports in the partner countries (it was assumed that there was no increase in the activity level of the "rest of the world"). The immediate impacts of these changes were significant, giving interesting and deep insight into the dependence of exports on the changes of partner's activity levels. This dependence was much stronger in the case of Belgium than for the other countries, which was to be expected. The detailed results seem to be of direct importance to business organizations and government agencies.

The authors also investigated the indirect impact of the above changes due to the feedbacks between the economies of France and the FRG. This impact appears, in fact, to be negligible. However, this result seems to confirm the authors' initial assumptions rather than describing real potential outcomes. They assumed for the simulation period that the capacities of the partner countries were exhausted and that therefore no income multiplier effects can be observed. The initial increase in exports will induce an increase only in the imports of intermediate products, with no additional effects on final consumption demand.

It is not easy to understand why the simulation experiments were conducted for a future period covering the years 1980—1987. This made necessary several arbitrary assumptions about the growth rates of GNP in the three countries in order to arrive at a base solution. Instead, a typical multiplier analysis, or at least a control solution covering the sample period (or the last 5 or 10 years of it), could have served as a convenient point of departure. In that case the specific changes in domestic and foreign activities would be known, leading to better understanding of the simulation exercises.

Nevertheless, it seems the authors have really pushed forward their research by demonstrating how large input—output models can be operationally linked. Despite the large size of the models, one would like to see them operating in the near future in a similar fashion to the linked systems of national econometric macromodels.

Part Five

Hybrid Models

GLOBAL INTERNATIONAL ECONOMIC MODELS
B.G. Hickman (editor)
Elsevier Science Publishers B.V. (North-Holland)
© IIASA, 1983

THE IMPACT OF PETROLEUM AND COMMODITY PRICES IN A MODEL OF THE WORLD ECONOMY

F. Gerard Adams and Jaime Marquez
*Economics Research Unit, Department of Economics, University
of Pennsylvania, Philadelphia, Pennsylvania (USA)*

1   INTRODUCTION

That increases in oil prices or in the prices of other primary commodities can upset the world economy has been amply demonstrated in recent years. What is not so clear, however, are the dimensions of the effects and the complex channels of interaction by which they operate.

When we trace the effects of commodity-price increases through to the consuming industrial economies and the producing economies we find complex channels of reaction. While the effects are generally in the direction that our own a priori judgment would predict, model simulation is necessary to establish their quantitative dimensions. The LINK model system augmented by commodity models to make COMLINK is a useful instrument for this purpose but its complexity and the diversity among the component country models make it difficult to evaluate clearly what is happening. Consequently there is some merit in first examining the impact of commodity and petroleum prices in a simpler system.

In this paper we examine the impact of oil and commodity prices on the GDP of the developed countries (DCs) and the less developed countries (LDCs). We contrast the impact of commodity-price increases with the effect of increases in oil prices. The orientation of the paper is primarily short run, focusing on business-cycle impacts rather than on long-term adjustments.

In Section 2 we consider a simple three-block model system of the industrial countries, the commodity-producing nonoil LDCs, and the oil producers to disentangle the impacts theoretically. (For simplicity the centrally planned economies are not included in the present version of the theoretical system.)

In Section 3 we examine simulations of the COMLINK system, a world model system adapted from Project LINK which treats the interactions in ways which are analogous to the simple theoretical system described in Section 2.

Finally in Section 4 we consider the additional elements which still need to be factored into the global models to allow for the full effect of increases in commodity and oil prices.

2   A THEORETICAL WORLD MODEL WITH OIL AND COMMODITIES

2.1   Structure of the Model

Our simple theoretical model is summarized in Table 1. It seeks to show the influence of the price of oil and other primary commodities on the GDP of the DCs and the nonoil LDCs. It highlights the channels through which a price increase affects the DCs and the

TABLE 1   Summary of the theoretical model.

DC model

$$Y^d = c^d(Y^d) + E^d + B^d \tag{1}$$

$$B^d = M_m^l + M_m^o - [(P_o/P_m)M_o^d + (P_p/P_m)M_p^d] \tag{2}$$

$$M_o^d = \delta_o^d Y^d \tag{3}$$

$$M_p^d = \delta_p^d Y^d \tag{4}$$

$$P_m = \pi + \pi_o P_o + \pi_p P_p \tag{5}$$

OPEC model

$$M_m^o = \beta P_o (M_o^d + M_o^l)/P_m \tag{6}$$

LDC model

$$Y^l = f(K^l, \bar{L}_o^l) \tag{7}$$

$$K^l = I^l + (1 - d)K_{-1}^l \tag{8}$$

$$I^l = i_t + i M_m^l \tag{9}$$

$$M_m^l = (R + P_p M_p^d - P_o M_o^l)/P_m \tag{10}$$

$$M_o^l = \delta_o^l Y^l \tag{11}$$

Notation

Variables: B, trade account; E, exogenous demand; I, investment; K, capital; L, labor; M, imports; P, prices; R, external credits; X, exports; Y, GDP.
Superscripts: d, DCs; l, LDCs; o, OPEC.
Subscripts: m, manufactures; o, oil; p, primary commodities.
Coefficients: c^d, propensity to consume and invest; f, production-function coefficients; i, investment coefficient; β, recycling coefficient; δ, import coefficients; π, price markup or indexing factors; d, depreciation rate

LDCs, and to what extent these channels reinforce or neutralize the effects. We now proceed to a description of the structure of the model. Three blocks of countries are interrelated only by trade of goods, and the only type of capital movement which is recognized is compensation for the flow of goods. The trade flows which are accounted for are petroleum from the oil countries to the LDCs and the DCs, other primary commodities from the LDCs to the DCs, and manufactured goods from the DCs to the oil countries and the LDCs. The structure of each of the bloc models is as follows.

2.1.1 The DCs

A Keynesian approach is used to determine GDP in the DCs, i.e., income is determined by the demand side. There are no supply-side constraints and supply responds rapidly enough to maintain equilibrium. It is assumed that both consumption and investment are endogenously determined depending on GDP, and these variables are combined in the term $c^d(Y^d)$. The trade balance which enters the GDP identity is defined in real terms by deflation by the price of manufactured goods. This is an important consideration because it means that the model recognizes the terms-of-trade effect of changes in oil or commodity prices since imports of these commodities are valued in terms of the exports of manufactured goods which would be required to pay for them. The imports of the DCs are directly related to real GDP. Initial versions of the system assume a zero price elasticity for oil demand; this assumption is close to reality in the short run but must be modified for the longer run. The price of manufactures is determined by a markup on the price of oil and other primary commodities.

2.1.2 The Oil Countries

Income determination is not considered explicitly for the oil countries. Instead we simply use the notion that these countries recycle part of their oil revenue into purchases of manufactures from the DCs, with no imports from the LDCs. It is assumed that the oil price is determined exogenously by OPEC. The price-determination mechanism is not considered until later.

2.1.3 The LDCs

In sharp contrast to the DCs, it is assumed that the GDP of the LDCs is determined by the supply side, e.g. via an aggregate production function with capital and labor as arguments. Capital accumulation equals some internal investment component plus some fraction of the imports of manufactures from the DCs, the latter representing imports of capital goods. Labor is assumed to be fixed. In addition to imports of manufactures the LDCs also import oil, the amount imported being determined by real GDP, as described earlier with a zero short-run price elasticity. The foreign-exchange constraint applies to the imports of manufactures. To pay for these the LDCs use the proceeds from their exports of primary commodities, first determining their oil imports and then using whatever is left over to finance imports of manufactures. This implies balance in their trade account, except for external credits.

2.1.4 Commodities and Petroleum

In the initial versions of the theoretical model we assume that commodity prices and the oil price are exogenously determined. We can also visualize a simple model of the commodity market which determines prices endogenously.

2.2   The Influence of Oil Prices on the DCs and the LDCs

One task of the model is to identify the possible channels through which an increase in oil (and commodity) prices may affect the consuming economies and to establish the direction of the effects.

We have divided the possible channels of oil-price effects into two types, direct and indirect. One direct channel is the obvious reduction in the resources available due to the higher oil bill that is caused by an increase in the oil price. In the case of the LDCs this takes the form of reduced foreign-exchange availabilities and subsequently produces indirect dynamic effects through the influence on imports of manufactured goods and the growth of capital stock. In the case of the DCs the direct effect is on the real balance of payments which deteriorates with the increased cost of imports (in terms of manufactured goods). As anticipated, the direct effects are negative.

With regard to the indirect effects, the channel of influence is through recycling, i.e., the increased imports of manufactures by the oil countries. This represents a stimulus to activity in the DCs — one which may or may not be offset by the direct effect. In turn the higher level of real activity in the DCs causes an increase in the volume of imports of primary commodities and hence enlarges the foreign-exchange resources that are available to the LDCs and their imports of manufactured goods, etc.

There are also other indirect channels. As suggested earlier, the price of manufactured goods is a markup on oil and primary-commodity prices. An increase in the price of oil when translated into an increase in the price of manufactured goods tends to decrease the real imports of manufactured goods by the oil countries and by the LDCs and tends to affect the GDP of the DCs in a negative direction. In contrast, an increase in the price of manufactured goods reduces the real burden of the oil prices to the DCs.

2.2.1 Solutions

The effects of oil-price increases on the GDPs of the LDCs and the DCs (dY^l/dP_o and dY^d/dP_o) depend on the values of the parameters, particularly the recycling coefficient β and the indexing parameters π_o and π_p for the prices of manufactured goods with respect to the price of oil and commodities, respectively. Results for these solutions are summarized in Tables 2 and 3.

For the LDCs the impact of oil-price increases is unequivocally negative. As the value of the indexing parameter increases, the effect of an oil-price increase on the GDP of the LDCs increases, i.e. becomes more negative. This result is reasonable since the available resources of the LDCs have been reduced not only through the higher oil prices but also

TABLE 2   Effects of oil prices on GDP: summary of dY^l/dP_o for LDCs.

β	π_o		
	0	$0 < \pi_o < 1$	1
0	—	—	—
$0 < \beta < 1$	—·	—	—
1	—	—	—

TABLE 3   Effects of oil prices on GDP: summary of dY^d/dP_O for DCs.

β	π_O		
	0	$0 < \pi_O < 1^a$	1^a
0	—	— or +	— or +
$0 < \beta < 1$	—	— or +	— or +
1	0	— or +	— or +

[a]See Appendix.

as a result of higher prices of manufactured goods (though the higher markup coefficient increases the income of the DCs and their purchases of primary products). For a given value of the markup coefficient, increases in the price of oil will reduce the LDCs' income by less the higher the recycling coefficient.

The effect of oil-price increases on the GDP of the DCs is not as clearcut (for an earlier discussion see Adams, 1979a). The impact of an increase in oil price will vary depending on the values of the recycling coefficient β and the markup coefficient π_O for the oil price.

A summary of the results for the DCs is presented in Table 3. The first impression is in line with what one might expect intuitively, i.e., that for any value of the recycling coefficient less than unity the impact of an increase in oil price will be negative when no markup for oil prices exists. However, when there is full recycling the effect is zero. Moreover, as soon as the markup takes positive values the impact of an oil-price increase on the GDP of the DCs may be positive or negative, and it becomes larger the greater is the markup coefficient. With respect to changes in the recycling coefficient β, we conjecture that the larger it is the less negative or more positive is the impact of an oil-price increase on the income of the DCs. The positive impacts appear on the surface to be counterintuitive. The ambiguity with regard to the sign of the multiplier of the GDP of the DCs is due to mutually offsetting effects arising from the multiple channels of influence. In particular, the increase in P_O worsens the trade account of the DCs and from there it worsens their GDP. However, OPEC imports more manufactured goods and this tends to offset this deterioration.

Depending on the relative magnitude of the variables involved, the effect of an increase in the oil price may result in a negative or positive impact on the GDP of the DCs (a condition to reduce the ambiguity of the sign of dY^d/dP_O is developed in the Appendix). It is important, however, to remember that no offsetting counterinflationary policy or capacity constraints have been assumed in the DCs so that the demand-side impacts can work out fully.

2.3   The Influence of Primary-Commodity Prices on LDCs and DCs

As in the previous section, there are direct and indirect channels through which an increase in primary-commodity prices may be transmitted. An increase in the prices of primary commodities directly raises the value of the exports of the LDCs (assuming a price elasticity less than unity) and a larger amount of financial resources becomes available for manufacturing imports to accelerate capital formation. This desirable result may be offset through one of the indirect channels to the extent that the prices of manufactured goods respond to the prices of primary commodities by the markup process. The ensuing increases in the prices of manufactured goods will reduce the purchasing power of the foreign-exchange resources of the LDCs, dampening the process of capital accumulation. Another possible indirect channel from the point of view of the LDCs is the effect of primary-commodity prices on the GDP of the DCs; this is a direct effect from the point of view of the latter countries. An increase in primary-commodity prices will raise the bill for imports of primary products in real terms. This will reduce real GDP in the DCs and this of course feeds back to the exports of the LDCs.

Another source of countervailing effects is the markup of manufactured-goods prices in response to variations in the prices of primary commodities. The larger the markup coefficient, the smaller is the amount of manufactured goods that needs to be exported by the DCs in order to secure a given amount of primary commodities, hence this will represent a stimulus to the income of the DCs.

At this point we note that the third block of countries, the oil countries, also plays a role in determining the effect of increases in primary-commodity prices. The markup response of manufactured-goods prices to an increase in primary-commodity prices will cause a reduction in the real volume of manufactures that are imported by the oil countries, and this reduction will dampen activity in the DCs, with other subsequent feedbacks.

As previously, we have computed solutions for the system in Table 4 for dY^l/dP_p and dY^d/dP_p under various assumptions for the markup coefficient. It should be noted

TABLE 4   The effect of commodity prices on GDPs.

π_p	dY/dP_p	
	Nonoil LDCs	DCs
0	+	—
$0 < \pi_p < 1^a$	+ or —	+ or —
1^a	+ or —	+ or —

^{a}See the Appendix for assumptions.

of course that the implicit recycling coefficient for the LDCs has a value of unity after oil imports have been taken into account. The OPEC recycling coefficient has been assumed here to have a value between zero and one.

In the case of the LDCs, the impact on GDP is positive when the markup coefficient is zero, as expected. As the markup coefficient takes positive values the result is less clear-cut. It is possible that higher values of the markup coefficient π_p will offset the initial positive impact of increases in P_p on the GDP of the LDCs. Moreover, this offset effect is larger the larger the markup coefficient. (The condition that invalidates our initial expectation of a positive impact is eqn. (A6) in the Appendix.)

In the case of the DCs, when the markup coefficient is zero, as expected, an increase in primary-commodity prices causes an unambiguous reduction in the income of the DCs. As for the LDCs, as the markup coefficient takes positive values, the net effect of an increase in primary-commodity prices becomes ambiguous. However, it can be shown that, as the markup coefficient increases, the change in DC income due to an increase in primary-commodity prices may take a positive sign and that the larger the markup the larger is the increase in DC income. (The condition that invalidates our initial expectation of a negative impact is eqn. (A7) in the Appendix.)

In the foregoing discussion we have assumed that commodity prices are exogenously determined. This is not altogether unrealistic with respect to petroleum prices under an OPEC-type regime or in connection with primary-commodity prices under an international price-stabilization scheme. However, it is more interesting to endogenize commodity-price determination. This can be done in a simple fashion. We can introduce a price response on the demand side simply by adding a term to the demand equation for primary commodities to the DCs. This price elasticity should reflect not only the response of demand to price in the consumption of the commodity but also the influence of price on inventory demand, assuming a negative relation between actual price and desired inventories. (This represents a regressive-expectations approach to price expectations which is typically used in commodity models. Alternative specifications are interesting but are not considered here in order to keep the model simple.) Secondly, we can assume that the available supply is exogenous. Changes in supply reflecting short-run influences on output such as the weather (e.g. droughts, frosts), inventory carry-over, or other supply interruptions (e.g. strikes, a mine disaster) can be assumed. We then solve for P_p/P_m. While this seems to be an oversimplification of the traditional commodity model it provides an endogenization that is useful for short-term simulation (for a discussion of the traditional commodity models see Adams and Behrman, 1976, 1978).

With regard to the oil market it is possible to endogenize the impact of changes in oil supply on the oil price in a similar way. It is not clear, however, that OPEC pricing behavior involves short-run profit maximization as described by such an approach.

3   PETROLEUM AND COMMODITY PRICES IN THE LINK SYSTEM

The aforementioned theoretical model is a greatly simplified representation of the relationships which are embodied in the empirical macromodel system of the world economy, Project LINK. The LINK system comprises models for 13 leading countries, area totals for the developing countries in the form of aggregative models for various areas in which the oil-producing LDCs are separated from the non-oil-producers, and finally models for the countries of the Council for Mutual Economic Assistance (CMEA), including the Soviet Union.

Since the country models are built at LINK centers at different locales, the structures are different for the various country models. Uniformity in specification is achieved only for the trade sector which considers exports and imports not by commodities but rather by Standard International Trade Classification (SITC) classes as follows: 0+1, food, beverages, and tobacco; 2+4, raw materials except fuel; 3, fuel (principally petroleum); 5—9, manufactured goods and semimanufactured goods.

One main feature of the LINK system is that it represents an interlinked model (for a detailed description, see Adams, 1979a, b) of the whole world economy and that it is able to assess mutual interactions through the channels of trade volumes and prices between various countries and trading blocks. Thus, it can serve as an instrument to measure the direct effect of increases in oil and commodity prices on the consuming countries as well as the feedbacks from them to the producers and back.

The COMLINK system is an augmented version of LINK that includes commodity models and the linkages from commodity prices to the trade prices operating in LINK. COMLINK was developed in order to endogenize the explanation of primary-commodity prices and to trace the impact of changes in commodity-market conditions on the exporting and importing countries. COMLINK contains 23 different commodities covering a large fraction of world primary-commodity trade but it does not yet encompass petroleum (for which an endogenous price-determination model would be hazardous in any case). In addition, COMLINK contains linkage equations which tie the export prices of primary commodities that are generated in the commodity models to the prices for SITC categories.

The propagation of a commodity-price increase through the system can be seen in the following sequence of steps.

(1) We begin with a conventional linked solution of the LINK country-model system. This solution takes into account the usual exogenous assumptions about policy, exchange rates, and other exogenous developments, including an initial assumption about foreign trade prices for the broad primary-commodity categories, i.e., SITC 0+1, 2+4, and 3. Typically, this solution already contains some adjustments to bring it in line with the latest known developments.

(2) The results of this solution are then entered into the commodity models. Specifically, the commodity models require information about economic activity in the consuming countries (which is a principal determinant of the demand for primary commodities) and an overall price deflator for the OECD which serves as a numeraire in the commodity models. Typically, the commodity models must then be lined up with real conditions. It is particularly necessary to ensure that the initial starting inventories are reasonably realistic. The solution of each of the commodity models then produces a set of commodity prices. The model solution also provides data on the consumption and production of each of the primary commodities as well as data on stocks, but this information is not utilized further in the COMLINK system, nor is any effort made to reconcile this information with the trade data of LINK.

(3) The commodity prices are then translated by linkage to the appropriately weighted commodity-price indexes into country-specific commodity-price indexes for export unit value for SITC 0+1 and 2+4. (For petroleum such equations have not been entered into the system, and the adjustments are made directly.)

(4) The LINK system then translates the export unit values into import unit values and import costs for the importing countries. It also translates the export unit values into earnings of foreign exchange by the producing countries.

(5) Finally, the LINK system solution translates this information into domestic prices and economic activities in the country models. An important aspect of this procedure is that the import prices for primary commodities are translated through the country models into export prices for manufactures.

The solution procedure is iterative, from a solution of the country-model system to a solution of the commodity models and then back to the country models until a stable solution is reached. The result is a consistent solution of the world model system which includes, in addition to economic activity and trade, the world primary-commodity markets.

However, while the system recognizes the commodity prices, we have noted before that it does not attempt to recognize commodity quantities. This is not a serious problem on the demand side since the import equations contain price terms and presumably take care of the price effects, which are small in the short run. However, on the supply side it poses a more serious problem since without specific adjustments LINK does not recognize country-specific commodity-supply disturbances.

The following are some of the behavioral attributes of the country–commodity model system.

(1) Economic activity in the developed countries is largely determined by Keynesian models, as in our simple theoretical system. Primary-commodity imports are closely tied to economic activity and the short-term price elasticities are low or nonexistent.

(2) The LDC model system assumes that the export earnings of commodity producers are fully recycled into imports but that the earnings of the oil producers are only partially recycled.

(3) The elasticities of trade unit values with respect to commodity prices are generally below unity and include significant lags; this result is not unrealistic in the light of the fact that commodity prices are spot prices while much trade travels under contract or internal accounting prices.

(4) Domestic considerations (Phillips curves and monetary factors) dominate price determination in most of the country models but imported materials and fuels do have an influence. It is important to note that the impact of import prices on domestic prices and export prices for manufactures is greatly attenuated.

As a consequence, the striking result of model simulations (as can be seen in the next section) is that commodity-price changes have attenuated though measurable effects on the world model system.

3.1   Some Empirical Results

In this section we summarize some empirical results from solutions of the LINK and COMLINK systems.

First, with regard to oil-price simulations there have been numerous such studies in recent years in response to the movements of world oil prices. Since there is no endogenous oil model, in LINK, the increase in oil prices is introduced by making explicit adjustments in the import unit value for SITC 3.

One recent computation suggests that a 100% increase in oil prices translates into an 8.6% decline in world GDP and a 4.3% increase in the GDP deflator of the OECD countries*. (The increase in the consumer-price index would be 8.3%.) These results are, however, sensitive to the size of the shock and the time at which it occurs. The other adjustments which are necessary to accommodate realistically the results of oil-price adjustments, particularly if they are very large, also make a significant difference in the results. Consequently it is difficult to generalize the impacts and it is better to evaluate the effects on a case-by-case basis.

---

*The effect is over two years. See also the oil-price simulation in Filatov et al. (1983).

With regard to commodity prices some of the same reservations apply. There are also significant differences depending on the commodities to which the price increases apply. (It should also be noted that the LDC commodity producers recycle all their earnings, in contrast to the oil producers which do not have full recycling.) The effects of 100% increases in the prices of primary commodities are summarized in Table 5. In each case the price of a commodity group is increased and the impact is measured relative to the base solution after a period of three years.

TABLE 5   The impact of 100% commodity-price increases on various indicators (percentage change from base solutions).

Commodity	Trade prices (unit values)		GDP (DCs)	GDP deflator (OECD)	GDP (LDCs)	Volume of LDC imports
	SITC 0 + 1	SITC 2 + 4				
Tropical beverages	+17.0	−0.1	+0.2	+0.3	+1.6	+3.9
Grains	+16.4	−0.1	—	+0.2	+0.4	−5.1
Nonferrous metals	—	+19.1	+0.2	+0.3	+0.9	+1.2

The effects on trade unit values and on domestic prices in the DCs are clear. However, the feedthrough to the trade unit values is smaller than one would have expected. The same is true of the effect on the OECD GDP deflator. The small response of the OECD GDP deflator may reflect the fact that the OECD GDP does not include production of tropical beverages and that the impact of trade prices on grains may fall far short of the actual impact (in the absence of a price policy) for grains. It is particularly interesting to note that, in contrast to the case of oil, the effect of the change in the prices of tropical beverages and nonferrous metals on the GDP of the industrial countries is positive; this result appears to reflect the positive impact on the GDP and imports of LDCs.

Some additional comments about the integrated modeling of countries and commodities are appropriate here. The foregoing simulations were obtained by adjusting the supply in the commodity markets to achieve desired price changes. In many commodity markets supply fluctuations lie behind the large swings in prices, making this an appropriate approach. Alternatively, we could have stimulated world economic activity in order to generate increases in demand and price. Unfortunately the commodity models, operating in the usual ranges, do not yield large enough responses to business-cycle swings to generate clearly visible results on world prices. One might argue that this is a problem since there are occasions when the pressure of demand on world capacity and speculation does create upsurges in commodity prices. However, it means that for many forecast applications it is not necessary to use the integrated country–commodity model system. If realistic assumptions about commodity prices are made in the first place, fluctuations in economic activity that are generated in the simulations of the LINK system will not produce vastly different commodity prices. However, the question of how to catch the speculative price swings remains troublesome.

4   SOME "MISSING LINKS"

So far the COMLINK system has focused on price interrelationships, tracing the effects of endogenously determined commodity prices through to export prices, import prices, and domestic inflation. We shall focus here on the "missing links" of the system insofar as they have special relevance to the question of the impact of commodity and oil prices on the world economy.

First, there is a need to reexamine and perhaps to complete the price interrelationships themselves. The degree to which commodity-price effects are attenuated is not altogether satisfactory. To some extent this may be because the estimated empirical relationships correctly reflect the real world at least during the estimation period. Nevertheless, to some extent the price linkages need reexamination. Do the trade unit values adequately capture the movement of world commodity prices? Do the price equations at the country level adequately incorporate the impact of imported-commodity prices? Are the impacts of world prices of commodities on the domestic markets represented realistically? (This is a serious question since the internal prices in many countries are reflections of world prices even if no imports occur!)

Second, is the price-determination mechanism in the commodity models themselves sufficiently responsive to changes in world economic conditions and/or to supply constraints? In practice the commodity models appear to attenuate the impact of changes in economic conditions and to average out price fluctuations which, at least in a time dimension of less than one year, are considerably more violent in the real world than in model simulations. In part this may be a question of properly specifying the impact of supply constraints but it may also reflect imperfect treatment of anticipations and their role in inventory purchasing.

Third, we may want to accommodate the information about quantities which is in the commodity systems but which does not now enter into the world model. We noted earlier that this is difficult to do from the point of view of the underlying statistical base. For most commodities data are available for production and consumption rather than for exports and imports, and it is difficult to reconcile these figures with the trade statistics by broad SITC category. However, especially where supply shortages originate in particular countries, unless the export volume data recognize the shift in supply the impact will be improperly distributed among the supplying countries, some of which will gain as a result of the high prices while others may lose (or gain to a lesser extent) as a result of the supply interruption (see Lord, 1981).

Fourth, there is the question of exchange rates. Work is proceeding in LINK to recognize exchange-rate determination and capital flows. This is a critical area for commodity markets and commodity-price determination. It is increasingly apparent that commodity prices are greatly influenced by both the actual and expected movements of exchange rates. Indeed, recent upsurges of commodity prices can be termed a "flight from money" into commodities. Nevertheless, few commodity-market models integrate this factor. One of the frontiers of the field is undoubtedly in the area of the relation between exchange rates and commodity prices. At the same time it should be noted that, in the country models as well, exchange rates may be an important channel (not always considered) in the impact of commodity prices on the world economy.

Finally, an important area of analysis must be the policy responses of the various countries. Apart from the broad issue of commodity-price stabilization through international buffer stocks (e.g. the "integrated program for commodities" of the United Nations Conference on Trade and Development) there are important questions of policy at the country level. In the producing countries passive and active policy responses may attenuate or amplify the impact of commodity-price movements (Adams and Behrman, 1982). At the level of the consuming countries, policies that are aimed at price stability or economic stabilization may also significantly alter the impact of commodity-price movements from what it might be in the absence of active or even passive intervention. For example, a fiscal or monetary policy designed to restrain inflation may turn price increases in primary-commodity markets into recessions in the DCs, while an accommodative monetary policy may result in higher inflation rates but may moderate the real impact of commodity-price increases. The impacts observed in the real world may, as a result of policy measures, be considerably different from those observed in model simulations.

REFERENCES

Adams, F.G. (1979a). Must high commodity prices depress the world economy? An application of a world model system. Journal of Policy Modeling, 1(2):201–205.

Adams, F.G. (1979b). Integrating commodity models into LINK. In J. Sawyer (Editor), Applications and Extensions of the LINK System. North-Holland, Amsterdam.

Adams, F.G. and Behrman, J.R. (1976). Econometric Models of World Commodity Markets. Ballinger, Cambridge, Massachusetts.

Adams, F.G. and Behrman, J.R. (1978). Econometric Modeling of World Commodity Policy. D.C. Heath/Lexington Books, Lexington, Massachusetts.

Adams, F.G. and Behrman, J.R. (1982). Commodity Exports and Economic Development: the Commodity Problem and Policy in Developing Countries. D.C. Heath/Lexington Books, Lexington, Massachusetts.

Filatov, V., Hickman, B.G., and Klein, L.R. (1983). Long-run simulations with the Project LINK system, 1978–1985. In B.G. Hickman (Editor), Global International Economic Models. North-Holland, Amsterdam; this volume, pp. 29–52.

Lord, M.J. (1981). Distributional effects of international commodity price stabilization: do the aggregate gains apply to individual countries? Journal of Policy Modeling, 3(1):61–76.

APPENDIX

This Appendix has two parts. Section A1 contains the theoretical expressions used in the derivation of Tables 2–4. Section A2 contains some of the conditions that will ensure the results of Tables 2–4.

A1   Theoretical Results

The approach taken here is to differentiate totally the model represented by eqns. (1)–(11). Then, using the identity that the exports of one country are the imports of another country, we can reduce the system of differential equations to a system of two differential equations. In order to reduce computational effort we assume that initial prices are equal to unity.

A1.1 Oil-Price Multipliers
We arrived at the following results:

$$
dY^l/dP_o = \left\{ \pi_o \left\{ -(R + M_p^d - M_o^l)[(1 - c^d) + \delta_p^d + \delta_o^d(1 - \beta)] - \beta\delta_p^d(M_o^l + M_o^d) \right. \right.
$$

$$
\left. + \delta_p^d(M_o^d + M_p^d) \right\} - M_o^l[(1 - \beta)(\delta_p^d + \delta_o^d) + (1 - c^d)]
$$

$$
\left. - M_o^d \delta_p^d(1 - \beta) \right\} if'/\Delta \tag{A1}
$$

$$dY^d/dP_o = \{\pi_o\,[(1 + \delta_o^1 f'i)(M_o^d + M_p^d) - (M_m^1 + M_m^o) - \delta_o^1 f'i(\beta M_m^1 + M_m^o)]$$

$$- (1 - \beta)M_o^1 - (1 - \beta)(1 + \delta_o^1 f'i)M_o^d\}/\Delta \tag{A2}$$

where

$$\Delta \equiv (1 - c^d - D_3)(1 + L_2 f') - D_2 f' L_3 > 0$$

$$D_2 \equiv \delta_o^1(\beta - 1)$$

$$D_3 \equiv \delta_o^d(\beta - 1)$$

$$L_2 \equiv \delta_o^1 i$$

$$L_3 \equiv \delta_p^d i$$

$$f' \equiv \partial f(K_i^1 \bar{L}^1)/\partial K^1$$

Equations (A1) and (A2) each contain two terms. One term has π_o multiplying an expression containing various variables of the model; this term captures the net effect of mark-ups in P_o on the oil-price multipliers. The other term is the net effect of an increase in the oil price alone on the GDPs of either LDCs (if eqn. (A1)) or DCs (if eqn. (A2)).

A1.2 Commodity-Price Multipliers

$$dY^d/dP_p = \Big\{\pi_p\{(1 + \delta_o^1 f'i)[(M_o^1 + M_o^d)(1 - \beta) - R] + \delta_o^1 f'i(1 - \beta)M_m^1\}$$

$$- \delta_o^1(1 - \beta)f'iM_p^d\Big\}/\Lambda \tag{A3}$$

$$dY^1/dP_p = \Big\{\pi_p\{\delta_p^d[(M_o^1 + M_o^d)(1 - \beta) - R]$$

$$- [(1 - c^d) + (1 - \beta)\delta_o^d](R + M_p^d - M_o^1)\} + [(1 - c^d)$$

$$+ (1 - \beta)\delta_o^d]M_p^d\Big\}f'i/\Lambda \tag{A4}$$

where

$$\Lambda \equiv K_2 T_3 + K_3 T_2 > 0$$

$$K_2 \equiv (1 - c^d) + \delta_o^d(1 - \beta)$$

$$K_3 \equiv \delta_o^1(1 - \beta)$$

$$T_2 \equiv if'\delta_p^d$$

$$T_3 \equiv (1 + \delta_o^1 f'i)$$

It should be noted that eqns. (A3) and (A4) have the same structure as eqns. (A1) and (A2). We can separate the effects of the markup π_p from the effects of increases in P_p. The term multiplied by π_p captures the net effect on the commodity-price multiplier of markups in P_p. The other term is the net effect of increases in P_p (alone) on the GDP of either LDCs (if eqn. (A4)) or DCs (if eqn. (A3)).

A2   Sufficient Conditions

In this section we develop sufficient conditions to eliminate the ambiguity in Tables 2–4. With respect to the ambiguity of dY^d/dP_o (Table 3) intuition suggests that dY^d/dP_o should have a negative sign. However, Table 3 shows the possibility of a positive sign for dY^d/dP_o. We develop here a sufficient condition for the positiveness of dY^d/dP_o. This amounts to finding a relationship between the variables that will make positive the numerator of eqn. (A2).

The condition is

$$(1 - \beta)[\pi_o (1 + \delta_o^1 f'i)]^{-1} [\pi_o \delta_o^1 f'i M_m^1 - (M_o^1 + M_o^d)(1 + \delta_o^1 f'i)] > B^d \qquad \text{(A5)}$$

where B^d is the trade account of the DCs and $\pi_o > 0$.

If B^d meets this requirement then dY^d/dP_o will be positive. Otherwise dY^d/dP_o will be negative.

With regard to the ambiguous results of Table 4, we expect a negative sign for dY^d/dP_p and a positive sign for dY^1/dP_p. However, for the case of LDCs if

$$R > (1 - \beta)(M_o^1 + M_o^d) - [(1 - c^d) + (1 - \beta)\delta_o^d](\delta_p^d \pi_p)^{-1} (\pi_p M_m^1 - M_p^d) \qquad \pi_p > 0 \qquad \text{(A6)}$$

then $dY^1/dP_p < 0$. This implies that the negative effect of the markup coefficient π_p overcompensates the positive effect of the increase in P_p. This is because the increase in the value of the exports of the LDCs due to the increase in P_p/P_m is more than offset by the reduction in the purchasing power of R due to the increase in P_m. Therefore a net reduction in imports of manufactures will occur and this will reduce capital accumulation. This last effect reduces the GDP of LDCs.

For the case of DCs, manipulation of eqn. (A3) suggests that if

$$R < (1 - \beta)(M_o^1 + M_o^d) + \delta_o^1 f'i(\pi_p M_m^1 - M_p^d)[\pi_p (1 + \delta_o^1 f'i)]^{-1} \qquad \pi_p > 0 \qquad \text{(A7)}$$

then $dY^d/dP_p > 0$; i.e. the markup coefficient π_p more than offsets the negative effect of the increase in P_p on the GDP of the DCs. Here, the reduction in the real value of R will not offset the increase in the real value of the exports so that the real external purchasing power and imports of the LDCs from the DCs are increased.

COMMENTS*

The paper presented by Adams and Marquez is an interesting attempt to explain what is happening in the triangle OPEC–LDC oil importers–developed countries during changes in petroleum prices. The authors extend the findings obtained, mutatis mutandis, to all primary products. As we are all well aware, these are rather controversial questions that have not yet been sufficiently explored, and there are no unanimously accepted answers.

The most valuable aspect of the theoretical approach presented here is the development of methodological tools, from a simplified world model to a flexible search for as-yet unknown linkages which could be interpreted as forming a coupling mechanism with the rest of the world economy.

The initial theoretical thesis, about the direct and indirect channels through which increases in oil and primary product prices may affect the consuming economies, both developed and developing, in my opinion constitutes a useful exploration of the basic problem.

Under certain assumptions I can accept the interpretation of the transmission mechanism of price increases through the world economy, including an increase in the developed-country prices of manufactured goods, as being due to markups of oil and primary commodity prices. It is therefore also an acceptable conclusion that for the non oil-producing LDCs the impact of oil-price increases is unequivocally negative. Equally evident is the fact that the developed countries have at their disposal a wide range of possible strategies for avoiding (or minimizing) the consequences of the oil-price changes under discussion.

In my opinion, certain technical details in the description of the theoretical model could be improved, for instance the way in which gradients are presented, and I would like to see a stricter acknowledgment of the basically identical positions of oil and other primary products in the model. Also, I find the absence of East European developed countries in the model a notable deficiency. On the other hand, the above-mentioned "triangle" approach should have been more strictly adhered to throughout the report. It is one valuable way to avoid the reduction of complex problems to a simplistic interpretation based on the immediate, first-step changes in the price system of the developed countries which neglects the effects on the developing countries and on the world economy as a whole.

The authors are on the right track in searching for a mechanism to transform a model with the prices as exogenous variables to one in which they are endogenous. But their real problem, and it is a problem we all face, is basically much more difficult to solve, since it is not just a technical question of model transformation but rather one of discovering qualitatively new phenomena in the world economy and of expressing them in terms of new paradigms.

It seems to me that even the highly respectable LINK or COMLINK models, with their business-cycle tradition and their rather restricted concepts concerning both the content and the forms of international economic relations, are not very well placed to overcome the growing difficulties in the analytical field. This is even more true for those projects that apply the general equilibrium approach.

---

*By Ivo Fabinc, Economics Faculty "Boris Kidric", University of Ljubljana, Ljubljana, Yugoslavia.

If we try to change the perspective, the increase of oil prices appears not as a unilateral act in a world of pure Walrasian interdependence but rather as a phenomenon that is deeply immersed in the stream of great historical changes and that is part of the continuing dynamic transformation of existing structures of economic strength and technological systems, and even of economic principles and values. The interdependence is obviously still there, but it now appears as a qualified interdependence. It is therefore questionable if the impact of the changes in oil and commodity prices can really be examined in an efficient and conclusive way on the basis of a short-run analysis.

But having said this, and having accepted these doubts and qualifications, we must now search elsewhere for the roots of inflation, certainly not overlooking the imposing military needs, the nonconventional behavior of powerful corporations, or the highly explosive monetary and financial situation, etc. The system of floating exchange rates, controlled or not, is really only a thin veneer over the surface of the underlying economic perturbations.

We must recognize that we are living in the middle of a deep structural crisis in the evolution of the world socioeconomic system. Nobody can remain completely unaffected although the intensity of the crisis is not evenly distributed over the world.

Economic isolation, or an insistence on selfish interests and a strong belief in the efficiency of national economic policies are not the right solutions. The existing socioeconomic structure of the world is an extremely complex totality that moves and changes under the interconnected influence of powerful national corporations and other social forces. What we need is a sincere explanation of what is happening and a frank international dialog about a commonly accepted strategy for development and means for its implementation. I have in mind not only the UN-sponsored global negotiations between the developed and developing nations, but also a constructive discussion along the lines of collective self-reliance between OPEC countries and the oil-importing LDCs.

Pursuing an honest and realistic international dialog is the real opportunity for solving more easily the challenges arising during this transitional period in a spirit of effective international interdependence and for discovering the best way of integrating the less developed countries into the world economy.

GLOBAL INTERNATIONAL ECONOMIC MODELS
B.G. Hickman (editor)
Elsevier Science Publishers B.V. (North-Holland)
© IIASA, 1983

AN EVALUATION OF THE EFFECTS OF COMMODITY-PRICE INDEXATION ON DEVELOPED AND DEVELOPING ECONOMIES: AN APPLICATION OF THE REMPIS MODEL

Carl B. Weinberg
Wharton EFA, Inc., and National Bureau of Economic Research, New York (USA)

M.I. Nadiri and J. Choi
New York University, and National Bureau of Economic Research, New York (USA)

1   INTRODUCTION

Developing nations which depend on exports of nonoil commodities for foreign exchange have long argued that the indexation of commodity prices to some price measure in developed countries would benefit rich and poor nations alike. This proposition has been dissected theoretically but no consensus of opinion has been established. In this paper we will attempt to evaluate the impacts of commodity-price indexation on the world economy using a specially designed global econometric simulation model. The model (the Regional Econometric Model for Price-Indexation Studies (REMPIS)) has been described elsewhere (see Nadiri and Weinberg, 1978).

The following section is a brief overview of some issues in the debate over commodity-price indexation. A summary of the REMPIS model is then presented in Section 3. Section 4 describes the simulation results, and in Section 5 we try to draw some conclusions from these simulations.

2   THE INDEXATION SIMULATION: SOME ISSUES

The most important element of the indexation scenario is the selection of the indexation rule. Any "real-world" application of commodity-price indexation will involve political compromise as well as economic benefit analysis. The selection of an appropriate indexation rule will most likely involve noneconomic elements, aligned along "North—South" political lines.

The specification of the political objectives is difficult. For example, would developing countries be satisfied with a substantial increase in their standard of living even if the income gap between richer and poorer economies widened? Are the structural changes sought by the less developed countries to be for protection against deterioration of their terms of trade? Should the benchmark be a fixed year or the (constantly improving) relative-price schedule of the previous year? (These issues are discussed in Bhagwati (1978), particularly the early article by H.G. Johnson (1956).)

The concerns of the developed economies are not mirror images of those of the developing nations. Rather than being concerned directly with real income levels they are more concerned with nominal price performance. For a given and slowly changing pattern of demand for primary commodities would a trend towards higher real commodity prices impose a permanently increasing rate of inflation? If so, then adjustment to commodity-price indexation would be costly during a period of transition in commodity demand, which is relatively price inelastic.

A related issue is the impact of commodity-price indexation on the balance of payments. In effect an indexation program is an attempt to make a transfer from the developed to the developing economies. However, the financing of the monetary transfer imposes some institutional accommodation. A permanent bias in payments against the developed economies would require a permanent accommodation in world capital markets. This could have both inflationary and contractionary effects on the developed countries since new world liquidity would have to be created (inflation) or funds would have to be borrowed on private capital markets, "crowding out" the private sector.

Indexation rules may be characterized as either price-stabilizing rules or price-maximizing rules. The price-stabilizing rules would act to support prices when markets were "weak" and to contain prices when markets were "strong". The rationale for such a program is that the marginal social welfare of an income windfall is less than the marginal loss of social welfare of an income shortfall. Clearly this depends on an assumption of decreasing marginal utility at all income levels. A price-maximizing rule would never allow prices to fall.

If commodity demand were perfectly inelastic then a price-maximizing rule would maximize income at all points in time. In the longer run, demand for commodities is expected to exhibit a significant price elasticity, suggesting that price-maximizing rules may not be long-run revenue-maximizing rules. Thus they may not give a desirable long-run path of development.

In the light of these issues in the choice of a commodity-price indexation rule, the specific rule selected for this study is stated as follows: the nominal price of any indexed commodity shall not increase in any period by less than some general index of inflation in the developed economies. If one defines the real price of a commodity as the ratio of its nominal price to the general price index of the developed economies then this rule may be restated to mean that the real price of a commodity shall not decline.

It should be noted first that this rule is a one-sided affair: there is nothing to restrain nominal prices from increasing by more than the general inflation rate, only by less than that amount. Next, the general inflation rate in this study is taken as the implicit deflator of gross domestic product (GDP) in an OECD regional model. This may be an imperfect measure of price inflation. Kravis (1975) suggests that GDP deflators converted at market exchange rates may not reflect relative purchasing powers. Other imperfections of the

GDP deflator as an inflation index have been frequently discussed. Further, if the developed economies are viewed as "specializing" in the export of manufactured goods, where export prices are loosely correlated in the general price deflator, then we have imposed the condition that the terms of trade of the developed countries can remain unchanged at best and will most likely worsen.

The simulated effects of imposing this rule on the system may vary depending on the initial conditions for the simulation. In any given year the indexation program will not affect a commodity price if the price of the commodity would have increased by more than the index price in the absence of indexation. The initial conditions of the baseline solution are reproduced in Table 1. During the simulation period from 1969 to 1973

TABLE 1   The baseline case: some inflation rates (measured as the percent change per year).

Variable[a]	1969	1970	1971	1972	1973
PCT	−6.4	3.4	8.6	12.3	36.7
PCO	25.3	−28.9	−21.2	17.0	82.3
PCF	1.9	29.0	−11.4	12.3	26.3
PRI	−3.8	−27.9	−2.9	10.8	83.2
PSU	15.5	7.1	7.7	45.8	−15.1
PWH	−5.4	−5.1	7.8	15.5	96.9
PWO	−11.6	−10.3	−7.7	60.2	97.4
OEPGDP	4.7	5.5	5.5	8.9	13.9

[a]The variable definitions are composed of a prefix P indicating price and a suffix denoting the commodity. The suffixes are as follows: CT, cotton; CO, cocoa; CF, coffee; RI, rice; SU, sugar; WH, wheat; WO, wool. $OEPGDP$ is the implicit deflator of GDP in the OECD regional model.

there were clearly wide variations in the rate of price increases and in the acceleration of prices. Most of the commodities in this study will be affected by the indexation program in the first three years of the simulation. However, only one commodity suffered a deterioration of its real price in the 1972–1973 period.

Technically, indexation is introduced by overriding the price equation in each of the commodity-market models whenever that equation predicts a real price decline. A typical commodity-market model can be summarized analytically in the following system of four equations:

$$\log Q^D = f_d[D, P, P(L)] \tag{1}$$

$$\log Q^S = f_s[Q^D(L), P(L)] \tag{2}$$

$$STK = STK_{-1} + Q^S - Q^D > 0 \tag{3}$$

$$\log(P/PDF) = f_p[STK/Q^D, STK/Q^D(L)] \tag{4}$$

In this system Q^D and Q^S are physical quantities that are demanded and supplied, P is the nominal commodity price in US dollars, and the STK are physical inventories. D and PDF are the world demand and general price levels, respectively. The L operator indicates the use of lag structures in estimation.

The indexation process operates on eqn. (4) of the system. If *P/PDF* as determined by the equation declines from one year to the next then the calculated value is replaced by the value for the previous year; thus real prices can never decline.

This indexation scenario does not explicitly account for the financing of the indexation scheme, nor for the mechanics of the program. Implicit in the simulation is a hypothetical stabilization stockpile, or buffer stock, that is increased whenever real prices fall below the level of the previous year. Even though indexation directly replaces eqn. (4), the market-clearing condition (3) indicates that higher prices, which reduce demand directly in the current period, will also increase inventories.

Supporting the accumulation of physical goods must be an accommodating source of funds for their purchase. This aspect of the indexation program plays no direct role in the model. Thus we have constructed a scenario in which the purchase of buffer stocks is financed by the creation of new international reserves. For example, new allocations of special drawing rights may be given to developing countries which can then be exchanged for US dollars for the support of commodity buffer stocks.

In this scenario there is a complete analogy of the indexation problem to the transfer issue. In this case, part of the transfer arrives "from a helicopter" and is dropped directly on commodity-producing economies. For this aspect of the transfer the question is simply this: how much of this nominal transfer can be translated into real terms, and what portion of it will simply generate increased inflation? The transfer is exactly the nominal increase in the revenues of the commodity producers. Here the issues are the distribution of the real effects of the transfer between the transferor nations (the importers) and the transferees (the exporters).

Clearly, there is a positive sum to the outcomes of this experiment. In the best of all possible worlds both the size of the "pie" would increase and the distribution of the slices could shift in favor of developing nations. The limitations facing this program are the degree to which these nominal transfers are translated into real gains and the degree to which monetary transfers generate inflation and concomitant slower growth. It is towards these issues that the following simulation analysis is directed.

3   THE REMPIS MODEL

The REMPIS model divides the world into four "super-regions". Countries are classified into sympathetic groups by their level of development and by their political/economic structure rather than by geographic grouping. The four regions recognized by this model are as follows: the developed market economies (OECD), including the 24 countries that are members of the OECD and South Africa; the less developed oil-importing market economies (DEVE) which include all countries not classified under one of the other four models (this country group follows United Nations classifications of countries by relative levels of economic development, as presented in the published tables of the UN Statistical Office); the oil-exporting economies (OPEC), including Iran, Saudi Arabia, Iraq, Qatar, Oman, Libya, Egypt, Syria, Indonesia, Venezuela, Kuwait, Yemen, and Nigeria; the centrally planned economies (CMEA), including the Union of Soviet Socialist Republics, Bulgaria, Czechoslovakia, the German Democratic Republic, Hungary, Poland, and Rumania. The structure of the model is described in Figure 1 and Table 2.

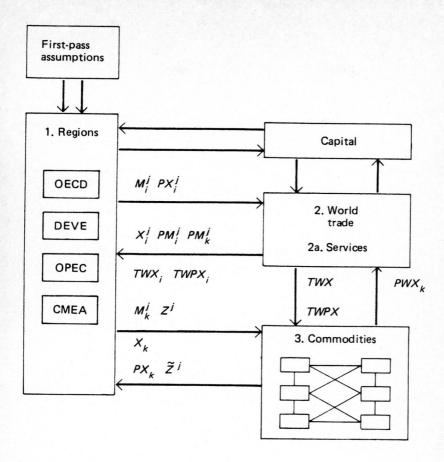

FIGURE 1   The overall structure of the REMPIS model.

While certain types of economic activity can be best modeled within the framework of national or regional macroeconomics the concept of a world model suggests that some activities may be better specified within a global framework. In the REMPIS system world trade markets are constrained so that world supply and world demand for merchandise are equal at all points in time and so that the world balance of payments on the merchandise account also comes to zero. This is equivalent to treating total world merchandise trade as being determined in a single world market, and it is accomplished through an export-allocation model (see Klein, 1976).

Exceptional treatment is given to the supply of primary commodities. Again, the assumption of a global market with supply and demand constraints is imposed. Supply functions are introduced explicitly for groups of commodities and these functions, together with a product-specific demand structure, are integrated with the regional macroeconomic

TABLE 2   The REMPIS model: the number of variables in each sector[a].

Sector	Behavioral variables	Identity variables	Exogenous A variables[b]	Exogenous B variables[c]
OECD	22	33	24	7
DEVE	12	14	17	4
OPEC	12	14	17	4
CMEA	10	4	9	0
ROW[d]	0	8	8	0
Linkage	25	20	41	0
Total	81	93	116	15

[a]The commodity-market models are not included in this table. They would add around 225 additional variables to the system.
[b]The exogenous A variables are required for the solution of a sector by itself.
[c]The exogenous B variables are the exogenous A variables that remain after subtracting those which are endogenized when all of the model sectors are linked together.
[d]ROW indicates the rest of the world. These are definitions which close the global system.

models. The essential result of this integration is that world primary-commodity production, demand, prices, and stocks are determined jointly with world demand and supply for other commodities (Adams, 1979).

The four regional macroeconomic components of the REMPIS model differ in other respects apart from the country coverage. In particular, the level of GDP is determined by either demand, supply, or fiat, depending on the structure of the prototype economy within each region. In the OECD model the aggregate demand determines the output of goods and services and the aggregate supply is assumed to adjust rather elastically to short-run fluctuations (Johnson, K.N., 1979). In the DEVE model the opposite case is presented (UNCTAD Staff, 1976; Glowacki and Ruffing, 1979). Supply constraints fix the maximum output obtainable, and demand fluctuations are reflected in price adjustments. The OPEC and CMEA models are trade models only, and fluctuations in output are not structurally modeled in them.

In the OPEC case, production may be interpreted as being primarily crude and refined petroleum, which is assumed to be available in perfectly elastic amounts at posted prices. The prices, however, are exogenous, reflecting supply-side considerations which may be either political, economic, or technological. The CMEA economies, in theory, use imports as primary inputs into their production process. Therefore an import shortfall would normally suggest a production shortfall. However, the production side of the CMEA region is not articulated in this model, and export goods are assumed to be provided at "world" prices and, again, in perfectly elastic supply.

Three of the models (the DEVE, OPEC, and CMEA systems) are constrained on their international transactions to reflect the availability of foreign exchange. Trade payments with the OECD group or with each other are assumed to be denominated only in convertible currencies, which are available to these regions only through export sales, through hoarding from previous transactions, or from "capital inflows". Therefore the commodity terms of trade, which measure the ability to import goods that can be derived from a given "basket" of export sales, are very important measures of well-being for these regions.

In fact, the currency constraint is imposed directly in the specification of the import-demand functions. The four classes that are recognized are SITC* groups 0 and 1 (foods),

*Standard International Trade Classification.

SITC groups 2 and 4 (nonfuel primary materials), SITC group 3 (mineral fuels and electricity), and SITC groups 5—9 (manufactured goods and miscellaneous). Rather than treating import groups independently for each category, available foreign-currency reserves are allocated to the alternative groups using an expenditure system specification (UNCTAD Staff, 1976). Thus an import shortfall or a decrease in foreign transfers received (or capital flows) directly decreases the ability to import in the DEVE, OPEC, and CMEA models.

Each of the regional models is estimated on aggregate data. The numeraire for aggregation has been arbitrarily selected as the US dollar. The implication of using a common numeraire currency is that exchange rates cannot appear explicitly in the models. However, they do appear implicitly in this system through fluctuations in the levels of reserves, which are endogenous in all of the regional model components. Following the balance-of-payments approach to exchange-rate determination (Johnson, H.G., 1956), exchange rates are assumed to adjust in response to payments imbalances so that reserves remain unchanged for any given country. It cannot be assumed that either a fixed or a flexible exchange-rate regime is in effect during the sample period. Changes in the reserves of one region relative to another require exchange-rate adjustment in either case. Given the intermediate-run perspective of this system we can realistically assume a mixture of fixed exchange rates and managed floating. In this environment, reserve changes indicate fundamental payment imbalances and lead to an adjustment of aggregate demand by reducing real money balances in deficit countries.

A world trade model is the centerpiece of the REMPIS system. The primary purpose of this sector is to bind together the regional macroeconomic models by imposing consistency in the world balance of trade and in the world balance of payments. In this usage, consistency means that two conditions are satisfied in the international accounts of the REMPIS system. First, exports must be allocated to the regional models so that the world trade balance, in both volume and constant-price terms, sums to zero. Together these two conditions impose the constraints that an import demand exists for every export supplied at equilibrium prices and that every international payment for merchandise supplied must have both a payer and a payee.

Operationally, the REMPIS system imposes these constraints using the simplest formulation of an export-allocation model: a constant trade matrix model. The technology for the utilization of such a matrix has been developed by the LINK Project (Waelbroeck, 1976). For the purposes of this study the constant shares matrix approach offers computational ease and reasonably small errors of prediction for short-term to medium-term simulation (Beaumont and Prucha, 1977).

Models of seven commodity markets are presently included in the REMPIS system. The models have been borrowed from the research of Adams and Behrman (Adams and Behrman, 1976) rather than being developed especially for this project. The essential elements of the models are the articulation of the demand and supply behavior of the seven agricultural commodities, disaggregating these components into three regional sources. These regions correspond to the OECD, DEVE, and CMEA components of the larger global system. Supply and demand are matched on a global basis, and world stocks of commodities can be calculated.

The "real world price" for each commodity is calculated using an adjustment equation. Changes in real prices are related to changes in the ratio of end-of-year stocks to final sales through a dynamic behavioral equation. The notion of real price, as opposed to nominal price, is derived from the concept that the behavior of the market is best captured by an analysis of relative prices rather than absolute price levels, which have no theoretical interpretation. The numeraire is the implicit GDP deflator for the OECD region, thus providing another linkage between the components of the models within the REMPIS system.

There are at least two bold assumptions involved in modeling world commodity markets with this type of model. First, it is assumed that there exists a unique world price for major commodity groups. While goods arbitrage could equate prices everywhere under competitive world markets (apart from transactions, information, and transportation costs), it is not clear that all world commodities are sold in purely competitive markets. The second major assumption is related to this point: namely, the structure of the markets is indeed competitive in the long run. While the price-determining mechanism in these models is disequilibrium in spirit in the short run, the longer-term implication of the model specification is that "invisible-hand" types of adjustment equilibrate world supply and demand in the longer-run picture. This assumption may not be valid in some of the markets that are being considered.

4   THE RESULTS OF THE INDEXATION EXPERIMENT

The first case to be considered is the comparison of a baseline simulation without indexation to a similar experiment with indexation imposed. The objective is to identify in the model results the issues discussed in the previous section. In the next section the multiplier properties of the model, both with and without indexation, will be analyzed in an attempt to evaluate the relative advantages and disadvantages of indexation in a changing world environment.

The first proposition of indexation is that the real price of a commodity cannot decline. As shown in Table 3, all the commodity prices increase by at least the same amount as the general commodity-price deflator *PDF*. This variable is linked directly to the price sector of the OECD model (*PDF* may not fluctuate exactly in the OECD deflator for GDP because of lags in the linking equation).

A second proposition is that the stocks of commodities should generally be higher under indexation than without indexation. Table 4 demonstrates this to be the case. With

TABLE 3   The indexed case: some inflation rates (measured as the percent change per year).

Variable[a]	1969	1970	1971	1972	1973
PCT	2.8	6.0	6.6	9.2	21.7
PCO	25.7	6.0	6.4	9.2	14.8
PCF	2.9	29.3	6.3	9.2	15.9
PRI	2.9	6.0	6.4	9.2	36.1
PSU	16.1	6.0	7.8	42.5	12.3
PWH	2.8	6.0	6.4	9.2	50.2
PWO	2.8	6.0	6.3	14.4	42.2
OEPGDP	5.0	6.7	6.9	10.0	13.5
PDF	2.8	6.0	6.3	9.2	12.2

[a]See footnote to Table 1. *PDF* is the deflator of commodity prices used by the commodity models.

TABLE 4 A comparison of the indexed and unindexed baseline solutions: the percent increase in commodity stocks in the indexed case over the baseline case.

Variable[a]	1969	1970	1971	1972	1973
STKCT	–	9.9	24.9	34.7	43.6
STKCO	··	5.6	26.7	58.6	154.3
STKCF	–	0.2	0.4	9.5	16.0
STKRI	1.3	11.9	30.3	68.7	114.9
STKSU	–	1.3	2.9	8.6	10.3
STKWH	10.3	45.3	83.4	178.6	196.8
STKWO	5.1	8.0	10.8	−5.6	33.6

[a]The prefix *STK* refers to stocks (in physical volumes). The suffixes refer to commodity markets, and are defined in the footnote to Table 1.

the exception of a few commodities in the first year of the indexation experiment and of wool in 1972, all the stocks increase each year as a result of the controlled higher prices. This is a direct result of lags in the demand and supply functions for the commodities. The other commodities which do not exhibit stock adjustments remain unchanged because indexation does not directly affect them in a specific year.

Table 4 also illustrates another implication of the indexation rule that we have specified. Since prices are always supported, stockpiles can only increase in the indexed case as compared with the baseline; there are no circumstances under which the buffer stocks would ever be sold off to decrease prices. This implies that the potential long-run cost of the programs could be infinite if there were a trend of the terms of trade against the commodity-exporting regions.

An unusual result occurs in the stock variable for wool. The indexed stockpile is actually less than the stockpile in the unindexed baseline solution in 1972. This is easily explained by noting that a nonnegativity constraint is imposed on the stockpile variables. This constraint limits the quantity demanded to be equal to the quantity supplied. In fact the baseline scenario causes the limitation to be imposed in 1972. As can be easily seen by the price pattern of wool in Table 1, there are certainly some unusual factors at work in that market. In this case the indexation rule eases these patterns by smoothing out the patterns of price adjustments over time.

Another prediction from the discussion of Section 3 is that the terms of trade would improve for the commodity-exporting regions. Table 5 compares the improvement or worsening of the simple commodity terms of trade for the four regional models. For the

TABLE 5 A comparison of the indexed and unindexed baseline solutions: the percent gain in terms of trade over the baseline[a].

Model	1969	1970	1971	1972	1973
OECD	−0.2	−0.1	+0.1	+0.1	+0.6
DEVE	+1.0	+2.8	+1.6	+0.9	−1.4
OPEC	−0.7	−2.3	−4.5	−4.3	−1.6
CMEA	−0.1	−0.3	−0.7	−0.4	−0.1

[a]The terms of trade are defined here as the ratio of export prices to import prices. Presented here are deviations in the terms of trade between the control and the indexed solutions for each year relative to the control solution.

developing-regions group the terms of trade under indexation improved over the unindexed solution every year except 1973. It should be pointed out that in the unindexed solution the terms of trade appreciated by 6.1% over the 1972 level so that the year-over-year changes still favor the DEVE group.

A surprising result is that the OECD also experiences an improvement in its terms of trade, most significantly in 1973. It is frequently overlooked that the primary-commodity trade of the developed economies is at least as great as that of the developing economies in absolute volume or value terms, although it is less important as a share of total trade. The level of the OECD terms of trade in 1973 declined in both simulations, but by less under indexation than in the baseline simulation.

In the OPEC and CMEA groups the terms of trade are worse in the indexed than in the baseline case. For OPEC the deterioration is significant even though the terms of trade do continue to improve strongly over time in both simulations. The exclusion of petroleum exports from the indexation group puts the region at a relative disadvantage.

The next step of the transmission mechanism leads us to examine the trade flows (Table 6). As suggested in the previous discussion, the direction of movement of the merchandise balances is towards improvement of the DEVE balance and worsening of the OECD balance in those years when indexation is affecting the commodity price. This can be seen in Table 6 to be true for the period 1969–1972 during which most commodities are affected by indexation.

A noteworthy element in the table is that there are no substantial shifts in the patterns of payments balances. This is true despite the fact that all the nominal trade flows are increased in value by indexation. For the DEVE, OPEC, and CMEA models this sort of behavior has been imposed in the linkage of import values to export revenues — the so-called "ability-to-pay" principle. For the OECD model, however, this behavior is not directly imposed although it is implicit in the constraints of the world balance-of-payments model.

In a four-region model the sum of balances of payments must be zero, i.e. $\sum_{i=1}^{4} B_i = 0$, where B_i is the dollar-denominated merchandise balance of region i. By model specification it has been imposed that the DEVE, OPEC, and CMEA regions can only import a value equal to or less than the sum of their export revenues plus capital inflows. If $B_i = X_i - M_i + F_i$ where X_i, M_i, and F_i are the dollar values of exports, imports, and capital flows, respectively, then this constraint implies that $dX_i = dM_i$ if $dF_i = 0$ for these three regions ($i = 1, 2, 3$). It is then also true that $dB_i = dX_i - dM_i + dF_i = 0$, for $i = 1, 2, 3$. Therefore, if $\sum_{i=1}^{3} dB_i = 0$, then $dB_4 = 0$. Thus an important property of the linkage system is illustrated.

Apart from the distributional effect on world trade there is also a level effect on world trade. Table 7 presents the effects of indexation on the price and quantity of world exports. In the 1969–1972 period when indexation is effective there are increases in world trade volume. The negative differential in volumes in 1973 does not suggest that the volume of world trade would be lower in 1973 under indexation than under free markets. Rather, it suggests that the increase in export volumes is less in the indexation simulation than in the free-markets case.

Table 8 makes the point clear by illustrating the growth rate of the value and volume of world trade in each case, year by year. The rate of growth of world trade volume under an indexation scenario is greater than or equal to the growth rate in the unindexed

TABLE 6 A comparison of the indexed and unindexed baseline simulations: world trade balances[a].

Model	Variable	1969 B	1969 I	1970 B	1970 I	1971 B	1971 I	1972 B	1972 I	1973 B	1973 I
OECD	VX	187.0	190.1	212.8	222.2	234.5	252.1	279.9	301.8	382.9	399.1
	VM	188.9	192.1	212.3	222.1	232.9	250.7	279.9	302.3	387.7	404.5
	VB	−1.9	−2.0	0.5	0.1	1.6	1.4	0.0	−0.5	−4.8	−5.4
DEVE	VX	33.0	33.8	35.6	37.8	38.4	41.7	44.0	47.2	67.4	69.2
	VM	42.8	43.4	47.1	48.0	53.5	56.3	58.7	61.8	87.5	87.0
	VB	−9.8	−9.6	−11.5	−11.2	−15.1	−14.6	−14.7	−14.6	−17.1	−17.8
OPEC	VX	16.2	16.3	17.8	18.1	22.2	22.7	26.9	27.7	40.6	41.9
	VM	8.7	8.8	9.7	9.9	11.3	11.7	13.9	14.3	20.0	20.2
	VB	7.5	7.5	8.1	8.2	10.9	11.0	13.0	13.3	20.6	21.7
CMEA	VX	18.9	19.5	25.7	27.3	31.9	34.5	36.4	39.2	53.8	55.4
	VM	14.5	15.2	22.9	24.4	29.4	31.8	34.7	37.3	52.5	53.9
	VB	4.4	4.3	2.8	2.9	2.5	2.6	1.7	1.9	1.3	1.5
Total world	VX	255.1	259.7	291.9	305.4	327.0	351.0	387.2	415.9	544.7	565.6
	VM	254.9	259.5	292.0	305.4	327.1	350.6	387.2	415.7	544.7	565.6

[a]World exports and world imports may not balance owing to rounding error. All flows are measured in billions of current US dollars. The B columns are the baseline simulation without indexation and the I columns are the indexed baseline simulations. VX indicates merchandise exports free on board (f.o.b.), VM indicates merchandise imports (f.o.b.), and VB is the balance.

TABLE 7   A comparison of the indexed and unindexed baseline solutions: the percent price and volume increase in world trade caused by
indexation.

Variable[a]	1969	1970	1971	1972	1973
X	0.3	0.3	1.0	2.0	− 2.4
PX	1.5	4.3	6.2	5.3	6.4

[a]X, volume of world trade; PX, price of world trade.

TABLE 8   A comparison of the indexed and unindexed baseline solutions: the growth rates of
world trade (value, price, and volume).

Variable[a]	1969		1970		1971		1972		1973		Total compounded	
	B	I	B	I	B	I	B	I	B	I	B	I
VX	14.7	16.9	14.5	17.6	12.0	14.8	18.4	18.6	40.7	36.0	145.0	154.0
PX	3.2	4.7	4.6	7.5	5.1	7.0	9.6	8.7	24.8	19.2	55.2	56.0
X	11.1	11.7	9.5	9.4	6.6	7.3	8.0	9.1	12.7	14.1	57.9	63.2

[a]VX, value of world trade; PX, price of world trade; X, volume of world trade.

case. Compounded over the five-year simulation period total world trade grows by 63.2%
under indexation compared with 57.9% in the baseline case, an increase of 70 basis points
in the average annual compound rate of growth.

The volume increase in world trade is interpreted as a measure of the real effect of
the financial transfer implicit in the accumulation of the larger commodity stockpiles.
Even though the nominal cost of these stockpiles is not explicitly measured in this model
the increments to the real "pie" may be calculated. Table 8 suggests that 5.3% of a 63.2%
cumulative increase in real world trade under indexation is directly attributable to indexation.

Earlier we noted that one fear of the developed economies is that indexation might
generate higher inflation rates than might otherwise prevail. Inspection of Table 8 shows
that in the first three years of the simulation, when indexation generally increased commodity prices, inflation of world trade prices was indeed high under indexation. However,
in the last two years of the experiment, when indexation played a minor role in commodity-
price determination, inflation was lower under indexation. Cumulatively over the five-
year simulation the inflation rate was insignificantly different in the two scenarios.

This result illustrates the smoothing process inherent in the particular indexation
rule that was selected for this experiment. By removing the downswings in prices it makes
the upswings less dramatic. A general smoothing of price fluctuations can be observed by
referring back to Tables 1 and 3. However, in the case of a trended deterioration of the
terms of trade against commodity prices there might very well be an increase in inflation
caused by indexation.

The performance of world trade prices masks the underlying rate of inflation of the
regional economies. In fact, as Table 9 demonstrates, the dynamic pattern of fluctuation
of import costs leads to a general increase in domestic inflation rates in the regions. After
1973 the cumulative price level in the OECD region stands 4.7 percentage points higher

TABLE 9   A comparison of the indexed and unindexed baseline solutions: inflation rates and growth rates (in percent per year) for the OECD and DEVE regions.

Variable[a]	1969		1970		1971		1972		1973	
	B	I	B	I	B	I	B	I	B	I
OECDPGDP	4.7	5.0	5.5	6.6	5.5	6.9	8.9	10.0	14.0	13.5
DEVEPC	2.5	2.6	2.7	2.9	1.0	1.2	3.8	3.6	16.9	15.3
OECDGDP	3.5	3.6	3.1	3.4	3.8	4.4	5.4	6.1	5.7	6.6
DEVEGDP	4.8	4.8	6.3	6.4	6.6	6.5	5.4	5.6	8.2	10.7

[a]*PGDP* is the implicit deflator of GDP, *PC* is the implicit deflator of consumption expenditures, and GDP is gross domestic product.

under indexation than without. For the DEVE group the difference in the compounded inflation is only 2.7 percentage points.

It is significant that inflation in the years when there is no effective indexation is lower than the inflation that would have prevailed in the absence of an indexation program. This further suggests the effects of smoothing: the OECD and DEVE regions trade off higher inflation today for lower inflation tomorrow, again assuming no trend in real commodity prices.

Higher nominal commodity-price levels provide a short-term boost to the ability of the DEVE economies to import by inflating export revenues quickly while import prices are slower to adjust. This surge in imports is reflected in both a surge in world trade and a surge in the contribution of real net exports to growth in the OECD. In the DEVE group the pattern of improvement in real product is cumulative and more inertial. Over the five-year period increments to imports allow a gradual increase in the capital stock and thus in output.

This pattern is visible in Table 9, where the OECD gains in real output are immediate. The benefits to the DEVE group are nil during the first three years and only become substantial in the fifth year. It must be argued that some momentum develops in this process: higher DEVE exports imply higher imports, and thus external stimulus to the OECD group. The OECD group closes the circle by importing more goods from the DEVE group and by demanding more commodities.

On looking underneath the rates of growth to the levels of output, it can be seen that the OECD group is clearly better off in each year of the simulation with indexation than without. The DEVE group achieves a level of GDP that is cumulatively 0.7% greater with indexation than in the baseline case. Most of this gain occurs in the last year of the simulation. There are really no substantial gains in the initial years.

5   CONCLUSIONS

It is difficult to isolate a single objective conclusion from this experiment. Analysts will have to impose their own subjective weights to many factors that are observed in this model and the companion assumptions. After taking into account the usual caveats that are relevant to any analysis based on an econometric model and qualifying each of the results to the specific period of simulation that was used for this experiment, we can make the following observations:

(1) The particular indexation program described in Section 2 can improve the merchandise terms of trade of commodity exporters.
(2) If commodity exporters can immediately absorb the increase in their export revenues as imports then an indexation program need not cause any chronic shift in the regional balances of payments.
(3) The value and volume of world trade can accelerate under an indexation scheme, especially in the case of immediate absorption of export revenues into imports.
(4) If there is a trend against commodity prices relative to general prices then the eventual cost of an indexation program is unbounded.
(5) There does not seem to be a tendency for world trade prices to cumulatively rise as a result of commodity-price indexation. The pattern of price adjustment over time is smoothed by the elimination of price downswings.
(6) Specific to the simulation period of this experiment, in which commodity prices would have dropped in the first few years and would have risen sharply in the last year without indexation, one observes a marked increase in inflation during the initial years and a decrease in the later years under indexation. Cumulatively, inflation within the regions would be higher in this scenario with indexation than without, more so than trade prices.
(7) At worst, the regional product of the DEVE group is unaffected by indexation. Cumulatively, the DEVE product increases with growing acceleration. However, the OECD region unambiguously benefits from indexation in each year. Thus, the "pie" grows larger and the "slices" are recut. The gap between the OECD and DEVE incomes widens, albeit at higher income levels.
(8) In general the impacts of indexation on the world economy are modest in magnitude. Not one observed element that changed between the indexed simulation and the baseline reversed the direction of an existing trend of development for that variable.

The results suggest an intermediate approach to the political—economic dialogue between the North and South on the indexation issue. Some aspects that have been revealed in these experiments may be summarized as follows:

(1) Both rich and poor countries export primary commodities. An indexation program that does not discriminate between regions of origin (which may not be possible on competitive world markets) must benefit both rich and poor nations.
(2) Global constraints on the balance of trade impose the condition that a redistribution of real exports away from the OECD countries cannot occur through a nominal transfer if developing countries can immediately absorb increased export revenues as real import purchases.
(3) A nominal transfer is implied by the creation of the stabilization stock. If money is created for this purpose then the world as a whole benefits from an injection of new resources, at least in the short run.
(4) Commodity prices do not rise or fall in unison; thus the direct impacts of indexation in any selected year are generally modest.

(5) If there is no trend in commodity prices relative to general prices then indexation as defined here smooths the fluctuation of commodity prices by eliminating declines in real and nominal prices. Cumulative changes in prices may be essentially unchanged, the more so if the trend in commodity prices is towards relative appreciation.

Thus if no source of funding for an indexation scheme is imposed then the world as a whole benefits in real terms from indexation. In the short run the richest countries, being driven by demand, should benefit more. Offsetting the real gains, moderately increased inflation rates and potentially expensive stockbuilding programs are the costs. However, neither the OECD nor the DEVE regional groupings would have had any real reasons to object to the implementation of commodity-price indexation as formulated in this model experiment. Conversely, neither region could expect to realize substantial gains. On the basis of this study we would therefore urge the view that the benefits of an indexation program are modest at best, while the potential cost is unbounded. Other forms of "transfer aid" may prove more powerful in improving life in developing countries.

ACKNOWLEDGMENTS

The research presented in this paper was carried out at the National Bureau of Economic Research under National Science Foundation Grant No. PRA7727048. The authors are grateful to the NSF, the NBER, and New York University for their support. The results presented here are preliminary and are offered for discussion purposes only. The views and opinions expressed here are solely those of the authors, who also claim full responsibility for any errors.

REFERENCES

Adams, F.G. (1979). Integrating commodity models in LINK. In J.A. Sawyer (Editor), Modelling the International Transmission Mechanism. North-Holland, Amsterdam.

Adams, F.G. and Behrman, J. (1976). Econometric Models of World Commodity Markets. Ballinger, Cambridge, Massachusetts.

Beaumont, P. and Prucha, I. (1977). Analysis of changes in a trade share matrix, 1971–1975. Paper presented at the World Meeting of Project LINK, 9th, Kyoto, Japan. (Mimeograph.)

Bhagwati, J. (Editor) (1978). The New International Economic Order. Ballinger, Cambridge, Massachusetts.

Glowacki, J. and Ruffing, K. (1979). Developing countries in Project LINK. In J.A. Sawyer (Editor), Modelling the International Transmission Mechanism. North-Holland, Amsterdam.

Johnson, H.G. (1956). The transfer problem and exchange stability. Journal of Political Economy, LXIV(3):212–215.

Johnson, K.N. (1979). Models for the rest of the world. In J.A. Sawyer (Editor), Modelling the International Transmission Mechanism. North-Holland, Amsterdam.

Klein, L.R. (1976). The five year experience of linking national econometric models. In H. Gleiser (Editor), Quantitative Studies of International Economic Relations. North-Holland, Amsterdam.

Kravis, I., Kraino, I.B., Kenessey, Z., Heston, A., and Summers, R. (1975). International Comparison of Gross Output and Prices. Johns Hopkins University Press, Baltimore, Maryland.

Nadiri, M.I. and Weinberg, C.B. (1978). REMPIS: A Regional Econometric Model for Price Indexation Studies. National Bureau of Economic Research, New York. (Mimeograph.)

Sawyer, J.A. (Editor) (1979). Modelling the International Transmission Mechanism. North-Holland, Amsterdam.
UNCTAD Staff (1976). Models for developing countries. In J. Waelbroeck (Editor), The Models of Project LINK. North-Holland, Amsterdam.
Waelbroeck, J. (1976). The Models of Project LINK. North-Holland, Amsterdam.

COMMENTS*

The ambition of the authors is high. The long-debated issue of regulating world market prices of those primary products which are major sources of export revenues of developing countries is the focus of the paper. The results of one specific kind of regulation or indexation are simulated in a model which produces effects at the level of the individual primary products as well as for four country-regions: OECD, developing countries (the DEVE region), OPEC, and the CMEA countries.

With the exception of a brief description of the model, the paper consists of reports of the computations of the effects of commodity-price indexation for eight agricultural products. The description of the REMPIS model is insufficient for the understanding of the year-by-year differences in effects during the period 1969—73. Partly as a consequence, almost all results at the commodity level which are easily understandable for the reader are results that follow more or less directly from the indexation or stockpiling programs.

However, the most interesting estimates in my opinion are the regional and global ones. Four results are particularly striking: the indexation leads to increased world trade; not only the DEVE region but also the OECD region experience terms-of-trade gains; the OECD gains gradually improve over the simulation period; and the CMEA countries suffer terms-of-trade losses during each of the five years with no decisive trend. These points are discussed below by questioning both the interpretation of results by the authors and the model used for the simulations.

According to the authors, the increased world trade is a result of the indexation and their explicit and implicit interpretation of this result is that there is a global welfare gain. In my view, however, both their conclusion and their interpretation are open to question. The combination of the indexation formulae and the fact that stockpiling is assumed to be costless lead to a rapid accumulation of stocks throughout the five-year period. It is therefore more likely that it is the no-cost assumption and the resulting increase in stocks which induce world trade to grow. Moreover, since world production and world consumption gradually deviate more and more from each other, it is quite possible that world consumption and welfare may decrease.

The finding that the OECD region countries obtain terms-of-trade gains after the first two years is emphasized in the paper. It is claimed that this effect is attributable to their large exports of the eight chosen commodities in absolute although not relative terms. Unfortunately, there is no comparison in the paper between the size of their

---

*By Lennart Ohlsson, Economic Research Institute at the Stockholm School of Economics, Stockholm, Sweden.

exports and imports of these commodities. The interpretation offered assures a substantial net export surplus which is larger in the last three years than in the first two. Since this is not explicitly shown to be the case, there might be alternative causes for the finding.

One such cause might have been the difference in adjustment flexibility assumed for the OECD and DEVE regions. The former region is very flexible in adjusting its supplies to demand changes but the latter has been given a fixed maximum output capacity. In other words, demand increases can only be met with price increases until investment has brought about an adjustment of its maximum output. In a multisectoral world this would have led to a tendency for the OECD region to alter its specialization flexibly in line with relative price changes whereas the DEVE region cannot. Moreover, it might have accounted for the successive improvements in the terms-of-trade effects of OECD.

Unfortunately, the OECD economy is a one-sector economy. Equally unfortunate is the fact that, of the two, only the DEVE region is a multisectoral economy which by assumption is prohibited from intersectoral resource shifts in the short run. Hence, the most likely explanation must be as follows. When the developing countries receive enhanced export revenues they devote at least part of them to investment. The investment growth induces increased purchases of machinery, most of which is imported from the OECD. This investment response is lagged, the probable explanation being that the initially negative terms-of-trade effects become less negative in the second year, and then successively more positive.

There is one additional piece of information that has been used in the derivation of this alternative interpretation. It is the fact that the indexation formulae use the GDP deflator as a norm of comparison for the eight commodity prices. This choice is unfortunate from two points of view. First, the most discussed norm is the (export) price of manufactures. Second, it is also analytically unfortunate since the initial terms-of-trade effect for the OECD is obscured. The high share of its trade-sheltered service sector means that an initial terms-of-trade improvement cannot be excluded.

The above alternative interpretation is able to explain both the positive terms-of-trade effects for the OECD region *and* the positive trend in these effects. If true, it also makes the model simulations somewhat uninteresting. Why use such an elaborate model to produce such simplistic results?

The fourth point above — that the CMEA region, in marked contrast to the OECD, is a persistent loser as regards terms of trade — is perplexing. After all, the REMPIS model describes the former region to be a price taker on the world market with a perfectly elastic supply of exports. Although the CMEA region is only incorporated in the form of a trade model the result is surprising if we believe the authors' assertions that these assumptions govern the trade performance of the CMEA region. As the results now stand, one is more inclined to believe that there is only one sector of the tradeable goods economy and that the only supply flexibility admitted is that it expands or contracts its traditional export products as excess world demands expand or contract. If this is the case, one must again ask the question: why employ so many elaborations when the permitted responses to commodity price indexation in the REMPIS model are so simplified in all four regions (although in different ways). The traditional transfer problem does not appear to be allowed to work through the ordinary adjustment of trade, production, and consumption to relative price changes in the world market.

GLOBAL INTERNATIONAL ECONOMIC MODELS
B.G. Hickman (editor)
Elsevier Science Publishers B.V. (North-Holland)
© IIASA, 1983

PROJECT FUGI AND THE FUTURE OF ESCAP DEVELOPING COUNTRIES

Yoichi Kaya
Faculty of Engineering, University of Tokyo, Bunkyo-ku, Tokyo (Japan)

Akira Onishi
Faculty of Economics, Soka University, Hachioji, Tokyo (Japan)

Yutaka Suzuki
Faculty of Engineering, Osaka University, Osaka (Japan)

1 INTRODUCTION

Project FUGI (FUture of Global Interdependence) was launched with the authors as coleaders in 1976 under the sponsorship of the Japan Committee of the Club of Rome and the Japan National Institute for Research Advancement. The first research report (Kaya et al., 1980) was presented in 1977, and the second report (Kaya et al., 1979) was presented jointly with two researchers from the office of the United Nations (UN) Economic and Social Commission for Asia and the Pacific (ESCAP) in 1979. The FUGI model was originally designed to investigate the long-term future of the world economy and industry but in the last two years it has been used mainly to investigate the future of the ESCAP economies at the request of the UN ESCAP office.

The FUGI model is a set of three different models that are loosely interrelated. The first model is a dynamic global macroeconomic model developed by a Soka University group headed by Onishi. The second is a static global input—output model developed by a group at the University of Tokyo headed by Kaya; this model gives various sectoral patterns of world industry, based on the macroframework of the world economy in a specific year given by the first model. The third model is a set of global metal-resource (namely copper and iron) models developed by an Osaka University group headed by Suzuki. Space limitations permit only a brief description of the model structures and some computational results for the first two models in this paper but the third model is extensively documented in Kaya et al. (1980).

The FUGI project is still active in collaboration with various institutions outside Japan. The Indonesian Institute of Science is studying the future of the Indonesian economy using the FUGI model under the sponsorship of the Japan Society for the Promotion of Science. Smit and his colleagues at the Free University, Amsterdam, are building a dynamic input–output model of the ESCAP developing countries in close contact with the FUGI group.

2   THE FUGI INPUT–OUTPUT MODEL

In this section we first describe the skeletal structure of the FUGI Input–Output Model (FIOM) and then investigate the feasibility of two different development patterns for the ESCAP developing countries, i.e. the industry-oriented pattern and the agriculture-oriented pattern.

2.1   Skeletal Structure of FIOM

FIOM was first developed in 1977 and was modified later for the purpose of investigating the future of the ESCAP developing countries. The main target area of the model is Asia, and in the model the world is divided into 14 regions, of which two (Japan and Oceania) are ESCAP developed regions and seven (India; the Republic of South Korea; Hong Kong and its neighbors; Indonesia; Malaysia, Thailand, and Singapore; the Philippines, other Asian developing countries of the market economy (mainly Pakistan, Bangladesh, Sri Lanka, and Afghanistan)) are ESCAP developing regions of the market economy. The whole industry of each region is divided into 14 sectors. The sectors and regions are listed in Table 1.

The skeletal structure of FIOM is shown in Figure 1, where TM is the trade module, IOM is the module for predicting the input–output coefficients of each region, FDM is the module for predicting domestic final-demand patterns, and LPM is the linear programming model.

TABLE 1   The regions and sectors used in the FUGI input–output model.

Region	Sector
1. United States and Canada	1. Agriculture, forestry, fisheries
2. EC and other developed countries	2. Mining
3. Middle East	3. Foods, beverages, tobacco
4. Latin America and Africa	4. Textiles, clothes, leather, wood products, furniture
5. Japan	
6. Australia and New Zealand	5. Pulp, paper, printing, publishing
7. India	6. Chemical products including petroleum and coal products, rubber, glass
8. South Korea	
9. Hong Kong, Macao, and Taiwan	7. Metal and metal products
10. Indonesia	8. Nonelectrical machinery
11. Malaysia, Singapore, and Thailand	9. Electrical machinery
12. Philippines	10. Transport equipment
13. Other Asian countries	11. Construction
14. Soviet Union and Eastern Europe	12. Electricity, gas, water
	13. Merchandise and services
	14. Transportation and communications

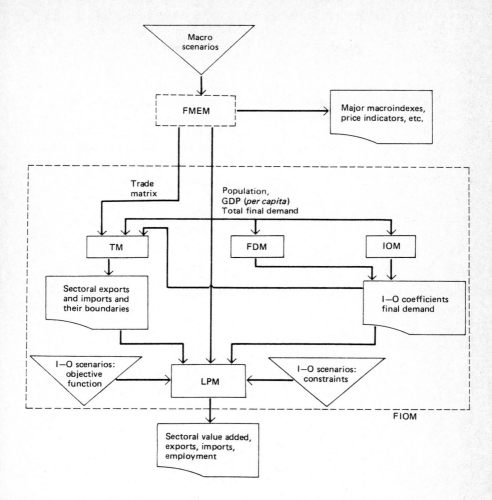

FIGURE 1   Skeletal structure of FIOM.

FIOM is designed to disaggregate the macroeconomic framework of each region in a specific year given by the FUGI ESCAP Macro Economic Model (FMEM) into sectoral variables by use of a modified simulation method or an optimization method. The modified simulation method gives standard scenarios or long-term projections of the industrial structure of each region within the given macroframework while the optimization method provides scenarios which emphasize the development of special sectors and/or countries.

2.1.1 The Trade Module

The function of the trade module is to provide central estimates of sectoral exports and imports for each region in a specified year and corresponding interval estimates. The former estimates are used in the projection scenarios while the latter are used as the upper and lower bounds of the trade variables in optimization scenarios. The basic characteristics of the estimates are as follows.

(i) A central estimate is the average of the upper and lower bounds of the corresponding interval estimate.

(ii) Estimates of both exports and imports are expressed in terms of free on board (f.o.b.) rather than cost, insurance, and freight (c.i.f.) values.

(iii) All the estimates are subject to the following constraints: (a) world trade must balance ($\Sigma_{ik} e_i = \gamma_k \Sigma_{ik} m_i$, $\gamma_k \approx 1$); (b) all the estimates must be nonnegative; (c) the total of all the exports of each region must equal the value predicted by FMEM; (d) the total of all the imports of each region must equal the value predicted by FMEM.

(iv) The central estimates are chosen to be as close to regressed sectoral trade estimates as possible within the constraints (iii).

(v) The interval estimates are originally chosen as those of regression analysis with a 1% level of significance but the width of the interval is increased roughly in proportion to the difference between the final central estimate and its original regressed value.

2.1.2 The Input–Output Module

The input–output coefficients for each region in a specified year are estimated in this module. A modified canonical regression analysis is employed which is particularly useful when applied to developing regions where the availability of data is limited (for details see Kaya et al., 1979).

2.1.3 The Final-Demand Module

The domestic final demand in each region is estimated in the following way.

Given the time-series data on the value added $\{x_i(t)\}$, exports $\{e_i(t)\}$, and imports $\{m_i(t)\}$, calculate

$$d_i(t) = k_{v_i}^{-1}(t)x_i(t) - A_i(t)k_{v_i}^{-1}(t)x_i(t) - e_i(t) + m_i(t) \tag{1}$$

where $k_{v_i}(t)$ is the vector of the value-added ratios of the ith region in year t and $A_i(t)$ is the input–output matrix of the ith region in year t. k_{v_i} and A_i are estimated in the input–output module. $d_i(t)$ in eqn. (1) is the estimated domestic final-demand vector expressed in terms of the purchase of goods.

The application of regression analysis to the time series $\{d_i(t)\}$ that is obtained from eqn. (1) provides future estimates of $d_i(t)$.

2.1.4 The Linear Programming Module

One of the important features of FIOM is its capability of investigating the possibilities of various types of development strategy by use of the linear programming technique. Sectoral value added, exports, and imports for each region are the variables to be determined as the solution of the optimization of a criterion function under certain equality and inequality constraints.

The choice of the criterion function depends on the purpose of the investigation. For instance, in the investigation of the upper bound of agriculture-oriented development of the ith region the criterion function F is chosen as

$$F = {}_1x_i \to \text{maximum} \tag{2}$$

where ${}_1x_i$ denotes the value added in sector 1 (agriculture, forestry, and fisheries) of the ith region.

The main constraints that are used in the module are as follows.

(i) The exogenous condition (linkage with FMEM)

$$\sum_k {}_kx_i = X_i \tag{3}$$

$$\sum_k {}_ke_i = E_i \tag{4}$$

$$\sum_k {}_km_i = M_i \tag{5}$$

where ${}_kx_i$, ${}_ke_i$, and ${}_km_i$ are the value added, the exports (f.o.b.), and the imports (f.o.b.), respectively in the kth sector in the ith region, and X_i, E_i, and M_i are the Gross Domestic Product (GDP), the total exports, and the total imports, respectively of region i given by FMEM.

(ii) The domestic material balance:

$$k_{v_i}^{-1} x_i = A_i k_{v_i}^{-1} x_i + d_i + e_i - m_i \tag{6}$$

(iii) The world trade balance:

$$\sum_i {}_ke_i = \gamma_k \sum_i {}_km_i, \qquad \gamma_k \approx 1 \tag{7}$$

(see Section 2.1.1).

(iv) Constraints on deviation from past trends:

$${}_ke_i{}^L \leqslant {}_ke_i \leqslant {}_ke_i{}^U \tag{8}$$

$${}_km_i{}^L \leqslant {}_km_i \leqslant {}_km_i{}^U \tag{9}$$

where ${}_ke_i{}^L$, ${}_ke_i{}^U$ and ${}_km_i{}^L$, ${}_km_i{}^U$ are the interval estimates of ${}_ke_i$ and ${}_km_i$, respectively.

(v) Constraints on change in industrial structure. The industrial structure of each region may change but only within a certain frame and at a limited speed. For instance the past data show that industrialization of a country normally begins with light industry and proceeds with more dependence on heavy industry. This characteristic is expressed in a linear inequality constraint. The details are described in Kaya et al. (1980).

(vi) Finally,

$$_k x_i \geqslant 0; \quad _k e_i \geqslant 0; \quad _k m_i \geqslant 0 \qquad \text{(for all } k \text{ and } i) \tag{10}$$

2.2 Development Strategy

Roughly, there are two alternatives for the industrialization of developing countries. One is to make concerted efforts to develop both light and heavy industries simultaneously, and the other is to stress agriculture and related light industries and to move only gradually to a structure that is more oriented towards heavy industry.

Two macroscenarios (described in Section 3.2) are given by FMEM as the framework for the sectoral scenarios: macroscenario A, the standard case; macroscenario B, the high-development case.

On the basis of the macroframework two scenarios, i.e. a manufacturing-industry-oriented scenario (M) and an agriculture-oriented scenario (AG), are calculated by use of FIOM.

In scenario M the criterion function is chosen as

$$J_M = \sum_i \sum_k {}_k x_i \rightarrow \text{maximum} \tag{11}$$

where the first summation is over developing regions except the Middle East and the second is over manufacturing sectors. In the AG scenario the criterion function is chosen as

$$J_A = \sum_i {}_1 x_i \rightarrow \text{maximum} \tag{12}$$

where the summation is over developing regions except the Middle East.

From the point of view of promoting rapid industrialization scenario M may be more efficient, as can be seen in Figure 2 where the results of the two extreme optimization scenarios are shown. The first is the M scenario in which the total production in the manufacturing industries of developing countries is to be maximized (see eqn. (11)) and the second is the AG scenario in which the total agricultural production of developing countries is maximized. Figure 2 indicates that the industrial production of developing countries will be much higher in the M scenario than in the AG scenario but it is still in question whether the M scenario is the better strategy since it has at least the following two difficulties.

(a) The development of both agriculture and manufacturing industry is almost a necessity in the ESCAP developing countries since agriculture provides food, which otherwise has to be imported by spending scarce foreign currency, and employment for a rapidly expanding population.

(b) Competition with advanced industrialized countries in the world market for manufactured goods will become a serious barrier. Most of the advanced industrialized countries rely on exports of industrial goods, and the goods produced in these countries will retain their nonprice competitive advantage over goods produced in developing countries for some years yet. The M scenario may in this sense be too optimistic.

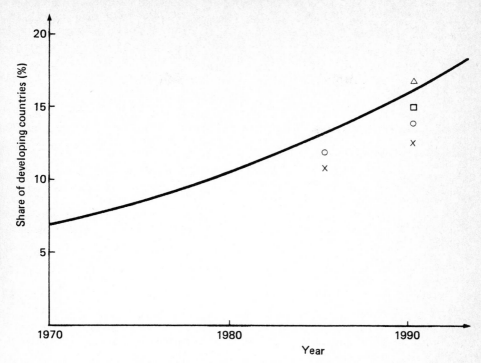

FIGURE 2   The share of the developing countries of the market economy in the world production of manufactured goods: —, Lima target path; ×, macroscenario A; ○, macroscenario B; □, scenario AG; △, scenario M.

These difficulties are basic and hence have been investigated in more detail as follows.

2.2.1 Agricultural Development

The average rate of growth of agricultural production in each ESCAP developing region is shown in Table 2 for the two scenarios in comparison with the rate of growth of Gross Regional Product (GRP). In the M scenario the growth rates of agriculture are very low in most ESCAP countries and average only 1.75%. In contrast, the AG scenario gives a reasonable picture of agricultural development, and the average growth rate of manufacturing industries in the ESCAP region is nevertheless 5.84% compared with a GRP growth rate of 4.84%. It is worth noting that the growth rate of manufacturing industry in the AG scenario is higher than that in the underlying macroscenario A (see Figure 2). From this viewpoint the AG scenario is another type of industrialization-oriented scenario. Eventually it may be said that the AG scenario is well balanced and closer to the optimum than the M scenario, at least in the decade of the 1980s.

2.2.2 The Effect of Competition in the World Market

The key point here is: How sensitive will scenarios of development be to the attitude of advanced industrialized countries in the world market for manufactured goods? Either

TABLE 2   Average annual rates of growth of agricultural production in the ESCAP developing countries for 1980–1990 under macroscenario A.

Region	Growth rate of agricultural production		Growth rate of GRP (%)
	M scenario (%)	AG scenario (%)	
7. India	0.90	1.96	3.37
8. South Korea	0.72	7.58	7.35
9. Hong Kong, Macao, and Taiwan	1.13	7.22	6.30
10. Indonesia	3.18	6.66	7.17
11. Malaysia, Singapore, and Thailand	4.88	7.14	5.40
12. Philippines	1.97	5.31	4.64
13. Other Asian countries	0.34	2.67	3.07
15. All ESCAP developing countries	1.75	4.34	4.84

of the following kinds of constraint may be introduced into the linear programming module to investigate the question.

(a) The total production of manufacturing industries in each advanced industrial region must not be less than that in the projection scenario: i.e.

$$\sum_{k\in\{\text{manufacturing industries}\}} {}_k x_i \geqslant \sum_{k\in\{\text{manufacturing industries of projection scenario}\}} {}_k x_i \tag{13}$$

where i indicates the region ($i = 1, 2, 3, 5, 6, 13$). (The Middle East has very different characteristics from other developing regions and so in this discussion is treated in the same way as the advanced industrialized regions.)

(b) Each sectoral production of manufacturing industries in each advanced industrial region must not be less than that in the projection scenario.

$$_k x_i \geqslant {}_k x_i \text{ in projection scenario} \tag{14}$$

where $k = $ sector $3, 4, 5, 6, 7, 8, 9, 10$ and i indicates the region ($i = 1, 2, 3, 5, 6, 13$).

Constraint (b) is apparently more severe for developing countries than constraint (a). The introduction of either of them will have negative effects on the industries of developing countries since advanced industrialized countries will not reduce their industrial production to make room for developing countries in the world market.

The results of the computations within macroframework B for 1990 are summarized in Table 3. The total production of the manufacturing industries in each developing region has been normalized by its value in the corresponding scenario without the constraints. It can be seen that the AG scenario is far more robust than the M scenario to competition in the world market. It is surprising that the introduction of the constraint (13) has so little effect on developing countries in the AG scenario.

In the AG scenario the developing regions are oriented towards agriculture and its related industries in which they have a high competitive power and room for expanding their exports; i.e. the AG scenario is one in which developing countries will develop themselves by fully utilizing their comparative advantage.

TABLE 3 The effect of constraints on manufacturing production in advanced industrialized countries on the manufacturing production in ESCAP developing regions (production for constrained cases is given as a percentage of the production for unconstrained cases).

Region	Total production of manufacturing industries in 1990 with macroframework B					
	M scenario			AG scenario		
	No con-straint	With (13)[a]	With (14)[a]	No con-straint	With (13)[a]	With (14)[a]
4. Latin America and Africa	100	93.8	91.4	100	100	91.3
7. India	100	90.5	90.5	100	100	99.4
8. South Korea	100	86.8	84.5	100	100	99.5
9. Hong Kong and its neighbors	100	94.4	87.0	100	100	100.1
10. Indonesia	100	71.6	71.9	100	100	91.4
11. Malaysia, Singapore, and Thailand	100	67.1	65.5	100	100	101.2
12. Philippines	100	86.7	86.7	100	100	96.4
13. Other Asian countries	100	89.4	91.8	100	100	98.1
15. All ESCAP developing countries	100	85.7	84.2	100	100	98.8

[a]Constraints (13) and (14) are explained in the text.

The AG scenario is therefore far more acceptable to both developing and developed countries at least in the 1980s. The reader is reminded, however, that the AG scenario represents a transitional stage for the ESCAP countries since they are poor in natural resources and hence in the long term will have to rely more on the production of industrial goods. Drastic changes in the attitude of the advanced industrialized countries will be needed to permit expansion of the share of developing countries in the world market for industrial goods.

3 THE FUGI MACROECONOMIC MODEL (FMEM)

3.1 The Basic Structure of FMEM (Type III 907–28)

FMEM (Type III 907–28) links 28 areas of the world, subdivided as follows:

Advanced Market Economies (AMEs):
  (1) Japan;
  (2) Australia and New Zealand;
  (3) Canada;
  (4) United States;
  (5) France;
  (6) Federal Republic of Germany (FRG);
  (7) Italy;
  (8) United Kingdom;
  (9) Other countries of the European Economic Community (EEC); and
  (10) Other advanced countries.

Developing Market Economies (DMEs):
(11) Hong Kong and Macao;
(12) Taiwan;
(13) South Korea;
(14) Indonesia;
(15) Malaysia;
(16) Philippines;
(17) Singapore;
(18) Thailand;
(19) Afghanistan, Bhutan, and Nepal;
(20) Bangladesh and Pakistan;
(21) India;
(22) Sri Lanka and the Maldives;
(23) Other Asian countries,
(24) Middle East;
(25) Africa; and
(26) Latin America (including the Caribbean).

Centrally Planned Economies (CPEs):
(27) Soviet Union and Eastern Europe; and
(28) China and the other Asian socialist countries.

While FMEM (Type III 907—28) represents a system which links together "submodels" reflecting the special characteristics of the 28 regions, each submodel in turn is composed of seven "subsectors" as follows: (i) production; (ii) expenditure on GRP at constant market prices; (iii) profits and wages; (iv) prices; (v) expenditure on GRP at current market prices; (vi) Official Development Assistance (ODA) and private direct overseas investment; (vii) the foreign exchange rate.

The regional submodels are mutually linked through the flows of trade, ODA, and private overseas investment.

The most important distinguishing feature of the model is the systems structure for determining interregional trade. The system at work is one whereby economic growth in each region does not take place completely on the basis of self-reliance but rather within a framework of interdependent relationships characterized by trade and financial flows.

The model treats ODA from industrially advanced regions to developing regions as a generally agreed policy aim of governments and intergovernmental bodies. ODA from the industrially advanced countries is of course distributed among several different developing regions, and this distribution ratio can be conceived as a "policy parameter".

The model recognizes that the present situation is one in which increases in ODA and private overseas investment depend very largely on income levels in the industrially advanced regions and such aid is seen by the developing regions as offering considerable promise as a supplementary factor for production, helping in turn to increase incomes in those regions.

Thus ODA and private overseas investment, together with trade, create important links between the developing and the industrially developed regions.

The technical details of FMEM (Type III 907—28) are presented in Onishi and Kaya (1980) and in Onishi (1981).

3.2 The Forecasting Scenarios

Using FMEM we attempted to derive outlooks for the economies of the ESCAP member countries based on the interdependent relations between the 28 regions in the world for the period 1980—1990.

3.2.1 Scenario A: the Standard Scenario
Reflecting the economic uncertainty of the era, projections of the economic development of the developing ESCAP region are best drafted in a scenario format. The question of whether the advanced industrialized nations will be able to maintain an appropriate level of economic growth while struggling to control inflation and to conserve energy in the face of the projected increases in the cost of energy in the 1980s will certainly be an important determinant of the progress of developing countries in the ESCAP region.

With regard to scenario A, particular attention was therefore given to the following considerations.

(1) In the 1980s the economies of the major advanced industrial countries will have increasingly strong international links, and any changes that might occur in the state of the economies in these countries will very soon make themselves felt throughout the entire world.

(2) Here it is hypothesized that oil prices will be indexed with respect to the average export price of the industrially developed countries for the period 1981—1990, increasing by 4.5% more than the annual rate of increase in their export prices.

(3) In addition to this indexation of oil prices it is assumed that the indexation of primary-commodity prices with respect to the average export price of the industrially advanced countries will be maintained in the 1980s (in the light of various UN Conference on Trade and Development (UNCTAD) discussions and propositions on the stabilization of prices for the major primary commodities exported from the developing countries).

3.2.2 Scenario B: Concerted-Growth Scenario for Decreasing the North—South Gap
Here we ask whether, under the supposition of a further widening in the gap in per capita incomes between the North and South, policies can be designed to diminish this gap. In this connection, if the industrially advanced regions slow their rates of economic growth, what impact will this have on economic development in the developing regions? Our forecast is that so long as there is no change in the structure of the present world economic system centered on the industrially advanced countries a lowering of the tempo of economic growth in these regions is likely to cause a corresponding lowering of the rate of economic development in the developing regions, which have strong links with the advanced countries, particularly through trade and ODA. Thus so long as the present mechanisms of world industry and trade move according to their previous patterns "zero growth" in the industrially advanced regions will not contribute to diminishing the North—South gap but will only tend to perpetuate the present state of inequality.

However, while efforts to accelerate economic development in the Third World and to narrow the income gap between the North and South are obviously desirable, development policy scenarios for these objectives must be realistic in order to promote dialog and cooperation between the North and South. Therefore after first building projections of the supply and price of Middle-East oil into the model we attempt to project in scenario B the extent to which it might be possible for the developing nations to accelerate their economic growth in the coming decade even while the growth of the advanced industrialized nations is limited by high costs and conservation efforts.

In both scenarios it is assumed that the major developed countries do not exceed the limits of oil imports from the Middle East laid down in the International Energy Administration agreement, although the developing countries may import oil without regard to such constraints during the period 1980–1990.

Furthermore, in order to realize the Lima target as a goal for the industrialization of the Third World, policy scenarios aimed at speeding up economic development and industrialization are necessary. This is because on the basis of a straight extrapolation of recent trends there is virtually no possibility that the Third World will be able to increase its share of the world market for manufactured products to 25% by the year 2000.

With regard to scenario B, particular attention was therefore given to the following considerations.

(1) A development-assistance policy calling for the advanced industrialized nations to achieve the target of ODA equivalent to 0.7% of their gross national product by 1990 will be incorporated in the Third UN Development Decade.

(2) It is also assumed that the distribution ratio of ODA towards the low-income countries (LICs) including Afghanistan, Bangladesh, Bhutan, Burma, India, Indonesia, Nepal, Sri Lanka, the Maldives, the Pacific island countries, and Africa will be increased in 1981–1999 (starting from the aid distribution pattern in 1980 we increase the share of ODA that is distributed to the LICs at an annual rate of 5% in order to accelerate aid flows toward the LICs).

(3) A trade-expansion policy calling for the industrially developed countries to increase imports of manufactured and semimanufactured commodities, particularly from the developing countries with low and medium incomes, will be introduced. In addition to this North–South trade-expansion policy, the developing countries will also encourage trade between themselves to achieve the goal of collective self-reliance through an intra-South trade-expansion policy.

(4) It is assumed that the per capita income of the LICs will at least double by the year 2000. In order to achieve this goal, an annual growth rate of the per capita income of at least 3.5% will be required for the LICs from 1981 to 2000.

Even in the LICs where the postulated GDP growth rates cannot be achieved by the above-mentioned policy mix of expansion of trade and aid we assume that the required GDP growth rate will be achieved by internal efforts to raise the domestic saving ratio and to increase labor productivity through education, manpower training, and the development of indigenous technology.

3.3 A Review of Forecast Results

3.3.1 Economic Growth

According to the projection based on scenario A the advanced industrialized countries will maintain a 3.5% annual growth rate of GDP for 1980–1990. With this low pace of economic growth in the advanced industrialized countries, it is expected that the annual growth rate of GDP in the developing countries will be 5.2% over the same period. It is worth noting that the annual average GRP growth rate of the developing ESCAP region will be 4.8%.

As shown in Table 4, the projection based on scenario A envisages continued higher rates of economic growth for the high- and medium-income nations such as the Asian

TABLE 4 Projections of annual growth and inflation rates for 1980–1990 and of the ratio of current-account balance (CAB) to GDP in 1990, for scenarios A and B.

Region	Growth rate of GDP (constant prices) (%)		Inflation rate (GDP deflator) (%)		CAB/GDP (current prices) (%)	
	A	B	A	B	A	B
Japan	5.4	5.7	6.2	6.0	−0.8	0.3
Australia and New Zealand	4.0	4.3	10.2	10.0	0.0	−0.9
Canada	3.8	3.8	7.5	7.4	−2.5	−2.8
USA	3.0	3.0	7.7	7.5	−0.9	−0.8
France	2.8	3.1	7.3	7.3	−0.2	−0.3
FRG	3.3	3.4	4.7	4.7	0.8	0.4
Italy	4.0	4.0	10.6	10.7	−2.2	−1.6
UK	2.6	2.8	9.6	9.5	−1.1	−0.8
Other EEC countries	3.1	3.1	8.8	8.5	−0.7	−1.2
Other advanced countries	3.5	3.5	9.0	8.7	−0.8	−1.0
The total of AMEs	3.5	3.5	8.0	7.8	−0.9	−0.9
Hong Kong and Macao	6.2	8.2	10.6	10.3	−7.6	−6.3
Taiwan	6.3	7.8	11.2	10.8	−1.3	−1.3
South Korea	7.6	10.6	19.0	18.9	−3.5	−3.2
Singapore	6.1	8.0	8.7	8.2	−10.6	−6.8
The total of Asian NICs	6.9	9.3	17.5	17.8	−3.6	−3.2
ASEAN	5.9	8.0	16.8	17.0	−1.6	−0.8
Indonesia	7.0	9.0	18.4	18.3	0.0	1.5
Malaysia	5.9	6.9	7.7	7.7	2.7	1.8
Philippines	4.8	8.0	18.1	18.3	−5.1	−4.9
Singapore	6.1	8.0	8.7	8.2	−10.6	−6.8
Thailand	5.3	7.3	10.8	11.1	−4.1	−4.6
Afghanistan, Bhutan, and Nepal	3.3	6.2	22.0	20.6	−1.3	−1.3
Bangladesh and Pakistan	3.1	6.3	11.9	11.7	−4.0	−3.3
India	3.4	5.9	8.0	7.6	−0.4	−1.4
Sri Lanka and Maldives	5.4	7.0	10.4	10.6	−4.4	−1.5
Other Asian countries	1.2	5.0	13.0	13.9	0.1	0.5
The total of all Asian DMEs	4.8	7.3	15.5	15.5	−2.4	−2.0
Africa	3.2	6.5	18.6	17.6	0.3	−0.2
Latin America	5.6	6.7	24.5	24.1	−0.3	−0.3
Middle East	6.5	7.6	10.1	9.7	19.6	16.3
The total of all DMEs	5.2	7.0	22.7	21.7	0.1	0.0
USSR and Eastern Europe	3.5	3.5	2.1	1.9	−1.9	−0.9
China and other Asian socialist countries	6.6	7.1	−0.1	−0.1	−0.9	−0.8
The total of CPEs	4.4	4.5	1.4	1.2	−1.7	−0.9
World total	3.9	4.3	15.7	15.9	−0.2	−0.2

Newly Industrializing Countries (NICs) (6.9%), and the countries of the Association of South East Asian Nations (ASEAN) (5.9%), the Middle East (6.5%), and Latin America (5.6%), and continued lower rates of economic growth for the LICs. For example, India (3.4%), Afghanistan (3.3%), Bangladesh and Pakistan (3.1%), other Asian countries (1.2%), and Africa (3.2%) will probably be unable to attain a 5% growth rate. China, although a member of the low-income group, can be expected to achieve a growth rate of 6.6%, in sharp contrast with the performance of the USSR (3.5%).

If the projection·is correct, the North—South per capita income gap in terms of 1970, 1973, and 1978 US dollars will be as follows: in 1970 dollars, 1:13.3 in 1980 and 1:12.0 in 1990; in 1973 dollars, 1:15.4 in 1980 and 1:15.4 in 1990; in 1978 dollars, 1:16.6 in 1980 and 1:16.8 in 1990. Thus under current trends no narrowing of the income gap can be anticipated.

A trend toward the widening of income differentials between Third World nations can also be recognized. The per capita income differential between the Asian NICs and the Third World is rapidly widening: in 1970 dollars, 1:1.8 in 1970, 1:2.8 in 1980, and 1:3.6 in 1990. This upward shift of the NICs can be seen as creating a new hierarchy within the bloc of developing nations. The Middle East is also moving upward within the ranks of the developing countries: in 1970 dollars, 1:2.0 in 1970, 1:3.2 in 1980, and 1:3.5 in 1990. In contrast, the ranking of the LICs such as India is dropping: in 1970 dollars, 1:0.5 in 1970, 1:0.4 in 1980, and 1:0.3 in 1990. Thus the LICs and their increasing relative poverty will continue to be a problem of grave concern.

It can therefore be realistically anticipated that the main objectives of the International Development Strategies for the Third UN Development Decade will be directed at decreasing the North—South income gap with special reference to the economies of the LICs. As shown in Table 4, the projection based on scenario B envisages a tendency for the industrially advanced regions to sustain an economic growth rate of 3.5% per year for the period 1980—1990 and for the tempo of economic growth in the developing regions to rise substantially. It is likely that income inequalities in our global society will be mitigated and that in the 1980s there will be a hope of greater cooperation between the North and South even under conditions of moderate economic growth in the industrially developed countries.

It is also worth noting that the annual rate of economic development of the developing ESCAP region will be 7.4% as a result of concerted North—South efforts.

On the basis of scenario B it is expected that the economies of the Asian NICs and the ASEAN countries will continue to grow faster at an annual average rate of 9.3% and 8.0% respectively. Even the low-income groups in Asia and Africa will be able to attain an annual growth rate of 5% or more. The projection also envisages that continued high rates of economic development will be feasible for the high- and medium-income groups such as the Middle East (7.6%) and Latin America (6.7%).

Under scenario B the projected per capita income gap between the North and South will narrow in the period 1980—1990 as follows: in 1970 dollars, from 1:12.0 to 1:10.2; in 1973 dollars, from 1:15.3 to 1:13.1; in 1978 dollars, from 1:16.6 to 1:14.3.

3.3.2 Prices

Next we ask whether a continuous increase in oil prices would tend to accelerate world inflation and in turn whether increases in the export prices of the industrially developed countries would lead to a vicious circle of continuous increases in oil prices because of oil-price indexation with respect to the export prices of the industrially advanced countries.

The results calculated from FMEM indicate that if oil-price increases exceed certain limits which allow for effective policy response then they are likely to accelerate world inflation. However, inflation is largely the result of factors in market economies such as higher wage costs, pressures from demand, and imbalances between money supplies and incomes. From the FMEM computations it can be seen that if the industrially advanced countries can succeed in controlling these factors moderate increases in oil prices can be absorbed under oil-price indexation as postulated in Table 5.

In this study the annual rate of increase in oil prices is assumed to be 34.2% in 1980. For the period 1981–1990, the annual average rate of increase is assumed to be 12.6% in scenario A and 12.4% in scenario B, i.e. 4.5% higher than the average increases in export prices of the industrially developed countries under the two scenarios.

In both scenarios the movement in the prices of primary commodities (including oil) is strongly linked to the export prices of the industrialized nations. From 1970 to 1979 primary-commodity prices had a very strong correlation with the export prices, and thus indexation has in fact been occurring for some time. On extrapolating this trend into the 1980s we find that the rise in primary-commodity prices will be for the most part linked to the inflation and growth rates of the industrialized nations. The annual average rate of increase in the export prices of the advanced industrialized countries is 8.1% in scenario A and 7.9% in scenario B and the rate of increase in the prices of primary commodities is 9.6% in scenario A and 9.2% in scenario B.

An important point to note here is that even if this type of indexation of primary-commodity prices does occur the vicious cycle of runaway world inflation that is sometimes predicted will not appear. On the contrary, without indexation the potentially even more troublesome problem of debt accumulation in countries that rely almost entirely on the export of primary commodities will intensify as their current balance of payments positions worsen.

For years the prices of the primary-commodity exports of developing countries have been bounced up and down by international speculation and fluctuations in their markets. The concept of a mutual fund to stabilize the prices of primary commodities has been a pending issue between the North and South since the Nairobi UNCTAD General Conference. The idea originated in the necessity for a buffer stockpile to stabilize the major primary commodities that constitute the majority of exports of the developing countries.

In terms of the management of the world economy, and particularly for the measurement of development trends in the Third World, the problem of price stability for primary commodities is of vital importance.

If price increases for primary commodities stay within the range of foregoing assumptions, our model simulations indicate that the advanced industrialized nations will be able to hold their inflation rates to the levels shown in Table 4.

3.4 Balance-of-Payments and Unemployment Issues

In both scenarios A and B as a result of raising oil prices during the 1980s the oil-exporting countries would have greater purchasing power to aid them in establishing

TABLE 5   Results of indexation of oil prices and primary-commodity prices with respect to average export prices of the AMEs, for scenarios A and B.

Year	Oil export price				Change in primary-commodity prices (%)		Change in average export prices of the AMEs (%)	
	A		B					
	Increase (%)	Price (US$/barrel)	Increase (%)	Price (US$/barrel)	A	B	A	B
1979 (actual)	59.4	20.3	59.9	20.3	17.4	17.4	10.0	8.9
1980 (estimates)	34.2	27.2	34.2	27.2	10.7	10.7	11.0	11.0
1981 (projection)	14.0	31.0	12.4	30.6	11.9	10.1	11.6	11.7
1982	14.6	35.3	14.7	35.1	13.8	14.0	10.5	9.6
1983	14.0	40.2	13.1	39.7	11.9	11.0	8.4	8.0
1984	11.9	45.0	11.5	44.3	9.4	9.0	8.7	8.4
1985	12.7	50.7	12.4	49.8	9.5	9.2	7.9	7.5
1986	11.9	56.7	11.5	55.5	8.6	8.2	7.5	7.2
1987	12.0	63.5	11.7	62.0	8.1	7.8	7.4	7.1
1988	11.9	71.1	11.6	69.2	7.9	7.7	7.0	6.7
1989	12.0	79.6	11.7	77.3	7.5	7.2	6.6	6.9
1990	11.6	88.8	11.9	80.5	7.0	7.3	5.3	6.0

themselves more squarely on a developmental course. Conversely, however, the oil-importing countries would lose purchasing power through negative current-account balances caused by the higher prices of oil (see Table 4).

Keynes argued in favor of a policy of creating more effective demand on a single-country level as a measure for dealing with increased unemployment caused by an economic slump in the industrially advanced countries. In today's global society, however, measures for dealing with unemployment problems caused by "oil crises" in the industrially advanced countries cannot be discussed without attention to the interdependent relations with the developing countries. Also, from a global point of view the mutual adjustment of economic policies and the maintenance of moderate economic growth by the industrially advanced countries is a precondition not only for coping with their internal unemployment problems but also for imparting greater purchasing power to the non oil-producing developing countries. Further, dynamic international arrangements must be established whereby the production levels, purchasing power, and absorptive capacity of employment in these developing countries can be raised through means such as increased exports, capital and technology transfers, rules and regulations on the conduct of multinational corporations to help developing economies, and a proper recycling of "petrodollars" toward the non oil-producing developing countries.

However, imbalances in the current balances of payments of the advanced industrialized nations with the non oil-producing developing countries are projected to develop further in future. Accordingly the advanced nations should set up a mutual fund for the stabilization of primary-commodity prices and constructively face the issue of indexation for the successful management of the world economy in the 1980s and, particularly, for the promotion of North–South dialog and cooperation.

4 CONCLUSION

The greatest task which global society faces is how to build a new international economic order. The aims of such a new order may be said to be more equitable utilization of global resources and greater equality on the plane of human and social welfare.

The principle that has up to now been dominant in the world economy has basically been that of "survival of the fittest". In the coming age of tightening global constraints one must ask whether human society can survive at all with a continuation of such behavior.

Without a change from the traditional principle of survival of the fittest to the principles of international cooperation and human solidarity or without changes from systems of wholly unrestrained free competition to systems incorporating a greater element of planning and coordination, it will probably be extremely difficult to overcome the various conflicts which we face in the world economy, to guarantee the economic security of every country, and to plan for a higher degree of social welfare.

In this regard a thoroughgoing strengthening of international bodies will be essential to attain global harmony in economic policies. With the present global system the mutual interdependence of all countries is in fact becoming greater. In such an international environment, unless the economic policies of each individual country (which take into consideration the "national interest" of each country) are adjusted for both the ESCAP region and the world as a whole, it will probably be impossible for us to solve the problems of economic security at either the regional or the global level. At this moment we are directly facing a period that demands a new perspective towards harmonized growth at both the regional and the global levels. However, little progress will be made without a change in methods and a reform of human value judgments.

REFERENCES

Kaya, Y., Onishi, A., Suzuki, Y., Ishitani, H., Ishikawa, M., and Shoji, K. (1980). FUGI – Future of Global Interdependence. In G. Bruckmann (Editor), Input–Output Approaches in Global Modeling. Proceedings of the IIASA Symposium on Global Modeling, 5th, September 26–29, 1977. Pergamon, Oxford, pp. 91–357.

Kaya, Y., Onishi, A., Abe, S., and Smit, H. (1979). Long-Term Projections of Economic Growth in ESCAP Member Countries. Paper presented at the International Conference on Input–Output Techniques, 7th, April 1979.

Onishi, A. (1981). Projections of Alternative Paths of Development of the ESCAP Countries in the Third United Nations Development Decade, 1981–1990. The Soka Economic Studies Quarterly, X (2, March):175–227.

Onishi, A. and Kaya, Y. (1980). Long-Term Projections of the Economies of ESCAP Countries. United Nations Economic and Social Commission for Asia and the Pacific, Development Planning Division, May 1980.

COMMENTS*

Global Modeling in Japan

There are a number of global models in use or under construction in Japan today. To the best of my knowledge, the following is a complete list:

FUGI (Y. Kaya and A. Onishi)
Tsukuba University Model (S. Shishido)
Economic Planning Agency Model (A. Amano et al.)
Institute of Developing Economies Model (T. Uchida et al.)
Asian Link Model (S. Ichimura and M. Ezaki)
Institute of Energy Economics Model (T. Tomitate et al.)

The first two are already used to forecast the future of the world economy and a breakdown of major countries. The Economic Planning Agency has organized a large project covering the main advanced countries, a few important trade partners of Japan among the LDCs, and the rest of the world: this seems the most promising project at present**. The Institute of Developing Economies is just starting model building. The Asian Link Model at Kyoto University is attempting to link the national models built by central banks in

*By Shinichi Ichimura, Center for Southeast Asian Studies, Kyoto University, Japan.
**See A. Amano, E. Kurihara, and L. Samuelson, "Trade Linkage Sub-Model in the EPA World Economic Model". Economic Bulletin No. 19. Economic Research Institute, Economic Planning Agency, July 1980. Comprehensive details of the EPA models are now (1983) available in EPA monographs.

East and Southeast Asia with Japanese and US models, using bilateral trade functions and a trade-share matrix. The Institute of Energy Economics model, which will deal mainly with world energy demand and supply, is still under construction. Most of these models should have become available by 1981. At the time of writing, however, none of the groups have given comprehensive quantitative details of the empirically estimated models, although partial descriptions are available in some cases[†]. Partly due to the lack of publications and reporting, mutual communication between the model-builders has unfortunately been limited.

The FUGI Macro-Economic Model

The present paper offers insufficient information on the FUGI model itself but a fair amount on the projected world economic conditions in the 1980s. The reader may wish that the emphasis of the paper had been reversed. It is not impossible, however, to perceive in outline the basic structure and usage of this model. It is an ambitious attempt on the part of a single econometrician to cover ten advanced countries, fifteen developing market economies, and two centrally planned economic regions, including the USSR and China. The empirical results are not given in the paper, so that comments must be limited to the general characteristics of the macro model; this will also be the case for the FUGI input—output and linear programming models discussed below[††].

The model described is not particularly different from other standard macro-models. This may not be suitable for the centrally planned and underdeveloped economies. The model specifications are, broadly speaking, too general. The same production functions or bilateral export functions can hardly be expected to fit fifteen LDCs in the same way, as we have learnt from our own research, even within the framework of macro-variables similar to those used here.

The bilateral export equations are critical for international linkage and they seem to contain some mis-specifications. The lag structure can hardly be uniform[§]. The exports of many LDCs are certainly price-elastic, although the authors do not assume so.

The authors distinguish between the potential and capacity GDP. In the model the capacity GDP (*GDPC*) is derived from the potential GDP (*GDPP*) by multiplying by a factor of oil import saving on the latter. Since *GDPC* divided by employed labor defines the labor productivity index (LPI), *GDPC* must be equal to *GDP**. Then it becomes critical how the authors determined $\lambda(\dot{M}^*_{oil}/G\dot{D}PP^*)$. If λ is given, then the system has one redundant equation. The authors impose a condition $GDP^* \leqslant \tilde{\beta}\ GDPC^*$, but they do not say how the system is adjusted if $GDP^* \geqslant \tilde{\beta}\ GDPC^*$.

[†]For example, ten articles on the Asian Link Model are available in Southeast Asian Studies (1979/80), volume 17 nos. 2, 3, and 4, and volume 18, no. 1.

[††]*Editor's note*: it was necessary to delete the equation specification to which Professor Ichimura refers from the paper by Kaya et al. because of space limitations. Full details of the model specification may be found in the references in the paper itself.

[§]See for example, S. Yasuda et al., "On Linking National Econometric Models of Japan, USA, and East and Southeast Asian Countries", Southeast Asian Studies, March 1980; see also, L.E. Sabater, "Econometric Models of Selected Countries in Asia", Southeast Asian Studies, December 1979.

The authors introduce a condition: $(G\dot{D}P^*)$ min $\leqslant G\dot{P}P^* \leqslant (G\dot{D}P)$ max. The upper and lower boundaries for the growth rate of GDP may be calculated for the past. But why does this set a boundary? The limits of growth must be set by scarce resources or by institutions. Imposing such conditions may be a device for easier computation but it has no economic rationale. For the same reason, the boundaries set for the average wage rate *WSEI* (or its rate of change) have no meaning. The rate of change in *WSEI* should depend on the rate of unemployment, not its rate of change.

The FUGI Input—Output and Linear Programming Models

Given a set of projected values for the macro-variables, the authors break them down into value added, exports, imports and the other final demands for fourteen industrial sectors. The paper's explanation of this division is inadequate. I, for one, fail to understand the methodology completely, when the paper says that "input—output coefficients of each region are estimated by employing a modified canonical regression analysis". Some of the procedures explained in the paper are understandable, but they leave me with a number of unanswered questions as follows.

For instance, the authors say that $d_i(t)$, the estimated domestic final demand vector, is calculated by eqn. (1) from the time-series data on $x_i(t)$, $e_i(t)$, and $m_i(t)$, with given coefficients k_{v_i} and A_i. Knowing the changes of industrial structure in the various countries over a number of years is it not too presumptuous to use the same coefficients? Or how are they adjusted? How did the authors "apply the regression analysis to the time-series data of $d_i(t)$ and then provide future estimates of $d_i(t)$"?

The authors impose constraints directly on exports and imports. They also introduce constraints on industrial structure, which are explained in their earlier paper presented at IIASA in 1977. A linear programming procedure is applied under these constraints. Then what matters most is the constraints in conditioning sectoral production. It is highly desirable not to impose the constraints directly on the variables which are to be determined but on the surrounding, external conditions such as scarce natural resources, foreign exchange reserves, foreign loans, government budget deficit, or the capacity levels of output for some sectors. If the $d_i(t)$ values are given, this implies that capital formation is given as a whole. Without going into the sectoral breakdown of this capital formation and setting the sum equal to the macro-economic model's nonhousing capital formation figures which play such an important role there, the capacity levels of sectoral production cannot be determined. For many developing countries in Asia in the 1980s, where a large number of new industries are going to develop, this aspect must be more carefully dealt with.

I agree with the authors that the agriculturally-oriented strategy is probably closer to the optimum development strategy for Asia. The general remarks in Section 2 are well taken. But, almost needless to say, the situations differ from one country to another. Even under the agriculturally-oriented strategy, Hong Kong's agriculture for one will not grow at the annual rate of 7.2%.

The Prognosis of the Asian Drama

Although it is true that East and Southeast Asia is a relatively bright spot in the generally dismal scene of the underdeveloped world, the prognosis given by the authors for the Asian economies seems a little too optimistic. The second oil crisis has spurred on hyperinflation in many Asian countries and their growth rates have slowed down. Developing countries with per capita incomes below US$1,500 per annum undergo an extremely difficult phase of worsening imbalances in income distribution and increasing social tension, as Kuznets, Huntington and others have shown. Almost all the Asian countries will experience this stage during the 1980s. Personally I remain fairly cautious about making an optimistic prognosis for the Asian Drama, on purely economic grounds. During the 1980s, social and political considerations are likely to be at least as significant as economic factors and they will probably cause more violent perturbations to economic conditions in Asia as well as the Middle East*.

---

*For the relevance of noneconomic factors to development in Asia, see S. Ichimura, "Institutional Factors and the Government Policies for Appropriate Technologies", ILO Working Paper, 1980.

GLOBAL INTERNATIONAL ECONOMIC MODELS
B.G. Hickman (editor)
Elsevier Science Publishers B.V. (North-Holland)
© IIASA, 1983

DYNAMICO: A MULTILEVEL PROGRAMMING MODEL OF WORLD TRADE AND DEVELOPMENT*

Antonio Maria Costa
*United Nations, New York (USA) and New York University,
Washington Square, New York (USA)*

1   INTRODUCTION

The most pressing reality of today's world economy is the existence of two major groups of countries — the underdeveloped countries of the Southern Hemisphere and the developed countries of the North — and their separation by an enormous income gap. The assessment and design of global policies for the bridging of this gap and the promotion of international development requires suitable analytical tools. This paper is a report on a new quantitative framework for projection and policy evaluation that has been devised and assembled at the United Nations Secretariat in New York.

Among the most striking features of the model are the way it addresses region-specific development priorities and the indications it provides — albeit crudely, as models inevitably do — with regard to the costs and benefits of the interaction of these priorities. Since regional development outcomes are devised on the basis of indigenous and endogenous policy assumptions, the model avoids the coalescence of these outcomes into arbitrarily identical molds (a frequent configuration in global models that have been built on the basis of positive rather than normative specifications). Because allowance is made for the supply of goods and services by several input mixes as well as by foreign sources, the model also displays some analytical capability in dealing with the issues of shifting international competitiveness and the underlying changes in technologies and production efficiency. The ultimate objective of the research is to forge an instrument that can contribute to the definition of national and international policies which then could enable rich and poor nations to pursue development in line with their dynamic long-term comparative advantage in an integrated world economic system.

The paper consists of two main parts. The first (Section 2) is a review of the purpose, coverage, structure, and analytical frame of reference of the model. The second (Section 3) sets forth preliminary informal results for 1980. Its aim is to provide the reader with a global view of the analytical capability of the model so as to facilitate assessment of its scientific validity. For the interested reader a Technical Appendix is available on request from the author.

---

*The views expressed in this study do not imply expression of any opinion whatsoever on the part of the United Nations.

2   DYNAMICO: A QUANTITATIVE FRAMEWORK FOR POLICY ANALYSIS

2.1   An Overview of the Coverage, Structure, and Analytical Frame of Reference of the Model

The general concern to provide the UN Secretariat with effective and flexible tools for policy assessment and design has stimulated the probing of several complementary procedures of economic analysis. Among the approaches that have been devised in recent years the one based on multiregion activity analysis has been singled out for its policy relevance, analytical power, and computational flexibility.

Although it is aggregate in scope and still unsatisfactory in its data base the resulting modeling framework (dubbed DYNAMICO) provides otherwise seldom-available information on inputs and outputs (activity levels and factor balances) as well as implicit price relations (terms of trade, interest rates, and commodity exchange values) in the world economy. Because of its normative nature the model also contributes to an order-of-magnitude assessment of the opportunity cost of alternative resource-management policies in each of the economies that it includes as well as in the world as a whole. The findings of the model are the product of previously seldom-realized interactions, not only between different world regions but also between the real (primal) and value (dual) economic variables in each of them. These combined results thus shed light both on the production and exchange linkages within and between each regional system and on the allocative implications of different patterns of world trade and development.

DYNAMICO is based on a geographical partition of the world into five developed and five developing regions. Each of these ten regions is treated as a homogenous whole on the basis of a representative matrix of intermediate and final flows of commodities and primary resources and of a vector of policy targets. The regions are as follows:

(1) North America;
(2) Western Europe;
(3) Soviet Union;
(4) Eastern Europe;
(5) Japan and Oceania;
(6) Latin and Central America;
(7) Oil-exporting countries of North Africa and the Middle East;
(8) Equatorial and Sub-Saharan Africa;
(9) India and the other market economies of Asia; and
(10) China and the other planned economies of Asia.

The sectoral breakdown, derived in part by aggregating the original information used in the Leontief model (Leontief et al., 1977) and in part from other sources, was devised in order to address a number of major socioeconomic concerns. It covers the following ten economic activities, nine of which produce tradable outputs:

(1) Renewable primary products, excluding grains;
(2) Grains;
(3) Nonrenewable primary products, excluding energy products;

    (4) Energy products, excluding petroleum;
    (5) Petroleum;
    (6) Intermediate goods;
    (7) Consumer goods;
    (8) Investment goods;
    (9) Construction (nontradable); and
  (10) Services.

The model is designed to find a possible set of regional development policies that are consistent with regional resource balances and also, in some sense, efficient — hence the normative nature of the model. The underlying mathematical algorithm (Dantzig and Wolfe, 1960; Kornai and Liptak, 1965) is known for its ability to reproduce bargaining processes for positive as well as, if desired, zero-sum games. Based on a sequence of simulations which assume limited information across regions, it can accommodate both rational and, again if desired, less-than-rational policy behaviors in the interaction between regions.

Results are obtained through a process which can be summarized as follows.

Each region first solves its own resource-allocation problem (the prelinkage models) under the assumption that the rest of the world is willing to purchase or sell commodities which are in excess supply or excess demand at the regional level. Outward linkages, expressed in terms of the import and export volumes of goods, services, and capital flows for each region, are thus extended.

In the next stage of computations (the postlinkage model) global consistency in world markets for all traded resources is tested. Whenever the aggregate world demand for a given resource diverges from its availability, policies are proposed to stimulate either demand or supply (depending on the type of disequilibrium) and to drive net resource balances toward zero. These inward linkages — expressed in terms of commodity terms of trade, implicit interest charges, or other signals — are then brought to bear upon the regional systems which are solved once again. The interaction of the external environment with the level and the structure of domestic activity in each region shifts regional development patterns and the international division of labor toward new configurations.

The process is repeated for several iterations until, after a finite number of experiments, conditions of zero excess demand prevail on all commodity and financial markets. The resulting regional development outcomes are then feasible and, within the world system, meet the Pareto condition for optimality. Therefore, both individually and globally, they are also the most efficient outcomes.

DYNAMICO is based on a decomposed activity-analysis procedure with one postlinkage core (the master or global problem) and hundreds of prelinkage modules (the satellite or regional structures). In order to determine the most desirable time profile in the allocation of world resources with policies, factor endowments, and production structures which change over time and reflect varying cost conditions, recursive programming is used. Recursive programming was selected from among the various dynamic simulation techniques available because of its ability to capture behavioral and structural shifts from one year to the next, within a time horizon which covers over a quarter of a century (1970–2000). The end result is a policy-oriented quantitative framework that is useful for investigating the development potential of the world economy, where the North–South and East–West frontiers inevitably remind one of the plurality of interests and the competition of goals.

2.2   Prelinkage Computations: the Prototype Regional Models

The analytical structure of DYNAMICO can be summarized by three sets of relationships.

(i) *The prelinkage module.* In this first system each of the ten satellite regional models is represented by a set of linear constraints which provide activity levels for regional production, factor requirements, the composition and nature of all interindustrial linkages, and the endowment of stock variables (population, capital assets, land, etc.). Since consistency over space is disregarded at this stage of computation, these regional solutions are referred to as prelinkage.

(ii) *The postlinkage module.* The second set of relationships is used to achieve overall consistency within the global module by means of a single worldwide global program. This postlinkage procedure handles all international flows of goods and services together with foreign capital and aid assistance.

(iii) *The dynamic module.* The third set of relationships links each set of solutions over time, thus making the global model a dynamic procedure.

Each prelinkage model consists of a regional strategy function and a broad array of linear inequalities concerning the domestic and external activities, all the fundamental expenditure components, all the factor demand and supply conditions, and all the major payment flows of each region.

In its present version a typical regional model includes ten types of sectoral output, each produced by several alternative technologies. The generalized production function for the ith output X_{ij} by the jth technology is given by the familiar material-balance relation

$$\sum_j^{z(k)} X_{ij} - \sum_k \sum_j^{z(k)} a_{ijk} X_{jk} - \sum_j c_{ij} C_j - \sum_j v_{ij} I_j - g_i G - s_i DS - (E_i - M_i) \geq 0 \qquad (1)$$

for $i = 1, 2, \ldots, N$, $k = 1, 2, \ldots, N$, and $j = 1, 2, \ldots, z(k)$, where $z(k)$ is the maximum number of technologies producing product k. The interindustrial coefficient a_{ijk} represents the output that is required from sector i to produce one unit of product k by technology j. In addition to multiple technologies there are also different consumption baskets C_j and several types of gross fixed investment I_j.

Each c_{ij} gives the share of the ith type of good in the jth type of basket. Similarly each coefficient v_{ij} gives the share of the ith type of good in the jth type of investment (plant, equipment, land improvement, irrigation, etc.).

Shares are also used to break down government consumption G and inventory accumulation DS. Naturally

$$\sum_i c_{ij} = \sum_i v_{ij} = \sum_i g_i = \sum_i s_i = 1 \qquad (2)$$

for $i = 1, 2, \ldots, N$, and $j = 1, 2, \ldots, Q$.

Shortages of capital assets place a severe constraint on the expansion of output and, more generally, of economic activity. The demand for each type K_i of capital asset is given by

$$K_i^D = \sum_y^{z(k)} \sum_j k_{ijy} X_{jy} + \sum_j k_{ij} C_j + k_i G + k_i UP$$

for $i = 1, 2, \ldots, F$. There are several types of capital asset, distinguished by usage or ownership: these are plant, equipment, arable land, inventories, and foreign-owned capital. The requirements for each of the first four types are determined by (1) production using the jth type of technology of each yth type of output ($y = 1, 2, \ldots, M$), (2) varieties of final demand, and (3) the need for infrastructural construction by the urban population UP. The sum of the requirements cannot exceed the availability K_i^S. Foreign-owned capital is treated differently, as seen later.

The supply of capital $K_{i,t}^S$ is given by an identity which adds investment resources stemming from either domestic or international sources to the existing depreciated stock of capital:

$$K_{i,t}^S = (1 - \delta)K_{i,t-1}^S + I_{i,t} \tag{3}$$

The investment function is determined on the basis of the flexible-accelerator principle which relates investment positively to the level of gross output and negatively to capital stock. To show its conceptual framework we assume that the demand for the kth type of capital asset ($k = 1, 2, \ldots, F$) by the ith activity ($i = 1, 2, \ldots, N$) is proportional to some weighted average of the output X_i in previous years represented by a series of geometrically declining weights λ_k ($0 < \lambda_k < 1$), i.e. we assume that

$$K_{ik,t} = \alpha_{ik} \sum_{j=0}^{\infty} \lambda_k^j X_{i,t-j}$$

where t represents time periods and α_{ik} is the capital/output coefficient for the kth type of asset in the ith activity,

$$\alpha_{ik} = K_{ik}/X_i$$

By the Koyck transformation (Koyck, 1954) the equation for $K_{ik,t}$ can be transformed into

$$K_{ik,t} = \alpha_{ik} X_{i,t} + \lambda_k K_{ik,t-1} \tag{4}$$

If we set D_{ik} as the sectoral depreciation ($D_{ik} = \delta_{ik} K_{ik,t-1}$), then

$$I_{ik,t} = \alpha_{ik} X_{i,t} - (1 - \lambda_k - \delta_{ik})K_{ik,t-1} \tag{5}$$

and for the economy as a whole

$$I_{k,t} = \sum_{j}^{z(j)} \sum_{i} \alpha_{ik} X_{ij,t} - (1 - \lambda_k - \delta_k)K_{k,t-1} \tag{6}$$

which yields the economy-wide requirement I_k for investment for the kth type of asset.

According to this flexible-accelerator formulation, net investment rises for several periods before the negative effect of the increased capital stock outweighs the positive effect of further increases in output.

An identity sums up the domestic demand for all types of investment and the net trade balance TB to determine the total investment demand I of each region. In another identity national saving S is found by adding the net factor income NFY from abroad to the total investment I. Thus

$$I = \sum_i I_i + TB \tag{7}$$

$$S = I + NFY \tag{8}$$

The net factor income NFY from abroad is measured on the basis of the rate of return charged on foreign-owned capital assets.

The labor factor is assumed to be characterized by a single homogenous skill. The total demand for labor is determined by (1) production using j alternative technologies for each kth type of product, (2) various types of final demand, and (3) the need for infrastructure of the urban population UP:

$$L^D = \sum_k \sum_j^{z(k)} l_{jk}^x X_{jk} + \sum_j l_j^c C_j + \sum_j l_j^i I_j + l^g G + l^n UP \tag{9}$$

The total labor supply L^s is determined on the basis of participation rates applied to exogenously given population estimates.

The stock H_0 of arable land available in the base period is exogenously given. Over time its supply is expanded by means of investment IR in irrigation and land improvement which is endogenously determined. The corresponding constraint states that the total land requirement cannot exceed the demand:

$$H_0 + \sum_t^T h_t IR_t \geqslant \sum_k \sum_j^{z(k)} r_{jk} X_{jk,t} \tag{10}$$

where h_t is a conversion factor and r_{jk} is the unit requirement (in hectares) of land by the jth sector using the kth technology.

Private consumption C is determined by means of a consumption function which incorporates some aspects of the permanent-income hypothesis:

$$C_t \geqslant \beta \sum_{i=0}^{\infty} \gamma^i GNP_{t-1}$$

where t represents time periods, γ^i are geometrically declining income weights, and β is the short-term marginal propensity to consume. By means of the Koyck transformation the consumption function can be reformulated into the simpler relation

$$C_t \geqslant \gamma C_{t-1} + \beta GNP_t \tag{11}$$

which assumes that the long-run consumption function passes through the origin if the above constraint is binding and has a positive intercept otherwise.

Government expenditure G is set on the basis of an exogenous parameter g, corrected by the tariff revenue that is charged on imports:

$$G = gGNP + \sum_i \tau_i M_i \tag{12}$$

The gross national product *GNP* is derived as the identity of its expenditure components:

$$GNP = C + G + S + (E - M) \tag{13}$$

which includes national saving, which is itself an identity, as seen earlier.

As is to be expected from a model that is geared to the study of the interaction of economic activities which take place in several world regions, the foreign sector commands the greatest attention. Its modeling takes into account several widely shared considerations concerning trade behavior. First, imports are significantly and positively related to movements in aggregate economic activity within each region. Second, in a number of regions the supply of foreign exchange places yet another major constraint on purchases from abroad. The price of imported goods relative to domestic goods is also an important determinant of comparative advantage and therefore of trade behavior.

Exports are thought to be less related to other economic activities within the region and to depend more directly on the income and policies of trading partners. However, this proposition is mitigated by several factors. First, there are economies in the world which for institutional or other reasons are constrained by supply. Second, exports (like imports) depend on the movement of the price of domestic goods and services that are produced for export relative to the price of the outputs of other regions. (Since at present the model uses exclusively real variables measured in constant (1970) US dollars the price of a commodity or service is understood here as the opportunity cost of the resources that are required for its supply.) Third, the expansion of GNP and therefore of imports in a given region affects the exports (and therefore GNP) of trading partners to an extent that depends on the size of the GNP of the impulse region and on its trade elasticity. Foreign-trade multipliers are thus set in motion: growing external demand is likely to affect the exports of the impulse region, and so on, in several rounds of feedbacks.

In the prelinkage format each regional model is constrained by nothing more than a maximum level of imports for tradable goods and services. This level is predetermined on the basis of import-propensity coefficients and balance-of-payments elasticities in order to capture the effects of foreign reserves. Exports implicitly reflect relative production efficiency. Since at the regional level nothing is known about the import-demand functions of the partner regions, exports take place only if, under a given regional development strategy, they can provide efficiently the foreign exchange that is required to finance imports.

This treatment of imports and, particularly, of exports in the prelinkage stage is greatly misleading in its apparent simplicity. Extensive regional linkages are at the very core of the model, as shown in the following sections, when the world module is used to determine relative prices.

2.3 Prelinkage Solutions

DYNAMICO is solved by means of an iterative procedure which, in the first place, identifies a large number of optimal solutions for each region taken in isolation: these are the prelinkage problems. Their solutions, often referred to as regional development proposals, are obtained on the basis of alternative, often radically different, policy assumptions. These include optimization of macroeconomic policies, factor utilization, and foreign-trade behavior.

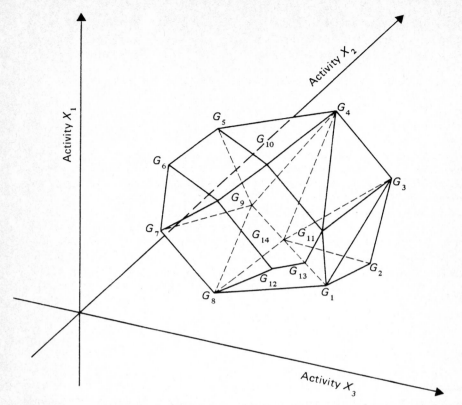

FIGURE 1   The carrying capacity of the rth region; a hypothetical example of the complexes G_i, for $i = 1, 2, \ldots, Z$, identified by means of multiple objective functions (prelinkage solutions).

The aim of this search for multiple prelinkage optimal solutions is to explore the production-possibility polyhedron (which, as shown in Figure 1, represents the carrying capacity of each regional economy) and to identify the corresponding solution values (or complexes). Each regional problem, which consists typically of some 80 equations and about 100 variables, is solved using over a dozen alternative objective functions. Therefore in the first stage of the computations nearly 200 linear programming problems are solved to scan the ten regional production-possibility polyhedrons at any time t.

Since each complex represents feasible and optimal prelinkage solutions, any convex combination of complexes will also be feasible and suboptimal. The task presented by the postlinkage problem is to find the appropriate weighting structure for which all the regional solutions are not only instantly compatible but also efficient. In the next phase a new procedure (a master, or global, program) is used to compute the weights that are to be assigned to each regional development proposal so that the world markets for all types of transaction (goods, services, and financial flows) are cleared. On the basis of these weights it is then possible to compute a preliminary (first-iteration) postlinkage solution of the world model. While individually optimal, these regional solutions may not as yet be the most efficient from a global perspective, and the search for additional complexes has to continue through several iterations. Over 100 additional regional problems are solved before the system converges to the desired postlinkage solution. As is to be expected, the master problem grows in size and complexity as more iterations go by (Vietorisz, 1968).

2.4 Postlinkage Solutions

The role of the postlinkage relations, and of the master problem which consists of these relations, is to guarantee the compatibility of the external sector of all the regional models. Since several convex combinations of regional proposals satisfy the world linkages, an optimality criterion is required for the master problem to single out the one combination which is most desirable from a global perspective.

Among the several global development-strategy functions that have been tested so far by the world module the following are prominent: (i) maximization of world GNP, or GWP (gross world product) at time t; (ii) minimization of the income gap between rich and poor regions; (iii) maximization of the discounted value of regional consumption.

For illustrative purposes let us elect to maximize the weighted sum of the regional GNPs:

$$\max GNP_{\text{world}} = \sum_r \sum_p^{q(r)} \mu_r \lambda_r^p GNP_r^p \tag{14}$$

for $p = 1, 2, \ldots, q(r)$ and $r = 1, 2, \ldots, R$.

The λ_r^p are the unknown variables of the problem. Each of them coincides with the weight to be assigned to the pth development proposal for the rth region. The other weights μ_r are exogenously provided and are used to simulate alternative policy situations. The maximum is constrained by the conditions of zero excess demand on the world markets for each ith commodity and service:

$$\sum_r \sum_p^{q(r)} \lambda_r^p (E_{r,i}^p - M_{r,i}^p) = 0 \qquad \text{for all } i, i = 1, 2, \ldots, N$$

and for the jth type of payment flow,

$$\sum_r \sum_p^{q(r)} \lambda_r^p KF_{r,j}^p = 0 \qquad \text{for all } j, j = 1, 2, \ldots, M$$

The convexity conditions require that for each region the sum of all the weights λ_r^p, which are constrained to be nonnegative, should be unity:

$$\sum_p^{q(r)} \lambda_r^p = 1 \qquad \text{for all } r, r = 1, 2, \ldots, R$$

The dual of the master problem consists of the minimization on a world basis of the resource costs RC that are required to attain given levels of regional GNPs:

$$\min RC_{\text{world}} = \sum_r RC_r \tag{15}$$

under the constraint that any discrepancy between these domestic resource requirements and the regional gross products has to be financed through the net trade position and interest charged (or earned) on world capital markets according to

$$\sum_i TT_i(E^p_{r,i} - M^p_{r,i}) + \sum_j IR_j + RC_r \geqslant GNP^p_r \tag{16}$$

where the TT_i are the terms of trade of commodities and services exchanged on world markets, the IR_j are the implicit interest rates charged on outstanding capital balances, and the RC_r are the resource costs required to run economic activity in each individual region at unit level.

The master problems include as many market-clearance equality constraints as there are commodity and other payment flows and as many convexity constraints as there are regions in the world model. The dual variables of the master problem, which provide the opportunity cost of these constraints, are also of fundamental importance. They show the gains and losses, in terms of the world gross product, of loosening trade and other world-wide consistency conditions. Since three types of equality constrain the maximum of the master problem there are three types of shadow price in this dual problem (see eqn. (16)): the terms of trade of commodities, the implicit interest rates, and the regional resource costs.

The sign of these three types of shadow price is also of fundamental importance. For example, the regional resource costs provide an indication of the extent to which the world GNP would be affected if the level of economic activity in a given region were allowed to change. In a very loose sense, a cross-regional comparison of these resource costs provides an order-of-magnitude indication of the contribution of each region to world development momentum and, as can happen in some cases, the extent to which some regions benefit from it.

The terms of trade for commodities and services and the implicit interest rate charged on capital flows provide an indication of the extent to which the world GNP would be affected if trade and payment flows were rearranged so as to pursue different comparative costs and capital-efficiency patterns.

The level and the structure of economic activity in each region interact with the external sector; the explanatory power of a world model critically depends on the ability of the model to address this problem. The iterative procedure which manages this interaction in DYNAMICO links serially the prelinkage and postlinkage problems by means of reaction functions and other types of feedback mechanism — the so-called outward and inward linkages. The iterations end when the world GNP ceases to grow as more computations are carried out; at that point no higher world income can be hypothesized by any rearrangement of trade and payment flows between the regions covered by the model.

At each iteration, exchange and payment flows are modified through the recycling of the commodity terms of trade and the interest that is charged on outstanding capital balances in each regional model system. If the behavioral assumption concerns, for example, the maximization of GNP, the objective function of the typical postlinkage problem for the rth region at the kth iteration is

$$\max GNP^k_r = GNP^{k-1}_r - \sum_i TT^k_i (E_{r,i} - M_{r,i}) - \sum_j IR^k_j (KF_{r,j}) \text{ for } r = 1, 2, \ldots, R$$

The last two terms on the right-hand side are the inward linkages, which include charges for exports E, imports M, and capital flows KF. This maximum is subject to constraints which concern domestic policies and resource availabilities within the region, as seen earlier. Therefore the domestic level and composition of production change at each iteration, as a reflection of, and at the same time as a prime mover of, shifts of comparative-advantage positions through space. The shifts through time are accounted for by means of dynamic linkages, as discussed later.

In any period the regional realignment of in- and out-payments is brought about by charging a premium on the demand for goods, services, and financial assets which are in short supply on world markets and by paying a subsidy for the supply of those items which are in excess demand. For each type of market the magnitude of the charges and the subsidies is usually identical; on the other hand, substantial differences between markets stem from scarcities which to varying degrees characterize goods and means of payment.

As iterations go by, the procedure finds new postlinkage vertices in the production-possibility polyhedron which represents the carrying capacity of each regional economy. These new solutions are based on regional development-strategy functions which are modified versions of the functions that were used under prelinkage conditions; however, they now incorporate the charges and subsidies which prevail on world markets.

The activity levels that are computed by each postlinkage problem give rise to new sets of outward linkages (the trade and payment position of each region) which are then added to the master problem as formulated in the previous iteration for recomputation of the weights in the next iteration.

The procedure ends when, in the given example, the increment of the world gross product between two successive iterations is less than a pre-established convergence parameter. Beyond this point, any further rearrangement of trade and payment will not benefit any one region without being detrimental to other regions. The Pareto condition for optimality is thus met. Naturally, nothing is said about interregional equity considerations or about the relative income positions of the regions covered by the system.

2.5   Dynamic Linkages

In addition to linkages through space the model includes extensive linkages over time; hence the name of the system, **DYNAMICO**. The end result is a recursive programming application of the decomposition procedure, whereby the level of the exogenous variables for any period is retrieved from the solution values of the model for the previous period. The control solution for the 1970–1980 period (the control solution of the system) is computed ex post on the basis of actual information concerning exogenous variables.

For each region the dynamic linkages concern resource endowments, technological change, extraction costs of nonrenewable resources, policy targets on final expenditure, foreign-exchange reserves, foreign-owned production assets, demographic behavior, etc.

The original statistical information used in the model covers four benchmark periods: the years 1970, 1980, 1990, and 2000. In order to investigate some aspects of the development trajectory of the world economy and of its regional and sectoral components, the benchmark data were interpolated yearly, for a total of 31 observations between

1970 and the end of the century, inclusive. Since over 350 regional linear programming problems are solved for each year, the entire time horizon 1970–2000 can only be covered by solving recursively over 10,000 problems. The model is therefore voracious in its use of computer resources. A tracking experiment is being tested to study how well the model can trace the world economy during the 1970s, with all its convulsions and turbulence.

In order to take into account exogenously projected rates of technological innovation and, above all, the expected increased costs in some economic activities, a series of cost-step functions are used which introduce discontinuities over time in the growth of the production-possibility polyhedron of each region. These cost parameters, which at present are computed by means of auxiliary computations outside the mainstream of the model solution, are recycled into the system, thus affecting the capital/output ratios in given sectors.

3   THE WORLD ECONOMY IN 1980: REALITY AND ITS PERCEPTION

The gross world product (GWP) for 1980 is estimated to be in the neighborhood of US$5090 billion measured in constant 1970 prices. About 80% of this total (US$4085 billion) is generated in the developed regions and the rest in the developing world. The magnitude of the income gap is put into sharp perspective when population levels are taken into consideration. Per capita income in the developed countries is estimated to be over US$3400 (at 1970 prices), while income per person in the Third World is about US$250, i.e. about one-fourteenth of the amount in the developed world. The estimated regional breakdown of total and per capita income and the share of the regions in the GWP are given in Table 1, while Tables 2 and 3 provide the 1980 distribution of regional GNPs according to end use and producing sector.

TABLE 1   Estimates of regional GNP, per capita income, and shares in GWP by region in 1980 (in constant 1970 US dollars).

Region	GNP (billions of US$)	Per capita GNP (US$)	Share in GWP (%)
1. North America	1492.6	5923.10	29.31
2. Western Europe	1147.3	2911.93	22.54
3. USSR	711.6	2650.28	13.97
4. Eastern Europe	250.4	2221.83	4.91
5. Japan and Oceania	483.4	2938.60	9.49
Total developed regions	4085.3	3427.62	80.22
6. Latin America	253.2	774.23	4.96
7. Oil-Exporting North Africa and Middle East	98.4	516.96	1.93
8. Sub-Saharan and equatorial Africa	123.2	317.08	2.42
9. Asia (market economies)	303.2	220.95	5.95
10. Asia (planned economies)	226.7	227.15	4.46
Total developing regions	1004.7	245.97	19.72
GWP	5089.4	1162.12	100.00

TABLE 2   Estimates of consumption and accumulation levels by region in 1980 (in constant 1970 US dollars).

Region	Consumption (billions of US$)	Accumulation (billions of US$)
1. North America	1164.1	328.6
2. Western Europe	766.92	380.6
3. USSR	501.90	209.7
4. Eastern Europe	175.90	75.3
5. Japan and Oceania	301.83	181.5
Total developed regions	2910.65	1175.7
6. Latin America	172.99	80.21
7. Oil-Exporting North Africa and Middle East	61.41	36.99
8. Sub-Saharan and equatorial Africa	86.60	36.69
9. Asia (market economies)	197.99	105.31
10. Asia (planned economies)	150.28	76.39
Total developing regions	669.27	335.59

TABLE 3   Estimates of the sectoral composition of gross output in 1980 by region (in constant 1970 US dollars).

Region	Primary products (billions of US$)	Manufactures (billions of US$)	Services (billions of US$)
1. North America	139.7	1204.4	877.6
2. Western Europe	67.0	992.8	604.2
3. USSR	79.7	577.0	378.6
4. Eastern Europe	33.9	203.2	136.3
5. Japan and Oceania	99.8	794.8	493.9
Total developed regions	420.1	3772.2	2490.6
6. Latin America	140.4	101.2	60.3
7. Oil-Exporting North Africa and Middle East	79.8	21.9	32.6
8. Sub-Saharan and equatorial Africa	52.8	49.5	58.7
9. Asia (market economies)	232.0	150.6	158.9
10. Asia (planned economies)	126.9	70.4	123.9
Total developing regions	631.9	393.6	434.4

The results shown in the tables fall short on many accounts. Among several sources of error are inevitable measurement and aggregation inaccuracies, the bias that is induced by conversion into a single currency, and the index-number problem stemming from the use of a constant-pricing rule. Also, no purchasing-power parity adjustment has been introduced. Nevertheless, because of their bare order of magnitude these numbers highlight the most critical concern of the world economy at the beginning of the 1980s: the persistence of a staggering income differential between regions and the urgent need for policy action to reduce it. One purpose of this paper and of the model developed to provide its quantitative framework is to contribute views on ways and means for such action.

The expansion of productive capacity in a given region (characterized by an increase in one or all of the factor inputs) inevitably results in some growth of the region where the change is postulated. The size of the change depends on the elasticity of output in relation to the variation of input. Depending on the size and nature of the linkages of the region with the rest of the world, external multipliers are also set in motion. The study of the transmission mechanism of economic events from one region to the rest of the world and, through various feedback channels, their return to the impulse region is therefore very important. DYNAMICO has been used to determine the impact on the world economy of the hypothetical expansion of production capacity in each of the ten regions covered by the model. Such an analysis is described in this section for a single year, 1980. A multistage investigation and an assessment of the dynamic linkages through the decade of the 1980s is at present under elaboration.

In an econometric exercise based on time-series analysis and the estimation of parameters by statistical inference, experiments of this sort are usually performed by means of ad hoc computations which take into account a given exogenous change; i.e. systems are shocked by a priori alteration of a variable level. Therefore the results inevitably reflect the implicit value judgments of the researcher on the size of the shock and the direction of change.

In the programming procedure which underpins this paper the impact on the world economy of greater factor endowment at the regional level is generated from within the model. To see how this takes place refer to Section 2.4, where the master (or global) problem is shown to be constrained by convexity conditions which guarantee that, in the optimal solution, the production potential of each region is exhausted. (This does not imply that the model forces full capacity utilization in all regions; such a restriction would be somewhat unrealistic.) As always occurs in optimization procedures, the shadow price associated with a given constraint (in this case the production capacity of the region) measures the gains in the maximum (in this case the GWP) following the loosening of the constraint. Therefore the effective contribution of each region to the world economy in a given year is measured by these regional shadow prices. As expected, they diverge from the national-accounts measurements of gross products; occasionally they do so by quite a margin. The conceptual difference between the GNP of a given region (as given by the solution of the model) and the contribution of that region to the world product (as given by the shadow price in the master problem) is fine, but fundamental. The former gives the gross product generated within a region; the latter gives the volume of world product generated by the productive capacity of that region. In short, the latter measurement adjusts domestic output for the externality generated by foreign economic activity. Both the nature and the magnitude of the difference between these two products reflect the production efficiency, the state of technology, the factor endowment, the final-demand composition, etc., all of which enter into the determination of the linkages of a given region within the world system, the competitiveness of the region in the world system, and the resulting trade behavior.

In some instances the contribution of a region to the GWP is greater than its own GNP; in other cases it is less. The regional national products (the estimate by the model of the national accounts for 1980) and the shadow prices (the model's perception of reality) are given in Table 4, both in terms of levels at constant 1970 US dollar prices and as percentages of the world total.

TABLE 4   Imputed contribution of regional activity levels to GWP in 1980 (in constant 1970 US dollars).

Region	Imputed GNP (billions of US$)	Share in GWP (%)	Variation from estimated GNP[a] (%)
1. North America	1501.3	29.50	+0.583
2. Western Europe	1113.3	21.88	−2.963
3. USSR	693.4	13.62	−2.557
4. Eastern Europe	222.7	4.38	−11.062
5. Japan and Oceania	492.1	9.67	+1.806
Total developed regions	4022.8	79.05	−1.500
6. Latin America	290.20	5.70	+14.463
7. Oil-Exporting North Africa and Middle East	116.7	2.28	+18.601
8. Sub-Saharan and equatorial Africa	120.2	2.36	−2.435
9. Asia (market economies)	310.2	6.10	+2.309
10. Asia (planned economies)	229.6	4.52	+1.281
Total developing regions	1066.9	20.96	+6.109
GWP	5089.4	100.00	

[a]The estimated GNPs are given in Table 1.

Of the ten regions covered by the model, North America, Japan and Oceania, Latin America, the petroleum-exporting and the Asian countries are estimated to contribute to the GWP to an extent that is greater than their own GNP. In the other regions the external multiplier is less than unity.

Before we proceed further, two points deserve attention. First, we must give a word of caution. The model is highly aggregated, both in terms of its trade configuration (there are nine groupings of tradables which lump together commodities whose market conditions are extremely diverse) and geographical composition (each region includes countries whose situations diverge substantially). Therefore the results mentioned only convey part of a more complex story, which hopefully one day may be probed by more appropriate and powerful tools. Secondly, it may also be useful to point out that similar findings have been obtained in regional studies at the national level when decomposition techniques have been applied. For example, Granberg has reported (Granberg, 1978) that the effective contribution of the Siberian region to the development of the USSR was found to be over 25% greater than its share in the net national product of the country. Similar asymmetry, often with even greater disparity, has been found in regional studies of Australia (Dixon and Powell, 1979), Italy (Costa, 1981), and the United States (Polenske and Skolka, 1977).

It can be easily shown that these findings reflect regional externalities; they are therefore a reflection of conditions that are found to prevail on world markets and of the role of each regional economy in these markets. Since in these markets all excess supplies and demands are eliminated by means of a combination of fiscal changes (penalties) for surplus commodities and incentives (subsidies) for commodities in shortage, regions which sell scarce commodities contribute to world development to a greater extent than their own GNP indicates. The entire world system would therefore benefit from the expansion of their productive capacity. Conversely, those regions which suffer from a low degree of comparative advantage on the world market and specialize in the export of commodities in excess supply benefit from participation in the international exchange of goods and services to a greater extent than they can actually contribute to this exchange. In short, the results in Table 4 are obtained on the basis of implicit external multipliers which, when they are triggered, tend to reduce or magnify at the global level the benefit accruing to a region following a capacity change. Oil is a good, if perhaps rather trite, example. For oil the model generates information which one would expect on the basis of common sense. Since oil is in short supply on world markets, the expansion of production capacity in the oil-exporting region propagates through space, thus inducing higher world production. Specifically, it is found that the contribution of the oil-exporting countries of the Middle East and North Africa to world development exceeds by 18% the volume of gross product actually generated in that region.

This consideration begs another, equally important, question. Since by definition equilibrium conditions prevail on all world markets (i.e. the sum of all imports is equal to the sum of all exports) how can we distinguish potential shortages from potential surpluses?

In DYNAMICO the typical market-clearance mechanism for each tradable commodity is expressed by two inequalities: first net exports and then net imports are forced to be nonnegative. The simultaneous satisfaction of these two constraints implies that the net trade balance for each commodity vanishes, so that its world demand is identically equal to the world supply. However, it is of great economic and policy relevance to distinguish whether the market equilibrium occurs through (a) the promotion of exports and the compression of imports (thus proving excess-demand conditions) or (b) the reduction of exports and the decompression of imports (under excess-supply conditions). It can be easily shown that nonzero shadow prices associated with the first of the two inequalities mentioned are the result of net import pressure. Conversely, nonzero shadow prices associated with the second inequality reflect net export pressure. Furthermore, since both types of adjustment are brought about by a system of fiscal instruments (penalties and subsidies) these shadow prices give the opportunity costs of reaching the market-clearance conditions.

As even the casual reader might have suspected on the basis of information that is readily available on current world economic conditions, in the control solution for the base year (1980) excess-demand conditions have been found to prevail on the markets for agricultural goods, grains, oil, and, to a lesser extent, all other energy products. According to the same preliminary computations, excess supply characterizes the markets for services, nonrenewable primary commodities (excluding all energy products) and, to various degrees, different types of manufactures. Table 5 gives these preliminary estimates.

With this trade information available it is now possible to propose a partial explanation of the difference that was found earlier between regional GNPs and the relative contribution of each region to the world product. Since agricultural products and grains are found to be in scarce supply on world markets, the implicit share of world output generated by North America — the major exporter of these two goods (respectively 65% and 34% of the total world trade) — is greater than the GNP of the region. As mentioned earlier, the same consideration holds for the oil-exporting countries of North Africa and the Middle East which practically monopolize the world trade of another scarce commodity (75% of

TABLE 5   Estimated excess-supply and excess-demand conditions on world commodity markets and product terms of trade in 1980.

Commodity	Excess demand (%)	Excess supply (%)	Shadow price
Agricultural products (excluding grains)	8.42		+ 1.2492
Grains	11.57		+ 1.6932
Raw materials (excluding fuels)		2.46	− 0.1062
Energy products (excluding oil)	6.57		+ 0.7360
Oil	17.29		+ 2.2389
Intermediate goods	5.58		+ 0.3671
Consumer goods		5.57	−0.1469
Investment goods		2.68	−0.3173
Services		4.30	−0.2702

oil exports are generated from this region). The case of Western and Eastern Europe is just the opposite: since they enjoy comparative advantage in, specialize in, and trade man-ufactures which are in excess supply, the contribution of these two regions to the world product is smaller than their GNP. External multipliers smaller than unity are also found for other regions.

Once again several caveats are required. First, the results presented at this stage of the computations should be seen as preliminary estimates. They may very well change if better data, more adequate econometric specification, and closer scrutiny are used. Second, although the linkage between trade behavior and the contribution of a region to the world product is at the very core of the DYNAMICO modeling procedure, other factors, which lie outside the present scope of the model, also play a role. The results in Table 5 should therefore be seen as an indication of a type of policy-oriented analysis that is of relevance in the context of world development studies rather than as a solid conclusive estimate of current conditions and development prospects.

ACKNOWLEDGMENTS

In the construction of the model the author was assisted by Saturnino Franco, Seiichi Itoh, Ahmet Ozbek, and Denis Sheridan. Peter Jennergren, Robert Dorfman, Walter Isard, and Merkk Kalio provided valuable advice.

REFERENCES

Costa, A.M. (1981). Development Planning: Techniques and Applications. Elsevier−North-Holland, Amsterdam.
Dantzig, G.B. and Wolfe, P. (1960). Decomposition principle for linear programming. Operations Research, 8:101−111.
Dixon, P. and Powell, A. (1979). Structural Adaptations in an Ailing Macroeconomy. Melbourne University Press, Melbourne, Australia.

Granberg, A.G. (Editor) (1978). Economiko-Matematicheskii Analiz Razmeshchenia Proizvoditel
    'nykh sil SSSR — Preimenenie Mezhotraslevykh Regional'nykh i Mezhregional nykh Modelei.
    Izdatelstvo Akademia Nauka SSSR, Novosibirsk, USSR.
Kornai, J. and Liptak, T. (1965). Two-level planning. Econometrica, 33(1):141–169.
Koyck, L.M. (1954). Distributed Lags and Investment Analysis. North-Holland, Amsterdam.
Leontief, W., Carter, A.P., and Petri, P. (1977). The Future of the World Economy. Oxford University
    Press, New York.
Polenske, K. and Skolka, J. (1977). Recent Advances in Input–Output Analysis. Ballinger, Boston,
    Massachusetts.
Vietorisz, T. (1968). Decentralization and project evaluation under economies of scale and indivisibili-
    ties. Industrialization and Productivity, 12:69–141.

COMMENTS*

Dr. Costa's paper really concerns much more than a normative analysis of trade and development in the 1980s. It deals with production interdependencies with and among ten comprehensive regions of the world, with opportunity costs of production activities and monetary flows, with excess supplies in worldwide factor markets, with foreign exchange and resource constraints on economic growth, and with socially desirable choices of production technologies. Even this list of topics is only a sample. They are all treated in a coherent analytical framework: the global model DYNAMICO.

Dr. Costa maintains that, at bare minimum, the model provides an empirical means for exploring the production possibility frontier of the world economy. It is certainly a rather refined means. Intersectoral production relations are not simply specified in terms of fixed input–output coefficients whereby each sector uses a single technology; instead, each sectoral output can be produced by various technologies, the choice of which is determined through efficiency criteria. Yet such an appraisal of the model involves an obvious and inexcusable understatement. The truly extraordinary feature of DYNAMICO is its normative framework. Through it, the global welfare effects of regional economic activities can be assessed empirically and thus one may inquire whether a particular region is overpaid or underpaid for the productive and extractive services it provides. In other words, interregional externalities are evaluated and these may be used to appraise the desirability not only of trade and development of underdeveloped regions, but also of monetary flows and of growth of developed regions.

In addition to an empirical specification of the productive structure of various regions, a global social welfare function provides another basic building block of DYNAMICO. Dr. Costa does not argue in favor of any particular social welfare function. He presents several alternatives (the maximization of world GNP, the minimization of the income gap between rich and poor nations, and the maximization of the discounted value of regional consumption) and chooses one (the first) to exemplify his empirical results. In this context, he presents some interesting conclusions. For example (p. 273), "Of the ten regions covered by the model, North America, Japan and Oceania, Latin America, the petroleum-exporting and the Asian countries are estimated to contribute to the GWP to an extent that is greater than their own GNP." Again (p. 275), "The case of Western and

---

*By Dennis J. Snower, Department of Economics, Institute for Advanced Studies, Vienna, Austria,
    and International Institute for Applied Systems Analysis, Laxenburg, Austria.

Eastern Europe is just the opposite: since they enjoy comparative advantage in, specialize in, and trade manufactures which are in excess supply, the contribution of these two regions to the world product is smaller than their GNP."

Aside from this issue of externalities, the model provides a novel approach to the possibility of unemployment and excess capacity under globally optimal conditions. Unlike the neoclassical macroeconomic models, the demands for and supplies of capital and labor services are not necessarily responsive to factor price changes in DYNAMICO. Instead, factor demands are derived demands (viz., derived from sectoral outputs) and factor supplies are given by technological (such as depreciation) and demographic considerations. Global optimality is defined with reference to sectoral outputs, not inputs; thus, unemployment and excess capacity may occur even after the global optimum has been attained. This possibility has not commonly been analyzed in normative macroeconomic models thus far. Of course, institutional and sociological constraints — not to be found in neoclassical macro models — are responsible for the economies' inability to take advantage of the gains from trade which unemployment and excess capacity imply; but given that such constraints exist, the resulting second-best optima are certainly worth exploring.

The normative nature of the model is brought into sharpest relief in the "master program," in which a global objective function (e.g., a weighted average of regional GNPs) is maximized subject to three constraints: (i) that a weighted average of regional trade balances sum to zero, (ii) that a weighted average of regional capital payment flows sum to zero, and (iii) that the weights computed for the commodities and regions all sum to unity. The model provides no mechanism whereby excess product demands and excess capital demands always collapse to zero on world markets. In fact, the model tells a story in which such a mechanism is manifestly excluded. The decomposition method, whereby the model is solved, does not guarantee that there exists a set of prices (suitably augmented by taxes and subsidies derived from the master program) which can induce the regional programs to generate the global optimum. The globally optimal solution is specified as a convex combination of solution sets from a sequence of iterations of the regional programs. No single iteration of the regional programs may yield the global optimum, since the worldwide constraints of the master program do not enter the regional programs. Hence, the global optimum may not lie on the boundary of the feasible regional production sets and no price system can induce the regions to produce in the interior of these sets.

In short, the globally optimal solution must be *imposed* on the regions through the explicit decree of a benevolent dictator; it cannot, in general, be found through a price system. The model is normative; its descriptive counterpart is conspicuously absent.

All that are relevant for the derivation of the real economic variables in the optimal solution are the global welfare function and the various constraints on production and capital payments as well as the above-mentioned market-clearing conditions. The objective functions of the regional programs — which would clearly be important in a descriptive account of global economic relations — are entirely irrelevant for this purpose. A transformation of a regional objective function from, say, minimization of production cost to maximization of personal consumption has no effect on the globally optimal real economic variables. However, it does affect the opportunity costs of regional economic activities. Insofar as these opportunity costs — i.e., the terms of trade for goods and services, the implicit interest rates on outstanding capital balances, and the resource costs of running the economic activity of each region at the unit level — are significant results of the model, the formulation of regional objective functions is significant as well.

But how important are these opportunity costs really in the formulation of global economic policy? It must be recalled that the opportunity costs are computed *at* the global optimum; moreover, at this global optimum, the worldwide market for goods and services and the worldwide market for capital payment flows both clear. Now, these two market-clearing conditions do not necessarily hold in practice. When they do not, the opportunity costs of regional economic activities may differ from the opportunity costs computed through the model. If the world economy faces non market-clearing conditions, the levying of taxes and subsidies prescribed by the model may not be desirable.

Besides, it has already been noted above that there may be *no* set of taxes and sub-sidies which can induce the regions — subject simply to their regional constraints — to produce the socially optimal set of goods and services. *Any* set of opportunity costs may provide an insufficient description of optimal policy measures.

Lastly, it may be well to recall that the opportunity costs depend on the specifica-tion of the regional objective functions. If the opportunity costs are to have any chance of yielding policy implications, then the regional objective functions of the model must be equivalent to the objective functions which these regions actually optimize. But what are these functions? How can they be determined? Or, more fundamentally, do such func-tions exist? Do regions or countries try to maximize anything? These are sticky questions indeed; yet they cannot be avoided if we are to attach any policy meaning to the op-portunity costs gleaned from DYNAMICO.

Hence, it is not clear whether the author is justified in stating (p. 259) that "Among the most striking features of the model are the ways it addresses region-specific develop-ment priorities and the indications it provides . . . as to the costs and benefits of [their] interaction." Some very basic and difficult questions must be answered before the useful-ness of DYNAMICO in this area is beyond doubt.

The dynamic linkages among optimal solutions of the global model give rise to an-other serious difficulty in determining the policy implications of the model. These dy-namic linkages enter in the form of resource endowments (the greater the amount of a resource used in the present period, the smaller the amount left over for the next period), foreign exchange reserves (the more of these reserves that are used to purchase foreign goods and services now, the fewer are available to purchase foreign goods and services in the future), and so on. Since resources and foreign exchange are not in unlimited supply, the intertemporal externalities generated in using them now may be quite important. For petroleum supplies, for example, these externalities are certainly important. In this case, the marginal social value of petroleum consumption should be set equal to the marginal cost of extraction *plus* the marginal user cost of petroleum (the latter embodying the intertemporal externality). Yet intertemporal externalities cannot be taken into account in a one-period model. An intertemporal global optimization program would be necessary for this purpose.

Since DYNAMICO is not intertemporal in this sense, it cannot describe the globally optimal economic activities in the longer run. The optimal set of economic activities period by period is not, in general, equivalent to the optimal set of economic activities for a conglomerate of these periods. The solutions of the model are optimal only if the global policy-maker's horizon is rather short, namely one year. Yet it is rather questionable that the common uses for a model such as DYNAMICO require such a short horizon. There appears to be no way of circumventing this difficulty other than making DYNAMICO dynamic. Restrictions on computational capacity may imply that the model may have to be aggregated before variables of different time subscripts can be accommodated. If so, it may be a price worth paying.

All in all, DYNAMICO is an impressive attempt to incorporate many of the world's most pressing macroeconomic issues within a single, logically coherent, analytical framework. Like all ambitious attempts in the early stages of creation, the model gives rise to a number of fundamental and challenging problems. Their solution would be important not only for DYNAMICO, but for vast areas of macroeconomics as well.

Part Six

Trade and Exchange Rate Models

GLOBAL INTERNATIONAL ECONOMIC MODELS
B.G. Hickman (editor)
Elsevier Science Publishers B.V. (North-Holland)
© IIASA, 1983

STRUCTURAL CHANGES AND DEVELOPMENT ALTERNATIVES IN INTERNATIONAL TRADE*

András Nagy
Institute of Economics, Hungarian Academy of Sciences, Budapest, (Hungary)

1   INTRODUCTION

The analysis of international trade flows is an approach by which, instead of the foreign-trade relations of a single country or bilateral trade between pairs of countries being surveyed, world commodity trade as a whole is examined in an attempt to demonstrate its structural changes in a consistent framework.

In the last decade a rearrangement of international trade relations has occurred as a result of relaxation of trade restrictions, economic integration of different regions, and decolonization; consequently the intensity of international trade relations has increased significantly. A new interest has emerged in the factors determining international trade, and the necessity of confronting abstract theories with facts has been increasingly felt. Such a confrontation is now much easier than it has ever been because of the improvement in international trade statistics; at present, time series covering more than 20 years are available regarding international trade flows disaggregated by commodities.

There is a considerable demand for projections regarding the probable evolution of international trade flows, particularly in developing countries and countries with centrally planned economies. Not only short-term forecasts regarding business-cycle fluctuations but also projections of the tendencies of structural development extending over longer periods are sought. Planners and policy makers in several countries ask questions such as the following. Will the previous dynamic expansion of the world market return or is its decline likely to continue? Can the export and import estimates of national development plans be fitted into the changing framework of international trade? Will evolution of the trade relations between developed and developing countries — or between the various integrated groups of countries — continue the present observed tendencies or will they deviate from these and, if so, in what sense and to what extent? What changes can be expected in the commodity structure of international trade?

A complex analysis of world trade as a whole is needed, bearing in mind that world trade is itself a part of a larger system (in fact a subsystem of the world economy).

---

*The original, extended version of this paper is available on microfiche from the Publications Department, IIASA, A-2361 Laxenburg, Austria.

Research on the structural analysis and projection of international trade was started in Hungary in the early 1970s (for more details see Nagy, 1977, 1979). On the basis of the experience thus gained a new Hungarian research project was started in 1979, supported by research grants from the Ford Foundation and the Hungarian Ministry of Foreign Trade. A team of about 30 research workers from the Institute of Economic and Market Research, the Institute of Economics, and the Institute of World Economy of the Hungarian Academy of Sciences is taking part in the project. Several regional consultants from the developing and socialist countries are also participating.

The project is expected to last two years and consists of two phases: (1) a Structural Analysis of International Trade (SAIT) in the first year and (2) the elaboration of a Development-Alternatives Model of International Trade (DAMIT) in the second.

For use during both phases of the project a data bank has been created where trade-flow data are stored in four dimensions: (1) exporting region, (2) importing region, (3) commodity group, and (4) year. Data from two sources are used: the SAIT study for the period 1955–1977 is based on current-price trade data from the United Nations Conference on Trade and Development (UNCTAD) Data Bank (the latest data are in UNCTAD, 1979); for the study of price changes (actually changes in unit value) in the period 1963–1975 we have used a data tape from the UNCTAD project containing current-price and constant-price trade-flow data in a somewhat different but comparable regional and commodity classification.

The model includes 12 regions and four regional aggregates; the commodity classification contains seven commodity groups and three aggregates (Table 1).

As can be seen, we have been obliged to restrict the project in several respects. We can deal only with the system of world trade, omitting (or at best treating perfunctorily) the connections between the domestic economies and the foreign trade of the regions as

TABLE 1   Regions and commodity groups included in the model.

Regions	Commodity groups	SITC[a]
1. Soviet Union	1. Food	$0 + 1 + 4$
2. Eastern Europe	2. Agricultural raw materials	$2 - 27 - 28$
3. Asian centrally planned economies	3. Ores and metals	$27 + 28 + 67 + 68$
4. Western Europe	4. Fuels	3
5. EEC countries	5. Chemicals	5
6. North America	6. Manufactured goods	$6 + 8 - 67 - 68$
7. Japan	7. Machinery	$7 + 9$
8. Other developed countries	8. Primary products	$0 + 1 + 2 + 3 + 4 + 67 + 68$
9. Latin America	9. Manufactures	$5 + 6 - 67 - 68 + 7 + 8 + 9$
10. Africa	10. Total world trade	$0 + 1, \ldots, + 9$
11. Western Asia		
12. East Asia and Oceania		
13. Total socialist countries		
14. Total developed countries		
15. Total developing countries		
16. Total world trade		

[a]Standard International Trade Classification.

well as the interdependences between international trade and other kinds of international economic relations such as financial flows, technological aid, labor migration, transportation, tourism and other services, etc.

A strong aggregation of both countries and commodities is unavoidable. The choice of the regional and commodity classifications is very restricted if trade-flow data in long time series are needed since the costs of regrouping the data stored in the UN Statistical Office are beyond the means of the project.

It would have been possible to go into more detail by country without commodity disaggregation but it was felt that models including only total exports or total imports of countries are aggregated to an extent that seriously hinders analysis of the factors affecting trade flows. The main characteristics and tendencies of structural changes in international trade can only be indicated with the aid of models containing a breakdown by main commodity groups.

The time series for analyzing past changes are for 23 years and development alternatives will be worked out for 1990, with the possibility of later extension to the year 2000.

The research project has both methodological and practical objectives: methods of analyzing and studying past and future structural changes in international trade are sought. The main aim will not be projection (i.e. to find the most likely outcome of future development) or planning (to achieve certain targets) but to study and compare the feasibility of change and the alternatives for development. The aim is to illuminate in a consistent way the limits within which international trade can develop and to point out specific alternatives in the future trade relations of developed, developing, and socialist regions. The alternatives, or scenarios, will differ as regards the structure and dynamism of the development of different regions, expected changes in the terms of trade or commodity groups and regions, trade-balance and capital-flow assumptions, and the application of instruments in economic and trade policy.

The study of the changing pattern of international trade has come into prominence with two major events in recent years: (a) unusual and spectacular changes in world market prices, terms of trade, and the exchange-rate system; (b) general recognition of the necessity for a new international economic order and the very divergent (very ambitious and rather pessimistic) expectations concerning this.

Following the extraordinary price and exchange-rate changes that occurred in the mid-1970s, for a few years the volume structure of international trade did not alter greatly, and this was manifested most conspicuously in trade-balance disturbances and the financial flows linked to them. Economic recession in several countries indicated the necessity for structural changes, and recent years have seen a process of adaptation whereby an attempt has been made to mitigate the consequences of the terms-of-trade changes and to utilize the advantages of trade in new conditions. Attention will be concentrated on these new features of structural changes and those characteristics which cannot be simply extrapolated from past tendencies.

It is nowadays widely acknowledged that a substantial reshaping is needed in the international economic order to end the inequalities of exchange and to promote faster and more-balanced growth of the developing countries. The debate is centered around such questions as the following. In what direction and how far should this transformation go? What are the realistic requirements and their limits? How can the different demands, aims, and expectations be reconciled? These problems can only be properly analyzed and solved by satisfying the consistency requirements of a global model, taking into account the interdependences of the world economy. Several global research projects dealing with the international economic order already exist and others are in preparation. It is intended to utilize their assumptions and to study more profoundly, in the limited area of international trade flows, the question of how the different assumptions, scenarios, and proposed measures of the new international economic order will affect the dynamism, balances, and commodity and market structure of world trade.

Special attention will be paid to probable changes in the economic relations of the socialist countries with the developed and developing market-economy countries. This problem has been neglected in several earlier research projects on international trade either because relevant data were lacking or because it was regarded as unmanageable. The structural problems of East—West trade are well known, as are the accumulating trade deficits of certain socialist countries. The consequences of discrimination, protectionism, and missed opportunities are less well known. We intend to study the feasibility of changes in this field by inserting alternative development strategies for the socialist countries into the international trade system.

In national plans and projections of foreign trade it is very difficult to achieve even internal consistency. By this we mean that national estimates of exports and imports should in principle be equal in every sector and commodity group to the differences between domestic output and consumption (including changes in stocks). Even less can independently prepared national foreign-trade projections be expected to satisfy the requirements of international consistency, i.e. to form a system in which the estimated exports of country i to country j will be equal to the estimated imports of country j from country i.

Several methods of ensuring internal consistency are known and are widely applied, e.g. the balance method of planning, input—output tables, and the constraints of linear programming models.

In comparison, international consistency is still a neglected field. One of the purposes of the present research was to draw attention to the importance of this problem.

The projected total-trade vectors will be based on development alternatives or scenarios of other global, regional, and global—sectoral models. Such models and scenarios are being prepared by various UN agencies, by the World Bank, by the Organization for Economic Cooperation and Development (Interfutures Project), the European Economic Community (EEC), the Council for Mutual Economic Assistance (CMEA), and a number of research institutes including the International Institute for Applied Systems Analysis and those represented at this conference. It will be assumed that the alternatives taken from these models are internally consistent (i.e. with regard to regional production and consumption) and feasible. In some cases of course these models also impose international consistency in our sense by integration of a trade matrix into the global model.

The project will concentrate on the international-consistency aspect of world trade, i.e. on how the development alternatives for the different regions in a commodity breakdown can be coordinated, or where and what are the main obstacles to consistency in this field. The detailed international-consistency aspect of global modeling which has been neglected in some global models will be more carefully analyzed.

2 A BRIEF OUTLINE OF THE MODEL AND METHODS

For each year a three-dimensional block of matrices has been constructed in which the exporting regions are shown in the rows, the importing regions are shown in the columns, and the commodity groups are shown along the third normal axis. With the help of dynamic structural analysis (details of the model as well as methods of structural analysis and projection can be found in Nagy, 1979) it was intended to decipher the intricate system of hidden attractions and resistances regulating intraregional and interregional commodity flows, which are influenced by a number of political, traditional, and noneconomic factors (in addition to the economic potential, the resource endowment, and the competitiveness of the partners). It is difficult even to enumerate all these factors, while their quantitative specification seems to be out of the question; however, it seems to be possible to classify all of them in two categories. In this sense, trade flows are determined by (a) volume factors regulating the total export supply and import demand of the regions and reflecting their economic or, rather, trade potential and (b) trade-policy and economic-distance factors indicating the characteristics of the partners' bilateral relations, with their intensity of trade regulating the individual commodity flows or the allocation of total exports and imports between markets.

By using trade-intensity indicators (to be defined later) it is possible to study changes in the factors that are shaping the total exports and imports of the countries or regions* separately from the factors that are regulating individual bilateral trade flows by commodities. In the next stage of the project a transformed linear programming technique (see Nagy, 1979) will be used either to coordinate the development alternatives for total trade turnover and the bilateral trade intensities projected separately in order to fit them into a consistent world-trade system if possible or to show the main obstacles to such coordination and contradictions in the basic assumptions of certain projection alternatives.

The method of projection consists of two steps: first, projections of regional total exports and imports and projections of structural coefficients of the commodity groups are elaborated and, second, a consistent projection of trade flows is obtained from these. The steps need to be repeated for each development alternative of international trade.

3 STRUCTURAL CHANGES IN INTERNATIONAL TRADE: 1955–1977

The first phase of the project, the SAIT, is now nearly complete. It consists of detailed studies by region and by commodity group of the changes in the past 23 years. We cannot go into all the details here but we will show the main features of change in a more-aggregated form. The 12 areas originally figuring in the model were distinguished mostly according to their geographical location and were aggregated into three regions according to sociopolitical system and development level. This is how the groups of socialist countries, developed market economies, and developing countries were formed. The groups of

---

*Trade statistics are of course drawn up from country data and are aggregated into regions. The difference from the point of view of this model is that the trade-flow matrices by country have zeros in their diagonals whilst in the matrices by region the diagonals represent trade between countries of the same region. As can be seen, we have used mixed trade-flow matrices in which both regions and countries can be found.

commodities were aggregated into primary goods and manufactured goods, although these denominations are rather inaccurate.

Thus the aggregated blocks of 4 × 4 × 3 matrices (comprising 48 flows) arose; they show a "bird's-eye view" of the main features of structural changes. From an initial 23 years our investigations were reduced to five: 1955, 1960, 1965, 1972, and 1977, which thus cover a series of five-year periods, except for the third which has been prolonged by two years up to 1972 in order to allow closer analysis of the post-1973 price rises.

3.1   The Distribution of World Trade

Table 2 shows the changes in the shares in world trade. The export shares of the three regions in 1977 hardly differed from those in 1955, though only because, under the effect of changes during the final five-year period, the economic structure which had undergone considerable changes between 1955 and 1972 was restored. The share of the socialist countries increased between 1955 and 1960 from 9.7% to 11.9% and then gradually decreased to 9.3% in 1977. The share of the developed market economies in world trade gradually rose from 64.9% in 1955 to 72.2% in 1972 but then fell to 65% in the last five years.

The export share of the developing countries shows a movement opposite to those of the two developed regions: from 25.4% in 1955 it gradually fell to 17.7% in 1972; it then increased to 25.7% by 1977.

By examining the breakdown into the two main commodity groups these movements can be traced back to stronger changes in the export shares of primary goods, since the changes in the shares of manufactured goods do not show any break under the influence of price changes after 1973. It may seem strange that the share of the developed countries in the exports of primary goods also increased between 1955 and 1972 (although the share of the socialist countries had already started to decline after 1965) but by 1977 it had fallen below its value in 1955. In contrast, the export share of the developing countries decreased from 40.5% in 1955 to 35.5% by 1972, before rising again to 48% by 1977. The share of the developed market economies in the export of manufactured goods is extremely high and stable (85.6% in 1955 and a constant 83.7% in the period 1960—1972) though it shows a slight decline under the influence of price changes. The export share of the developing countries is extremely low, though it shows a definite rise from 4.4% in 1965 to 7.6% by 1977. The export share of the socialist countries in manufactured goods rose only in the late 1950s and has been steadily declining since then. The rise of 3.2% between 1965 and 1977 in the share of the developing countries can be mainly attributed to the declining share of the socialist countries — to the extent of 2.5%.

On the import side the share of the developing countries in the trade in manufactured goods is obviously much higher and that of the developed countries correspondingly lower. Here too it is clear that between 1955 and 1972 the share of the developed economies was rising (from 56.3% to 69.3%) and that of the developing countries was diminishing (from 34.2% to 20%). Then, following the rise in prices, both tendencies turned; the share of the developed market economies fell to 63.7% by 1977 while that of the developing countries rose to 26.3%; thus neither region attained its 1955 level.

On examining the distribution of exports between the main regions (Table 3) it can be seen that the trade between the socialist countries declined throughout the period: from

TABLE 2 The distribution of world trade by main regions and main groups of commodities (in percent)[a].

	Year	Total				Primary goods				Manufactured goods			
		TS	TD	TG	TW	TS	TD	TG	TW	TS	TD	TG	TW
TS	1955	7.4	1.8	0.5	9.7	7.2	2.3	0.5	10.0	7.9	1.0	0.8	9.7
	1960	8.6	2.3	1.0	11.9	7.4	3.1	0.6	11.1	9.7	1.2	1.3	12.2
	1965	7.4	2.5	1.6	11.5	6.5	3.7	1.3	11.5	8.3	1.4	2.2	11.9
	1972	6.5	2.4	1.2	10.1	4.9	3.8	0.9	9.6	7.5	1.5	1.5	10.5
	1977	5.4	2.6	1.3	9.3	4.4	4.1	1.1	9.6	6.2	1.5	1.7	9.4
TD	1955	1.4	45.4	18.1	64.9	1.3	39.7	8.5	49.5	1.5	53.1	31.0	85.6
	1960	2.1	47.6	17.2	66.9	2.4	40.5	9.3	52.2	2.3	55.3	26.1	83.7
	1965	2.7	51.8	14.6	69.1	2.5	42.2	8.4	53.1	2.7	60.3	20.7	83.7
	1972	2.9	55.9	13.4	72.2	2.9	44.4	7.6	54.9	3.0	63.9	16.8	83.7
	1977	3.0	46.4	15.6	65.0	2.5	32.5	7.4	42.4	3.7	53.7	22.0	83.0
TG	1955	0.7	18.4	6.3	25.4	1.0	30.4	9.1	40.5	0.1	2.2	2.4	4.7
	1960	0.9	15.5	4.8	21.2	1.7	27.4	7.6	36.7	0.0	2.2	1.9	4.1
	1965	1.2	14.1	4.1	19.4	2.4	26.4	6.6	35.4	0.1	2.5	1.8	4.4
	1972	0.8	13.2	3.7	17.7	1.8	26.9	6.8	35.5	0.2	3.9	1.7	5.8
	1977	1.2	18.4	6.1	25.7	2.2	35.5	10.3	48.0	1.0	4.9	2.6	7.6
TW	1955	9.5	65.6	24.9	100.0	9.5	72.4	18.1	100.0	9.5	56.3	34.2	100.0
	1960	11.6	65.4	23.0	100.0	11.5	71.0	17.5	100.0	12.0	58.7	29.3	100.0
	1965	11.3	68.4	20.3	100.0	11.4	72.3	16.3	100.0	11.1	64.2	24.7	100.0
	1972	10.2	71.5	18.3	100.0	9.6	75.1	15.3	100.0	10.7	69.3	20.0	100.0
	1977	9.6	67.4	23.0	100.0	9.1	72.1	18.8	100.0	10.0	63.7	26.3	100.0

[a]TS, socialist countries; TD, developed market economies; TG, developing countries; TW, total world trade.

TABLE 3 The distribution of the exports of main commodity groups and of total exports by main regions (in percent)[a].

	Year	Total			Primary goods			Manufactured goods		
		TS	TD	TG	TS	TD	TG	TS	TD	TG
TS	1955	74.7	18.5	6.8	70.2	24.0	5.8	81.1	10.8	8.1
	1960	72.7	18.8	8.5	65.4	27.7	6.9	80.6	9.3	10.1
	1965	64.4	21.8	13.8	56.6	32.6	10.8	71.4	12.1	16.5
	1972	63.4	24.4	12.2	50.4	39.0	10.6	71.8	15.0	13.2
	1977	56.8	29.0	14.2	45.1	43.2	11.7	66.5	17.3	16.2
TD	1955	2.2	70.0	27.8	2.8	80.1	17.1	1.7	62.1	36.2
	1960	3.5	70.8	25.7	4.5	77.7	17.8	2.7	66.1	31.2
	1965	3.9	75.0	21.1	4.9	79.7	15.4	3.3	72.1	24.6
	1972	4.0	77.8	18.2	5.1	81.0	13.9	3.6	76.3	20.1
	1977	4.7	71.3	24.0	5.8	76.8	17.4	4.3	69.1	26.6
TG	1955	2.5	72.8	24.7	2.5	75.2	22.3	2.3	45.4	52.3
	1960	4.4	73.1	22.5	4.7	75.1	20.2	2.5	53.3	44.2
	1965	6.6	72.2	21.2	6.9	74.4	18.7	4.9	53.3	39.8
	1972	5.1	73.8	21.1	5.4	76.0	18.6	4.4	64.9	30.7
	1977	4.1	72.2	23.7	4.5	74.0	21.5	2.4	63.3	34.3

[a]The notation is the same as for Table 2.

a 74.7% share in the total exports of the socialist countries in 1955 it fell to 56.8% by 1977. The share of trade between the socialist countries is considerably smaller in the export of primary goods than in the export of manufactured goods, and the declining tendency is much stronger too: for primary goods the share of this "intratrade" fell from 70.2% to 45.1% while for manufactured goods it fell from 81.1% to 66.5%.

The changes in the share of exports to the developing countries are different for the socialist countries and the developed market economies. In 1955 36.2% of the manufactured exports of the developed market economies went to the markets of the developing (then mostly colonial) countries; by 1972 this figure had fallen to 20.1% but it rose to 26.6% by 1977. The intratrade of the developing countries in manufactured goods also shows a similar movement: from 52.3% in 1955 it fell to 30.7% by 1972 and rose again to 34.3% by 1977. In a less-marked form similar changes can be observed in the export of primary goods and consequently in total exports. This is not the case in the total exports of the socialist countries, where the share of the developing countries shows a steady rise from 6.8% in 1955 to 14.2% by 1977. It is true that this rise occurred mostly in the first decade and that in 1972 there was some decline (mainly in manufactured goods) but this does not change the opposite tendencies in the exports to the markets of developing countries that can be seen between the socialist and the developed market economies. However, we must not lose sight of the fact that the share of exports to developing countries in the total exports of the socialist countries is much lower than the corresponding share in the total exports of the market economies: in 1977 the developing countries had a 14.2% share in the exports of the socialist countries but a 70% higher share in the exports of the developed and developing countries (i.e. 24%).

3.2 The Intensity of Trade

A particularly revealing view can be given of the structural features of world trade and the changes therein with the aid of the intensity (so-called "delta") indicators which measure precisely the political and trade policy impacts. These impacts cause trade flows to deviate from what might be expected on the basis of the share in world trade of the individual exporting and importing regions. (The "delta indicator" is defined in the foot-notes to Table 4; for further details see Nagy, 1979.) In the regional breakdown that is analyzed here the most intensive flows are found between the socialist countries, mainly in the trade in manufactured goods; however, this extremely high intensity of mutual trade is declining gradually, with corresponding increases in the trade transacted with the developed market economies and the developing countries (Table 4).

TABLE 4   Trade-intensity indicators[a] in the trade by main regions and main commodity groups[b].

	Year	Total			Primary goods			Manufactured goods		
		TS	TD	TG	TS	TD	TG	TS	TD	TG
TS	1955	7.92	0.28	0.27	7.43	0.33	0.32	8.60	0.19	0.24
	1960	6.19	0.29	0.37	5.69	0.39	0.39	6.67	0.16	0.35
	1965	5.68	0.32	0.68	4.95	0.45	0.68	6.34	0.19	0.68
	1972	6.22	0.34	0.68	5.26	0.52	0.70	6.77	0.22	0.66
	1977	6.04	0.43	0.62	5.08	0.60	0.63	6.75	0.27	0.62
TD	1955	0.23	1.07	1.12	0.30	1.11	0.95	0.18	1.11	1.06
	1960	0.30	1.09	1.12	0.40	1.10	1.02	0.23	1.13	1.07
	1965	0.34	1.10	1.05	0.43	1.11	0.97	0.29	1.13	1.01
	1972	0.40	1.09	1.01	0.53	1.09	0.92	0.34	1.11	1.01
	1977	0.51	1.06	1.05	0.66	1.07	0.93	0.44	1.09	1.02
TG	1955	0.26	1.11	0.99	0.26	1.04	1.24	0.25	0.81	1.53
	1960	0.38	1.13	0.99	0.41	1.06	1.17	0.22	0.91	1.52
	1965	0.58	1.06	1.05	0.60	1.03	1.17	0.46	0.86	1.63
	1972	0.51	1.04	1.17	0.55	1.02	1.23	0.42	0.94	1.54
	1977	0.44	1.08	1.04	0.50	1.03	1.15	0.24	1.00	1.31

[a] The trade-intensity (or "delta") indicator $= z_{ijk}/Z_{i.k}Z_{.jk}$ where z_{ijk} is the share of exports in commodity k from region i to region j in the total world trade of k, $Z_{i.k}$ is the total exports of region i in commodity k, and $Z_{.jk}$ is the total imports of region j in commodity k.
[b] The notation is the same as for Table 2.

The rate at which the export intensity of the socialist countries with the other regions rises differs greatly according to commodity group and importing region. While the export intensity of primary goods rose nearly twofold in both receiving regions, the intensity of exports of manufactured goods to the developed market economies stagnated in the period 1955—1965 and increased thereafter only moderately. The intensity of the export of manufactures to developing countries almost tripled in the first decade but declined by 9% between 1965 and 1977. The export intensity of manufactured goods directed from developed market economies to the socialist countries rose rapidly and by 1977 it was nearly twice as strong as the intensity of trade in the opposite direction.

The export intensity of developing countries' exports to the socialist countries shows an unfavorable picture: though between 1955 and 1965 the export intensity of primary goods was rising fast (from 0.26 to 0.60) and the export intensity of manufactured goods also rose, though more moderately (from 0.25 to 0.46), in the following 12 years both intensities fell (the intensity for primary goods quite moderately (to 0.50) but the intensity for manufactured goods extremely steeply to below the 1955 value (to 0.24)). This shows that, over the 12-year period, the socialist countries increased their purchases of manufactured goods from the developing countries to a significantly smaller extent than one might expect based on either their own total imports of manufactured goods or on the increase in manufactured exports of the developing countries over the same period. In contrast with this tendency, the intensity of export of manufactured goods from developing countries to the developed market economies considerably increased over the same period and attained in 1977 the "normal" level (i.e. an indicator value of 1.00).

The trade-intensity indicators of the developed market economies show great stability, particularly in their intratrade; the strong rise in the intensity of trade transacted with the socialist countries mentioned above is slightly offset by a decline in the intensity of trade with the developing countries.

The trade intensity of the developing countries with each other is not strong and the rising tendency in the period 1955–1972 gave way to a decline during the next period. It can be considered as favorable that the intensity of trade in manufactured goods is relatively strong and showed a definite rise over the period 1955–1965 (from 1.53 to 1.63) but it is unfortunate that it has fallen back since then (to 1.31 in 1977).

3.3   Trade Balances

The trade balances show with great sensitivity the structural changes (Table 5), i.e. the relative shifts in the ratios of exports and imports between the regions. Our data assume that the total exports of the world equal the total imports in every commodity group; thus the balance of total world trade is zero. Further, our data do not show the balances within the main regions, and thus the diagonal elements are also zero.

The summarized data for the regions show very balanced trade up to 1972, the two sides of turnover differing by only US$1–2 billion, i.e. by 1–4%. Bigger differences do not occur until after 1972; however, the data in the table show only the figures for 1977. A deficit of US$27.5 billion for the developed region is set against a surplus of US$29.3 billion for the developing countries, behind which we find a 3.7% import surplus for the developed countries and an 11.5% export surplus for the developing countries. This emerges even more sharply if we consider only the balance between the developed market economies and the developing countries; between 1955 and 1972 the balance was almost always in equilibrium, and only after 1973 did a considerable import surplus deriving from the developed region appear, amounting to US$53.9 billion in 1974 and to US$32.2 billion in 1977.

Though the aggregate balance of the socialist region is in equilibrium, the balances of the trade transacted with the developed and the developing regions are of opposite sign and of continually rising tendency. The socialist countries regularly have an import surplus from the developed market economies and an export surplus with regard to the

TABLE 5 Trade balances by main regions and main commodity groups (in millions of US dollars)[a].

	Year	Total				Primary goods				Manufactured goods			
		TS	TD	TG	TW	TS	TD	TG	TW	TS	TD	TG	TW
TS	1955	—	387	49	436	—	558	−219	339	—	−171	268	97
	1960	—	−166	38	−128	—	545	−629	−84	—	−711	667	−44
	1965	—	−310	556	246	—	990	−1,067	−77	—	−1,300	1,623	323
	1972	—	−1,762	1,300	−462	—	1,772	−1,365	407	—	−3,534	2,665	−869
	1977	—	−4,607	2,888	−1,719	—	8,002	−5,079	2,923	—	−12,609	7,967	−4,642
TD	1955	−387	—	−385	−772	−558	—	−11,725	−12,283	171	—	11,340	11,511
	1960	166	—	2,009	2,175	−545	—	−12,218	−12,763	711	—	14,227	14,938
	1965	310	—	935	1,245	−990	—	−16,311	−17,301	1,300	—	17,246	18,546
	1972	1,762	—	−366	1,396	−1,772	—	−31,819	−33,591	3,534	—	31,451	34,987
	1977	4,607	—	−32,197	−27,590	−8,002	—	−137,786	−145,788	12,609	—	105,589	118,198
TG	1955	−49	385	—	336	219	11,725	—	11,944	−268	−11,340	—	−11,608
	1960	−38	−2,009	—	−2,047	629	12,218	—	12,847	−667	−14,227	—	−14,894
	1965	−556	−935	—	−1,491	1,067	16,311	—	17,378	−1,623	−17,246	—	−18,869
	1972	−1,300	366	—	−934	1,365	31,819	—	33,184	−2,665	−31,451	—	−34,118
	1977	−2,888	32,197	—	29,309	5,079	137,786	—	142,865	−7,967	−105,589	—	−113,556
TW	1955	−436	772	−336	—	−339	12,283	−11,944	—	−97	−11,511	11,608	—
	1960	128	−2,175	2,047	—	84	12,763	−12,847	—	44	−14,938	14,894	—
	1965	−246	−1,245	1,491	—	77	17,301	−17,378	—	−323	−18,546	18,869	—
	1972	462	−1,396	934	—	−407	33,591	−33,184	—	869	−34,987	34,118	—
	1977	1,719	27,590	−29,309	—	−2,923	145,788	−142,865	—	4,642	−118,198	113,556	—

The data appear in the table twice with opposite signs since the surplus of one region over another also appears as a deficit for the latter.
[a] The notation is the same as for Table 2.

developing countries. The considerable passive and active balances mostly neutralize each other in the aggregate balance. The sums can be read from Table 5; to get some idea of their proportions we note that the exports of socialist countries to the developing countries exceeded their imports therefrom by 34.8% in 1972 and by 24.7% in 1977. Balancing this, exports to the developed market economies lagged behind imports therefrom by 4.9% in 1972 and by 3.4% in 1977.

Of course the balances by the main commodity categories show bigger differences; they testify that in the trade between the major regions the raw-material imports and the industrial exports of the developed countries are still predominant. The import surplus of the developed market economies in the trade in primary goods rose from US$12.2 billion in 1955 to US$33.6 billion by 1972 and then soared to US$145.8 billion in 1977. In the same years their export surplus in the trade in manufactured goods increased from US$ 11.5 billion to US$35 billion and then jumped to US$118.2 billion in 1977. The total trade balances partly cover these extreme export and import surpluses in the two main groups of commodities. For example, it is characteristic that, concealed behind the deficit of the trade in 1972 between the developed and the developing countries of US$366 million, there was an import surplus of US$31.8 billion for the developed countries in the trade in primary goods and an export surplus of US$31.4 billion in the trade in manufactured goods.

The balances of the socialist countries by the main groups of commodities are quite different for trade with the developed market economies and for trade with the developing countries. The socialist countries had large surpluses in primary goods exported to the developed countries in every year, and up to 1972 these were almost balanced by their import surpluses in materials from the developing countries. In the period after the price explosion the export surplus towards the developed economies considerably exceeded the import surplus from the developing countries, so that in 1977 the surplus of the aggregate balance of primary goods was almost US$3 billion. The trade in manufactured goods, where the surplus of imports to the socialist countries from the advanced market economies is considerable and continually rising provides a mirror image of the primary goods case: in 1955 the export of manufactured goods still paid for 71% of imports, at the end of the 1960s for only half of them, and in 1977 for only 43.5% of them. In contrast, the trade in manufactured goods with the developing countries shows a considerable export surplus: it rose from US$268 million in 1955 to US$2.7 billion in 1972 and to almost US$8 billion in 1977. It is a conspicuous and unfavorable phenomenon that the trade in manufactured goods with the developing countries is not becoming more balanced over time and that for developing countries the export/import ratio in their trade with the socialist countries is less advantageous than the corresponding ratio in their trade with the developed market economies. This is shown in Table 6.

TABLE 6   Exports as a percentage of the imports of manufactured goods of the developing countries.

Year	Importing region	
	Socialist countries	Developed market economies
1955	13.8	6.9
1960	8.8	8.6
1965	11.8	12.6
1972	19.3	22.9
1977	12.6	22.4

REFERENCES

Nagy, A. (1977). A világkereskedelem strukturája és jövője (The structure and future of international trade). Közgazdasági és Jogi Könyvkiadó, Budapest.

Nagy, A. (1979). Methods of structural analysis and projection of international trade. Studies, No. 13. Institute of Economics, Hungarian Academy of Sciences, Budapest.

UNCTAD (1979). Handbook of International Trade and Development Statistics, United Nations, New York.

GLOBAL INTERNATIONAL ECONOMIC MODELS
B.G. Hickman (editor)
Elsevier Science Publishers B.V. (North-Holland)
© IIASA, 1983

A MODEL OF TRADE AND EXCHANGE RATES

Dennis L. Warner
Department of Economics, Michigan State University, East Lansing, Michigan 48823 (USA)

1 INTRODUCTION

This paper outlines a model of world trade and exchange rates. The modeling effort to date has focused on combining previous research on individual equations into a large logically consistent empirical model. The model is designed to give projections of trade volume and exchange rates, given various assumptions on alternative developments in the economies of the Organization for Economic Cooperation and Development (OECD), developing countries, and Centrally Planned Economies (CPEs). The model covers 26 regions of which 23 are members of the OECD. The non-OECD world is covered by regions (8), (9), and (10). The regions are as follows:

(1) Canada	(10) the CPEs	(19) Norway
(2) France	(11) Australia	(20) Portugal
(3) the FRG	(12) Belgium/Luxembourg	(21) Spain
(4) Italy	(13) Austria	(22) Sweden
(5) Japan	(14) Denmark	(23) Switzerland
(6) the UK	(15) Finland	(24) Greece
(7) the USA	(16) Iceland	(25) New Zealand
(8) the LDCs	(17) Ireland	(26) Turkey
(9) OPEC countries	(18) the Netherlands	

The model presented here is not a closed system. It contains equations for international trade and exchange rates only. To operate, the model must be linked to a set of country macromodels or must be driven by exogenous time series for real Gross Domestic Product (GDP) and domestic production costs.

It is designed to project changes in the pattern of international trade in goods and services. The channels through which trade patterns change are relative price changes and differential rates of growth in the domestic economies. The changing volume and patterns of trade will determine the current-account position, net foreign assets, and movements of the exchange-rate and/or official-reserves position of a country. Exchange-rate changes affect imports through the relative prices of foreign and domestic goods and affect exports through the relative level of the export prices of competitors. Exchange rates themselves are determined by countries' holdings of net foreign assets, and holdings of assets in other countries.

The equations of the model are specified in Section 2, and Section 3 contains summary results of two simple simulation exercises. Summary comments and a discussion of work in progress are given in Section 4.

For this early version of the model we did not carry out our own estimation of the parameters. The sources of the estimates are described in detail in Working Paper No. 390 of the National Bureau for Economic Research. Currently the model is being expanded and estimated with data through 1978 or 1979.

2   THE INTERNATIONAL LINKAGE MODEL

The variables used in the model are described in Table 1.

2.1   Imports

In the preliminary version of the model imports are separated into nonoil merchandise MG, nonfactor services MS, and oil MP. For the total-import equation MG and MS are aggregated into MGS since in our initial search we found few estimates for separate service-import equations.

The share of real nonoil imports out of the real GDP depends on the ratio of the actual to the potential real GDP and the ratio of imported to domestic prices of goods and services. This formulation has the property that when the economy is on its full-employment output path the income elasticity of imports is unity and the import/GDP ratio is consistent if relative prices do not change:

$$MGS_i/Y_i = a_{1i}(Y_i/Y_i^*)^{a_{2i}}(PD_i/PMGS_i)^{a_{3i}} \tag{1}$$

The split between nonoil merchandise and nonfactor services is taken to be constant and equal to the historical average:

$$MS_i = b_{1i}MGS_i \tag{2a}$$

$$MG_i = (1 - b_{1i})MGS_i \tag{2b}$$

Petroleum imports MP are related to real GDP, petroleum prices PMP, and lagged petroleum imports. The following formulation was used by the energy study group at Project Interfutures:

$$MP_i/Y_i^{C_{4i}} = c_{1i}(PD_i^{C_{2i}C_{3i}}/PMP_i)(MP_{i,t-1}^{1-C_{3i}}/Y_{i,t-1}^{C_{4i}}) \tag{3}$$

TABLE 1   Glossary of variable names.

Name	Description	Unit
Imports		
MG	Nonoil merchandise imports	Billions of 1975 US$
MP	Oil imports (SITC 331)	Billions of 1975 US$
MS	Nonfactor service imports	Billions of 1975 US$
MGS	MG + MS	Billions of 1975 US$
MGSP	MG + MS + MP	Billions of 1975 US$
Exports		
XG	Nonoil merchandise exports	Billions of 1975 US$
XP	Oil exports (SITC 331)	Billions of 1975 US$
XS	Nonfactor service exports	Billions of 1975 US$
XGSP	XG + XS + XP	Billions of 1975 US$
Prices		
PD	GDP deflator (in US$)	1975 = 1.0
E	Foreign price of domestic currency (US$/unit of local currency) (equals currency exchange rate divided by its 1975 value)	1975 = 1.0
PMG	Price index for MG	1975 = 1.0
PMP	Price index for MP	1975 = 1.0
PMS	Price index for MS	1975 = 1.0
PMGS	Price index for MGS	1975 = 1.0
PMGSP	Price index for MGSP	1975 = 1.0
PXG	Price index for XG	1975 = 1.0
PXP	Price index for XP	1975 = 1.0
PXS	Price index for XS	1975 = 1.0
PWG	Weighted index of PXGs of competitors	1975 = 1.0
PWS	Weighted index of PXSs of competitors	1975 = 1.0
Trade shares		
TMG_{ij}	Imports of nonoil merchandise from j to i divided by MG_i	
TMP_{ij}	Imports of oil from j to i divided by MP_i	
TXG_{ij}	Exports of nonoil merchandise from i to j divided by XG_i	
TS_i	Exports of nonfactor services from i to rest of the world divided by total world nonfactor service imports	
Other items		
C	Current account	Billions of current US$
F	Total net foreign assets (valued at purchase prices)	Billions of current US$
G	Net unrequited transfers (private and official)	Billions of current US$
R	The world interest rate (0.06)	Decimal fraction
S	Total net foreign assets accumulated since 1975	Billions of current US$
Z	Other items in the current account (errors and omissions, net labor incomes, and 1975 interest incomes)	Billions of current US$

TABLE 1   *Continued.*

Name	Description	Unit
Y	Real GDP	Billions of 1975 US$
$Y*$	Potential real GDP	Billions of 1975 US$
$YW*$	Weighted average of potential GDPs of competitors	Billions of 1975 US$
ΔM	Change in nominal money supply	Billions of local currency

This form has the properties that MP responds to GDP with a constant elasticity of c_4 and to relative price changes with an elasticity of $c_2 c_3$ in the short run and c_2 in the long run.

The import functions for the three non-OECD regions are handled differently. Total OPEC imports are set exogenously, total CPE imports depend on export earnings and capital inflows, and total LDC imports respond to relative prices with an elasticity of 0.7 and to real GDP with an elasticity of 1. For these three regions ($i = 8, 9, 10$) total imports are split into nonoil goods, nonfactor services, and oil by the historical shares:

$$MS_i = b_{1i} MGSP_i \tag{4a}$$

$$MP_i = b_{2i} MGSP_i \tag{4b}$$

$$MG_i = (1 - b_{1i} - b_{2i}) MGSP_i \tag{4c}$$

2.2   Bilateral Trade Flows

For nonoil goods changes in an exporter's share of an importer's market depend on changes in the ratio of the exporter's export price to a weighted average of the export prices of its competitors in that market (both in the importer's currency) and the ratio of the exporter's potential GDP to a weighted average of the potential GDPs of its competitors. Nonfactor services are modeled in the same way except that the dependent variable is not the exporter's share of a certain import market but rather its share of the world market for traded services. The trade-share matrix for petroleum is exogenous.

Samuelson's estimates (Samuelson, 1973) of the elasticities of substitution for each import market and of the effects of exporters' relative output growth are used here. The form of the equation for the import shares of nonoil goods is

$$T\hat{M}G_{ij} = d_{1i}(P\hat{X}G_j - P\hat{M}G_i) + d_{2i}(Y_j^* - \hat{Y}w_i^*) \tag{5a}$$

For an exporter's share of the world market in traded services

$$T\hat{S}_i = f_1(P\hat{X}S_i - P\hat{M}S) + f_2(\hat{Y}_i^* - Y\hat{W}S^*) \tag{5b}$$

Because of the lack of bilateral data on trade in services we are forced to assume a globally unified market in traded services. There is one import price, *PMS*, which in the absence of trade barriers is the import price facing all importers.

2.3 Exports

Real exports of each commodity are derived from the country imports and the market shares:

$$XG_i = \sum_j TMG_{ji}MG_j \tag{6a}$$

$$XS_i = TS_i \sum_j MS_j \tag{6b}$$

$$XP_i = \sum_j TMP_{ji}MP_j \tag{6c}$$

2.4 Import Prices

Import prices are simple weighted averages of export prices:

$$PMG_i = \sum_j TMG_{ij}PXG_j \tag{7a}$$

$$PMS_i = PMS = \sum_j TS_jPXS_j \tag{7b}$$

$$PMP_i = \sum_j TMP_{ij}PXP_j \tag{7c}$$

Aggregated price indexes are used in the import equations:

$$PMGS_i = b_{1i}PMS_i + (1 - b_{1i})PMG_i \qquad \text{(for the OECD countries)} \tag{7d}$$

$$PMGSP_i = b_{1i}PMS_i + b_{2i}PMP_i + (1 - b_{1i} - b_{2i})PMG_i \qquad \text{(for } i = 8, 9, 10) \tag{7e}$$

2.5 Export Prices

With the assumption of imperfect competition in international markets the supply function of exports should be specified as some type of price-setting behavior. For a small country with no market power in the export markets the price of exports will be given in foreign currency. If the country has some market power its export prices change less than the export prices of its competitors if there are no changes in domestic costs of production. If production costs do change a country with export market power will be able to pass on some of the change in the form of changes in the foreign-currency export prices.

If we assume constant price elasticities of export supply and demand then the relative change in export prices can be expressed as a weighted average of the relative change in competitors' prices and the relative change in domestic costs. We have used the domestic price level as a crude substitute for domestic production costs. The price elasticity of demand for exports is implicit in eqns. (1), (2), and (5)–(7) and changes as trade shares and import volumes change. To simplify the model we have assumed for the export-price equation that the elasticity is constant at the implicit 1975 value.

The measure for the competitors' prices is a doubly weighted average of the competitors' export prices. For each import market an index of competitors' prices is obtained by weighting each export price by that country's share of the import market. The aggregate index of competitors' prices is the sum of the market-specific indexes, each weighted by the share of total exports going to that market. For traded services the index of competitors' export prices is simply the import price facing each country.

$$PXG_i = g_{1i}PWG_i + (1 - g_{1i})PD_i \tag{8a}$$

$$PXS_i = g_{1i}PWS_i + (1 - g_{1i})PD_i \tag{8b}$$

$$PXP_i = \overline{PXP}_i \tag{8c}$$

$$PWG_i = \sum_j TXG_{ij} \sum_k TMG_{jk}PXG_k \tag{8d}$$

$$PWS_i = \sum_j TS_j PXS_j = PMS \tag{8e}$$

2.6 Domestic Price

We assume that the domestic price responds to changes in production costs. These costs are crudely disaggregated into two foreign components and one domestic component. The costs of imported raw materials and intermediate goods are represented by the nonoil merchandise import-price index PMG. The cost of imported oil is PMP. Domestic costs (factor prices) are ignored in this discussion. When the international model is linked to a set of domestic macromodels this is one of the primary links. Here we seek to highlight the international transmission of inflation while ignoring the more important motive forces for inflation:

$$\hat{PD}_i = h_{2i}\hat{PMP}_i + h_{1i}\hat{PMG}_i + (1 - h_{2i} - h_{1i})(\hat{E}_i + \hat{W}_i) \tag{9}$$

In the simulations presented below the domestic cost variable W_i is set to zero.

2.7 Exchange Rates

From the early 1970s onwards countries have adopted a wide variety of exchange-rate systems. Major OECD countries have had more or less floating exchange rates since 1973 while several small OECD economies and LDCs have chosen to peg their currencies to some basket or a single currency.

We have tried to capture some basic aspects of the present policies. The currencies of the "big seven" OECD countries are floating, smaller OECD countries and the LDCs peg their currencies (with adjustments) to a trade-weighted basket of currencies, and the CPEs and OPEC countries trade in US dollars. A major drawback of this scheme is that the European Monetary System is not modeled in this preliminary version.

The trade block of the model generates projections for the current account. The link from the current account to the exchange rate for the big seven OECD countries is obtained by applying a version of the asset-market approach to determine the exchange rates. Equations from Branson (Branson, 1977; Branson and Halttunen, 1978; Branson et al., 1978; Branson and Papaefstratiou, 1978) have been used to determine the US-dollar/local-currency exchange rates for Canada, France, the FRG, Italy, Japan, and the UK. With flexible exchange rates the sum of balances on capital and current accounts is identically zero (central-bank foreign reserves stay constant). If the current account shows a surplus then the capital account remains in deficit and the private sector accumulates foreign assets. Given these changes in net private holdings of foreign assets, the exchange-rate equations determine changes in the exchange rates. Changes in the exchange rates affect relative export and domestic prices and hence affect trade flows and the overall current accounts.

In the model a current-account deficit (surplus) in a country will cause its currency to depreciate (appreciate). This in turn improves (worsens) the current account. The long-run dynamic adjustment thus occurs through the interaction of the exchange-rate equations and the trade block.

The 16 smaller OECD countries (and the LDCs) are handled in a less-satisfactory way. These countries revalue or devalue the effective exchange-rate index according to an arbitrary formula based on recent movements in their current accounts.

$$\Delta E_i = q_{1i} \Delta F_i + q_{2i} \Delta F_j + q_{3i} \Delta M_i + q_{4i} \Delta M_j \tag{10a}$$

where j = FRG for i = UK, France, or Italy; and j = United States for i = FRG, Canada, or Japan. Using the subscripts S for the 16 smaller OECD countries and the LDCs and B for the big seven OECD countries, the OPEC countries, and the CPEs,

$$e_S = k_S(I - T_{SS})^{-1} T_{SB} E_{SB} \tag{10b}$$

where T is the matrix of total trade weights, i.e.

T_{ij} = (exports from i to j + exports from j to i)/(exports of i + imports of i),
T_{SS} = the $S \times S$ upper-left submatrix of T,
T_{SB} = the $S \times (B - S)$ upper-right submatrix of T,
$e_i = E_i/E_{i75}$,
e_S = the S-element vector of small-country exchange-rate indexes,
E_{SB} = the $(B - S)$-element vector of large-country exchange-rate indexes, and
k_S = an $S \times S$ diagonal matrix of parameters.

Finally, $k_{ii} = k_{ii,t-1} + rC_{i,t-1}/REV_{i,t-1}$ (10c)

Using the list of regions and their numbers given in Section 1, the LDCs and the smaller OECD countries are denoted by $i = 8$ and $11-26$, respectively; and the big seven OECD members, the OPEC countries, and the CPEs are denoted by $j = 1-7$, 9, and 10, respectively. Equations (10a) describe the behavior of the exchange rates for the big seven OECD countries. For the 16 smaller OECD countries plus the LDCs eqns. (10b) and (10c) describe the adjustable peg rule we have adopted. For the big seven the private capital flows are endogenous to the model and result from the equations estimated by Branson and Halttunen. For the other 17 the system is entirely arbitrary and should be replaced by some system capable of empirical verification.

2.8   Closing the Model

In order to obtain current-account equations for each region, the determination of aid flows, factor incomes, and net private transfers are needed. The total amount of aid received by non oil-exporting LDCs is projected exogenously. The increase in total aid flows is allocated among donor countries according to constant 1975 shares. Net interest incomes from abroad are generated as a multiple of the exogenously specified "world interest rate" and the endogenously generated cumulative current account.

Net private transfers and net labor incomes are exogenous. For the CPEs the current account is exogenous (being set equal to projected capital inflows) and the value of imports adjusts as the residual item. For the other 25 regions the current account is:

$$C_i = PXG_i XG_i + PXS_i XS_i + PXP_i XP_i - PMG_i MG_i - PMS_i MS_i - PMP_i MP_i$$

$$+ G_i + Z_i + R_i S_i \tag{11a}$$

Revenue is simply the current account plus import expenditures:

$$REV_i = C_i + PMG_i MG_i + PMS_i MS_i + PMP_i MP_i \tag{11b}$$

Net foreign assets are simply the cumulative current account:

$$F_i = F_{i,t-1} + C_i \tag{11c}$$

$$S_i = S_{i,t-1} + C_i \tag{11d}$$

No term for capital gains is included in eqns. (11c) and (11d) because they are the only wealth items in this version of the model. Both F_i and S_i are denominated in foreign currency; hence they do not need to be adjusted for changes in the domestic exchange rates. When the model is fully linked to a system with explicit alternative assets then it will be necessary to measure accumulated wealth in domestic currency units and to make the proper adjustments for revaluation of the foreign assets in response to exchange-rate changes.

3   SIMULATIONS WITH THE MODEL

In this section three simulations with the described model for trade and exchange rates are compared. The simulations were designed to illustrate the flexibility of the model and the type of information it generates. These experiments can describe only partially the usefulness of the model structure since the model is not yet linked with a set of domestic macromodels. There are three channels of feedback missing in these runs which would be most important in a fully linked simulation.

(1) The effect of exports and imports on the level of domestic activity is missing. In the following runs both Y and Y^* are set exogenously. It is assumed that the respective governments take whatever fiscal-policy decisions are necessary to maintain GDP at the exogenous level.

(2) The effects of money-supply growth on exchange rates and the domestic price level are not illustrated since we have not included any projections of money-supply growth.

(3) Interest-rate effects are missing because the money markets are not modeled.

3.1 Exogenous Inputs

For these simulations it is assumed that GDP follows the path described in the OECD Interfutures Report of 1979. This report contained optimistic projections of real growth for the OECD countries through 1990. Table 2 illustrates the projected average growth rates. For this run we have assumed that the OECD economies will reach their potential output paths by 1990. This implies very high growth of actual GDP for all countries.

For Greece, New Zealand, Turkey, the non oil-producing LDCs, and the CPEs the GDP growth rate is arbitrarily set. The aid inflow to the LDCs is taken from the World

TABLE 2   Average annual growth rates of potential output (in percent).

Region	Period			
	1975–1980	1980–1985	1985–1990	1975–1990
Australia	5.4	4.5	4.4	4.8
Austria	6.4	5.7	4.6	5.6
Belgium/Luxembourg	5.3	4.5	3.4	4.4
Canada	4.6	3.4	3.1	3.7
Denmark	4.0	4.0	3.6	3.9
Finland	4.7	5.3	4.6	4.8
France	5.3	5.0	3.8	4.7
FRG	5.4	5.0	3.0	4.5
Iceland	5.6	4.1	4.5	4.7
Ireland	5.7	5.6	5.8	5.7
Italy	6.3	6.2	4.9	5.8
Japan	7.6	6.8	6.0	6.8
Netherlands	6.8	5.8	4.3	5.6
Norway	4.7	4.1	3.4	4.0
Portugal	8.2	7.5	6.8	7.5
Spain	6.7	6.3	5.8	6.3
Sweden	2.7	2.8	2.7	2.8
Switzerland	3.9	3.8	3.4	3.7
UK	3.3	3.6	3.5	3.5
United States	4.4	2.7	2.4	3.2

Bank 1976 SIMLINK projections. The capital inflow to the CPEs declines steadily from its 1976 value to zero by 1990. The final exogenous time series are those for the price of oil and OPEC imports. For these runs we set the oil-price index equal to the actual index for 1975–1979 (as of July 1980) and to the 1979 values for 1981–1990. The OPEC imports are equal to their actual value for 1975–1979 and then increase so that OPEC has a zero balance on current account by 1990.

3.2   The Three Simulations

Three simulations are compared here. First a flexible-exchange-rate simulation is compared with a fixed-exchange-rate simulation. The fixed-rate simulation is of no interest in itself; it is useful only in that it allows an illustration of the importance of the flexible-rate model. The third simulation is a flexible-rate run with an exogenous increase in the FRG's rate of growth of actual GDP. The comparison between this and the original flexible-rate run is meant to illustrate some aspects of the importance of the FRG as a "locomotive" in pulling the European "train" toward potential output paths.

3.3   The Standard Simulation

Tables 3 and 4 show some results from the standard flexible-exchange-rate run. Table 3 shows differences between the simulations for flexible and fixed exchange rates. The cumulative current-account figures show that impossibly large net foreign-asset positions would result if exchange rates were fixed. The FRG, Italy, the UK, and the United States would accumulate very large net foreign assets without flexible rates while the LDCs and several smaller OECD countries would have huge net liabilities. In general, the fastest-growing countries (the LDCs and the smaller OECD countries) are forced to depreciate to reduce their foreign liabilities while the relatively slow-growing major OECD countries appreciate and decrease their foreign assets compared to a fixed-rate regime.

Table 3 shows also the changes in export market penetration caused by the flexible-exchange-rate system. Countries which depreciate gain market share and conversely for the appreciating countries.

Table 4 gives further results for the standard flexible-rate simulation: the real exchange rates, world market shares, balance on petroleum, and incremental inflation rates.

All the large OECD countries (except France), the OPEC countries, the CPEs, Australia, and Switzerland have an increased real exchange rate at the end of the simulation while the rest depreciate to varying degrees. However, surpluses (or deficits) and thus appreciation (or depreciation) will occur for different reasons.

Fast-growing Japan is capturing markets but it also exports a remarkable share to the fast-growing markets of the LDCs. The FRG, being among the major exporters to developing countries, also has a remarkable share of the LDC markets. The UK surplus is generated mainly as a result of slowly growing import demand but also because of fast-growing markets for UK exports in LDCs. The appreciation is also reflected in market shares; in general, appreciating countries are losing markets owing to the weakening of their price competitiveness compared with the projection under the regime of fixed

TABLE 3   Changes caused by flexible exchange rates.

Region	Change in share of world nonoil goods exports (%)			Change in cumulative current account (billions of 1975 US$)		
	1979	1985	1990	1979	1985	1990
Canada	0.1	0.1	−0.1	−6.2	−29.2	− 52.0
France	0.2	0.5	0.4	−2.6	9.0	20.6
FRG	− 0.4	−0.4	−0.1	−17.6	−78.2	−137.9
Italy	0.0	− 0.4	−0.6	−4.8	−58.0	−168.9
Japan	−1.2	− 1.3	−1.2	−36.2	−183.6	−383.3
UK	0.4	−1.3	−1.5	−11.4	−112.1	−288.3
United States	−0.6	−1.0	−1.0	−33.7	−180.9	−406.5
LDCs	2.9	3.5	2.9	94.9	465.7	884.7
OPEC countries	− 0.5	−0.6	−0.6	0.3	18.0	61.6
CPEs	−0.1	−0.3	−0.4	−0.3	−1.1	− 1.4
Australia	0.0	0.0	−0.1	−0.4	−6.3	−15.9
Austria	0.0	0.1	0.1	0.9	4.4	14.0
Belgium/Luxembourg	0.1	0.0	0.0	−2.9	− 14.5	−19.5
Denmark	0.0	0.1	0.1	3.0	22.3	55.0
Finland	0.0	0.2	0.2	1.5	13.4	36.0
Iceland	0.0	0.0	0.0	0.1	0.1	0.6
Ireland	0.0	0.0	0.1	0.5	8.3	26.6
Netherlands	−0.1	−0.1	0.1	−6.5	−31.4	−35.5
Norway	0.1	0.1	0.0	10.7	116.4	91.5
Portugal	0.1	0.2	0.4	1.3	13.6	36.9
Spain	0.1	0.2	0.3	8.6	54.4	132.2
Sweden	0.1	0.1	0.2	2.7	28.6	74.9
Switzerland	−0.2	−0.2	0.0	11.3	−42.6	−77.2
Greece	0.1	0.1	0.2	2.8	14.6	53.0
New Zealand	0.1	0.1	0.1	2.3	9.6	18.0
Turkey	0.1	0.3	0.5	4.1	29.4	80.5

exchange rates, as is shown in Table 3. The Scandinavian countries, the Mediterranean countries, and the non oil-producing LDCs are devaluing their currencies in real terms as a consequence of running current-account deficits with fixed exchange rates. This is increasing their shares of world markets from what they would be under the assumption of fixed exchange rates.

It should be noted here that the good export performances of Japan and the non oil-producing LDCs in the model occur for different reasons. Japan's success comes from better nonprice competitiveness measured by relative growth of capacity output (i.e. expanding productive capacity is assumed to be linked with the rapid introduction of technological innovation, intensified export promotion, etc.) while at the same time Japan is experiencing losses because of the appreciating yen. In the case of the non oil-producing LDCs both better price and better nonprice competitiveness are helping to increase market share. The channel through increased price competitiveness due to a large devaluation of LDC currencies is much more important, as indicated by a comparison between the runs with fixed and flexible exchange rates (see Table 3); under fixed-rate assumptions the world market share of the non oil-producing LDCs increases from 11.1% in 1979 to 12.6% in 1990 but under flexible-rate assumptions it jumps 4.4 percentage points from 11.1% to

TABLE 4 Projections of selected variables in the flexible-rate run.

Region	Real exchange rate[a]			World market share[b]			Balance on petroleum			Inflation[c]	
	1979	1985	1990	1979	1985	1990	1979	1985	1990	A	B
Canada	106	112	113	4.5	3.8	3.4	1.4	0.8	0.9	0.1	0.0
France	95	86	86	7.4	7.9	7.6	−20.3	−25.3	−28.4	0.2	0.4
FRG	109	105	102	11.5	11.7	11.3	−16.9	−21.9	−24.3	0.1	0.1
Italy	105	117	120	4.4	4.4	4.4	−14.0	−18.4	−21.7	0.3	−0.4
Japan	116	119	121	9.0	9.8	10.7	−34.5	−46.9	−57.7	0.3	0.0
UK	108	133	137	5.4	4.5	3.8	−2.9	0.0	0.3	0.2	−0.6
United States	106	113	117	14.2	12.2	11.1	−25.8	−23.1	−25.1	0.1	0.0
LDCs	71	71	76	14.0	15.2	15.5	4.0	2.6	2.9	0.0	0.0
OPEC countries	105	112	116	4.1	4.3	4.8	150.7	188.4	217.0	–	–
CPEs	105	112	116	4.0	4.2	4.5	3.7	4.1	4.6	–	–
Australia	96	104	108	1.7	1.7	1.7	−0.7	−0.8	−0.9	0.1	0.0
Austria	99	96	92	1.1	1.2	1.2	−1.3	−1.9	−2.2	0.1	0.3
Belgium/Luxembourg	109	105	97	4.1	4.0	3.8	−4.9	−6.5	−7.3	0.2	0.5
Denmark	87	72	67	1.1	1.1	1.0	−2.4	−3.2	−3.5	0.1	1.0
Finland	73	50	42	0.8	0.9	0.9	−2.4	−3.2	−3.6	0.2	2.2
Iceland	90	87	84	0.0	0.0	0.0	0.0	0.0	0.0	0.0	0.6
Ireland	100	96	91	0.4	0.4	0.5	−0.4	−0.5	−0.6	0.1	0.8
Netherlands	114	106	96	5.0	5.3	5.4	−12.2	−17.5	−20.1	0.3	0.6
Norway	76	73	72	1.0	0.9	0.8	0.0	0.0	0.0	0.0	0.8
Portugal	71	42	34	0.3	0.5	0.7	−1.1	−1.4	−1.6	0.3	3.7
Spain	86	71	70	1.3	1.5	1.7	−8.8	−12.0	−14.4	0.3	0.9
Sweden	85	63	56	2.2	2.0	1.9	−5.7	−8.0	−8.5	0.1	1.0
Switzerland	126	119	110	1.6	1.5	1.6	−0.7	−0.9	−1.0	0.1	−0.2
Greece	96	82	75	0.4	0.4	0.5	−1.6	−1.9	−2.2	0.5	1.7
New Zealand	69	70	73	0.4	0.4	0.4	−0.3	−0.4	−0.4	0.1	0.3
Turkey	63	37	28	0.4	0.6	0.8	−2.3	−3.0	−3.4	0.1	1.8

[a] Index of the ratio of the US$-denominated GDP deflator to the total trade-weighted average of trading partners' US$-denominated GDP deflators (1975 = 100).

[b] Percentage share of total world nonoil goods exports in 1975 US$-denominated prices.

[c] A is the percentage increase in the average annual inflation rate due to oil-price increases and B is the percentage increase in the average annual inflation rate due to exchange-rate changes.

15.5% by 1990 since the introduction of the flexible-exchange-rate run overestimates the share of the non oil-producing LDCs.

The final two columns in Table 4 show the incremental inflation rates. Since there is no money growth or excess demand for goods in this model there are only two causes for an increase in the domestic GDP deflators: exogenous oil-price increases and exchange-rate changes. The first of the two columns shows the average increase in the inflation rate due to the exogenous oil-price increase while the second gives the changes in inflation rates due to changes of exchange rates. For the appreciating countries there are deflationary pressures while for depreciating countries there are inflationary pressures. The effects of exchange-rate movements on the domestic price level are more pronounced for the smaller and more open economies.

3.4   Higher Growth in the FRG

For this simulation it was assumed that the growth rate of output in the FRG was on average 1% higher than in the standard run. Here we compare the results of the two simulations to illustrate some of the cross-country linkages present in the model.

Because of the higher growth the current account of the FRG is worsened (see Table 5) and its real exchange rate depreciates by 23.1% by 1990. This depreciation lowers the relative price of FRG exports, giving the FRG an additional 1.4% of the world's non-oil goods market by 1990 and causing a 0.4% increase in the average domestic inflation rate.

The countries affected most strongly are France, Italy, the UK, Belgium and Luxembourg, and the Netherlands. For all the countries there are two primary channels of influence: the exchange-rate determination system and the current account. The exchange rates of France, Italy, and the UK are linked directly to the current account of the FRG. Initially this current account worsens owing to higher import demand while the French, Italian, and UK current accounts improve because of higher exports to the FRG. This causes the French, Italian, and UK exchange rates to appreciate and the FRG's import demand and the current accounts of France, Italy, and the UK to weaken. All three lose market shares and experience a decline in their inflation rates.

For the smaller European countries the effects are somewhat different. With the exception of Ireland, whose exchange rate is closely linked to that of the UK, all experience an improved trade balance and hence an improved current-account balance because of increased FRG demand. All their exchange rates appreciate slightly and their inflation rates are lowered. Here it must be remembered that output is always kept at an exogenous level so there is no change in labor-market pressure on costs, but only a reduction in prices of imported goods because of the exchange rate appreciation.

The effects on the non-European countries are relatively small. The OPEC countries do experience a significant increase in their current accounts due to increased oil exports to the FRG. The effects on Canada, Japan, the United States, Australia, and New Zealand are very small.

The simulation results indicate that the model produces a smooth slow adjustment process for exchange rates and current accounts. They also show that with the higher growth target for an individual country large current-account deficits may occur or large

TABLE 5   Changes caused by increased growth of the FRG.

Region	Change in share of world nonoil goods exports (%)			Change in real exchange rate (%)			Change in cumulative current account (%)			Change in inflation rate (%)
	1979	1985	1990	1979	1985	1990	1979	1985	1990	
Canada	0.0	-0.1	0.0	0.0	-1.1	0.1	0.1	0.2	0.1	0.0
France	0.0	-0.2	-0.4	0.3	9.6	13.3	-0.2	-6.7	-5.3	-0.3
FRG	0.0	0.9	1.4	-0.6	-15.6	-23.1	-0.7	-38.1	-57.2	0.4
Italy	-0.1	-0.1	0.0	0.7	12.7	8.8	-0.2	-20.1	-55.7	0.0
Japan	0.0	-0.2	-0.2	0.0	-0.9	-0.8	0.2	1.7	1.7	-0.2
UK	-0.1	-0.1	-0.1	0.5	10.4	14.1	-0.2	-9.0	-19.1	-0.1
United States	0.0	-0.2	-0.3	-0.1	-0.8	-0.4	0.4	3.5	4.2	0.0
LDCs	0.0	-0.3	-0.4	0.0	1.4	2.1	0.2	8.6	8.6	0.0
OPEC countries	0.0	-0.1	-0.1	0.0	-0.8	-0.4	0.2	12.2	47.0	-0.1
CPEs	0.0	0.0	-0.1	0.0	-0.8	-0.4	0.0	0.5	0.6	--
Australia	0.0	-0.1	0.0	0.0	-0.4	-0.4	0.0	-0.3	-0.4	0.0
Austria	0.0	0.0	0.0	0.2	0.2	2.6	0.1	2.5	4.9	-0.2
Belgium/Luxembourg	0.0	0.1	0.1	-0.1	1.9	4.6	0.2	5.1	10.0	-0.3
Denmark	0.0	0.0	0.0	0.0	1.9	3.9	0.0	2.1	4.1	-0.2
Finland	0.0	0.0	0.0	0.0	2.2	3.8	0.1	2.1	4.7	-0.2
Iceland	0.0	0.0	0.0	0.0	1.4	2.4	0.0	0.1	0.0	-0.2
Ireland	0.0	0.0	0.0	0.2	2.2	2.0	0.0	-0.2	-0.5	-0.1
Netherlands	0.0	0.2	0.0	-0.1	2.1	4.9	0.4	10.0	19.5	-0.3
Norway	0.0	0.0	0.0	0.0	1.3	2.3	0.0	0.5	0.7	-0.1
Portugal	0.0	0.1	0.0	0.1	2.7	4.0	0.0	2.1	5.1	-0.3
Spain	0.0	0.1	0.0	0.1	2.7	3.5	0.0	2.6	2.9	-0.2
Sweden	0.0	0.1	0.1	0.0	2.5	4.3	0.0	3.4	6.3	-0.1
Switzerland	0.0	0.0	0.0	0.0	1.9	2.3	0.0	1.1	1.7	0.0
Greece	0.0	0.0	0.0	0.0	0.9	1.3	0.1	0.9	1.6	-0.2
New Zealand	0.0	0.0	0.0	0.0	1.5	2.0	0.0	0.2	0.1	0.0
Turkey	0.0	0.0	0.0	0.0	1.8	2.6	0.0	1.8	4.1	-0.1

changes in real exchange rates are needed to reach external equilibrium. However, it must be emphasized that the projected changes in market shares and exchange rates reflect the growth assumption and the introduction of different exchange-rate regimes as well as historical income and price elasticities in international trade. This is why the projected changes are conditional and should not be interpreted as forecasts of future developments of trade flows and exchange rates.

REFERENCES

Artus, J.R. and Rhomberg, R.R. (1973). A multilateral exchange rate model. IMF Staff Papers, XX(3). International Monetary Fund, New York.

Basevi, G. (1973). Commodity trade equations in Project LINK. In R.J. Ball (Editor), The International Linkage of National Economic Models. North-Holland, Amsterdam.

Branson, W.H. (1977). Assets markets and relative prices in exchange rate determination. Sozialwissenschaftliche Annalen, I.

Branson, W.H. and Halttunen, H. (1978). Asset-market determination of exchange rates: initial empirical and policy results. In J.P. Martin and A. Smith (Editors), Trade and Payments Adjustment Under Flexible Exchange Rates. Macmillan, London, to be published.

Branson, W.H., Halttunen, H., and Masson, P. (1978). Exchange rates in the short run: the dollar–deutschemark rate. European Economic Review, 10.

Branson, W.H. and Papaefstratiou, L. (1978). Income instability, terms of trade and the change of exchange rate regimes. Paper presented at the Nobel Symposium, Stockholm.

Deppler, M.C. and Ripley, D.C. (1978). The world trade model: merchandise trade. IMF Staff Papers, March. International Monetary Fund, New York.

Dornbusch, R. and Krugman, P. (1976). Flexible exchange rates in the short run. Brookings Papers on Economic Activity, No. 3. Brookings Institution, Washington, D.C.

Houthakker, H.S. and Magee, S.P. (1969). Income and price elasticities in world trade. Review of Economics and Statistics, II.

Jonson, P.D. and Butlin, M.W. (1977). Price and quantity responses to monetary impulses in a model of a small open economy. Research Discussion Paper 7703. Reserve Bank of Australia.

Samuelson, L. (1973). A new model of world trade. OECD Economic Outlook, Occasional Studies, December. Organization for Economic Cooperation and Development, Paris.

Stern, R.M., Francis, J., and Schumacher, B. (Editors) (1976). Price Elasticities in International Trade. Macmillan, London.

Taplin, G.B. (1973). A model of world trade. In R.J. Ball (Editor), The International Linkage of National Economic Models. North-Holland, Amsterdam.

COMMENTS*

The Theoretical Structure of the Model

My comments here will be very brief, although this may imply a certain amount of oversimplification and therefore increase the possibility of misunderstandings. Basically, the paper presents a model of the balance of payments of the world broken down into different regions; some of these regions are countries and some of them are groups of

---

*By Hanns Abele, Wirtschaftsuniversität Wien, Vienna, Austria.

countries. Several items such as commodities and services are considered as well as foreign assets. All other parts of the economies are left exogenous.

Changes in the exchange rates influence the relative prices of the commodities in different countries and thus the volume of trade which determines the current account. Different regimes govern the changes in exchange rates depending on the exchange rate policies pursued by the various countries in the past. One can, however, think of conflicts in the goals of governments which force them to change the conduct of their exchange rate policy because of serious deterioration in their exchange rate (both depreciation and appreciation may be undesirable, as cases like Switzerland or the UK show).

The fundamental assumptions underlying the model are of a typically "Walrasian" spirit. Changes of prices, and especially of exchange rates, govern the adjustment process which is assumed to be stable. But can we be sure about the validity of this assumption?

One of the main results of disequilibrium theory and the non-market-clearing paradigm is a shift with respect to adjustment processes. Forcing a model into equilibrium via price signals only may lead to serious mis-specifications, because of the additional, binding, quantity constraint. Allowing for the influence of quantities offers a clear justification for a more Keynesian approach.

As an example, one can put the argument in another way. Recently, Frenkel and Mussa* stated:

> "Second, while as a technical matter, government policy can reduce exchange-rate fluctuations, even to the extent of pegging an exchange rate, it may not be assumed that such policies will automatically eliminate the disturbances that are presently reflected in the turbulence of exchange rates. Such policies may only transfer the effect of disturbances from the foreign exchange market to somewhere else in the economic system. There is no presumption that transferring disturbances will reduce their overall impact and lower their social cost."

This remark seems to deny either the existence or the stability of a general equilibrium. In any case, it raises doubts about modeling the equilibrium of an economy by focusing on an equilibrium in the market for foreign exchange.

Concerning the dynamics of the model and especially the adjustment process one gets the impression of a period-by-period adjustment on an annual basis by solving the model simultaneously every year. What would be the effect of a shift to another period, aggregating or disaggregating the basic time unit? With respect to exchange-rate developments, I doubt whether the period chosen in Dr. Warner's paper is the most promising for modeling exchange-rate dynamics.

This leads to another important problem. The structure of a model must depend on the questions to be answered. If one is concerned with policy problems in connection with exchange rates one should have a model that allows the questions posed to be answered. I am afraid that I did not totally grasp the aim of Dr. Warner's modeling exercise, because I must question the problem solving ability of the model. It is not an econometric model, but it is not a forecasting model either. It represents a merger of historical developments

---

*J.A. Frenkel and M.L. Mussa, The Efficiency of Foreign Exchange Markets and Measures of Turbulence, *American Economic Review*, 70 (1980), p. 379.

with exogenously projected variables. Implied in the structure of the model are assumptions about the conduct of economic policy in the countries concerned, like pegging the exchange rate. Pegging the exchange rate depends, however, on the reserves available. Besides that, the development of the domestic economies may put another constraint on the trade and exchange-rate policy. Therefore the results of the model depending on the structure described can be rendered totally useless if any one of these constraints becomes binding. It appears to me that the "automatic" aspect of the process dominates entirely the decision- or behavior-oriented approach. Thus it cannot be a policy model. The author himself warns at the end of his paper against possible overinterpretation of his results but the question remains: in what respect does the model further our understanding of the working of the international economy? Without pretending that the state of the theory of international economic relations is such that all relevant problems have been solved, I am inclined to recommend a more theoretically oriented approach. If there is a trade-off between further disaggregation and covering longer time periods on the one hand, and theoretical improvements on the other, I prefer the latter option.

Comments on Specific Points

I wonder whether there is a serious mis-specification in eqn. (11) which influences the results and conclusions given in Table 2. All variables are flow variables with the exception of the variable "net foreign assets", F_i, which is a stock, thus being the only intertemporal link in the model. But this means that any change of the exchange rate will change the value of F_{it-1} directly, and not only indirectly through its influence on the current account. The importance of this influence can be seen by the changes in the competitive positions of German, Swiss, French, or Japanese banks vis-à-vis US banks as a consequence of the declining dollar.

A second remark concerns the data. In OECD's economic outlook the aggregated balance of payments on current account is given. Beginning in 1975, it shows a total sum of about 20 billion dollars instead of almost zero. How reliable are these data sources? What is the sense of using in the model a condition which exactly balances the current accounts in the aggregate?

In Table 3, the results for the UK, Italy, and Switzerland startle me somewhat. Although these countries experience different exchange-rate developments, according to the simulations the effects of exchange rates on their domestic inflation rates are the same in all cases. What is the reason for this result?

Finally, a few remarks concerning the exogenous variables and parts of the model. To my mind, these are dependent on the endogenous variables of the model. Particularly for small countries, the foreign contributions to the determination of GNP are very important. As long as the feedbacks to the domestic economies are excluded, the conclusions are of very limited value. Even the excellent feature of relying on the ratio of GNP to potential GNP, both being exogenous projections, does not overcome these deficiencies.

Therefore I conclude that the usefulness of the approach taken in the paper is rather limited. I do not hesitate to express a preference for taking up more limited questions but adding more economic content, instead of producing long-term simulations with inadequate models.

AUTHOR INDEX